A Natural History of Infixa

OXFORD STUDIES IN THEORETICAL LINGUISTICS

GENERAL EDITORS: David Adger, *Queen Mary College London*; Hagit Borer, *University of Southern California*

ADVISORY EDITORS: Stephen Anderson, *Yale University*; Daniel Büring, *University of California, Los Angeles*; Nomi Erteischik-Shir, *Ben-Gurion University*; Donka Farkas, *University of California, Santa Cruz*; Angelika Kratzer, *University of Massachusetts, Amherst*; Andrew Nevins, *Harvard University*; Christopher Potts, *University of Massachusetts, Amherst*; Barry Schein, *University of Southern California*; Peter Svenonius, *University of Tromsø*; Moira Yip, *University College London*

PUBLISHED

1 *The Syntax of Silence*
   Sluicing, Islands, and the Theory of Ellipsis
   by Jason Merchant
2 *Questions and Answers in Embedded Contexts*
   by *Utpal Lahiri*
3 *Phonetics, Phonology, and Cognition*
   edited by *Jacques Durand and Bernard Laks*
4 *At the Syntax-Pragmatics Interface*
   Concept Formation and Verbal Underspecification in Dynamic Syntax
   by Lutz Marten
5 *The Unaccusativity Puzzle*
   Explorations of the Syntax-Lexicon Interface
   edited by Artemis Alexiadou, Elena Anagnostopoulou, and Martin Everaert
6 *Beyond Morphology*
   Interface Conditions on Word Formation
   by Peter Ackema and Ad Neeleman
7 *The Logic of Conventional Implicatures*
   by Christopher Potts
8 *Paradigms of Phonological Theory*
   edited by Laura Downing, T. Alan Hall, and Renate Raffelsiefen
9 *The Verbal Complex in Romance*
   by Paola Monachesi
10 *The Syntax of Aspect*
   Deriving Thematic and Aspectual Interpretation
   Edited by Nomi Erteschik-Shir and Tova Rapoport
11 *Aspects of the Theory of Clitics*
   by Stephen Anderson
12 *Canonical Forms in Prosodic Morphology*
   by Laura J. Downing
13 *Aspect and Reference Time*
   by Olga Borik
14 *Direct Compositionality*
   edited by Chris Barker and Pauline Jacobson
15 A Natural History of Infixation
   by Alan C. L. Yu
16 *Phi-Theory*
   Phi-Features Across Interfaces and Modules
   edited by David Adger, Susana Béjar, and Dan Harbour
17 *Dislocation in French: Syntax, Interpretation, Acquisition*
   by Cécile De Cat

The Oxford Handbook of Linguistic Interfaces
edited by Gillian Ramchand and Charles Reiss
[*published in association with the series*]

For titles in preparation see page 265.

A Natural History of Infixation

ALAN C. L. YU

OXFORD
UNIVERSITY PRESS

OXFORD
UNIVERSITY PRESS

Great Clarendon Street, Oxford OX2 6DP

Oxford University Press is a department of the University of Oxford.
It furthers the University's objective of excellence in research, scholarship,
and education by publishing worldwide in

Oxford New York

Auckland Cape Town Dar es Salaam Hong Kong Karachi
Kuala Lumpur Madrid Melbourne Mexico City Nairobi
New Delhi Shanghai Taipei Toronto

With offices in

Argentina Austria Brazil Chile Czech Republic France Greece
Guatemala Hungary Italy Japan Poland Portugal Singapore
South Korea Switzerland Thailand Turkey Ukraine Vietnam

Oxford is a registered trade mark of Oxford University Press
in the UK and in certain other countries

Published in the United States
by Oxford University Press Inc., New York

British Library Cataloguing in Publication Data

Data available

Library of Congress Cataloging in Publication Data

Data available

Typeset by SPI Publisher Services, Pondicherry, India
Printed in Great Britain
on acid-free paper by
Biddles Ltd., King's Lynn, Norfolk

ISBN 978–0–19–927938–8 (HB)
     978–0–19–927939–5 (PB)

1 3 5 7 9 10 8 6 4 2

Contents

Preface   ix
General Preface   xi

1 Introduction   1

2 What is infixation?   9
  2.1 Defining infixation descriptively   9
  2.2 Infixes as formal objects   14
  2.3 Infixation as a phonological process   17
  2.4 Infixation as morpho-phonological mismatch   21
  2.5 Phonological Readjustment and Phonological
     Subcategorization compared   25
    2.5.1 On the ethological view of infixation   26
    2.5.2 On the issue of empirical coverage: Problems of
      undergeneration   31
    2.5.3 On the predictive power of the theory: Problems with
      overgeneration   37
  2.6 Conclusion   45

3 Subcategorization in context   47
  3.1 Subcategorization as Generalized Alignment   48
  3.2 Phonological Subcategorization in Sign-Based Morphology   53
  3.3 Phonological Subcategorization and constraint overgeneration 58
  3.4 Understanding the Edge-Bias Effect   62

4 Pivot Theory and the typology   67
  4.1 The Pivot Theory   67
  4.2 Sampling procedures   73
  4.3 First consonant   76
  4.4 First vowel   89
  4.5 Final syllable   108
  4.6 Final vowel   111
  4.7 Stress and related metrical units   118

4.8 Other potential pivots   124
   4.8.1 Final consonant   124
      4.8.1.1 Takelma frequentative reduplication   125
      4.8.1.2 Hunzib   128
      4.8.1.3 Hausa Class 5 Plural formation   130
   4.8.2 First syllable   133
4.9 Conclusion   135

5 The secret history of infixes   137

5.1 Background   137
5.2 Toward a diachronic typology of infixation   138
   5.2.1 Metathesis   139
      5.2.1.1 The phonetic origins of metathesis 141
      5.2.1.2 Metathesis without faithfulness   142
      5.2.1.3 Infixation in Pingding Mandarin   144
      5.2.1.4 Summary   147
   5.2.2 Entrapment   148
      5.2.2.1 Muskogean infixation   148
      5.2.2.2 Symptoms and predictions of entrapment 151
      5.2.2.3 Hua   154
      5.2.2.4 Summary   156
   5.2.3 Reduplication mutation   157
      5.2.3.1 Hausa pluractionals   157
      5.2.3.2 Hopi plural formation   159
      5.2.3.3 Trukese durative   162
      5.2.3.4 Yurok intensive   163
      5.2.3.5 Northern Interior Salish diminutives 165
      5.2.3.6 Summary   171
   5.2.4 Morphological excrescence and prosodic stem association 172
      5.2.4.1 The emergence of Homeric infixation 174
      5.2.4.2 Summary   177
5.3 Conclusion   177

6 Beyond infixation   181

6.1 Fake vs. true infixation   181
6.2 Infixation in language games and disguises   190
   6.2.1 Iterative infixal ludling   192
   6.2.2 A general theory of iterative infixing ludling 199

6.3 Endoclisis 206
  6.3.1 Udi 208
  6.3.2 Pashto 212
6.4 Feature and subcategorization 218
  6.4.1 Kashaya Pomo 220
  6.4.2 Tiene 222
6.5 Conclusion 229

Appendix 231
References 235
Language Index 255
Subject index 259

Preface

We shall not cease from exploration
And the end of all our exploring
Will be to arrive where we started
And know the place for the first time.

T. S. Eliot, Little Gidding

This book is ostensibly a revision of my 2003 dissertation from the University of California at Berkeley. However, while the main thesis has not changed, this book differs from, and far exceeds if I dare say, the earlier manuscript in several important respects. I have included considerably more data as well as discussion on how the different parts of my theory work together as a coherent model. In lieu of reproducing the three case studies discussed in the dissertation, I have, on the suggestion of one of the reviewers for Oxford University Press, opted to provide many short illustrations instead. My aim is not only to increase the empirical coverage but also to give the reader a better sense of how the diversity of infixes is analyzed within the framework defended in this monograph. To be sure, it was at times difficult to maintain the delicate balance between the desire to offer a breadth of coverage and the necessity to achieve a certain depth of analysis. Decidedly, short case studies are not meant to be exhaustive analyses. I have focused instead on attending to the basic pattern and highlighting the more peripheral aspects of the pattern only when relevant. A central thesis of this book is the idea that typological tendencies of language may be traced back to its origins and the mechanisms of language transmission. As such, this book is more than just a natural history of infixation; it is an apologia for a holistic approach to linguistic explanation. It echoes much previous work that has tirelessly combated the confusion in regard to the role diachronic and functional factors play in synchronic argumentation. When a diachronic explanation for typological tendencies is advanced, it is not an attempt to attribute some psychic ability of the speakers that can pierce into the past to uncover the hidden secret histories of their language. Such a naïve interpretation of the diachronist's agenda is misguided and certainly not conducive to the advances of the field. I hope that this work, like the work of many others before me, will advance the dialogues, if only in a small way, in a fruitful direction.

Ideas presented in this work did not come out of a vacuum. This project began at Berkeley where I have had the great fortune of working with Sharon

Inkelas and Andrew Garrett. I benefited tremendously from their sage guidance. They have both been a consistent source of support and inspiration throughout my years at Berkeley and beyond. I shall like to think that this work reflects an adequate synthesis of the ideas they have imparted to me throughout the years.

I am also happy to have another opportunity to express my thanks to all those people who helped me in writing the thesis and contributed to the wonderful Berkeley experience. Many of them were mentioned in the dissertation. However, I would like to single out a few of these individuals who have made the experience particularly enjoyable; among these are (in alphabetic order) Juliette Blevins, Jeff Good, Larry Hyman, Mary Paster, Johanna Nichols, Ruth Rouvier, and Tess Wood. I am also grateful and indebted to many people for various comments and suggestions along the way: (in alphabetic order) Bill Darden, Daniel Kaufman, Josh Viau, Moira Yip, Cheryl Zoll, and the reviewers for Oxford University Press (who gave extensive and very helpful comments for which I am grateful). I would also like to thank the students in my classes and seminars at the University of Chicago for the patience with which they have listened to many ideas presented in this book, and for their questions, comments, and challenges. Additional editorial comments and assistance on portions of the manuscript from Robert Peachey and Jett McAlister have been extremely valuable. I would like to thank John Davey, my editor at Oxford University Press, for his patience and support. Last but not least, I thank my parents and my brothers who have provided constant encouragement and much love.

General Preface

The theoretical focus of this series is on the interfaces between subcomponents of the human grammatical system and the closely related area of the interfaces between the different subdisciplines of linguistics. The notion of 'interface' has become central in grammatical theory (for instance, in Chomsky's recent Minimalist Program) and in linguistic practice: work on the interfaces between syntax and semantics, syntax and morphology, phonology and phonetics etc. has led to a deeper understanding of particular linguistic phenomena and of the architecture of the linguistic component of the mind/brain.

The series covers interfaces between core components of grammar, including syntax/morphology, syntax/semantics, syntax/phonology, syntax/pragmatics, morphology/phonology, phonology/phonetics, phonetics/speech processing, semantics/pragmatics, intonation/discourse structure as well as issues in the way that the systems of grammar involving these interface areas are acquired and deployed in use (including language acquisition, language dysfunction, and language processing). It demonstrates, we hope, that proper understandings of particular linguistic phenomena, languages, language groups, or inter-language variations all require reference to interfaces.

The series is open to work by linguists of all theoretical persuasions and schools of thought. A main requirement is that authors should write so as to be understood by colleagues in related subfields of linguistics and by scholars in cognate disciplines.

In this volume Alan Yu examines a process at the interface of phonology and morphology—infixation—and argues that infixes are epiphenomenal. They emerge from a misalignment of phonology and morphology: the infix phonologically subcategorizes a phonological unit that is not a morphological unit. Yu combines this grammar-internal analysis with a plea for the importance of grammar-external factors which influence the typological profile of infixation and similar phenomena.

David Adger
Hagit Borer

For my parents,
Paul and Carol Yu

1

Introduction

My subject—infixation—is at once exotic and familiar. Russell Ultan in his pioneering study of the typology of infixation (1975) noted that infixes are rare compared to the frequency of other affixes. The presence of infixes in any language implies the presence of suffixes and/or prefixes, and no languages employ infixation exclusively (Greenberg 1966: 92). The term 'infixation' is also less familiar to students of linguistics than are such terms as prefixation and suffixation. The *Oxford English Dictionary* goes as far as defining infixes as what prefixes and suffixes are not:

A modifying element inserted in the body of a word, instead of being prefixed or suffixed to the stem. (May 14, 2003 Web edition)

Infixes are not at all difficult to find, however. English-speaking readers will no doubt recognize some, if not all, of the following infixation constructions:

(1) Expletive infixation (McCarthy 1982)
    impórtant   im-*bloody*-pórtant
    fantástic   fan-*fuckin*-tástic
    perháps   per-*bloody*-háps
    Kalamazóo   Kalama-*goddamn*-zóo
    Tatamagóuchee   Tatama-*fuckin*-góuchee

(2) *Homer*-ic infixation (Yu 2004*b*)
    saxophone   saxo*ma*phone
    telephone   tele*ma*phone
    violin   vio*ma*lin
    Michaelangelo   Micha*ma*langelo

(3) Hip-hop *iz*-infixation (Viau 2002)
    house   h*iz*ouse
    bitch   b*iz*itch
    soldiers   s*iz*oldiers
    ahead   ah*iz*ead

Given the relative rarity of infixes in the world's languages, it is perhaps not surprising that infixes are often afforded a lesser consideration. Yet their richness and complexity have nonetheless captured the imaginations of many linguists. Hidden behind the veil of simplicity implied in the term 'infix', which suggests a sense of uniformity on par with that of prefixes and suffixes, is the diversity of the positions where infixes are found relative to the stem. The range of infixation patterns in English presented readily illustrates this point. While the expletive in its infixal usage generally appears before the stressed syllable (1), the Homeric infix must come after a trochaic foot (2). The -*iz*- infix popularized by hip-hop singers is attracted by stress as well. However, it differs from the first two patterns by lodging itself before the stressed vowel (3). Besides the diversity in infixal location, the semantic function of infixation is also wide-ranging. While the English language makes use of infixation mainly for paralinguistic purposes, languages as diverse as Greek, an Indo-European language (4), and Atayal, an Austronesian language (5), rely on infixation to signify important grammatical functions.

(4)   Greek present stem formation -*N*- (Garrett, forthcoming)

Aorist stem	Present stem	Gloss
e-dak-	daŋk-an-	'bite'
e-lab-	lamb-an-	'take'
e-lat^h-	lant^h-an-	'escape notice'
e-lip-	limp-an-	'leave'
e-pat^h-	pant^h-an-	'suffer'
e-put^h-	punt^h-an-	'inquire'
e-p^{h}ug-	p^{h}uŋg-an-	'flee'
e-t^{h}ig-	t^{h}iŋg-an-	'touch'
e-mat^h-	mant^h-an-	'learn'

(5)   Atayal animate actor focus -*m*- (Egerod 1965: 263–6)

qul	qmul	'snatch'
kat	kmat	'bite'
kuu	kmuu	'too tired, not in the mood'
hŋuʔ	hmŋuʔ	'soak'
skziap	kmziap	'catch'
sbil	smbil	'leave behind'

In fact, based on the languages surveyed in this work, infixes may signal a wide array of morphosyntactic functions: agreement (person, gender, number, focus), possession, intensification, nominalization, verbalization, diminution, derision, expletive, distribution, durative, frequentative, perfective/imperfective, completion, aorist, intransitive, passive, negation, past, verbal/nominal plural, reflexive/reciprocal, and resulting state.

This apparent richness and diversity, however, mask another striking feature of infixes, namely, the asymmetric typology of the placement of infixes. It has long been recognized that the placement of infixes converges to two locales, despite its diversity in shape and function. A survey of 154 infixation patterns from more than 100 languages revealed that infixes invariably appear near one of the edges of a stem or next to a stressed unit (see Chapter 4 for details of the typological survey). However, while 137 of these infixes (i.e., 89 percent) are edge-oriented (6), only 17 are prominence-driven ($p < 0.01$, Fisher's exact test). That is, infixes predominately lodge themselves close to one of the edges of the domain of infixation, which may be a root, a stem (i.e., root or root plus some affixes) or a free-standing word (cf. Moravcsik 2000; Ultan 1975). I refer to this asymmetric distribution of infixes as the *Edge-Bias Effect.*

(6)   Distribution of edge-oriented and prominence-driven infixes

	Fixed	RED	Total
Edge-oriented	94	43	137
Prominence-driven	6	11	17
Total			154

Thus, one of the fundamental problems motivating this research is the search for a principled explanation for this typological skewing. A theory of infixation must be able to account for the bias toward edge-oriented infixes without losing sight of the prominence-driven ones.

Infixes are also remarkable from a functional point of view. Hawkins and Cutler (1988) argue that the position of an affix relative to the stem is influenced by factors in language processing. Affixes tend to follow the stem rather than precede it (i.e., the typological bias toward suffixation over prefixation (Greenberg 1966)) because the stem-affix order facilitates the processing and recognition of the contentful and unpredictable part of a word, namely, the stem. Infixed words should therefore be relatively difficult to process assuming that structural discontinuities complicate language processing. This disadvantage offers a compelling explanation for the paucity of infixes in the world's languages, yet the fact that infixes keep emerging over the ages suggests that there might be historical factors at work that favor the creation of infixes.

Moravcsik's pioneering 1977 monograph, *On Rules of Infixing,* was the first to articulate the basic challenges to linguistic theory presented by infixes. While the answers she supplies reflect the theoretical mode of the time, the questions she poses remain relevant to this day. A complete theory of infixation has to address three major questions: (i) What is the total range of infix patterns? (This is an empirical question that concerns the typology.) (ii) What are the mechanisms and principles in terms of which such patterns are based? That is, what are the primitives and the principles for combining these primitives into representations of specific infixes? (iii) What are the metatheoretical constraints which permit just these mechanisms and principles and their particular language-internal co-occurrence and exclude others?

This book is devoted to an exploration of these issues, laying out and comparing different theories which address them. It aims to provide an overview and synthesis of the results of current research on infixation, to highlight questions which remain open, and to lay out the challenges such phenomena present for linguistic theory. Groundbreaking studies exploring this issue include McCarthy and Prince (1986), Inkelas (1990), McCarthy and Prince (1993*a*), and Prince and Smolensky (1993). Over the years many studies have dealt with the placement properties of infixes and several general theories of infix placement have been developed (Broselow and McCarthy 1983/84; Buckley 1997; Chiu 1987; Clements 1985; Crowhurst 1998; Davis 1988; Halle 2001; Hyman and Inkelas 1997; Inkelas 1990; Kaufman 2003; Kiparsky 1986; Kurisu and Sanders 1999; Lubowicz 2005; Marantz 1982; McCarthy 1982, 2000, 2003*b*; McCarthy and Prince 1986, 1990, 1993*a*, 1993*b*, 1994*b*; Moravcsik 1977, 2000; Rose 2003*a*, 2003*b*; Spaelti 1995, 1997; Urbanczyk 1993). Broadly speaking, there are two main traditions of analyzing infixes. One approach embraces the morpho-phonological mismatching nature of infixes by treating them as affixes that subcategorize for a phonological element, rather than for a morphological one (see e.g., Broselow and McCarthy 1983/84; Cohn 1992; Inkelas 1990; Kiparsky 1986; McCarthy and Prince 1986). I shall refer to this approach as *Phonological Subcategorization*. On the other hand, some have argued that infixes are 'defective' adpositional affixes, and that their underlying prefixing or suffixing nature is obscured by synchronically motivated (morpho)phonological factors (see e.g., Halle 2001; McCarthy and Prince 1993*a*; Moravcsik 1977; Prince and Smolensky 1993). This movement-based view of infixation is referred as *Phonological Readjustment*. The theoretical context in which the Phonological Readjustment view of infixation comes under intense scrutiny is the claim by the fathers of Optimality Theory (McCarthy and Prince 1993*a*; Prince and Smolensky 1993) that the placement of an infix is intimately linked to its prosodic shape and the phonotactics of the language. From this perspective, infixes are predominantly edge-oriented because they are adpositional underlyingly; they are driven minimally inward due to the optimizing forces operating in the phonological grammar of the language.

The source of this long-standing suspicion that infixes are really adpositional affixes or adfixes (i.e., prefixes and suffixes) gone awry differs from theorist to theorist. Some reject the notion of phonological subcategorization out of methodological constraints against representation- and constituent-internal heteromodality (Halle 2001; Moravcsik 1977). Such theorists generally subscribe to a strictly modular model of the grammar in which morphological/syntactic operations are prohibited from referring to phonological information, a concept otherwise celebrated by the proponents of phonological subcategorization. Others object to phonological subcategorization out of the suspicion that generalizations would be missed in appealing to such a powerful device. For example, it has often been noted that infixes often have adpositional variants. One generalization that seems to hold across languages is that if an infix is concatenated adpositionally, it would have resulted in a phonotactically ill-formed output. Consider an example from Latin. Latin imperfective stems are formed by the infixing of a homorganic nasal before the root-final consonant (e.g., *rump* 'break' $<$ $\sqrt{rup}$). However, when the root is vowel-final, the nasal appears suffixing (e.g., *sin* 'allow' $<$ $\sqrt{si}$ (Matthews 1974: 125)). Many researchers were impressed by the fact that had the nasal been suffixed after a consonant-final root, it would have resulted in an illegitimate coda cluster in Latin (e.g., **rupm*). The homorganic nasal is infixed to avoid phonotactically illicit clusters. No infixation is needed with respect to vowel-final roots since no illicit cluster may result by the suffixation of the nasal.

This concern over the underlying motivation for infixation has gained a renewed sense of urgency in recent years. Many current theories of infixation and of grammar in general, assume that, all else being equal, naturalness and the universal typological tendencies in phonology and morphology should be captured in the theory of grammar itself in order to attain explanatory adequacy (Chomsky 1986). That is, besides arriving at a formalism that describes what happens, many linguists consider it imperative to also restrict the formalism to capture why a phenomenon unfolds only the way it does. From this point of view, the theory of grammar not only should 'account' for what is found in language, but also 'explain' the source of the variations. This view has prompted some, for example, to incorporate into synchronic models articulatory and perceptual constraints in speech to account for cross-linguistic sound patterns (Boersma 1998; Flemming 1995; Gordon 1999, 2001, 2002; Hayes 1999; Kirchner 1998, 2000; Pater 1999; Silverman 1995; Smith 2002; Steriade 1994, 1995, 1997, 2000, 2001; Walker 2000*a*).

Such an all-encompassing view of the grammar is not without detractors, however. Many linguists argue that the sources of naturalness and typological tendencies do not reside in the nature of the grammar *per se*, but must be recovered from grammar-external sources, such as diachronic factors or psycholinguistic constraints. These authors contend that, while the formal system should model productive grammatical effects, Universal Grammar-specific explanations should be appealed to only when a phenomenon cannot be accounted for by psychological or historical means. As Anderson (1988: 325) succinctly puts it,

Allowing one part of the grammar to 'overgenerate' in the context of constraints imposed by its interaction with other areas [e.g., morphological change, AY] often makes it possible to bring order and coherence to each independently—order and coherence that would be impossible if the principles determining the range of possible phenomena in each part of the grammar had to be limited to statements internal to that domain alone. Such a modular conception of grammar thus seems in many cases the only path to a constrained account.

Many phonological phenomena can be successfully understood in this perspective (e.g., Barnes 2002, 2006; Dolbey and Hansson 1999; Hale and Reiss 2000; Hume 2004; Kavitskaya 2001; Mielke 2004; Yu 2004*a*). Juliette Blevins's program of Evolutionary Phonology (2004) has consolidated and extended this approach of linguistic explanation to a new level. To be sure, this perspective finds champions outside the domain of phonology as well. For example, Harris and Campbell (1995) have forcefully argued that many morpho-syntactic phenomena can be more insightfully analyzed if the contexts of their historical emergence are taken into account.

This book presents a treatment of infixation from the latter perspective. One of the main goals of this book is to provide a bridge between the line of linguistic research that emphasizes the synchronic forces operating in language and those that recognize the forces of diachrony that help shape them. Synchronists are most often interested in broad generalizations concerning nature of infix placement based on a small set of languages without paying sufficient attention to the actual typology. On the other hand, the diachronists often ignore the synchronic forces that often simultaneously drive and constrain linguistic change. In this book I attempt to synthesize and evaluate these strands of work, placing them in a unified perspective.

This book is organized as follows. Chapter 2 addresses the question of what infixes are. The focus is to adequately account for infixation from both descriptive and theoretical perspectives. The descriptive account allows us to delineate the scope of the problem to be addressed in this work. From the perspective of linguistic theory, however, infixes are formal elements that stand in combinarial relation with other linguistic elements. As such, an adequate theory of infixation is also a theory of affix placement that is sufficient to account for infixation as well as the more canonical concatenating morphology. In Chapter 2, I review different formal accounts that have been advanced to model infixation. I begin by laying out the basic properties of two main approaches to infixation mentioned above: Phonological Readjustment and Phonological Subcategorization. I show that the Phonological Readjustment approach includes much that is local and parochial and should be discarded in favor of principles of broad applicability.

As laid out in Chapter 3, the model of infix placement defended in this book is that of Phonological Subcategorization, formalized in terms of Generalized Alignment. Infixes are treated as affixes that subcategorize for a phonological unit (called the pivot point), rather than a morphological one. When the morphological domain coincides with the phonological one, adpositional affixation (or adfixation) obtains. However, when there is a mismatch, infixation may result. This theory of phonological subcategorization is couched within the framework of Signed-Based Morphology (Orgun 1996, 1998, 1999; Orgun and Inkelas 2002), which is a declarative, non-derivational theory of the morphology-phonology interface that utilizes the basic tools one finds in any constituent structure-based unificational approach to linguistics (e.g., Construction Grammar (Fillmore and Kay 1994) and HPSG (Pollard and Sag 1994)). Subcategorization restrictions are treated as declarative constraints and thus may never be violated. As such, the interaction between morphological alignment and the phonological grammar is much more limited.

The analysis of infixation cannot be conducted in a vacuum, however. The theory of affix placement, and indeed of grammar as a whole, must be embedded within a temporal axis. That is, the diachronic evolution of infixes is as much an integral part of the explanation as are their treatments within the synchronic grammar. As summarized in (7), the model of infixation advocated in this work has three parts. A holistic theory of infix distribution must elucidate the set of grammar-external forces that shape the synchronic profile of infix distribution, in addition to supplying a theory of phonological subcategorization (i.e., a source of grammar-internal constraints). Two important grammar-external factors are identified: the diachronic mechanisms that drive the emergence of infixation and the inductive biases in morphological learning that allow or, in some cases, favor the emergence of infixes.

(7) **A holistic theory of infix distribution**
     a. Grammar-internal constraints:
        A theory of phonological subcategorization

b. Grammar-external constraints:
constraints on morphological learning
constraints on morphological change

c. A theory of interaction between these grammar-internal and grammar-external constraints

Since the starting point for discussions of language change is acquisition in the context of current linguistic theory, I first articulate a theory of inductive bias in morphological learning in Chapter 4. This will pave the way for the discussion of the diachronic typology in Chapter 5. The main idea advanced in Chapter 4 is that learners are biased toward setting up subcategorization restrictions of a certain sort. In particular, I introduce a specific type of inductive bias, called the Pivot Theory, which proposes that the most subcategorizable elements are also the most salient and the easiest to recover. I show that the set of predicted salient pivots are also the same pivots that are subcategorized by infixes. The rest of Chapter 4 is dedicated to laying out the synchronic landscape of infixation patterns organized in terms of the different pivot points.

Chapter 5 is a survey of the diachronic pathways through which infixes emerge. I show that infixes are the results of morphological misparsing introduced by four mechanisms: phonetic metathesis, morphological entrapment, reduplication mutation, and morphological excrescence.

It is in the context of the synchronic and diachronic typologies of infixation laid out in Chapters 4 and 5 and the nature of morphological change and acquisition argued in this work that the Edge-Bias Effect can be fully understood. The diachronic typology shows that infixes originate predominately from adpositional affixes. Thus, it is not surprising that infixes are biased toward the edges to begin with. The birth of infixation also hinges on speakers misanalyzing in the direction of infixation, rather than reverting back to the historical antecedent. The nature of the inductive bias in morphological learning itself also favors pivot points close to the edge since such units are psycholinguistically more salient and can be more reliably recovered. Non-edge pivots that are not prominence-based are difficult to obtain either because no historical pathways may give rise to them or because they are rejected in the acquisition process.

In Chapter 6, I conclude by considering a set of residual issues raised by the theory of infixation advocated in this work. First, I examine the possibility of the so-called 'genuine' infixation. I then take a brief foray into the realm of infixal ludlings and endoclisis. Finally, I close by exploring further the ramifications of adopting a phonological subcategorization approach to infixation.

2

What is infixation?

Since the phenomenon of infixation tends to be less familiar to students of linguistics than other morphological operations are, and the term 'infixation' is often used in the literature quite liberally, it is instructive to discuss at the outset what sort of patterns falls within the scope of the present study.

2.1 Defining infixation descriptively

It is often stated that an affix is considered an infix when it 'occur[s] within stem' (Payne 1997: 30). This, however, is not quite adequate. Many instances of discontinuous morphology may fall under this definition. For example, the well-known vocalism marking tense and aspect in the verbal system of Semitic languages is 'interdigitated' with the consonantal root (e.g., Egyptian Arabic *ktb 'write', kita:b 'book', katab 'he wrote', yektub 'he is writing'; (Nida 1949: 68)). Likewise, internal modification (a.k.a. ablaut or replacive morphology) also involves surface discontinuity. It has, for example, been suggested that English irregular past tense and participle formations may be analyzed as a matter of infixation. That is, like the verbal morphology of the Semitic languages, the roots in (1) can be analyzed as C__C where the empty slot is filled in by the 'infixal' vowel.

(1) | Present | Past | Past Participle |
|---------|-------|-----------------|
| sing | sang | sung |
| drink | drank | drunk |
| fling | flang | flung |
| sink | sank | sunk |
| ring | rang | rung |

Yet there are fundamental differences between the types of discontinuity found in the 'interdigitation' of the Semitic languages or the internal modification of English, and the discontinuity found in the infixation patterns presented in this work. What is missing from the conventional definition is the idea of *derived discontinuity*. The Semitic vocalism and the 'infixal' vowel in English internal modification cannot be said to have created a disruption in the roots or stem since the discontinuity of the consonantal roots in Semitic languages or the C_C roots in the case of English internal modification is *intrinsic*. The Semitic consonantal roots are always interrupted by the vocalism; they never surface as fully continuous strings per se. The contiguity between segments within the consonantal root is therefore the exception rather than the norm (see, for example, Gafos 1998, 1999; McCarthy 1979, 1981; Ussishkin 1999, 2000 for more discussion on the templatic morphology of the Semitic languages). Discontinuity in the infixed word is *extrinsic* since infixes create derived discontinuous morphs by splitting apart meaningful roots or stems that otherwise surface as a unitary whole.

Operationally, I consider an affix infixing if it appears as a segmentally distinct entity between two strings that form a meaningful unit when combined but do not themselves exist as meaningful parts (2).[1]

(2)   An affix, whose phonetic form is A, is infixed if
      the combination of B_i & B_j constitutes exhaustively the non-null parts
            of the terminal
      phonetic form of a continuous stem, B,
      and the terminal phonetic form of A is both immediately preceded by B_i
      and also immediately followed by B_j,
      without any part of A being simultaneous with any part of B,
      and such that B_i and B_j do not by themselves correspond to meanings
            that would
      jointly constitute the total meaning of B.

Thus, English expletive (e.g., *abso-bloody-lutely*) is considered an infix since the expletive (i.e., *bloody*) is both preceded and followed by non-null and non-meaningful parts (i.e., *abso* and *lutely*) of a meaningful non-discontinuous stem (i.e., *absolutely*) without being simultaneous with any non-null part of the stem.

Note, however, an affix should not be discounted as an infix based on the decomposability of the interrupted stem alone. The morphological hosts of an infix may in fact be complex. In the Timugon dialect of Sabah Murut (Austronesian), for example, the infix -*in*-, which marks 'Past Temporal Aspect, Object focus' in verbs or 'something resembling X' in nouns, comes before the first vowel of the stem. Depending on the nature of the stem itself,

---

[1] This is an amended version of the definition provided in Moravcsik's 1977 pioneering study on the formal properties of infixing.

the infix may appear internal to a root (3a), a reduplicant (3b), or a prefix (3c) (Prentice 1971: 126–39).

(3) a. kinandoy   ←   kandoy   'S works [on O]'
        linopot   ←   lopot   'S wraps up O'

     b. minamato   ←   ma-mato   ←   mato   'eye'

     c. pinooŋoy   ←   po-oŋoyon ←   oŋoy   'S causes O to go'
        pinaakan   ←   pa-akanon   ←   akan   'S causes O to eat [A]'
        pinansaduy ←   pan-saduyon ← saduy   'S causes O to swim'

The definition in (2) does not preclude infixes from lodging between two morphemes by happenstance either. For example, while the two parts separated by the expletive infix in forms such as *un-bloody-believable* do in fact constitute continuous morphs themselves, the infixal status of the expletive can nonetheless be unequivocally established by examples such as *e-bloody-nough* or, better yet, by infixed proper names, such as *Tatama-fuckin-gouchee* (see McCawley 1978 and McCarthy 1982 for more discussion on where the expletive might appear).

The infixal status of certain affixes can be difficult to access sometimes. For example, the direction object pronouns and subject/object relative markers in Old Irish are said to be infixes (Fife and King 1998). However, they only appear 'infixed' in verbs that are comprised of minimally a preverb and a stressed main verb (e.g., *as-beir* 'says' (< *as* + *beird*)), never in verbs lacking the preverbal element (e.g., (3 SG pres.) *berid* 'come'). Some examples with the 1 SG, *-m-* (basic form) and *-dom-* (expanded form) are given below:

(4) Old Irish
     ad-cí   'see'   atom-chí   'sees me'
     ni accasi   'does not see'   nim accai   'does not see me'
     ro-n-ánaic   'he reached'   ro-n-**dom**-ánaic 'he reached me'
     intí do-eim   'he who protects'   intí do-**dom**-eim 'he who protects me'
     for-comai   'preserve'   for-**dom**-chomaither 'I am preserved'

Given that the preverbs are synchronically analyzable apart from the main stressed verb, the direction object pronouns and subject/object relative markers cannot be considered 'infixing' when they appear in the Old Irish stems. As will be discussed in detail in Chapter 5, however, the scenario found in Old Irish is often the precondition from which infixes arise: should the preverb and main verb complex lose their independent meanings and form a distinct meaningful whole together, the trapped personal affixes, previously prefixed to the main verb, would have to be considered infixing. Ultan, in his pioneering 1975 study of the diachronic origins of infixation, termed this 'entrapment'. Thus, while the Old Irish person markers might appear to be on the way to becoming infixes, they still have not yet achieved this status given that, to the best of my knowledge, the person markers always occur between parts that are decomposable based on the synchronic data available.

Decomposability of the host alone might not suffice to rule out the possibility of infixation, however. The morphology of a number of Bantu languages illustrates this point. According to Orgun (1996), certain affixes in these languages must be regarded as infixed before the last vowel of a verb stem even though the last vowel is co-extensive with the causative morpheme. For example, in ChiBemba, labials change to [f] (e.g., -*lob*- 'be extinct' → -*lof-i* 'exterminate') and non-labials to [s] (e.g., -*lung*- 'hunt' → -*lúns-i* 'make hunt') before the causative suffix [i]. Nasals do not undergo this consonant mutation. Mutation overapplies, however, when the causative and applicative suffixes are both present in a stem. Both the root-final consonant and the /l/ of the applicative -*il* undergo mutation even though only the latter precedes [i] on the surface (Hyman 1994).[2]

(5) -leep-el-   'be long for/at'   -leef-es-i-   'lengthen for/at'
     -up-il-   'marry for/at'   -uf-is-i-   'marry off for/at'
     -lub-il-   'be lost for/at'   -luf-is-i-   'lose for/at'
     -lob-el-   'be extinct for/at'   -lof-es-i-   'exterminate for/at'
     -fiit-il-   'be dark for/at'   -fiis-is-i-   'darken for/at'
     -ónd-el-   'be slim for/at'   -óns-es-i-   'make slim for/at'
     -lil-il-   'cry for/'at'   -lis-is-i-   'make cry for/'at'
     -buuk-il-   'get up for/at'   -buus-is-i-   'get [s.o.] up for/at'
     -lúng-il-   'hunt for/at'   -lúns-is-i-   'make hunt for/at'

Thus the applicative seems to have infixed before the last vowel of a causativized stem (e.g., -*leef-es-i*- 'to lengthen for/at' from -*leef-i*- 'to lengthen'). It would not do to simply analyze the applicative as suffixing to the root directly since the root-final consonant would not have mutated appropriately (e.g., *-*leep-es-i*-). To be sure, it is also not viable to analyze the observed mutation as a matter of iterative right-to-left application of mutation triggered by the causative suffix. For example, mutation does not apply across the intransitive reversive suffix -*uk* even though the suffix itself undergoes mutation.

---

[2] The vowel of the applicative -*il*- harmonizes in height with the preceding vowel.

(6) | Verb | Intransitive | Intransitive-Causative | |
|---|---|---|---|
| -kak- | -kak-uk- | -kak-us-į-/*-kas-us-į- | 'tie' |
| -ang- | -ang-uk- | -ang-us-į-/*-ans-us-į- | 'feel light' |
| -sup- | -sup-uk- | -sup-us-į-/*-suf-us-į- | 'be lively' |

At first glance, the applicativization appears to be an instance of interfixation. For example, in German, constituents within compounds are often interjected with the segment *s* (e.g., *Geburt-s-tag* 'birthday') or *en* (*Schwan-en-gesang* 'swan song'). The linker morphemes, *-s-* and *-en-*, are interfixes, rather than infixes, since they do not appear within a monomorphemic continuous morph. However, the interfixation analysis of the applicative is insufficient. The parts that appear before and after the applicative marker do not themselves correspond to meanings that would jointly constitute the total meaning of the causative stem in the sense that the mutated root itself does not exist as a root independent of the causative suffix. That is, the applicative must take a mutated causative stem as its input (i.e., *lof-į* 'exterminate' is the input to *-lof-es-į-* 'exterminate for/at' not *-lob-* 'be extinct'). From the perspective of applicativization, a derived discontinuous stem is created out of the causative stem. The infixal nature of the applicative marker is thus established not only by the meaning (i.e., the applicative element is clearly an addition to a base already containing the meaning of the causative), but also by the phonological fact that mutation on the root-final consonant by the causative suffix is preserved after the addition of the infix, which results in a situation where the mutated root-final consonant is no longer adjacent to the mutation-inducing vowel.

As a final note, it is also important to maintain a clear distinction between sporadic infixation and systematic infixation. Sporadic infixation refers to a discernible infix that is perhaps a relic of a previously productive infixation process. For example, some researchers have noted that the *-n-* in *stand*, *tangential*, and *succumb* could be considered an infix in English (Sapir 1921). However, this nasal marker is a historical relic that largely occurs only in loanwords from French. The distribution of this *-n-* is extremely restricted and its function is by no means recoverable synchronically. This and other erratic appearances of intruding segment(s) are excluded as viable cases of infixation and will not be consider further in this study. The cases of infixation that fall within the scope of the present study must, therefore, be at least partially productive, if not fully, and their function must be recoverable.

While the descriptive apparatus discussed above helps us delineate the scope of the present study, the analysis of infixation is ultimately a theoretical matter. That is, how should infixes be treated as a formal object within the context of a theory of grammar? This is the topic of the next section.

2.2 Infixes as formal objects

Theories of infixation differ in their understandings of the nature of the interruption in the linear order between morphological constituents that is infixation. There are two broad classes of theories concerning the placement properties of infixes: *Phonological Readjustment* and *Phonological Subcategorization*. While these approaches espouse quite opposing views on the nature of infixation, in practice, individual analyses do not always fall straightly on either end of the analytic spectrum. As I cannot evaluate all in detail, I focus on arguments that affect most instantiations of each particular approach, paying specific attention to those properties which have gained currency in recent research. My goal here is to present the core of these ideas and explicate how these views should be understood in the context of infixation research.

But before diving into the specifics of these two approaches, it is useful to point out at the outset that all theories of infixation assume, at the very basic level, that infixes are adpositional affixes, formally no different from prefixes and suffixes. This assumption is derived from the premise that a Morphological Hierarchy, such as (7), does not distinguish between the different types of affixes since it does not prescribe the linear order between morphological constituents.

(7) Morphological Hierarchy
     MWd   →   Stem*
     Stem →   Stem, Affix
     Stem →   Root

A complete theory of morphology must provide a means to encode two types of relations between morphological elements—morphological dependence and linear precedence. Morphological dependence concerns the requirement of a morphological sister. One way to capture such a dependency is by way of subcategorization frames (Inkelas 1990; Kiparsky 1983; Lieber 1980; Selkirk 1982; Sproat 1985):

(8) English suffix -*ity*   N[A[ ] ity]
     English suffix -*ic*   A[N[ ] ic   ]
     English prefix *un*-   A[un A[ ]   ]

However, morphological structure represents only a commitment to the hierarchical organization of the constituent morphemes, not necessarily to linear ordering (Inkelas 1993; Sproat 1985: 80–1). Several formalisms for capturing linear precedence relation between linguistic entities have been proposed in the past. To this end, some theorists have extended the notion of morphological subcategorization to the phonological domain, based on evidence for a phonological structure distinct and parallel to the morphological structure within the lexicon (Booij 1985; Booij and Rubach 1984, 1987; Cohn 1989; Inkelas 1990, 1993; Sproat 1985, 1986). In particular, it is argued that while morphological subcategorization frames encode dominance relations in morphological structure, phonological subcategorization frames encode linear precedence relations. Thus while the morphological subcategorization frames in (8) encode the type of morphological sister each suffix takes, the phonological subcategorization frames in (9) specify the linear precedence between the affix and its sister.

(9) English suffix -*ity* $[[\ ]_{p\omega}$ ity $]_{p\omega}$
     English suffix -*ic* $[[\ ]_{p\omega}$ ic $]_{p\omega}$

This distinction between phonological vs morphological subcategorization is obscured in the context of Generalized Alignment (McCarthy and Prince 1993*a*) since the morphological element can align directly with the phonological one and vice versa. Generalized Alignment (GA) is a family of well-formedness constraints which 'demands that a designated edge of each prosodic or morphological constituent of type Cat1 coincide with a designated edge of some other constituent of Cat2' (McCarthy and Prince 1993*a*: 80). Although the formalism was originally developed within the context of Optimality Theory, GA is 'relatively abstract, and not tied to the particular details of phonological or morphology sub-theory' (McCarthy and Prince 1993*a*: 81).

(10) Generalized Alignment
      Align (Cat$_1$, Edge$_1$, Cat$_2$, Edge$_2$)$=_{\text{def}}$
          $\forall$ Cat$_1$ $\exists$ Cat$_2$ such that Edge$_1$ of Cat$_1$ and Edge$_2$ of Cat$_2$ coincide.
      Where Cat$_1$, Cat$_2$ ϵ PCat $\cup$ GCat
          Edge$_1$, Edge$_2$ ϵ {Right, Left }

The set of admissible GCat is derived from the morphological hierarchy stated below:

(11) Morphological Hierarchy (McCarthy and Prince 1993*a*: 85)
      MWd $\rightarrow$ Stem*
      Stem $\rightarrow$ Stem, Affix
      Stem $\rightarrow$ Root

On the other hand, the PCat is taken to be categories within the Prosodic Hierarchy. McCarthy and Prince recognize that the moraic and skeletal levels may also be part of this hierarchy. However, based on the evidence available to them, these levels subordinating to the syllable were left out due to lack of examples illustrating their relevance to edge alignment in morphological and phonological processes.

(12)   Prosodic Hierarchy

       Prosodic Word   PrWd

                                   |

       Foot   Ft

                                   |

       Syllable   σ

As will be illustrated below, many of the approaches to infixation discussed below and the theory defended in this work in particular adopt the basic formalism of GA for the purpose of encoding the edge-alignment relations between linguistic elements. A more detailed discussion of this formalism and its implementation appears in Chapter 3. It is sufficient to note at this juncture that GA provides a means to capture the diverse ways in which constituent edges figure in morphological (and phonological) processes. GA also provides a handy way to capture the distinction between the Phonological Readjustment and the Phonological Subcategorization approach to infixation. The first approach, Phonological Readjustment, regards infixation as a by-product of phonological operations. All affixes align with respect an edge of some morphological entity, be it root, stem or another affix. Phonological Subcategorization, on the other hand, takes infixes to be a by-product of mismatches between boundaries of phonological and morphological categories. On this view, the affix in question must align with respect to the edge of some phonological element, rather than a morphological one. When the edges of the phonological element and the morphological host coincide, the affix will surface as adpositional. However, when the phonological element is properly contained within the domain of the morphological host, the affix might appear infixal. The basic distinction between these two approaches is summarized in (13). On the view of Phonological Readjustment, both arguments of the alignment constraint are taken from the set of GCat.[3] On the view of

---

[3] To be sure, some Phonological Readjustment analyses treat prefixes and suffixes as aligning with respect to the PrWd. For example, while McCarthy and Prince (1993*a*: 102) analyze the actor focus marker -*um*- in Tagalog as aligning with respect to the stem (i.e., Align([um]$_A$, L, Stem, L)), Kager (2000: 122) treats -*um*- as aligning with respect to the PrWd.

Phonological Subcategorization, however, the universally quantified argument (Cat1) is of the GCat set while the existentially quantified argument (Cat2) is of the PCat set.

(13)	ALIGN	(Cat1	Cat2)
Phonological Readjustment		GCat	GCat
Phonological Subcategorization		GCat	PCat

In Sections 2.3 and 2.4, I survey the basic claims of these two approaches, rather than comparing and contrasting the myriad proposals for infixal placement. Section 2.4 is a critical discussion of these approaches. In particular, I focus on several issues which are highly problematic for the Phonological Readjustment approach and conclude that this line of analysis cannot be maintained. In the following chapters, I show that the Phonological Subcategorization approach, properly understood in the context of a holistic view of the theory of grammar, contains the machinery necessary for an explanation of the data which is problematic for the Phonological Readjustment analysis.

2.3 Infixation as a phonological process

Phonological Readjustment analyses share the unifying, but often implicit, assumption that infixes are underlyingly adpositional morphologically; that is, they are sisters to some morphological constituent. The surface appearance of infixation comes about as the result of readjustments (see Buckley 1997; Halle 2001; Hyman and Inkelas 1997; Kaufman 2003; McCarthy 2003b; McCarthy and Prince 1993a, 1994b; Moravcsik 1977; Stemberger and Bernhardt 1998). Derivational theories implement this idea differently from constraint-based approaches, however. From the perspective of a derivational theory of the grammar, infixation does not exist as a morphological process. The semblance of infixation is taken to be the result of segmental metathesis (Halle 2001; Moravcsik 1977). For example, Halle (2001) argues that many of the so-called VC infixes in many Austronesian languages are in fact CV prefixes. The apparent surface infixing pattern is a matter of Onset Metathesis. Take, for example, the [+realis] construction in Tagalog, as illustrated by the data below taken from Schachter and Otanes (1972: 370):

(14)	/in, ?awi/	→ ?-in-awit	'sang'
	/in, bigy, an/	→ b-in-igy-an	'gave to'
	/?i, in, bilih/	→ ?i-b-in-ilih	'bought for'
	/?i, ka-takoh/	→ ?i-k-in-a-takoh	'caused to run for'

Contrary to Schachter and Otanes's morphological analysis, Halle (2001) proposes that the [+realis] morpheme is underlyingly a CV prefix, *ni-*. The prefix appears to be infixed due to a rule of onset metathesis.

(15) UR *á la* Halle   SR   Gloss
     /ni, ʔawit/   →   ʔi-nawit   'sang'
     /ni, bigy, an/   →   bi-nigy-an   'gave to'
     /ʔi, ni, bilih/   →   ʔi-bi-nilih   'bought for'
     /ʔi, ni, ka-takboh/   →   ʔi-ki-na-takboh 'caused to run for'

Schematically, Halle's *Onset Metathesis* analysis of infixation can be stated as follows:

(16) Onset Metathesis

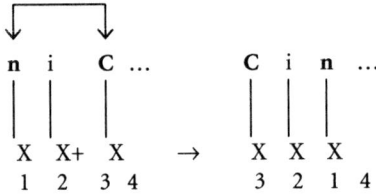

This understanding of 'infixation' follows from generative theories of grammar that are strictly modular. Operations in one module, like Syntax, are prevented from accessing or referring to information derived in another module, such as the phonological component. This view was reflected in Moravcsik's 1977 seminal treatise on the rules of infixing which implements the separation of information by proposing a metaconstraint against hetero-modality in grammatical statements. However, nowhere is this modular view of the grammar and its implication for the analysis of infixation more succinctly articulated than in Halle's 2001 rebuttal against the Optimality Theoretic analysis of infixation:

[F]rom the point of view of syntax, morphemes are indivisible, atom pieces. The syntax is systematically oblivious of phonological aspects of the morphemes. In the theory of Distributed Morphology (Halle and Marantz 1993) this obliviousness is formally reflected by the absence—in syntactic representations—of the phonetic exponents of the morphemes. In the syntax proper, morphemes are nothing but complexes of syntactic and semantic features; their phonetic exponents are inserted by Vocabulary Insertion, which is part of the morphology. Since the phonetic exponents of morphemes are thus not present in the syntax, it is literally impossible within the syntax to infix /um/ or /in/ before the first vowel of the Tagalog stem. This can only be done in the morphology or phonology, after the phonetic exponents of the morpheme have been spelled out. (Halle 2001: 153)

While this analysis duly handles the data discussed by Halle, the status of Onset Metathesis within Tagalog and in the theory of infix placement in general remains obscured. Onset Metathesis cannot be a general phonological process in the language since there are many instances of prefixation that do not involve infixation (e.g., the irrealis *ma-* and realis *na-* are straightforwardly prefixing; *ma-takot* 'fear.irrealis.perfective' and *na-takot* 'fear.realis.perfective'). Thus, Onset Metathesis must be treated as a morpheme-specific rule that is triggered only when the [+realis] morpheme is applied. On this view, 'infixation' is accounted for by stipulations. No general principle in the grammar triggers the application of segmental metathesis rules *per se*. The readjustment rule is specific to the morpheme in question.

On the other hand, for constraint-based models of phonology which eschew structure-building and structure-changing rules in favor of static well-formedness conditions evaluating output forms, interface between domains, if modularity still plays any substantial role at all in such a model, is often celebrated rather than avoided. The rationale behind this type of Phonological Readjustment analysis is not imposed by the intrinsic architecture of the grammar per se, but is rather a matter of methodological priorities. As McCarthy and Prince noted, the goal of all linguistic theories 'is to achieve greater empirical coverage with fewer resources—maybe with no resources at all that are specific to the domain under investigation' (McCarthy and Prince 1994: B13). In particular, the goal of Prosodic Morphology, the rubric under which infixation falls, is '[t]o explain properties of morphology/phonology dependency in terms of independent, general properties' (McCarthy and Prince 1994*b*: B1). On this view, motivations for the Phonological Readjustment approach stem from (i) a concern of formal economy, that is, the elimination of infixes as formal objects by deriving infixes from other morphological primitives, such as prefixes and suffixes, and (ii) the drive to achieve explanatory adequacy in a theory of grammar. Within the context of a constraint-based framework like Optimality Theory, this was taken to mean that infixation should be derived, rather than stipulated, through constraint interaction. Consider, for example, the case of agreement infixation in the Siouan language, Dakota. The Dakotan agreement system consists of a set of person/number affixes which are prefixed to monosyllabic verb roots and some polysyllabic ones, but are infixed after the initial syllable into other polysyllabic verb roots of a lexically specified subclass.

(17)   Dakota agreement infixation (Moravcsik 1977: 95–6, based on Boas and
       Deloria 1941)

ća.pa	'stab'	ća.**wa**.pca	'I stab'
ʔi.kto.mi	'Iktomi'	ʔi.**ma**.ktomi	'I am Iktomi'
ma.nç	'steal'	ma.**wa**.nç	'I steal'
na.pca	'swallow'	na.**wa**.pca	'I swallow it'
la.kᶜota	'Lakota'	la.**ma**.kᶜota	'I am a Lakota'
na.wizi	'jealous'	na.**wa**.wizi	'I am jealous'

McCarthy and Prince (1993*a*) analyze the agreement markers as formally
prefixes which are subject to the ALIGN-IN-STEM constraint in (18). This
constraint states that the left edge of the agreement marker must coincide
with the left edge of the stem.

(18)   ALIGN-IN-STEM(Dakota)
       Align([AGR]$_{Af}$, L, Stem, L)

For the infix-taking subclass of verb roots, however, the agreement morphemes are prevented from surfacing as prefixes by the dominant ALIGN-
ROOT constraint in (19).

(19)   ALIGN-ROOT(Dakota)
       Align(Root, L, PrWd, L)

As shown in Tableau (20), the agreement marker -*wa*- is infixed after the first
CV of the root (20c) because of the dominance of ALIGN-ROOT over ALIGN-
IN-STEM (see the failure of (20a)). Minimal displacement of the agreement
markers from the absolute initial position, i.e., *ćwa.a.pa*, does not suffice to
derive the optimal output. McCarthy and Prince argue that the constraint
ONSET is involved, disfavoring candidates with syllables that are onsetless.

(20)

wa, *ćapa*	ONSET	ALIGN-ROOT	ALIGN-IN-STEM
a. [-<u>wa</u>.lća.pa[4]		*!	
b. [lć-<u>wa</u>.a.pa.	*!		ć
c.☞ [lća.-wa.pa.			ća

---

4 The left edge of the root is denoted by '|', the left edge of the affix by '–', and the left edge of PrWd by '['.

Thus, unlike the derivational theories of Phonological Readjustment, which derive the surface appearance of infixation by way of some phonological operation, on the view of the constraint-based approach, affix movement is key. As illustrated above, 'infixation shows that phonological constraints can determine even the linear order of morphemes and morpheme parts' (McCarthy and Prince 1993*a*: 85). In a constraint-based approach, affix reordering is motivated by reifying a long-standing intuition that the position of an infix is functionally linked to its shape. That is, affixes 'migrate' only when the infixed outcome yields 'better' surface realization (Anderson 1972; Buckley 1997; Cohn 1992; McCarthy and Prince 1993*a*; Prince and Smolensky 1993). What counts as the functional motivating factors for infixation are many, although not all of them have equal explanatory values. Some argue that affixes move away from the edge in order to improve syllable structure well-formedness (McCarthy 2003*b*; McCarthy and Prince 1993*a*, 1994*b*; Prince and Smolensky 1993). Others consider it a matter of featural preservation (Buckley 1997). Like the case of Dakota, many have also argued that infixation serves to preserve morphotactics (Lubowicz 2005; Stemberger and Bernhardt 1998).

In this section, I reviewed the logic of the Phonological Readjustment approach to infixation in both derivational and non-derivational frameworks. The fundamental assumption that unifies all Phonological Readjustment-based analyses is the insistence that the motivation for infixation must be exogenous. The Phonological Subcategorization approach, to be reviewed in the next section, eschews this analytic bias.

2.4 Infixation as morpho-phonological mismatch

Proponents of the Phonological Subcategorization approach embrace the mismatch between morphological and phonological representations. On this view, an infix is an affix that is sensitive to the phonological properties of its sister. Phonological sensitivity is often encoded in the form of *phonological subcategorization*, that is, an infix is an affix that subcategorizes specifically for a phonological constituent as its sister, rather than a morphological one. Simplifying the analysis at this juncture, the expletive infix in English, for example, can be treated as lodging before a stressed trochaic foot (FT'). Such a subcategorization requirement may be stated in terms of a subcategorization frame or a GA constraint (21). Crucially, when the left edge of the stressed foot and the left edge of a stem coincide, the expletive appears prefixing (e.g., *bloody-(háppy)*). When the left edge of the stem is to the left of the stressed foot, the expletive appears infixing (e.g., *fan-bloody-*(*tástic*), *Kalama-**goddamn**-*(*zóo*)).[5]

(21)   English expletive
        Subcategorization frame: 'expletive' $[(\sigma_s \dots)]$
        Generalized Alignment: Align ('expletive', R, FT', L)

Likewise, some theories analyze infixes as *bi-dependent* in that infixes subcategorize for two entities simultaneously (Inkelas 1990; Kiparsky 1986). That is, infixes subcategorize for some prosodic constituent (i.e., the frame-internal $[\ ]_p$ in (22)) and the material across which they are attached (i.e., the X in (22)).

(22) $[X\_[\ ]_p\ ]_p$

Thus, for example, the infix *-in-* in the Timugon dialect of Sabah Murut (see (3)) has the subcategorization frame $[(C) \_ [\ ]_p\ ]_p$ where *-in-* is understood to take a prosodic stem, in the sense of Inkelas 1990, as its right constituent and may optionally be preceded by a consonant.

To be sure, the ability for an affix to subcategorize for a phonological constituent is not unique to infixes. Adpositional affixes often have phonological subcategorization requirements as well. A typology of subcategorization types and examples of each type are given in (23).

(23) Subcategorization	Examples
Morphological (Adpositional affix)	English nominalizing *-ness*
Morphological/Phonological	German perfective participle *ge-*
Phonological (Infix)	English *ma*-infixation, Ulwa *ka*-infixation

From the perspective of learning, phonological subcategorization takes place under two scenarios. When the placement of a morpheme can be determined by both morphological and prosodic/phonological means simultaneously, this analytical ambiguity often gives rise to selection of either one or both modes of affixation. Examples of simultaneous subcategorizations at the morphological and phonological levels are not difficult to find in the literature. For example, the German perfective participle, *ge-*, only attaches to stems that begin with a stressed syllable; the Lappish illative plural has two allomorphs: *-ide*, which appears after a stem with an even number of syllables, and *-ida*, which appears after a stem with an odd number of syllables (Bergsland 1976; Hargus 1993). Similarly, in Dyirbal, the ergative suffix is *-ŋgu* with disyllabic V-final nouns

---

   [5] In this work, I shall focus strictly on the purely phonologically governed distribution of the expletive and leave aside the issue of the interaction between expletive placement and morphological boundary for future research (but see McCawley 1978).

(24a), but is *-gu* when the stem is longer (24b). Stress is initial and alternating in Dyirbal although final syllables are never stressed (Dixon 1972: 274–6).

(24) a. yaɽa-ŋgu   'man'
      b. yamani-gu   'rainbow'
          balagara-gu 'they'

According to McCarthy and Prince (1993*b*), the *-ŋgu* suffix subcategorizes for the head foot as its left-sister (i.e., AFFIX-TO-FOOT). When direct suffixation to a disyllabic stem is not possible (i.e., when the right edge of the head foot does not coincide with the right edge of the stem), the general, non-phonological subcategorizing, suffixal allomorph, *-gu*, is used instead (see also Paster 2006). The subcategorization requirement of an infix is formally no different from that of these ergative suffixes. The only difference is in the response to the failure of Phonological Subcategorization satisfaction. In Dyirbal, for example, when the Phonological Subcategorization of the ergative *-ŋgu* cannot be satisfied adpositionally, instead of infixation (e.g., **yama-ŋgu-ni*), an alternative general suffixal allomorph, *-gu*, is used instead. Other languages may return no output (in which case, ineffability obtains) or make use of periphrasis. I will return to this topic in Section 6.4 in Chapter 6. The main point here is that, from this perspective, infixes are really just affixes without any subcategorization requirement stated at the morphological level. 'Infixation' is essentially epiphenomenonal; nothing in the grammar requires morpheme interruption *per se*. There is no reordering of segments or movement of affixes. Infixation simply falls out from the cross-level edge-alignment property of phonological subcategorization; no stipulated mechanism is needed to account for infixation.

Before turning to the comparison between Phonological Readjustment and Phonological Subcategorization, it should be noted that phonological sensitivity in morphology, particularly in the context of infixation, may also be encoded indirectly, for example, in the form of stem alternation. For example, within the theory of Prosodic Morphology prior to the advent of Optimality Theory (McCarthy and Prince 1990, 1993*a*, 1993*b*), infixation is analyzed in terms of *operational prosodic circumscription*, which is a factoring function that allows a peripheral constituent to be parsed from a string. Operations can then be performed on that element (positive circumscription) or on the remainder (negative circumscription). In particular, prominence-driven infixes are analyzed in terms of positive operational prosodic circumscription while edge-oriented infixes are analyzed in terms of negative operational prosodic circumscription. Consider, for example, that in Samoan, a Polynesian language, plural is marked by reduplicating the penultimate, thus stressed, syllable. Syllables are always open, thus the reduplicant is CV in shape. When the stem is more than two syllables long, the reduplicant appears to infix before the stressed syllable.

(25)   Samoan plural (Mosel and Hovdhaugen 1992: 221–2)[6]

tóa	'brave'	totóa
má:	'ashamed'	mamá:
alófa	'love'	a:lolofa
galúe	'work'	ga:lulúe
a:vága	'elope'	a:vavága
atamái	'clever'	atamamái
maʔalíli	'cold, feel cold'	maʔalilíli
toʔúlu	'fall, drop'	toʔuʔúlu

Under positive prosodic circumscription, one first selects the prosodic constituent to be copied (represented by the function Φ), in this case, a stressed foot (step i). The Φ-delimited portion of the word is assembled with the non-Φ-delimited part of the stem (step ii). The reduplicative prefix O is then affixed to this circumscribed foot (step iii), followed by the reassembling in step iv.

(26)   i.   O: $\Phi(\text{a}[\text{lófa}]_{\text{Ft}})$ = $\text{a}[\text{lófa}]_{\text{Ft}}/\Phi * O(\text{a}[\text{lófa}]_{\text{Ft}}{:}\Phi)$

    ii.   = $\text{a} * O([\text{lófa}]_{\text{Ft}})$

    iii.   = $\text{a} * \text{lolófa}$

    iv.   =   alolófa

In negative prosodic circumscription, the circumscribed prosodic constituent, rather than serving as the base of affixation, is stripped away temporarily for the purpose of affixation.

(27)   Timugon Murut (McCarthy 2000; Prentice 1971)

a.

bulud	**bu**-bulud	'hill/ridge'
limo	**li**-limo	'five/about five'
ulampoy	u-**la**-lampoy	no gloss
abalan	a-**ba**-balan	'bathes/often bathes'
ompodon	om-**po**-podon	'flatter/always flatter'

b.   Circumscriptional analysis

Φ(Onsetless Syllable, Left), O   =   Prefix σ_{μ} (reduplicative prefix)

O/Φ(ompodon)   =   O(ompodon/Φ) * ompodon:Φ

    =   O(podon) * om

    =   popodon * om

    =   Ompopodon

---

[6] While stress is not marked in the source, stress marking is indicated to facilitate the presentation.

For example, partial reduplication in Timugon Murut, an Austronesian language spoken in Malaysia, can be analyzed in terms of negative circumscription where an initial onsetless syllable, if any, is circumscribed and stripped away temporarily (McCarthy 2000). The reduplicative morpheme is then attached to the residue (see (27b) for a step-wise illustration of this operation). Operational prosodic circumscription was abandoned in the wake of the advent of Optimality Theory. McCarthy (2000), for example, contends that infixation can be more insightfully analyzed in terms of the OT implementation of Phonological Readjustment. As reviewed in the next section, however, such a conclusion is not warranted.

2.5 Phonological Readjustment and Phonological Subcategorization compared

The differences between Phonological Readjustment and Phonological Subcategorization approaches to infixation can be summarized schematically as in (28). On the view of Phonological Subcategorization, an affix, *A*, takes a phonological constituent, *X*, as its left sister. When the right edge of *X* is within the domain of the morphological host (and if *A* is to be realized faithfully), the infixal distribution of *A* obtains. Infixation is epiphenomenal in the sense that no mechanism in the grammar requires the intramorphemic distribution of the affix in question. The infix does not undergo any movement at any level of the analysis either. If the stem boundary coincides with the edge of *X*, the affix will appear adpositionally. It is only when the morphological and the phonological edges misalign that the affix manifests as an infix.

From the perspective of Phonological Readjustment, on the other hand, infixation is the result of displacement. The affix *A* is prefixed to the stem *XYZ*. The phonology then repositions the terminal phonetic form of *A* (or the morpheme *A* itself) inside the terminal phonetic form of *XYZ* and infixation obtains. It should be noted that the nature of the displacement differs between the derivational and constraint-based approaches to Phonological Readjustment. From the perspective of the constraint-based model, it is the morpheme that moves. As McCarthy and Prince (1993a: 85) emphasize, 'infixation shows that phonological constraints can determine even the linear order of *morphemes* and *morpheme parts*'. On the view of the derivational model, however, it is the phonological strings that permute, never the morpheme itself.

(28)   Phonological Readjustment Phonological Subcategorization

Input	/A, XYZ/	/A, XYZ/
Morphology	A+XYZ	XAYZ
Phonology	XAYZ	XAYZ
Output	XAYZ	XAYZ

This work is a defense of the Phonological Subcategorization view of infixation. Before introducing in more detail the theoretic apparatus for the understanding of Phonological Subcategorization, I review in some detail arguments against the Phonological Readjustment approach. Since much research has demonstrated the need for simultaneous reference to phonological and morphological structures in languages (Booij 1985; Booij and Rubach 1984, 1987; Cohn 1989; Inkelas 1990, 1993; Sproat 1985, 1986), I see no reason to restrict our theoretical apparatus from accessing cross-modular information. This freedom with respect to cross-module interaction is particularly acute in the context of constraint-based approaches to language (see more discussion of this issue in the next chapter). As such, I shall limit my discussion of the derivational view of Phonological Readjustment and focus my attention instead on the constraint-based view of Phonological Readjustment, particularly as it is implemented in Optimality Theory (henceforth OT-PR). However, when appropriate, I will highlight critiques that are equally applicable to both views of Phonological Readjustment.

2.5.1 *On the ethological view of infixation*

One of the main arguments for OT-PR rests on the premise that the infixability of an affix is partly determined by the phonological composition of the affix itself and the context in which it appears. Similar ethological observations have been made repeatedly in the literature (Anderson 1972; Buckley 1997; Cohn 1992). Formally, this intuition is captured by the constraint-ranking schema, P >> M, one of the three basic tenets of Prosodic Morphology within Optimality Theory.

(29)   Prosodic Morphology within OT (McCarthy and Prince 1993*b*: 110)
   a. Prosodic Morphology Hypothesis
      Templates are constraints on the prosody/morphology interface, asserting the coincidence of morphological and prosodic constituent.

   b. Template Satisfaction Condition
      Templatic constraints may be undominated, in which case they are satisfied fully, or they may be dominated, in which case they are violated minimally, in accordance with general principles of Optimality Theory.

c. **Ranking Schema**
   P >> M

The main innovation of this conception of Prosodic Morphology lies in (29c), which embodies the idea that prosody-governed morphology is the result of phonological constraints (P) taking precedence over morphological ones (M). Phonological constraints may be of several varieties (e.g., segmental faithfulness, syllable well-formedness, segmental markedness, etc.). On the other hand, morphological constraints generally include constraints on faithfulness (e.g., FAITH-Root, FAITH-Affix, etc.) and linear precedence (i.e., alignment constraints). It is the latter that is most relevant in the case of infixation. For example, McCarthy (2003*b*) proposes that the affix -*um*- in Tagalog should be treated formally as a prefix and is infixed to avoid onsetless word-initial syllables in the outputs. The affix -*um*- is infixed after the stem-initial consonant since prefixing -*um*- would have resulted in a fatal violation of ONSET, which penalizes any onsetless syllables (30b). It serves little purpose to ameliorate the fatal ONSET violation by supplying the prefix with an onset (30c) due to the dominance of DEP-C, a constraint that penalizes consonant epenthesis. To be sure, gratuitous additional inward migration of -*um*- is not encouraged since it does not improve the standing of the candidate (see (30d)).

(30) EDGEMOST(L, *um*)   The morpheme *um* is located at the left edge;
                          is a prefix.
      ONSET   Syllables must begin with a consonant.
      DEP-C   Do not epenthesize consonants.

/um, tata /	DEP-C	ONSET	EDGEMOST(L, *um*)
☞ a. tumata			*
b. umtata		*!	
c. ʔumtata	*!		
d. tatuma			*!**

If infixation were indeed the result of phonological constraints taking precedence over morphological ones, and phonological constraints are constraints penalizing marked structures, it follows that one should never expect to find instances of infixation that yield structures that are more marked than their prefixing or suffixing counterparts. This observation has prompted, for example, Buckley to revel at the dearth of examples of 'CV infixes which occur after the onset' (1997: 14).

Blevins (1999) reports just such a case in Leti, an Austronesian language spoken on the island of Leti, east of Timor.[7] Leti nominalizing affixation has eight distinct phonological forms: three infixes -*ni*-, -*n*-, -*i*-; three prefixes *ni*-, *i*-, *nia*; a parafix *i*-+-*i*-; and a zero allomorph. Each of these allomorphs has very specific distribution. The infix -*ni*- appears before the first vowel of the stem when the stem has an initial non-nasal or non-alveolar consonant followed by a non-high vowel (31a). The infix -*ni*- is realized as -*n*- when the stem contains a high vowel after the initial consonant (31b).

(31) Nominalizing -*ni*- in Leti (Blevins 1999)

a.	kaati	'to carve'	k-ni-aati	'carving'
	kasi	'to dig'	k-ni-asi	'act of digging'
	kakri	'to cry'	k-ni-akri	'act of crying'
	pèpna	'to fence'	p-ni-èpna	'act of fencing, fence'
	polu	'to call'	p-ni-olu	'act of calling, call'
	n-sai	'to climb, rise, III (3SG)'	s-ni-ai	'act of climbing, rising'
	n-teti	'to chop, III (3SG)'	t-ni-eti	'chop, chopping'
	n-vaka	'to ask (for), III (3SG)'	v-ni-aka	'act of asking, request'
b.	kili	'to look'	k-n-ili	'act of looking'
	kini	'to kiss'	k-n-ini	'act of kissing, kiss'
	surta	'to write'	s-n-urta	'act of writing, memory'
	tutu	'to support'	t-n-utu	'act of supporting, support'
	n-virna	'to peel, II (3SG)'	v-n-irna	'act of peeling'

Another allomorph of -*ni*- is -*i*-, which surfaces before the first vowel of the stem when the initial consonant is a sonorant or an alveolar consonant.

(32)   Nominalizing -*i*- in Leti

davra	'cut'	d-i-avra	'act of cutting, cut'
dèdma	'to smoke'	d-i-èdma	'act of smoking'
l-lèvra	'to disperse s.t.'	l-i-èvra	'dispersal'
l-lòi	'to dance'	l-i-òi	'act of dancing'
mai	'to come'	m-i-ai	'arrival'
n-nasu	'to cook'	n-i-asu	'cooking'
n-navu	'he sows'	n-i-avu	'the act of sowing'
n-resi	'to win'	r-i-esi	'victory'
n-ròra	'to draw (a line)'	r-i-òra	'line'

---

[7] Consonants [t, n, s] are dental in Leti, while [d, l, r] are alveolar. Following Blevins's transcription, v = [β]; è = [ɛ]; ò = ɔ.

The fact that the nominalizing morph, -*ni*-, is infixed is puzzling within a prosodic optimization view of infixation. It is unclear what problems confront the strategy of simply prefixing -*ni* to the stem (e.g., *ni-teti instead of *t-ni-eti* 'chop, chopping'). The infixal outputs invariably contain initial onset clusters and vowel-vowel sequences;[8] both are marked structures typologically. To be sure, Leti infixation cannot be analyzed on the par as Dakota agreement infixation, that is, as an instance of edge avoidance. When the stem is vowel-initial, the nominalizer is prefixed. According to van Engelenhoven (2004), the *i*-prefix sometimes nominalizes the verb as an instrument while the *ni*- prefix nominalizes the verbal act.

(33) Nominalizing -(*n*)*i*- in Leti

n-osri	'to hunt'	i-osri, ni-osri	'act of hunting'
n-otlu	'to push'	i-otlu, ni-otlu	'act of pushing'
n-atu	'to know'	i-atu, ni-atu	'knowledge'
n-odi	'to carry'	i-odi, ni-odi	'pole, load, act of carrying'
n-èmnu	'to drink'	i-èmnu, ni-èmnu	'act of drinking, drink, beverage'
n-òra	'to be with'	i-òra, ni-òra	'companion'

A similarly puzzling case of infixation is found in Pingding Mandarin. As in most Mandarin dialects, Pingding has a diminutive/hypocoristic affixation process. However, unlike the other dialects, where this process is marked by the suffixing of a retroflexed morpheme (i.e., -*r*), the cognate morpheme in Pingding, -ɭ-, is infixed before the rhyme of a syllable.

(34) Pingding -ɭ-infixation (Lin 2002; Xu 1981; Yu 2004*b*)

mən tuɤŋ	+	ɭ	→	mən tɭuɤŋ	'hole on the door'
lɔɔ tʰɤu	+	ɭ	→	lɔɔ tʰɭɤu	'old man'
çiɔɔ pɤŋ	+	ɭ	→	çiɔɔ pɭɤŋ	'small notebook'
xɤu mɤŋ	+	ɭ	→	xɤu mɭɤŋ	'back door'
çiɔɔ kuɤ	+	ɭ	→	çiɔɔ kɭuɤ	'small wok'
xuɑŋ xuɑ	+	ɭ	→	xuɑŋ xɭuɑ	'yellow flower'
ŋɤ	+	ɭ	→	ŋɭɤ	'moth'

Outside the domain of infixation, Pingding Mandarin has the canonical Chinese syllable structure, (C)(G)V(C) where G stands for a glide. The very fact that onset clusters should be tolerated just in the case of infixation should be evidence enough for rejecting the hypothesis that infixation is a matter of prosodic optimization. Lin (2002) notes that there is at least one redeeming aspect of ɭ-infixation, that is, it follows the Sonority Sequencing Constraint.

---

[8] The high vowel in a vowel-vowel sequence is realized as a glide.

However, recent work on the positional markedness effects of retroflexion (Steriade 1995) has demonstrated that retroflexion is perceptually most salient in post-vocalic positions. Thus, the 'migration' of [ɭ] to post-consonantal position only endangers the identification of the retroflex feature, rather than enhancing it.

What the Leti and Pingding cases illustrate is that infixation can occur for no obvious prosodic or phonotactic gains. The optimization approach offers us no insight as to why such infixation patterns exist at all. One may appeal to edge avoidance to account for certain cases, but the fundamental appeal of the OT-Phonological Readjustment approach is lost in such an analysis. That is, the functional motivation for an affix to migrate inward is to minimize output prosodic or phonotactic markedness. This functional connection is not readily available for the edge-avoidance analysis.

The list of non-functionally motivated infixes may be expanded to include infixes that do not either improve or worsen output markedness. For example, in Hua, a Papuan language of the Eastern Highlands of New Guinea, the negative marker -ʔa- appears before the final syllable.

(35)   Hua negative formation (Haiman 1980)
zgavo   zgaʔavo   'not embrace'
harupo   haruʔapo   'not slip'

Prosodically speaking, the suffixal counterpart of this CV marker would have resulted in equally well-formed outputs (see also the Budukh case in (40)). No obvious functional motivations can be adduced for the infixing of such a morpheme.

In light of the cases reviewed above, the purported functional bond between the shape of an infix and its position with respect to the host is at best suspect. A closer look at the typology of infix shape and its placement property supports this position. Claims with regard to the functional connection between morpheme shape and infix position were established previously based on the perceived prevalence of VC affixes that infix after an onset consonant. Upon closer examination, however, the purported functional connection may actually reflect a bias introduced by impoverished sampling. Of the forty cases of fixed-segment VC infixation, twenty-three are from the Austronesian languages, eleven are from Austro-Asiatic languages, while only six are from other languages.[9] More importantly, of the thirty-four VC infixes that appear after the first consonant or before the first vowel of the stem, all

---

[9] The ethological connection between infix shape and its location was first noted in Anderson's (1972) study of nasalization and infixation in Sundanese, an Austronesian language.

but one belongs to the Austronesian and the Austro-Asiatic families.[10] The fact that the majority of the post-onset VC infixes belong to one of two language families suggests that such cases might be features inherited from their respective protolanguages.[11] In contrast, about 20 percent of the fixed-segment infixes surveyed are CV in shape, about 10 percent are just a single vowel, and about 44 percent are monoconsonantal. Of these coda- or cluster-generating monoconsonantal infixes, only five are from Austronesian and three from Austro-Asiatic.

(36) Breakdown of fixed segment infixes by shape (and position)

	Austronesian	Austro-Asiatic	Other languages	Total
VC after C_1 or before V_1	22	11	1	34
VC elsewhere	1	0	5	6
C	5	5	34	44
CV	3	0	17	20
V	3	1	6	10

Thus, a closer look at the cross-linguistic evidence shows that an ethological understanding of infixation cannot be substantiated. Since the OT-PR approach to infixation was built upon this ethological assumption of infix placement, the rejection of this premise left the foundation of the theory badly shaken. In the next section, I turn to the empirical adequacy of the OT-PR approach. Upon closer scrutiny, the theory crumbles as I reveal deep-rooted problems with both the derivational and constraint-based versions of Phonological Readjustment.

2.5.2 On the issue of empirical coverage: Problems of undergeneration

Both derivational and constraint-based Phonological Readjustment approaches to infix placement suffer from an inherent limitation on empirical coverage. The most effective demonstration of this limitation comes from the domain of iterative infixation. Iterative infixation is commonly found among language games and disguises (see Section 6.2 for more discussion). For example, a language game in Hausa involves inserting -*bV*- after the vowel of each word-internal syllable. The vowel of the infix is a copy of the preceding vowel.

---

[10] The lone exception comes from the intensive -*eg*- infix in Yurok, an Algic language. The origin of this infix is discussed in Section 5.2.3.4 in Chapter 5.

[11] The Austronesian VC infixes are mainly reflexes of the actor focus **mu-/-um-* or the perfective **ni-/in-* in Proto-Austronesian (Dahl 1976: ch. 22).

(37) Hausa word game (Newman 2000: 297)
      gidā   gibìda   'house'
      maskī   mabàski   'oily'
      Màimunà   Maibàimubùna   'Maimuna (name)'
      hatsī   habàtsi   'grain'

Similarly, in Tagalog, the infix -*gVVdV*- is inserted after the vowel of each syllable. The unspecified vowels of the infix copy the adjacent vocalism of the basic form (Conklin 1956, 1959).

(38) Tagalog *baliktad* speech-disguise game (Conklin 1956)
      hindí?   higíidindigíidi?   'not, not'
      taŋháali?   tagáadaŋhagáadaligíidi?   'noon'

It is unclear what type of phonological readjustment can account for the multitude of infixal locations if infixes are underlyingly adpositional. (Iterative infixation finds natural expression within a Phonological Subcategorization approach, however. See Section 6.3 in Chapter 6 for more discussion.)

The limitation of Phonological Readjustment extends beyond the domain of language games and disguises. For example, recall that Halle (2001) reanalyzes VC infixation as a matter of CV prefixation followed by Onset Metathesis. Thus, the fact that the passive completive marker in Toba Batak has two allomorphs (the allomorph *ni*- is prefixed to vowel-initial roots, while the allomorph -*in*- is infixed after the first consonant of consonant-initial roots (39a)) can be straightforwardly analyzed under the Onset Metathesis analysis. Yet, not all VC infixes can be reanalyzed in this way. Halle himself points out that the nominalizing marker -*al*- in Toba Batak is a bona fide infix (Halle 2001: 163). That is, while -*al*- is infixed before the first vowel when the stem begins with a consonant, it is straightforwardly prefixed to vowel-initial stems (39b). Onset metathesis is not applicable here since vowel-initial stems are genuinely vowel-initial (rather than beginning with a glottal stop as in Tagalog). Instead, infixation of the nominalizing -*al*- is treated as the result of *al*-prefixation followed by Stem Onset Preposing (e.g., *al-bátuk* → *b-al-átuk* 'ladder').

(39) a. ni-ulÓs-an   'have been covered' (completive passive)
          b-in-úat   'has been taken' (completive passive)
          j-in-oú-an   'have been called repeatedly' (completive passive)
      b. b-al-átuk   'ladder'
          al-ógo   'wind'

Onset Metathesis also offers no recourse when the infix is CV in shape. As illustrated in (40), the prohibitive infix -*mE*- in Budukh, a Lezgic language spoken in the Caucasus, always appears after the initial vowel of the stem.

Onset Metathesis predicts the wrong results (e.g., *mə+yixər* → **yəmixər*, not *yiməxər*).

(40)   Budukh prohibitive (Alekseev 1994*a*: 279)

Root	Gloss	Prohibitive
yeči	'to arrive'	yemeči
yixər	'to be'	yiməxər
yuc'u	'to give'	yumoc'u

Derivational accounts are particularly uninsightful when dealing with *tmesis*, that is, instances of infixation involving a whole word into another (e.g., English expletive infixation: *abso-bloody-lutely*). Rule-based formulations of *tmesis* are riddled with shortcomings. Aronoff (1976: 70), for example, proposes the rule in (41) for expletive infixation in English. This rule dictates that the expletive infix must be preceded by a tertiary stress and follow immediately by the primary stress.

(41)   Expletive infixation in English

$$
\begin{array}{cccccc}
 & 3 & & 1 & & \\
[\text{X} & \text{V} & \text{Q} & \text{V} & \text{Y}] & \\
1 & 2 & 3 & 4 & 5 & \rightarrow \quad 1 \quad 2 \quad 3 \quad \text{Expletive} \quad 4 \quad 5 \\
 & & & & & 3
\end{array}
$$

Condition: Q does not contain V

Not only does this rule fail to account for many attested examples (e.g., *Ne-bloody-braska*), as McCarthy (1982) noted, it crucially fails to explain the relationship among stress, syllabification, and the infixed expletive that is encoded into the rule.

Like its derivational cousin, OT-PR is limited in empirical coverage as well. There exists one class of infixes that has always been outside the purview of OT-PR, that is, the stress-driven infixes. From the outset, stress-driven infixes are treated in terms of prosodic subcategorization, a subtype of phonological subcategorization (see e.g., McCarthy and Prince 1993*a*). For example, in Ulwa, a Misumalpan language spoken in Nicaragua and Honduras, the construct-state (CNS) markers are affixed to the right edge of an iambic foot.

(42)   Ulwa construct state (Green 1999: 64)

súːlu	súː-**ma**-lu	'dog-CNS2'
áytak	áy-**mana**-tak	'paper-CNS22'
aláːkuṃ	aláː-**ka**-kuṃ	'Muscovy duck-CNS3'
waráẉwa	waráẉ-**kana**-wa	'parrot sp.-CNS33'
káːsiráːmah	káː-**ki**-siráːmah	'lizard sp.-CNS1'

To account for these infixal markers, McCarthy and Prince (1993*a*) set up the prosodic subcategorization constraint in (43), formulated in the schema of Generalized Alignment.

(43) Ulwa infixal construct noun marker
      ALIGN-TO-FOOT
      ALIGN ([POSS]$_{Af}$, L, FT', R)
      'The left edge of the construct noun marker is aligned to the right edge
      of the head foot.'

The Ulwa example thus highlights an important point about OT-PR. Unlike
its derivational cousin, the constraint-based approach does not reject
Phonological Subcategorization. It remains an integral part of its analytic
arsenal. However, there is an implicit priority in analytical preference. OT-PR
bears the main burden of explaining the Edge-Bias Effect. Phonological
Subcategorization is invoked only when no OT-PR option is available.
This analytic priority of Phonological Readjustment over Phonological Subcategorization is a reflection of two presuppositions. The first is the
ethological attitude OT-PR analysts take toward infix placement. As demonstrated in the last section, however, the ethological view lacks empirical
substance and should not be maintained. The second stems from a theory-
internal bias against invoking sub-prosodic constituents in phonological
analysis.

The theory of Prosodic Morphology, first articulated in McCarthy and
Prince (1986), requires morphological processes that interact with phonology
to refer to genuine prosodic constituents. The basic tenets of this theory are
given in (44).

(44) Basic tenets of Prosodic Morphology (McCarthy and Prince 1993b: 109)

      Prosodic Morphology Hypothesis: Templates are defined in terms
      of the authentic units of prosody: mora (μ), syllable (σ), foot (Ft),
      prosodic word (PrWd).
      Template Satisfaction Condition: Satisfaction of templatic constraints is
      obligatory and determined by the principles of prosody, both universal
      and language-specific.
      Prosodic Circumscription of Domains: The domain to which morpho-
      logical operations apply may be circumscribed by prosodic criteria as
      well as by the more familiar morphological ones.

The admittance of sub-prosodic unit into alignment or subcategorization
relation has traditionally been seen as an embarrassment to the theory of
Prosodic Morphology since the unit referred to by such an affix often does not
match the units generally licensed by the Prosodic Hierarchy (see e.g.,
McCarthy and Prince 1993a). For example, on the view of Phonological
Subcategorization, the animate actor focus marker, -*m*-, in Atayal is treated

as subcategorizing for the first consonant of the stem as its left-sister.[12] Yet, most theories of prosodic phonology do not admit a consonant as a possible constituent within the Prosodic Hierarchy (see Broselow 1995 for an overview of the evidence for and against skeletal units below the level of the mora).

(45)   Atayal animate actor focus (Egerod 1965: 263–6)

qul	qmul	'snatch'
kat	kmat	'bite'
kuu	kmuu	'too tired, not in the mood'
hŋuʔ	hmŋuʔ	'soak'
skziap	kmziap	'catch'
sbil	smbil	'leave behind'

While the need to refer to sub-prosodic units remains controversial in the phonological literature, suggestive supportive evidence abounds. For example, in speech-error studies, many have found that consonants and vowels within words are often exchangeable.

(46)   a. Consonantal exchange (Fromkin 1980)
       Error (target)
       my hetter baff (My better half)
       The Folden Gleece award (The Golden Fleece award)

       b. Vocalic exchange (Shattuck-Hufnagel 1986)
       f[i]t the b[ʊ]ll (foot the bill)
       st[ɪ]rred the sh[i]p (steered the ship)
       al[i]minum an' st[u]l (aluminum an' steel)
       ch[i]ps 'n tw[ɚ]ts (chirps 'n tweets)

Such an independent awareness of consonants from vowels is also observed in poetic devices such as alliteration and assonance.

(47)   *Alliteration*:   In clichés: *sweet smell of success, a dime a dozen, bigger and better, jump for joy*
               Wordsworth: *And sings a solitary song | That whistles in the wind.*
       Assonance: 'fleet feet sweep by sleeping geeks.'

Language games and language disguise, which have provided some of the most useful evidence for investigating cognitive representations in sound

---

[12] Between consonants at syllable margins, a phonetically predictable weak vowel is often heard (e.g., /blaq/ 'good' [bəlaq] and /slaq/ 'farmland' [silaq]; Huang 2005). Egerod (1965) and Li (1980) argued against positing underlying schwas in the Atayal due to the predictability of the excrescent vowel. However, Kaufman (2003), following the analysis of Rau (1992), contends that the animate actor focus marker is underlyingly /əm/. Further investigation is needed to ascertain the underlying status of the weak vowel.

structures (Alidou 1997; Bagemihl 1988, 1995; Campbell 1986; Harrison and Kaun 1999, 2001; Hombert 1986; Lehiste 1985; Piñeros 1998; Vago 1985), have been argued to support the existence of sub-syllabic constituents, such as, mora, onset/rhyme, and CV skeleton (cf. Yip 2003). For example, a language game in Tigrinya inserts a -*gV*- sequence, where *V* is a copy of the preceding vowel, after every vowel in the word.

(48)   Tigrinya (Bagemihl 1988)

Natural Lg	Play Lg 1	
s'äḥifu	s'ägäḥigifugu	'he wrote'
bïč'a	bïgïč'aga	'yellow'
?intay	?igïntagay	'what'
k'arma	k'agarmaga	'gnat'

Akin to the speech-error examples, there are also reports of apparent segmental and sequence exchange in language disguise (Bagemihl 1995).

(49)   Segmental exchanges

Tagalog:	dito	>	doti		'here'	(Conklin 1956)
Javanese:	satus	>	tasus		'100'	(Sadtano 1971)

Sequence exchanges

Hanunoo:	rignuk >		nugrik	'tame'	(Conklin 1959)
Thai:	khab rod	>	khod rab	'to drive'	(Surintramont 1973)
Mandarin:	ma >	ma key >	mey ka		(Bao 1990; Yip 1982)

These phenomena provide strong support for the psychological reality of sub-syllabic and skeletal units in language. A theory that bans such possibilities a priori is far too restrictive. The bias against sub-prosodic units cannot be maintained on theory-internal grounds either. The need to refer to skeletal segmental units, like consonant and vowel, in the formulation of alignment is not new. Prosodic constraints such as ONSET and NoCODA, have been formulated in terms of Generalized Alignment (Ito and Mester 1999; McCarthy and Prince 1993*a*; Prince and Smolensky 1993; Yip 2003), which crucially refer to edges of consonants and vowels directly.

(50)   ALIGN (σ, L, C, L)   ONSET
        ALIGN (σ, R, V, R)   NoCODA

Formally, the alignment restriction of an infix that targets the first consonant or the first vowel is no different from the syllable alignment constraints in (50). In particular, skeletal units such as C and V occupy the existentially quantified argument. The only distinction is that, in a morphological constraint, it is the affix that occupies the universally quantified first argument, rather than a syllable. Thus the vexing question is not whether skeletal units can enter into alignment relations, but why only skeletal units at particular positions within a domain can be targeted.

In sum, the empirical and theoretical arguments demonstrate that the bias against sub-prosodic constituents has no place in deciding the merit between the Phonological Readjustment and the Phonological Subcategorization approaches to infixation. Given that both presumptions for the analytic bifurcation (i.e., the ethological view of infix placement and the prejudice against sub-prosodic constituents) symptomatic of the constraint-based approach to OT-PR are demonstrably not viable, it is difficult to justify maintaining Phonological Readjustment as a distinct analytic tool from Phonological Subcategorization for the analysis of infixation.

2.5.3 On the predictive power of the theory: Problems with overgeneration

Limitations of OT-PR run deeper than what has been mentioned thus far, however. The basic appeal of OT-PR is that infixation is explained as essentially a repair strategy. Following the logic of the P $>>$ M constraint schema, output ill-formedness is ameliorated through affix movement. Taken to its logical extreme, this approach makes a queer prediction: under the right conditions, an affix may appear at the opposite edge of what its underlying subcategorization specifies. That is, a prefix may end up surfacing as a suffix, and vice versa. To illustrate this, let us reconsider the case of Dakota agreement infixation. As noted earlier, agreement morphemes in Dakota are infixed after the initial syllable into polysyllabic verb roots of a lexically specified subclass. However, the second-person dual marker *ų (k)* is prefixed to vowel-initial roots, but is infixed to consonant-initial ones.[13]

(51) Patterning of Root Type and Infix Type in Dakota[14]

		CV affix /wa/ '1sg.'	VC affix /ų(k)/ '1du.'
[C root	manų	ma-wa-nų	ma-ų-nų
[V root	ali	a-wa-li	ų̨k-ali

---

[13] The allomorphs of the first-person dual morpheme are actually *uŋ*, which is used before consonants and *uŋk* before vowels (Moravcsik 1977: *n.* 57l).

[14] These examples are taken from McCarthy and Prince (1993a: n. 26) who in turn cited them from or constructed them on the basis of the description in Boas and Deloria 1941: 78–9.

According to McCarthy and Prince (1993*a*), this state of affairs is due to the force of the ONSET constraint. Since ONSET dominates ALIGN-ROOT, the optimal, prefixal, candidate is *ų.ka.li* since it incurs one less onset violation than the infixing variant, *a.ų.li*. When the root is consonant-initial, however, the prefixal candidate, *ų.ma.nu*, holds no such an advantage since both the prefixal and infixal candidates incur an equal level of ONSET violations.

(52)

ų(k), ali	ONSET	ALIGN-ROOT	ALIGN-IN-STEM
a. ☞[-ų.kla.li.	*	*	
b. [la- ų.li.	**!		*

This analysis, however, fails to account for why a candidate such as *al-ų k-i* (← *ali*), which shows the agreement morpheme embedded further inside the root, does not prevail over the prefixal candidate *ų k-ali*. As shown in (53), the hyper-infixed candidate, *alų ki* (53c) should be preferred over the prefixal one (53a) since (53c) not only minimizes violations of ONSET, but also satisfies the high-ranking ALIGN-ROOT constraint. The prefixal candidate, on the other hand, will always fatally violate ALIGN-ROOT. McCarthy and Prince contend that the prefixal candidate is the preferred output in Dakota because of a constraint enforcing integrity of root syllables. No independent empirical support for this claim is forthcoming, however. The effect of root syllable integrity notwithstanding, the significance of this illustration is clear. If infixes are indeed the result of the inward migration of peripheral affixes (as predicted by the P >> M schema of constraint interaction), hyperinfixation should be the norm, rather than the exception.

(53)

ų(k), ali	ONSET	ALIGN-ROOT	ALIGN-IN-STEM
a. ☞[-ų.kla.li.	*	*!	
b. [la-ų.li.	**!		*
c. ●*[la.l-ų.ki.	*		**

Consider now the case of Tagalog -*um*- infixation. As described in (30), -*um*- is treated formally as a prefix under OT-PR and is infixed to avoid word-initial onsetless outputs. Tagalog bans the occurrence of -*um*- after a labial sonorant (i.e., OCP-*um*). When confronted with forms like *mumeri for *um* + *meri* 'to marry', the Tagalog speaker returns an absolute ungrammaticality judgment (see Orgun and Sprouse 1999 for further discussion). The fact of ineffability notwithstanding, it is not hard to imagine a situation where a speaker must produce an output. In such a case, the OT-PR approach predicts hyperinfixation. Consider the scenario where -*um*- is applied to the hypothetical loanword, *wawana*. From the point of view of avoiding onsetless syllables, the optimal candidate should have been (54c). However, the high-ranking OCP-*um* constraint, which prohibits -*um*- from appearing after a labial sonorant, precludes this possibility. As it turns out, infixing -*um*- further inward offers no relief since the medial consonant of the stem is also a labial sonorant (54d). In order to avoid fatal violations of the high-ranking constraints, the -*um*- prefix must realize as a suffix.

(54)   OCP-*um*, DEP-C, ONSET >> EDGEMOST(L, *um*)

/um, wawan/	OCP-*um*	DEP-C	ONSET	EDGEMOST(L, *um*)
a. **um**wawan			*!	
b. **?um**wawan		*!		
c. w**um**awan	*!			
d. waw**um**an	*!			***
e. ☞wawan**um**				*****

To be sure, this is not a problem unique to the gradient interpretation of alignment. In his attempt to eliminate gradient constraint evaluation in OT, McCarthy (2003*b*) reconceptualizes the nature of Alignment constraints by proposing a family of quantized alignment constraints, like those in (55).

(55)   Quantized ALIGN (Ft, Wd, R) (McCarthy 2003*b*: 3)
   a. ALIGN-BY-FT(Ft, Wd, R)
      No foot stands between the right edge of Ft and the right edge of Wd.
   b. ALIGN-BY-σ(Ft, Wd, R)
      No syllable stands between the right edge of Ft and the right edge of Wd.
   c. ALIGN-BY-SEG(Ft, Wd, R)
      No segment stands between the right edge of Ft and the right edge of Wd.

Thus, for example, a constraint such as ALIGN-BY-SEG(-*um*-, Wd, L) requires that no segment comes between the left edge of -*um*- and the left edge of a word. Likewise, ALIGN-BY-σ requires the left edge of a word and the left edge of -*um*- not be separated by a syllable. Violations of these constraints are accessed categorically because each constraint can be violated only once by a candidate. As shown in (56), hyperinfixation obtains when the OCP-*um* dominates these quantized alignment constraints.

(56)

/um, wawan/	OCP-*um*	DEP$_C$	ALIGN-BY-σ	ALIGN-BY-SEG
☞ a. wu.ma.wan	*!			*
⊛ b. wa.wa.num			*	*
c. ?um.wa.wan		*!		
d. wa.wu.man	*!		*	*

McCarthy (2003*b*) notes that hyperinfixation can be curtailed if MPARSE(-*um*-), a constraint that demands the realization of -*um*-, were ranked between ALIGN-BY-σ and ALIGN-BY-SEG. In this case, the null parse candidate, (57c), emerges victorious over the other outputs in (57), since (57c) vacuously satisfies all high-ranking constraints.

(57)

/um, wawan/	OCP-*um*	ALIGN-BY-σ	MPARSE	ALIGN-BY-SEG
a. wu.ma.wan	*!			*
b. wa.wa.num		*!		*
☞ c. ∅			*	

While it is possible to contrive a solution to the hyperinfixation problem, it nonetheless misses the mark. To the best of my knowledge, hyperinfixation is not attested in any of the world's languages. A theory that predicts, as the normal case, that infixes should behave this way seems fundamentally misconceived.[15] To be sure, the hyperinfixation problem is really a problem for the OT approach to Prosodic Morphology in general. Hyperinfixation will

---

[15] Featural affixation, which has been treated in terms of affix displacement (e.g., Akinlabi 1996), displays what appears to be 'hyperinfixation'. However, the viability of this featural alignment

always remain a theoretical possibility as long as phonotactic/prosodic constraints can take precedence over constraints on affix placement as licensed by the P >> M schema. Thus a rejection of hyperinfixation also calls for a reevaluation of the nature of the morphology-phonology interface. I will address this issue directly in the next chapter. Finally, it is also worth highlighting the fact that the family of Align-by-X constraints exists solely for the purpose of maintaining an OT-PR treatment of infixation. No other application of this family of constraints has thus far been identified. Thus, if a theory can be called successful only to the extent that 'it avoids positing its own special rules, constraints, or principles that are invoked to analyze a phenomenon but not applicable elsewhere' (McCarthy 2003a: 177), then the Align-by-X-based Phonological Readjustment analysis of infixation is doubly undesirable.

The converse of hyperinfixation is what I referred to as *frivolous infixation.* The logic of the OT-PR framework dictates that an affix is only coerced to move when the result of infixation produces a more well-formed output; otherwise, an affix should remain at the periphery. Yet, non-prominence-driven infixes that have no adpositional counterpart are not difficult to find. For example, in Alabama, a Muskogean language, the mediopassive -*l*- must surface after the first vowel of the stem, regardless of whether the stem is consonant- or vowel-initial.

(58) Alabama mediopassive (Martin and Munro 2005)

takco	'rope (v.)'	talikco	'be roped'[16]
hocca	'shoot'	holicca	'be shot'
o:ti	'make a fire'	o:lti	'kindling'

Or in Oaxaca Chontal, one method of plural formation is by infixing -*ɫ*- before the final syllable of the singular regardless whether the singular form is vowel-initial or vowel-final.

(59) Oaxaca Chontal (Waterhouse 1962)

Singular	Plural	Gloss
cece	ceɫce	'squirrel'
tuwa	tuɫwa	'foreigner'
te?a	teɫ?a	'elder'

approach has been called into question in recent years. Piggott (2000), for example, argues that featural affixation is better understood as a consequence of featural licensing, rather than the result of displacement.

[16] According to Martin and Munro (2005), an epenthetic *i* is inserted before consonant clusters in Alabama and Koasati while a copy of the preceded vowel is inserted in the Western languages.

akanʔoʔ	akaɫnʔoʔ	'woman'
ɫipo	ɫiɫpo	'possum'
mekoʔ	meɫkoʔ	'spoon'
kwepoʔ	kweɫpoʔ	'lizard'

If infixation is motivated by prosodic well-formedness (e.g., avoidance of initial cluster or final coda consonant, etc.), it is puzzling why the adfixal option is not available in these languages (e.g., in Alabama *lo:ti* or *o:til* instead of *o:lti* 'kindling'). Similarly, in Archi, a Daghestanian language spoken in the Caucasus, the number/class markers, *-w-*, *-r-*, and *-b-*, always appear after the first vowel of the stem, regardless of whether the stem is vowel-initial or vowel-final (Kibrik and Kodzasov 1988).

(60) daχi   dabχdi 'to churn (AOR, III)'   (Kibrik and Kodzasov 1988: 33)
      ak'a   abk'u   'to drive (AOR, III)'   (Kibrik and Kodzasov 1988: 33)
      aχa   abχu   'to lie down (AOR, III)' (Kibrik 1989: 458)

To be sure, a prefixal variant of the class markers is available. However, such an option is only available when the post-initial vowel position is filled, for example by the durative infix *-r-* (e.g., *ak'ar* 'to drive' → *ark'ar* 'to drive, DUR' → *b-ark'ar* 'to drive, DUR, III'). On the view of the OT-PR approach, all else being equal, the prefixal variant should be preferred since it reflects the underlying adpositional nature of the affix. The fact that the infixal variant has priority over the prefixal option in Archi highlights the fact that the infixal variant is the canonical position of the affix while the prefixal variant is used only when infixation is not possible.

Kaufman (2003) proposes that the infixability of an affix is predictable based on the affixal properties of its paradigmatic neighbor. That is, if a phonotactically suboptimal affix belongs to a paradigm that contains phonotactically optimal neighbors, then no infixation is predicted due to paradigm uniformity. Conversely, if a phonotactically suboptimal affix belongs to a paradigm with other similarly suboptimal affix(es), infixation is predicted. For example, in Ilokano, an Austronesian language spoken in the Philippines, actor voice can be marked by either the prefix *ag-* or the infix *-um-*.

(61) Ilokano active voice (Vanoverbergh 1955)

		active voice₁	active voice₂
isem	'smile'	**um**isem	**ag**isem
kagat	'bite'	**kum**agat	**ag**kagat

At first glance, the fact that these affixes have different surface distribution is puzzling since both are VC in shape. Couched within the theory of Optimal

Paradigm (McCarthy 2003*a*), Kaufman (2003) contends that the reason why /ag/ is prefixing in Ilokano is because it belongs to an aspectual paradigm containing a consonant-initial form /nag/. On the other hand, /um/ is in a paradigm with another VC affix, /im(m)/. Assuming that the affixes within the same paradigm must be uniformed with respect to their alignment, a VC-shaped affix will be prefixed if it has a prefixal paradigmatic neighbor, but will be infixed if it has an infixal paradigmatic neighbor. Following McCarthy's (2003*b*) OT-PR approach to infixation, Kaufman argues that the infixation of /um/ and /im(m)/ is motivated by the avoidance of onsetless syllables in the language (note the failure of (63b)).[17] Onset violations may be avoided by way of onset epenthesis (63c), but that would incur fatal violations of DEP$_{IO}$-C, which penalizes any epenthetic segment in the output.

(62) ALIGN-BY-σ-L   No syllable stands between the left edge of an affix and the left edge of a stem (McCarthy 2003*b*)

      ALIGN-BY-SEG-L   Assess a violation when the left edge of an affix is aligned with or past the first segment of the stem (McCarthy 2003*b*)

      ANCHORING-OP   Assess a violation mark when the left edge of the stem coincides with the left edge of the prosodic word in one paradigm member but not in another.

(63) Ilokano active voice$_1$

stem: *kagat* 'to bite' morph: *um* (L); *im* (L)	ONSET	*COMPLEX	ALIGN-BY-σ-L	ANCHOR-OP	DEP$_{IO}$-C	ALIGN-BY-SEG-L
a. ☞ \<k<u>u</u>magat, k<u>i</u>magat\>						**
b. \<<u>um</u>kagat, <u>im</u>kagat\>	**!					
c. \<ʔ<u>um</u>kagat, ʔ<u>im</u>kagat\>					**!	

The effect of paradigm uniformity comes into play when paradigmatic members incur different markedness violations. As shown in (64), paradigm (64d), where /ag/ is infixed after the first consonant of the root while /nag/ is prefixed, is ruled out since it fatally violates ANCHOR-OP, which penalizes

---

[17] The first member within each bracketed voice paradigm is the *irrealis* inflection and the second is the *realis*.

paradigms with members showing non-matching stem-alignment relations. An ANCHOR-OP violation cannot be ameliorated simply by infixing both /ag/ and /nag/ (see (64a)) due to a fatal violation of *COMPLEX incurred by the infixing of /nag/. While infixing /nag/ further inward would avoid the *COM-PLEX violation (64b), the infixing paradigm remains suboptimal due to a fatal violation of ALIGN-BY-σ-L. The least costly strategy, as it turns out, is to realize both /ag/ and /nag/ as prefixing (64c).

(64)   Ilokano active voice₂

stem: *kagat* 'to bite' morph: *ag* (L); *nag* (L)	ONSET	*COMPLEX	ALIGN-BY- σ-L	ANCHOR- OP	DEP$_{IO}$-C	ALIGN-BY- SEG-L
a. <kagagat, knagagat>		*!				**
b. <kagagat, kanaggat>			*!			*
c. ☞<ʔagkagat, nagkagat>					*	
d. <kagagat, nagkagat>				*!		*

This Optimal Paradigm approach to infixation is appealing since it avoids the necessity of positing parochial alignment constraints that stipulate the pre-fixing nature of /ag/ and the infixing distribution of /um/. The distribution of these VC affixes is derivative of the distribution of their paradigmatic neighbor. This line of analysis, at first glance, might provide a solution to the frivolous infixation problem. On this view, the affixes in (58)–(60) might be infixing because their paradigmatic neighbors are of the nature that favors infixation. But a closer look at these cases suggests otherwise. To begin with, while paradigm-based explanation is often invoked to better understand inflectional morphology, it is unclear how paradigmatic relations should be established in the case of derivational morphology. That is, in what paradig-matic relationship should the mediopassive in Alabama or the plural marker in Oaxaca Chontal participate? This quandary highlights a major weakness of paradigm-based explanations. That is, paradigm-based explanations have no explanatory force unless the notion of a paradigm can be defined in some rigorous fashion (Kenstowicz and Kisseberth 1977). To be sure, even within the domain of inflectional morphology, the Optimal Paradigm is still hard pressed to provide a principled explanation for the existence of frivolous infixation. For example, in the case of Archi, the class-number markers are first and foremost infixal (65a–c). Only when in the constative/durative aspect

(CONST) are the class-number markers prefixal (65d). Like any OT-PR analysis, the Optimal Paradigm approach to infixation still requires some displacement-triggering constraint to motivate phonological readjustment. Yet, no obvious phonotactic or prosodic advantage can be adduced for infixing the class-number markers. Edge avoidance offers no real solution in this case since prefixing the class-number marker is in fact possible (65d).

(65)   aχas 'lie down' (Kibrik 1998: 457)
   a. o-w-χ-u[18]   AOR.1SG
   b. o-w-χ-u-qi   FUT.1SG
   c. o-w-χa-s   INF.1SG
   d. w-a-r-χa-r[19]   CONST.1SG

True to the spirit of the ethological approach to infixation, the Optimal Paradigm approach to infixation offers an intriguing way to understanding why morphemes of similar prosodic shape nonetheless have different surface distributions within the same language: namely, by capitalizing on the paradigmatic nature of a certain type of morphology. However, such an approach falters when the paradigmatic relation is either difficult to motivate or provides no useful information.

2.6 Conclusion

This chapter presents an overview of the nature of infixation from both descriptive and theoretical perspectives. Formally, infixes have been treated as either the result of phonological readjustment or as the result of morpho-phonological mismatch due to phonological subcategorization. Previous scholars have suggested that the Phonological Readjustment account, particularly within the context of a constraint-based framework, is superior to the subcategorization approach on the grounds of simplicity (e.g., Kaufman 2003; McCarthy and Prince 1993a). That is, phonological readjustment-induced affix reordering, which results in surface infixation, can be derived from constraint interaction alone, an integral part of the explanatory machinery of Optimality Theory. In particular, it is argued that the goal of simplicity demands that predictable aspects of a surface form not be treated as part of its underlying representation. However, following the logic of Occam's Razor, simplicity may only determine the superiority between theories that make comparable predictions. As reviewed above, the Phonological Readjustment treatment of

---

[18] The perfective suffix is -*u̦*; *a* → *o* before *w*.
[19] The constative/durative aspect is marked by the discontinuous transfix -*r* . . . -*r*.

infixation is neither sufficient nor necessary. Phonological Readjustment is inherently deficient as a theory of infixation since it is applicable only to a subset of infixal patterns in the world's languages. In order to account for the prominence-driven infixes, advocates of Phonological Readjustment must appeal to phonological subcategorization, the very machinery Phonological Readjustment is ostensibly trying to eliminate. It should also be noted that Phonological Subcategorization is no more complicated, if not in fact simpler, than Phonological Readjustment since Phonological Subcategorization is stated in terms of Generalized Alignment, a formal device that is also part of the theoretical arsenal of Phonological Readjustment. Some researchers reject Phonological Subcategorization on the grounds that it admits segmental units into alignment relationship. But as noted earlier, the hypothesis that only units in the prosodic hierarchy may enter into alignment relations, as pointed out in McCarthy and Prince (1993*a*), is a matter of empirical observation, rather than a theoretical necessity. In fact, alignment involving segmental-level information has been part of the theoretical arsenal since the inception of Optimality Theory. Thus, to claim that Phonological Subcategorization is somehow theoretically more burdensome than the Phonological Readjustment approach due to its need to refer to segmental information in alignment relations is misleading to say the least. Furthermore, as I will be demonstrating in detail in the following chapters, not just any segmental level unit may enter into alignment relations. Only a restricted set of subcategorizable phonological units is observed.

Thus while it has achieved some significant descriptive and analytic successes, Phonological Readjustment includes much that is local and parochial and therefore should be replaced by principles of broad applicability. Phonological Subcategorization, understood in the context of a holistic framework of linguistic explanation, provides just the right balance of empirical and explanatory adequacy. To be sure, aspects of the Phonological Subcategorization approach require further qualification. For example, some might argue that Phonological Subcategorization is overly powerful as it predicts alignment relationships between affixes and phonological constituents in odd positions within a word. That is, in its most basic formulation, it is possible to set up a GA constraint that requires an affix to subcategorize for, for example, the third consonant of the root. At first glance, such a prediction seems to seriously undermine the viability of phonological subcategorization as an insightful theory of infix placement. Such an objection, however, is misplaced from the perspective of the theory adopted in this monograph. The next chapter explains why.

3

Subcategorization in context

The fundamental puzzle presented by the Edge-Bias Effect often confronts the typologist: which factor(s) reduce the amount of conceivable variation across languages down to the observed set? One method for the study of typology and universals, which Greenberg refers to as dynamic comparison or diachronic typology (1969), is to show that typological patterns emerge from common diachronic changes in related and unrelated languages. This model of linguistic evolution and change, in which the grammars of individual languages emerge from the processes of change operative in all languages at all times, as Bybee (forthcoming) points out, suggests that 'the true universals of language are the mechanisms of change that propel the constant creation and re-creation of grammar.'[1] The emphasis on the mechanisms of change does not lessen the synchronic relevance of such an endeavor. Weinreich, Labov, and Herzog (1968) were among the first to recognize that the diachronic and synchronic research programs share the same fundamental goals; that is, the 'constraints' problem of determining possible and impossible changes and the synchronic question of determining possible and impossible human languages are essentially the one and the same pursuit.

From the point of view of current theories of linguistics, the starting point for discussions of language change is acquisition, that is, the individual's acquisition of a grammar distinct from the one which underlies the output of the preceding generation. The key to understanding the 'error' in grammar transmission lies in the nature of the input for acquisition. The input data is often wrought with ambiguities. The learner's task is to find a good match between the input and the output of candidate grammars. In this chapter, I will articulate a concrete, crucially holistic, model for understanding the distributional properties of infixes, as summarized in (1).

(1) **A holistic theory of infix distribution**
    a. Grammar-internal constraints:
        A theory of phonological subcategorization (this chapter)

---

[1] The quote is taken from the original pre-translated English version of the paper.

b. Grammar-external constraints:
   constraints on morphological learning (Chapter 4)
   constraints on morphological change (Chapter 5)

c. A theory of interaction between these grammar-internal and
   grammar-external constraints (this chapter)

There are three main components to this model. First, I offer a formal theory of phonological subcategorization and, by extension, morphological subcategorization that can express the full range of subcategorization relations in language (Section 3.1). As illustrated in Chapter 2, when phonological constraints take precedence over constraints on affix placement, as in the case of OT-PR, the undesirable effect of hyperinfixation results. A more restrained model of the morphology-phonology interface is needed to adequately model the distributional properties of infixes. I show in Section 3.2 that such a theory is indeed possible if the present theory of phonological subcategorization is situated within a declarative unification-based framework of grammatical analysis. Allowing affixes to target phonological constituents *per se* is not sufficient to explain the restricted typology of infix placement, however. As argued in Section 3.3, the model must also include a theory of how phonological subcategorization interacts with grammar-external constraints imposed on morphological learning and morphological change. Section 3.4 shows that a proper understanding of the synchronic typology of infix distribution requires the theory of affix placement, indeed of grammar as a whole, to be embedded within a temporal axis. The diachronic evolution of infixes is as much an integral part of the explanation as is their treatment within the synchronic grammar.

3.1 Subcategorization as Generalized Alignment

The approach to infix placement argued in this work is the theory of Phonological Subcategorization. Under this theory, infixes are formally no different from prefixes and suffixes, except for the fact that, while prefixes and suffixes target morphological constituents, infixes target phonological ones. When there is a mismatch between the targeted phonological constituent and the morphological host, infixation obtains. When the morphological and phonological boundaries coincide, we find adpositional affixation. For example, while the English prefix *re-* targets verbs (e.g., *re-visit, re-read* but never *re-beautiful* since *beautiful* is an adjective), the expletive *-bloody-* in certain varieties of English targets the left edge of a stressed foot (e.g., *fan-bloody-tástic*, never **fantás-bloody-tic* or **fantá-bloody-stic*). Phonological

Subcategorization inherits the insight of earlier subcategorization-based theories, such as *prosodic subcategorization* (also known as prosodic alignment (McCarthy and Prince 1986)) and the *Bi-dependent* approach to infixation (Inkelas 1990; Kiparsky 1986), that infixation involves the alignment of a morphological entity with respect to a phonological one. However, it breaks with *Prosodic* Subcategorization by eliminating the restriction that allows only genuine prosodic categories to take part in morpho-phonological alignment relationships (see also Inkelas 1990; Kiparsky 1986).

The present theory is anticipated in part by Anderson (1992), who proposes a parameterized approach to affix placement:

(2)   Parameters for the placements of affixes within a word:
      (Anderson 1992: 210)
      a. The affix is located in the scope of some constituent which constitutes its domain. This may be either a morphological constituent (the word-structure head vs the entire word) or a prosodic one (prosodic word).

      b. The affix is located by reference to the {first vs last vs main stressed} element of a given type within the constituent in which it appears.

      c. The affix {precedes vs follows} the reference point.

In this work, I formalize an affix's subcategorization requirement in terms of Generalized Alignment (McCarthy and Prince 1993a: 80). Subcategorization restrictions are therefore constraints on proper edge alignment between categories. A G(eneralized) A(lignment) constraint has four arguments: two linguistic categories and one of the edges of each of the respective category. The general formulation of a GA constraint is stated below:

(3)   Align (Cat_1, $Edge_1$, Cat_2, $Edge_2$) $=_{def}$
      $\forall$ Cat_1 $\exists$ Cat_2 such that $Edge_1$ of Cat_1 and $Edge_2$ of Cat_2 coincide.
      Where Cat_1, Cat_2 $\in$ PCat $\cup$ GCat
      $Edge_1$, $Edge_2$ $\in$ {Right, Left}

The set of admissible GCat is derived from the morphological hierarchy stated below:

(4)   Morphological Hierarchy (McCarthy and Prince 1993a: 85)
      MWd $\longrightarrow$ Stem*
      Stem $\longrightarrow$ Stem, Affix
      Stem $\longrightarrow$ Root

The set of PCat, on the other hand, includes not only the categories within the Prosodic Hierarchy including the level of the mora (i.e., ProsCat), but also units on the CV skeletal tier.

(5)   Prosodic Hierarchy

Prosodic Word   PrWd
                       |
Foot   Ft
                       |
Syllable   σ
                       |
Mora   μ

Standard adpositional affixation (i.e., morphological subcategorization) is
captured in this formalism in terms of the alignment of a GCat with respect
to another GCat. Phonological Subcategorization obtains when a designated
edge of a morphological constituent (CAT_1) coincides with a designated edge
of a phonological pivot (CAT_2) or vice versa. To illustrate this point more
concretely, let us revisit the case of Ulwa briefly alluded to in Chapter 2. In
Ulwa, nouns have two forms: bare and affixed. The affixed variant is referred
to as the construct state. The construct state may appear as either an infix or
a suffix, depending on various factors including the length of the stem and
its morphological make-up. Disyllabic roots may have either initial or final
stress (see (6i)). In the construct state, however, stress is always iambic (6ii).
That is, main stress on a construct-state noun is on the first syllable if it is
heavy; otherwise, it is on the second syllable. Crucially, the construct-state
marker always appears after the leftmost iambic foot of the stem.

(6)   Ulwa construct state (Green 1999: 61, 64)
      a. i. awa, awá: ii. awá:-**ki**   'silkgrass-CNS1'
            súru, surú: surú:-**kina**   'log-CNS11'
            (?)yápu, yapú: yapú:-**kana**   'crocodile-CNS3'
            (?)ábu, abú: abú:-**ma**   'stingray-CNS2'

      b. i. sú:lu   ii. sú:-**ma**-lu   'dog-CNS2'
            áytak   áy-**mana**-tak   'paper-CNS22'
            alá:kuṃ   alá:-**ka**-kuṃ   'Muscovy duck-CNS3'
            waráẇwa   waráẇ-**kana**-wa   'parrot sp.-CNS33'
            ká:sirá:mah   ká:-**ki**-sirá:mah 'lizard sp.-CNS1'

Within the formalism of GA, the construct-state marker in Ulwa is formally
analyzed as aligning with respect to the right edge of the head iambic foot (7)
(i.e., the iambic foot that carries the main stress). Thus when the size of
the morphological host and the leftmost iambic foot coincide, the construct-
state marker appears suffixing (6a). When the morphological host of

construct-state affixation is larger than an iamb (i.e., in the case of a polysyllabic noun or a disyllabic stem where the initial syllable is heavy), however, infixation obtains (6b).

(7) Ulwa infixal construct noun marker (McCarthy and Prince 1993*a*: 110)
ALIGN-TO-FOOT
ALIGN ([POSS]$_{Af}$, L, FT', R)
'The left edge of the construct noun marker is aligned to the right edge of the head foot.'

A notion central to the present theory of infix placement is that of the *pivot point*, which refers to the phonological unit to which an infix attaches.[2] To be sure, the notion of the pivot is orthogonal to the notion of the *base*. Throughout this study, the term *base* will be reserved for discussion specific to reduplication. The term *base* will be taken as the morphological and/or phonological domain from which the reduplicant copies.[3] For example, in the Pama-Nyungan language, Uradhi, pluractionality (PLR in gloss) is marked by (C)CV reduplication:

(8) Uradhi pluractional reduplication (Crowley 1983: 364)
wi.li	wi-li-li	'run'
a.ŋa	a-ŋa-ŋa	'dig'
i.pi.ɲi	i-pi-piɲi	'swim'
wampa	wa-mpa-mpa	'float'
i.kya	i-ki-kya	'speak'
u.ɲɟa	u-ɲɟa-ɲɟa	'sleep, lie down'
u.ɲya	u-ɲi-ɲya	'eat'

Following the present terminological scheme, the pivot of internal reduplication is after the first vowel of the stem; the base of reduplication is to the right of the reduplicant:

(9) ROOT ⟶ PIVOT-*RED*-BASE
u.ɲɟa ⟶ u-ɲɟa-ɲɟa 'sleep, lie down.PLR'

---

[2] Kiparsky (1986) uses the term 'pivot' to refer to the portion of a root over which an infix 'skips'. The Kiparskyan understanding of the pivot is analogous to that of negative circumscription (McCarthy and Prince 1990). A pivot is treated as a unit ignored for the purpose of affixation. The notion of pivot adopted here is similar to that of positive circumscription. A pivot is treated as the circumscribed constituent to which an affix attaches.

[3] This dichotomy has been implicitly and explicitly assumed in the previous literature as the distinction between affix location and the direction of association (e.g., Broselow and McCarthy 1983/84; Clements 1985; Kiparsky 1986; Marantz 1982).

Based on a typological survey (see Chapter 4 for details), I identify the following set of phonological constituents that may enter into phonological subcategorizing relations that result in infixation:

(10)   Potential pivots of infixation
        Edge pivots   *Prominence pivots*
        First consonant   Stressed foot
        First vowel   Stressed syllable
        (First syllable)   Stressed vowel
        Final syllable
        Final vowel
        (Final consonant)

The set of pivot points is subdivided into two types: pivots that occur at the edge of a domain (edge pivots) and pivots that are defined with respect to lexical stress (prominence pivots). The GA formalization allows a four-way typology of alignment relations between an affix and its pivot (11).[4] The affix and the pivot may enter into what is referred to as different-edge alignment. The right edge of an affix may align with respect to the left edge of a pivot or the left edge of an affix may align with respect to the right edge of a pivot. Such alignment relations essentially amount to the phonological analogs to morphological prefixation and suffixation. More interesting, however, is the notion of same-edge alignment, in which the left edges or right edges of the affix and the pivot coincide. As such, this type of alignment relation is unlike traditional adpositional relations. The affix and the pivot invariably overlap in the output when they are in a same-edge alignment relationship.

(11)   Different-edge alignment   Same-edge alignment
        Align (Affix, R, Pivot, L) Align (Affix, L, Pivot, L)
        Align (Affix, L, Pivot, R) Align (Affix, R, Pivot, R)

I shall return to the issue of the pivot points in the next chapter. I will first articulate in more detail some of the formal issues raised by the adoption of a GA formulation of subcategorization relations. GA is a tool for capturing possible alignment relations between elements. Depending on the framework in which this formalism is implemented, different consequences obtain. For example, as reviewed in Chapter 2, when GA is implemented

---

[4] Here, I restrict my focus on just the range of alignment constraints predicted when the affix occupies the universally quantified argument. Section 6.4 in Chapter 6 briefly considers the reverse situation where the pivot point is in the universally quantified argument while the affix is in the existentially quantified one.

in OT as rankable and violable constraints, the different predictions of the OT-PR approach to infixation obtain. In the next section, I show that a more restrictive theory of the morphology-phonology interface results when phonological subcategorization as formalized in terms of GA is implemented within a declarative model of the morphology-phonology interface.

3.2 Phonological Subcategorization in Sign-Based Morphology

The theory of Phonological Subcategorization presented in this work is couched within the larger framework of Sign-Based Morphology (SBM) (Orgun 1996, 1998, 1999; Orgun and Inkelas 2002). SBM is a declarative, non-derivational theory of the morphology-phonology interface which utilizes the basic tools one finds in any constituent structure-based unificational approach to linguistics (e.g., Construction Grammar (Fillmore and Kay 1994) and HPSG (Pollard and Sag 1994). It assumes that terminal and non-terminal nodes bear features and that non-terminal nodes also include phonological information along with the usual syntactic and semantic information (i.e., co-phonology (Inkelas 1998; Inkelas, Orgun, and Zoll 1997; Inkelas and Zoll 2005; Orgun 1996, 1999; Orgun and Inkelas 2002; Yu 2000); and similar co-phonological approaches (Anttila 1997, 2002, 2006; Kiparsky 2000)). Morphological constructions are organized into a type hierarchy, represented as a lattice with the maximally general type at the top and the specific type at the bottom. This approach captures generalizations across constructions by extracting such generalizations into a super-type, thus providing a natural way to express which features are appropriate to which kinds of items and what range of specifications are possible for the value of a given attribute. A partial type hierarchy proposed in Koenig and Jurafsky 1994 for English is given below (much detail is omitted to make the hierarchy simpler):

(12)

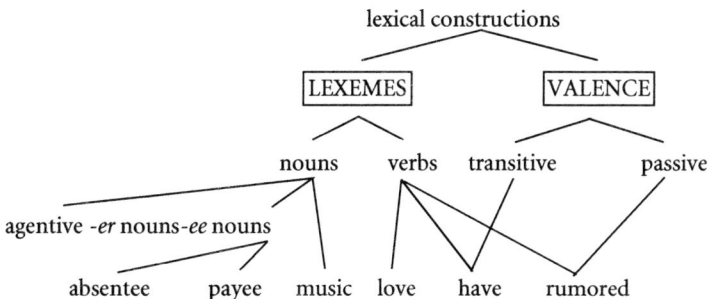

Constraints imposed on all items of a given type are also stated as holding on the general type. Constraints are signs represented as Attribute-Value Matrixes (AVM). Signs are pairings of sound and meaning (Saussure 1916 [1986]). In SBM, a sign is a linguistic unit containing phonological information as well as morphosyntactic and semantic features. Signs are represented as typed feature structures (Carpenter 1992) with attributes such as PHON and SYNSEM. Since we are interested in the morphology-phonology interface here, the value of the SYNSEM attribute will be used here as a convenient placeholder for glosses, or, when convenient, I will simply omit this attribute. Thus, the sign representing the noun *áytak* 'paper' in Ulwa will be:

(13)
$$\begin{bmatrix} \textit{noun-stem} \\ \text{SYNSEM} \qquad \text{paper} \\ \text{PHON} \qquad \textit{áytak} \end{bmatrix}$$

Affixes may be treated in several ways in SBM. Here, I assume that affixes are represented as fixed arguments to the phonological function (i.e., the φ-function), specified in affixational constructions.[5] Consider the schematic representation of a morphologically complex structure in (14), which shows the dominance relation between two signs, *complex-stem* and *stem*. The indices ①, ②, and ③ indicate identity. This construction specifies that a well-formed sign of the type *complex-stem* consists of the SYNSEM information of the type *stem* (i.e., ①) mediated by the *ı*-function. The phonological content of the *complex-stem* is an amalgamation of the phonological content of the *stem* (i.e., ②) plus some affixal element (i.e., ③). The affixal element essentially corresponds to the 'underlying' form of the affix. The φ-function is responsible for any phonological adjustments (e.g., stress assignment, vowel harmony, etc.) that are required to render the phonological content of the *complex-stem* well-formed. The main innovation here is the addition of the feature SUBCAT, which specifies the linear position of an affix relative to some other unit. In the present case, the affix (i.e., ③) is aligned with respect to some phonological pivot.[6]

---

[5] For a discussion of the advantages of the affix-as-fixed-argument approach over other conceptions of the affix in SBM, see section 3.2.2 in Orgun 1996.

[6] Previous SBM approaches to affixation adopt the basic premise of OT-PR and assume that the subcategorization requirement of the affix is supplied as part of the constraint set of the φ-function.

(14)
$$
\begin{bmatrix}
\textit{complex-stem} & \\
\text{SYNSEM} & \iota(\boxed{1}) \\
\text{PHON} & \varphi(\boxed{2},\boxed{3}) \\
\text{SUBCAT} & \text{ALIGN}\,(\boxed{3},\text{EDGE}_1,\text{PCAT},\text{EDGE}_2)
\end{bmatrix}
$$
$$
|
$$
$$
\begin{bmatrix}
\textit{stem} & \\
\text{SYNSEM} & \boxed{1} \\
\text{PHON} & \boxed{2}
\end{bmatrix}
$$

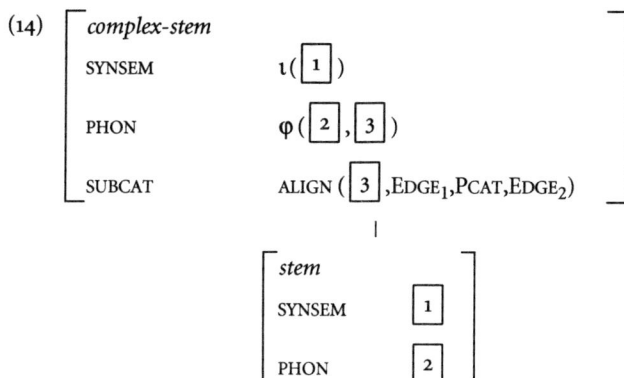

For example, the construct-state noun *áy-**mana**-tak* 'paper-CNS22' in Ulwa is licensed by the construction in (15). It shows that the input to forming a construct-state noun is a noun stem. The affix -*mana*- subcategorizes for the right edge of a stressed foot. The subscript annotation on the φ-function is a reminder to the reader of which phonological alternations are enforced by φ. In the present case, the construct-state construction requires a construct-state noun to bear iambic stress. Since stress is on the initial syllable, -*mana*-appears as an infix in the noun *áytak* 'paper'.

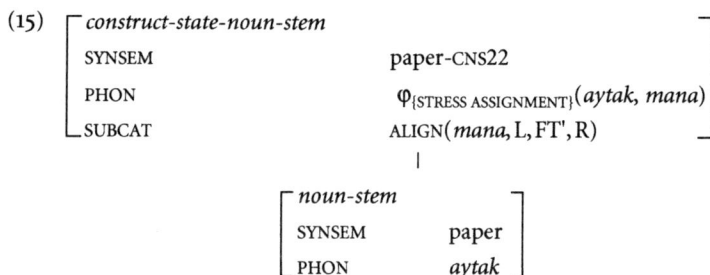

(15)
$$
\begin{bmatrix}
\textit{construct-state-noun-stem} & \\
\text{SYNSEM} & \text{paper-CNS22} \\
\text{PHON} & \varphi_{\{\text{STRESS ASSIGNMENT}\}}(\textit{aytak, mana}) \\
\text{SUBCAT} & \text{ALIGN}(\textit{mana},\text{L},\text{FT}',\text{R})
\end{bmatrix}
$$
$$
|
$$
$$
\begin{bmatrix}
\textit{noun-stem} & \\
\text{SYNSEM} & \text{paper} \\
\text{PHON} & \textit{aytak}
\end{bmatrix}
$$

In the last chapter, we saw that OT-PR enshrines the spirit of the ethological view of affix movement in the constraint-ranking schema, P $>>$ M. Such an approach is demonstrably inadequate not only because it runs into problems of under- and overgeneration (by allowing affixes to move around for phonological repair reasons), but also because the ethological view of infix placement, which serves as the premise for the P $>>$ M approach in the first place, is empirically suspect. Recent work has also highlighted other problems associated with the P $>>$ M theory (e.g., Paster 2006).

In light of these shortcomings, the idea that phonological considerations may trump morphological subcategorization ones is best avoided if the goal of a restrictive and explanatory theory of infixation is to be realized.

In the present theory, the inviolability of the subcategorization requirement follows straightforwardly from the architecture of this model. Subcategorization information is stated as part of the sign of the morphological construction. As declarative constraints are not violable, subcategorization restrictions may never be violated as well. Given that affix alignment cannot interact with phonological constraints that are part of the phonological function of the mother node, the phonological function is incapable of moving affixes around. The locus of the interface between morphology and phonology is the interaction between constraints on prosody/phonotactics and faithfulness within the φ-function of the PHON feature. In particular, non-suppletive phonologically conditioned allomorphy (e.g., English plural -*s* allomorphy) occurs when prosodic/phonotactic constraints outrank the faithfulness constraints (i.e., P >> FAITH). Allomorphy involving a difference in affix alignment is thus treated as an instance of suppletive allomorphy; that is, the allomorphs are assigned different subcategorization requirements (see Paster 2006 for a thorough defense of this approach to other cases of phonologically conditioned suppletive allormorphy). Consider once again the example of Ulwa. As reviewed in the last chapter, the construct-state (CNS) markers in Ulwa are generally affixed to the right edge of an iambic foot. However, there is a lexically arbitrary class of nouns that takes the construct-state morpheme as a simple suffix (16).

(16)   Suffixal -*ka*   (Hale and Lacayo Blanco 1989; McCarthy and
                        Prince 1993*a*)

gobament	gobament-ka	'government'
abana	abana-ka	'dance'
bassirih	bassirih-ka	'falcon'
ispiriŋ	ispiriŋ-ka	'elbow'

Since the classes of lexical items that take the infixing rather than the suffixing allomorphs of the construct-state morpheme are arbitrary, two inflectional classes in the lexical type hierarchy must be posited: *class 1* and *class 2*. Noun stems must belong to one of these two classes. There are two methods of forming construct-state nouns in Ulwa (17). Each construct-state construction specifies which noun class may serve as its morphological daughter.

(17)   Infixing allomorph

$$
\begin{bmatrix}
\textit{class 1 construct-state noun} \\
\text{SYNSEM} \qquad\qquad\qquad \iota(\boxed{1}) \\
\text{PHON} \qquad\qquad\qquad \varphi(\boxed{2},\boxed{3}) \\
\text{SUBCAT} \qquad\qquad \text{ALIGN}(\boxed{3},\text{L},\text{FT}',\text{R})
\end{bmatrix}
$$

$$
\begin{bmatrix}
\textit{class 1 noun} \\
\text{SYNSEM} \quad \boxed{1} \\
\text{PHON} \quad \boxed{2}
\end{bmatrix}
$$

Suffixing allomorph

$$
\begin{bmatrix}
\textit{class 2 construct-state noun} \\
\text{SYNSEM} \qquad\qquad\qquad \iota(\boxed{1}) \\
\text{PHON} \qquad\qquad\qquad \varphi(\boxed{2},\boxed{3}) \\
\text{SUBCAT} \qquad\qquad \text{ALIGN}(\boxed{3},\text{L},\text{STEM},\text{R})
\end{bmatrix}
$$

$$
\begin{bmatrix}
\textit{class 2 noun} \\
\text{SYNSEM} \quad \boxed{1} \\
\text{PHON} \quad \boxed{2}
\end{bmatrix}
$$

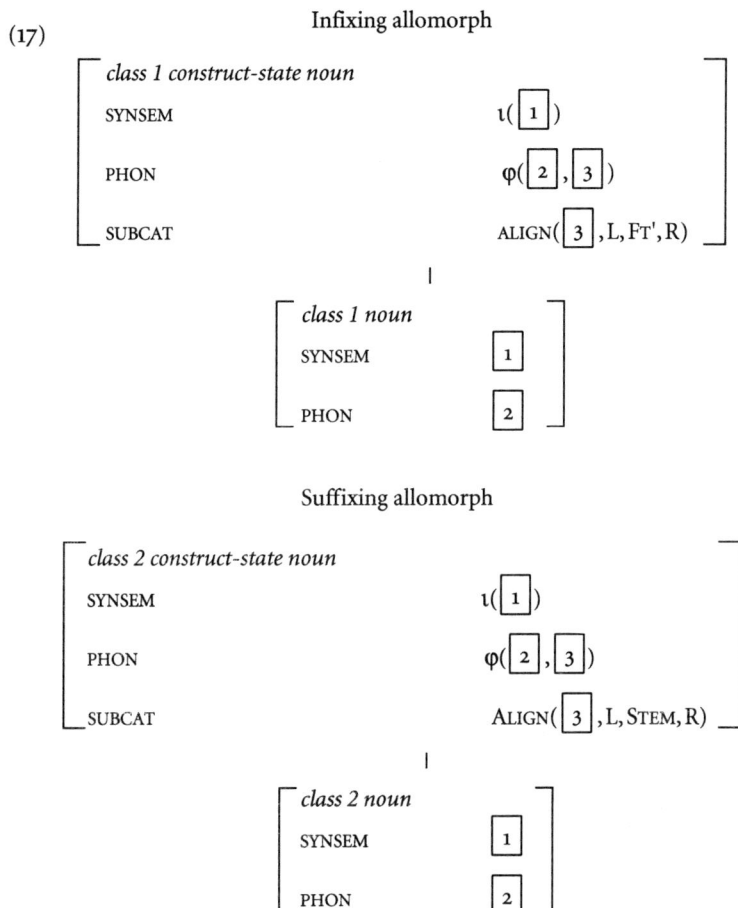

Phonological Subcategorization, when implemented properly in SBM, provides a restrictive account of the morphology-phonology interface. In particular, the phonological function is strictly evaluative; it interprets the phonological exponents of a morpheme in accordance with the phonotactics of the language, but does not alter the morph's underlying distributional restriction.

Recall now that the Phonological Readjustment approach accounts for the Edge-Bias Effect by assuming that edge-oriented infixes are underlying prefixes and suffixes; movement from its original position is minimal, hence the peripheral distribution. This explanation of the Edge-Bias Effect is therefore grammar-internal; ethological/functional motivations for infixation are derived from the intrinsic properties of the grammar. In Chapter 2, I reviewed the obstacles such an explanation faces and concluded that Phonological Readjustment is not a viable theory of infixation. The present theory of Phonological Subcategorization is formulated in terms of Generalized Alignment. GA is a constraint schema that makes possible the encoding of the formal relations between basic grammatical elements in a transparently compositional fashion. Specific phonological subcategorization constraints are therefore language-specific constraints since they operate at the level of individual affixes rather than on general universally available constituents. Such a model of constraint building invariably leads to the problem of constraint overgeneration. That is, not all formally possible combinations of PCat and GCat arguments lead to alignment constraints that are attested. For example, it would be quite unexpected to find an affix that subcategorizes solely for the third syllable of a word or the fourth mora of the root. As such, the formalism of GA shows no intrinsic bias toward any particular grammatical element; the Edge-Bias Effect is thus not part of the explanatory purview of GA or that of Phonological Subcategorization *per se*. In the next section, I will argue that the unabashedly non-ethological nature of GA and its overgenerating capacity is not only not an obstacle toward a restrictive theory of infixation; it is, in many respects, desirable.

3.3 Phonological Subcategorization and constraint overgeneration

Constraint overgeneration is not unique to GA/Phonological Subcategorization. As reviewed in Smith (2002, 2004), constraint overgeneration is symptomatic of theories that generate constraints from a small set of formal relations and basic grammatical elements. For example, a generalized feature co-occurrence schema, such as *[Fea_1, Fea_2], would generate co-occurrence constraints for all pairs of features, regardless of whether the features are physically incompatible or not. Solutions to the constraint overgeneration problem have generally assumed that excess constraints can be ruled out with constraint filters. Many such constraint filters are argued to be functionally or substantively motivated (Hayes 1999; Smith 2002, 2004). Within the framework of Optimality Theory, the grammar is conceived as a set of violable constraints and their interactions. Languages differ only in terms of the ranking of the members of the universal set of violable constraints, CON. With these assumptions in mind, Smith (2002, 2004) proposes a Schema/Filter model of the CON component, in which a set of constraint filters inspects the constraints that are freely generated by the schemas and admits into CON only those formally possible constraints that meet the criteria of the filters. The filters may be functionally motivated in that they make use of articulatory, acoustic, perceptual, or other substantive information to distinguish between legitimate and undesirable constraints.

(18)   The Schema/Filter model of CON (Smith 2002, 2004)

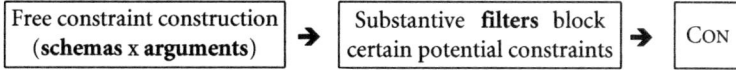

| Free constraint construction (**schemas** x **arguments**) | → | Substantive **filters** block certain potential constraints | → | CON |

While I agree with this approach of using filters to combat the overgeneration problem, the main innovation of this work, and its chief divergence from previous work dealing with the constraint overgeneration problem, is the proposed division of labor between components within a holistic theory of language. Recall that while OT constraints are assumed to be universal, declarative constraints in sign-based models of the grammar are language-specific constraints that are post hoc generalizations over a lexicon. Information on subcategorization requirements is no exception. It may thus be hypothesized that the task of a language learner is to construct declarative constraints on subcategorization requirements based on the ambient language environment. Formally, a learner is assumed to be equipped with the knowledge of the GA schema and her task is to fill the variable slots with arguments of the correct type based on the available data. Subcategorization requirements might change as the lexicon is updated. Evidence for this dynamic and usage-based view of subcategorization requirement formation can be found in the case of variable infixation. For example, in Tagalog, the agentive focus marker may be analyzed as aligning with respect to either the first vowel or the first consonant, if only the native lexicon is considered.

(19)   b-**um**-ilih   'X buys/bought'
       t-**um**-alikod   'X turns/turned his back to'
       b-**um**-agsak   'X fails/failed'
       ?-**um**-akyat   'X climbs/climbed'

Given the ambiguity inherent in the identification of phonological pivots, it is to be expected that, if subcategorization is usage-based, speakers should be able to exploit this analytic ambiguity. The variable infixation evidence (20) is consistent with this prediction. That is, when the root begins with a consonant cluster, the infix -*um*- can appear after the first consonant, thus interrupting the cluster, or before the first vowel (see Orgun and Sprouse 1999; Zuraw 2005 for more discussions).

(20)   Tagalog focus construction (Orgun and Sprouse 1999)
       gradwet   grumadwet   ~   gumradwet   'to graduate'
       plantsa   plumantsa   ~   pumlantsa   'iron'
       preno   prumeno   ~   pumreno   'to brake'

A similar, but more complicated pattern is observed with respect to the perfective affix -*in*- in Tagalog. Avery and Lamontagne (1995) report that -*in*- may appear after the first consonant or before the first vowel of the stem. However, this variation is partly conditioned by the placement of stress. Two patterns are reported in particular. Avery and Lamontagne describe Pattern A as follows: '[i]f the base-accent is an odd number of syllables from -*in*-, -*in*- will occur after C1 and an epenthetic vowel appears immediately following -*in*-.' An epenthetic vowel is capitalized in Avery and Lamontagne's transcription.

(21)   Pattern A of Tagalog perfective infixation
       plahiyó   p-in-<u>A</u>lahiyó   'plagiarized'
       premyuhán   p-in-<u>I</u>remyuhán   'rewarded'
       plántsa   p-in-<u>A</u>lántsa   'ironed'
       drówing   d-in-<u>U</u>-rówing   'drew'
       príto   i-p-in-<u>I</u>-ríto   'fried'

Pattern B shows that 'if the base-accent is an even number of syllables from -*in*-, -*in*- will occur after either C1 or C2. If it occurs after C1, metathesis may apply [see (22b), A. Y.].'

(22)   Pattern B of Tagalog perfective infixation
       a. prenúhan   pr-in-enúhan   'braked'
          gradúhan   g-in-radúhan   'graded'
          klipán   k-in-lipán/kl-in-ipán   'cremated'
          promót   p-in-romót/pr-in-omót   'promoted'
       b. trabáho   t-in-arbáho   'worked'

Variable infixation in Tagalog, as is obvious from the examples above, is the consequence of loanword borrowing (Yip 2002, 2003, 2006; Zuraw 1996, 2005). The native Tagalog lexicon lacks initial consonant clusters. Thus, a speaker of Tagalog must decide where the infix may appear when confronted with the need to perform infixation on loanwords with initial consonant clusters. Since the existing pattern of the actor focus and perfective infixation patterns support both the post-first-consonant and the pre-first-vowel analyses, speakers are free to entertain either analysis.[7]

---

[7] Zuraw (1996) accounts for the variable infixation patterns in Tagalog by proposing the possibility of floating constraints in Optimality Theory, whose ranking has never been crucial to the language in question until the proper test case is introduced, for example, in loanword borrowing.

That grammatical constraints may be derived rather than supplied by fiat is not itself a radical idea. Much research from the usage-based perspective has argued for the viability and indeed necessity of such an emergent approach to linguistics (e.g., Bybee 2001; Bybee 1985*a*, 1985*b*, 1995; Elman *et al.* 1996; Goldberg 1999, 2006; MacWhinney 1999; Tomasello 2003). Hayes (1999), for example, proposes an algorithm to derive the appropriate set of formal phonological constraints through inductive grounding. The question that must be addressed here is what the filters are that regulate the formation of alignment requirements. I share with Smith the assumption that filters are functionally based. That is, they are grounded in constraints on speech perception and production and cognitive factors in language acquisition. However, unlike the Filter/Schema model, which assumes that the filters serve an inspection role, weeding out undesirable constraints after the set of constraints has already been constructed, I maintain that the relation between filters and grammatical constraint construction is indirect. While certain filters prevent grammatical constraints from emerging during the language acquisition process, the effects of other filters are apparent only in the corpus of data available to the learner. That is, such filters eliminate impossible utterances or restrict the frequency and distribution of highly improbable ones. As I shall argue below, in the case of subcategorization restriction formation, there are two main filters that eliminate improbable or impossible alignment relations. On the one hand, there are inductive biases in morphological acquisition that block certain alignment relations from being admitted to CON, or from being set up as proper signs. On the other hand, the nature of morphological change itself restricts the range of reanalysis-inducing, ambiguous contexts that are conducive to the creation of infixes. The diachronic filter does not weed out constraints per se. Certain alignment relations are not possible because no available data, or not enough data, support their construction in the first place. The general model of the interplay between grammar-external forces and formal theory in the construction of linguistic signs is presented below:

(23) A generalized model of the interplay between external forces and formal theory in the construction of linguistic SIGNS (i.e., cognitive representations)

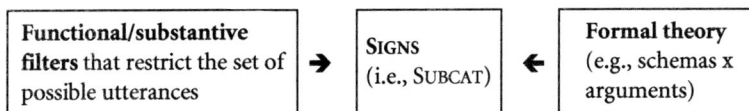

| Functional/substantive filters that restrict the set of possible utterances | ➜ | SIGNS (i.e., SUBCAT) | ← | Formal theory (e.g., schemas x arguments) |

This model is similar to the model proposed in Hume and Johnson 2001 for the interplay of external forces and phonological theory in that external factors may directly influence cognitive representations, but have only an indirect influence on formal phonological theory itself (see also Barnes 2002, 2006; Hume 2004; Kavitskaya 2001; and Mielke 2004 for similar proposals). To the extent that linguistic patterns are shaped by external factors, these factors are only *reflected* in the formal theory; the formal theory itself does not make direct reference to such functional factors. This model of sign construction and its relation to the filters thus diverges significantly from the assumptions of the traditional OT model, which assumes that the constraint set is universal across all languages. The present model has several advantages over the traditional OT model. The language-specific nature of alignment constraints has been a constant source of embarrassment for Optimality Theory since GA constraints are often formulated for language-specific affixes. The force of such an objection is much diminished if the subcategorization constraints are consigned to the declarative component of the grammar. The fact that alignment constraints are gradiently evaluated has also come under attack in recent years. This has led McCarthy (2003*b*) to propose eliminating gradiently evaluated alignment constraints entirely. However, in order to preserve the Phonological Readjustment analysis of infixation, a new set of categorically evaluated alignment constraints are posited (see discussion in Section 2.5.3 in Chapter 2). The necessity of such Alignment-by-X constraints, where X stands for a host of segmental and prosodic constituents, is suspect, given that they are only needed to preserve an OT-PR account of edge-oriented infixes; the Alignment-by-X constraints have no application outside of this very restricted domain. In the present theory, there is no need for such infixation-specific constraints since the categorical nature of subcategorization constraints follows naturally from the declarative nature of a sign-based grammar. Thus, from the perspective of the present theory, the burden of the explanatory power is distributed. The mechanism of Phonological Subcategorization governs what subcategorization requirements may be formulated and SBM regulates how such subcategorization restrictions are situated within the grammar. These two components of the theory are unabashedly silent with respect to the Edge-Bias Effect. The distributional bias of infixes is derived from external factors (i.e., the "filters"), which I shall elaborate further in the next section.

3.4 Understanding the Edge-Bias Effect

Thus far, I have articulated only a theory of phonological subcategorization. Phonological subcategorization is formalized in terms of Generalized Alignment, which, in turn, is couched within the theory of Sign-Based

Morphology. The declarative nature of linguistic signs in SBM captures straightforwardly the non-violability of subcategorization requirements in general. I have proposed that the overgenerating nature of the Generalized Alignment schema is curbed by external filters operating on the linguistic inputs through which subcategorization restrictions are derived. Two main grammar-external factors are crucial to understanding the current state of infix distribution. The next two chapters are dedicated to explicating the nature of these external filters. However, to put them in perspective, in this section, I briefly lay out the overall framework.

As foreshadowed in the beginning of this chapter, the starting point of understanding the synchronic typology of infixation, indeed any linguistic phenomenon in general, is the study of its diachronic typology. The study of language change is, however, inextricably linked to the study of language acquisition. That is, changes in language are by and large the results of misanalysis or misperception of the input data to learning (e.g., Blevins 2004; Ohala 1983, 1993). Misparsing, from the level of features to the level of phrasal constituents, may lead to reanalysis (Hopper and Traugott 1993: ch. 3). The reanalyzed structures may then propagate through analogical extension. There is ample evidence in support of this view of new construction emergence. Infixation is no exception. Infixes emerge out of ambiguity-induced morphological misparsing. Infixes are predominantly edge-oriented because the set of ambiguity-induced changes that lead to the development of infixation and the mechanism of subcategorization formation during language transmission conspire toward outcomes that favor edge-oriented infixes.

Consider the following scenario: let us assume that there exists historically an affix, X, and a set of different affixes, A. X must prefix directly to a set of roots, B, while A may prefix directly to B or XB. For simplicity's sake, let us also assume that A is present in all output forms that contain X. At some later stage, the morphological independence of A is lost and the AB complex fused to form a set of new roots, $R_A R_B$, where R_A corresponds to the set of historical affixes A, while R_B corresponds to the set of historical roots B. At this stage, the distribution of X is ambiguous: X may be subcategorizing for R_A, for R_B, or for some prosodic correlates of them. Principles of morphological learning help the learner decide on the proper subcategorization relation for X. The new distribution of X may then be extended to roots that are historically monomorphemic.

(24) Stage 1 A+B ≈ A+X+B   Straightforward adfixation to roots and stems.

$\Downarrow$

The fusion of A with B creates morphological parsing ambiguity.

- $A + B > R_A R_B$
- $A + X + B > R_A X R_B$

Stage 2 $R_A R_B \approx R_A X R_B$ Historical polymorphic forms are synchronically not decomposable.

Principles of morphological learning winnow down the possible set of subcategorization requirements, that are consistent with the input data (e.g., Align(X, R, R_B, L), Align(X, L, R_A, R) ... etc.)

$\Downarrow$

Stage 3 $R_A R_B \approx R_A X R_B$:   The infixing pattern is analogically
          $R_i R_j \approx R_i X R_j$ extended to roots that were historically monomorphemic.

Given this understanding of the origins of infixation, the main task of explaining the Edge-Bias Effect is to understand the range of linguistic changes that might give rise to ambiguities in morphological parsing, as well as the principles of morphological learning that facilitate the formation of appropriate subcategorization relations. For example, as will be reviewed in detail in Chapter 5, the particular linguistic change scenario presented in (24) is known as entrapment. The historical prefix, X, is sandwiched in between a set of historical prefixes and roots. Chapter 5 explores in detail this and other mechanisms of language change that can give rise to infixes. I will show that the set of diachronic pathways that lead to infixation is very small, which in turn has the effect of restricting the set of possible infixes that might be generated. In particular, these pathways point to the fact that infixes are predominately historical adpositional affixes. Their original peripheral distributions are reflected in their peripheral infixal distribution (i.e., the first source of the Edge-Bias Effect).

To be sure, the trajectory of change is often non-deterministic. That is, ambiguities can often be resolved in multiple ways. Infixation is often only one of many competing solutions. Ideally, a theory of language and of language change in particular should provide principled explanations for what Weinreich, Labov, and Herzog (1968) refer to as the 'actuation' problem. Here, I shall not attempt to accomplish such a tall order. In the next chapter, I have limited my goal to answering a more modest question. That is, given an ambiguous context in which a speaker is presented with multiple subcategorization analyses, what types of inductive bias might help the speaker settle on a unique solution? For example, which factor(s) decide which pivot (e.g., R_A or R_B) the infix, X, in (24) should subcategorize for? Thus, equally important to the understanding of the Edge-Bias Effect is the mechanism that allows learners to decide what subcategorization restriction is appropriate for a particular morphological construction. A theory of inductive bias, called the Pivot Theory, is introduced in the next chapter. The Pivot Theory is essentially a bootstrapping mechanism in morphological learning that helps the learner narrow down the space of possible subcategorization restrictions describing the distribution of an emergent infix to variable degrees of success. Since edge pivots (and prominence pivots) are more salient and more reliable than other potential pivot points, learners are more likely to set up phonological affixes that target these edge pivots (i.e., the second source of the Edge-Bias Effect). Chapter 4 also lays out the synchronic typology of infixation using the different pivot points as a classification scheme. I will also demonstrate how these infixes may be analyzed within an SBM-based Phonological Subcategorization approach to infixation. The presentation of the synchronic typology of infixation will set the stage for the presentation of the diachronic typology in Chapter 5.

4

Pivot Theory and the typology

In the preceding chapter, I have asserted that the distribution of infixes is governed by a restricted set of phonological pivots that enter into phonological subcategorization relations with morphological units. This limited set of phonological pivots can be subdivided into two main categories: edge pivots and prominence pivots (1).

(1)   Potential pivots of phonological subcategorization

Edge pivots	*Prominence pivots*
First consonant	Stressed foot
First vowel	Stressed syllable
(First syllable)	Stressed vowel
Last syllable	
Last vowel	
(Last consonant)	

The main problem to be addressed in this chapter is to what extent it is possible to delineate the set of attested phonological pivots without resorting to stipulation. This chapter is devoted to articulating and substantiating a theory of what constitutes a possible phonological pivot in language. Section 4.1 advances a theory of one major source of inductive bias that is crucial for morphological learning, called the Pivot Theory. Up till this point, I have refrained from laying out the synchronic typology of infixation in detail. This chapter confronts this head on. The heart of this chapter is an exploration of the general typology of infixation organized by pivot positions (Sections 4.2–4.8). I will set out any broad descriptive generalizations which emerge from the typological investigation, as well as illustrations of how infixes might be accounted for within the declarative framework laid out in Chapter 3.

4.1 The Pivot Theory

The main proposal defended in this section is the idea that the morphological learning algorithm is biased toward a phonological subcategorization relationship that is built upon certain phonological pivot points. In particular, phonological pivots must be perceptually and psycholinguistically salient, where salience may include factors such as ease of recoverability and facilitation in language processing and lexical retrieval. I shall refer to this as the Salient Pivot Hypothesis:

(2)   Salient Pivot Hypothesis
       Phonological pivots must be salient at the psycholinguistic and/or phonetic level.

The idea that certain positions in a word are privileged in the grammar has a long pedigree. As early as Trubetzkoy (1939: 22), it has been recognized that phonological contrasts are sustained to variable degrees depending on the positions of the word. Most relevant to the present discussion is the fact that certain positions in a word are 'strong' in that they are either the sole locus licensing a contrast, or that they are more resistant to reduction (e.g., Barnes 2002, 2006; Beckman 1997, 1999; J. L. Smith 2002, 2004; Zhang 2001). For example, Smith (2004) argues that positional augmentation constraints are relativized only to phonologically prominent or 'strong' positions, which include the stressed syllable, the released consonants (often the onset of a syllable), the long vowel, the initial syllable, and the morphological root. The final syllable is also a domain of some prominence. Phonologically, certain contrasts are found to be preferentially licensed in final syllables (e.g., tone and vocalic contrasts: M. Gordon 1999; Zhang 2001). In acquisition, children are most likely to retain internal-stressed syllables and first and final syllables (Kehoe and Stoel-Gammon 1997; Peters 1983). Past research has also shown that the edges of words are psycholinguistically prominent. For example, Shattuck-Hufnagel (1992) argues that the first consonant of a word is prominent based on lexical retrieval evidence. Beckman (1999) argues that initial and stressed syllables are more prominent based on the fact that they generally license a greater array of phonological contrasts than syllables in other positions. As summarized in (3), the set of phonological pivots is a proper subset of the phonologically and psycholinguistically prominent positions.

(3)   Psycholinguistically salient/   Infixal pivots
       phonologically prominent positions
       Initial syllable   First consonant
                                                 First vowel
                                                 First syllable

       Final syllable   Final consonant
                                                 Final vowel
                                                 Final syllable

       Stressed syllable   Stressed vowel
                                                 Stressed syllable
                                                 Stressed foot

This correlation is significant. The fact that the set of phonological pivots converges with the set of phonologically and psycholinguistically prominent positions suggests that the Salient Pivot Hypothesis is on the right track. As noted in Chapter 3, a learner is equipped with knowledge of the GA schema and her task is to fill the variable slots with arguments of the correct type based on the available data. The representation of morphological processes, which involves generalizations over the distinction between stems and affixes, emerges as the result of appropriate associations between formatives (e.g., Albright 2002; Albright and Hayes 2003; Bybee 1995; Bybee 2001). The reliability of a 'rule' or subcategorization requirement, in the present context, posited by the learner, depends on how well the subcategorization restriction accounts for the data and how widely a pattern is attested. Albright (2002), for example, proposes the following evaluation metric to quantify the reliability of a rule.

(4)   Definition of a rule's reliability:
$$\frac{\text{\# of forms included in the rule's structural change } (=\text{hits})}{\text{\#of forms included in the rule's structural description } (=\text{scope})}$$

Extending this metric to evaluating the reliability of subcategorization restrictions, I propose that subcategorization restrictions with the highest reliability value are the ones that are adopted. Thus, for example, consider the hypothetical language in (5), where verbs are inflected with the infix *-ka-*.

(5)   verb root   inflected form
      mata   ∼   makata
      vire   ∼   vikare
      famile   ∼   famikale
      tenupik   ∼   tenukapik

Assuming the inflected forms are derived from the verb roots, at least three subcategorization frames are possible for deriving the *ka*-inflected forms (in order to simplify the complexity of the example here, only subcategorizations stated at the level of the syllable are considered):

(6)   a. ALIGN $(ka, \text{L}, \sigma 1, \text{R})$ i.e., #$[\sigma]$ka...
      b. ALIGN $(ka, \text{L}, \sigma 2, \text{R})$ i.e., #$[\sigma\sigma]$ka...
      c. ALIGN $(ka, \text{R}, \sigma_{\text{LAST}}, \text{L})$ i.e., ...ka$[\sigma]$#

The post-initial syllable subcategorization (6a) has a structural description that covers all four words, but *-ka-* is after the first syllable in only two words. Thus, the reliability of this subcategorization restriction is $2/4 = 0.5$. Similarly, the post-second syllable subcategorization (6b) has the same reliability ratio as (6a), since (6b) also has a structural description that covers all four words, but only two show *ka* appearing two syllables away from the left edge of the word. The pre-final syllable subcategorization (6c), on the other hand, has a reliability ratio of 1, since its structural description covers all four words and all four show -*ka*- before the final. (In Albright's model, the reliability ratios are further adjusted using lower confidence limit statistics to yield a confidence value (Mikheev 1997); thus a reliability ratio of $2/4 = 0.5$ is assigned a confidence of 0.31). A learner of this hypothetical inflectional pattern is predicted to select (6c) as the subcategorization restriction for -*ka*- since it has the highest reliability value.

Based on this metric for evaluating the reliability of a subcategorization requirement, it is hardly surprising that salient pivot points are singled out for the purpose of establishing subcategorization relations. The phonological pivots in (1) are most reliable since such pivots are most likely to be established across stems. That is, if a language were to have any phonologically subcategorizing affixes at all, it is likely to have affixes subcategorizing for some phonological element within the first or the last syllable since subcategorization frames that target these pivots have the best chances of holding true across most roots/stems (7). Prominence (i.e., lexical stress) is predicted to be a legitimate pivot as well, since it is likely to be a feature of all content words in the stress-marking language.

(7) a.   First and last syllable pivots

$$\begin{bmatrix} \sigma \\ \sigma\sigma \\ \sigma\sigma\sigma \\ \sigma\sigma\sigma\sigma... \end{bmatrix} \qquad \begin{bmatrix} \sigma \\ \sigma\sigma \\ \sigma\sigma\sigma \\ ...\sigma\sigma\sigma\sigma \end{bmatrix}$$

   b.   First consonant, first vowel, and last vowel pivots

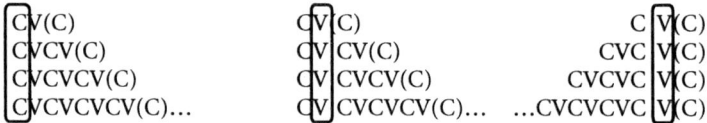

$$\begin{bmatrix} CV(C) \\ CVCV(C) \\ CVCVCV(C) \\ CVCVCVCV(C)... \end{bmatrix} \quad \begin{bmatrix} CV(C) \\ CV|CV(C) \\ CV|CVCV(C) \\ CV|CVCVCV(C)... \end{bmatrix} \quad \begin{bmatrix} C|V(C) \\ CVC|V(C) \\ CVCVC|V(C) \\ ...CVCVCVC|V(C) \end{bmatrix}$$

   c.   Prominence pivot

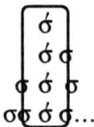

$$\begin{bmatrix} \acute{\sigma} \\ \acute{\sigma}\sigma \\ \sigma\acute{\sigma}\sigma \\ \sigma\sigma\acute{\sigma}\sigma... \end{bmatrix}$$

A similar rationale has been invoked to account for the property of demarcative stress. Hyman (1977), in his treatment of the typology of primary stress location, observes that demarcative primary stress is most often assigned to the first or the last syllable. In his survey of 444 languages, he found 114 languages with initial stress and 97 with final stress. Hyman explains this tendency for demarcative stress to be at the word boundary in the following way (see also Kurylowicz 1958: 375 *n.*):

One problem with assigning stress too far from a boundary is that short words may require a separate treatment. In a language with third syllable stress, a bisyllabic word should presumably get initial stress, while a monosyllabic word would receive stress on its only syllable. It is only initial and final stress which allow a general statement without complication. (Hyman 1977: *n.* 16)

The basic tenor of Hyman's observation is clear. All else being equal, one expects the site of a linguistic operation, be it stress assignment or infixation, to be easily identifiable regardless of the shape of the word. The edges and the stressed domain of a stem are just such locations. The difference between stress and infix placement is that the proper placement of stress often hinges on other factors (e.g., syllable weight, foot form/structure, etc.), while infixation shows no such dependencies. The pressure to posit a subcategorization restriction with maximal generality might also have to do with the nature of abductive reasoning involved in language learning. Abductive reasoning, in contrast with inductive and deductive reasoning, 'proceeds from an observed result, invokes a law, and infers that something may be the case' (Andersen 1973: 775). Thus when a learner confronts an ambiguity in morphological parsing, she may reason that, given that grammatical rules are generally transparent and exceptionless, the distribution of an affix must also be maximally reliable and exceptionless. Generalizations that are exception-ful (or demonstrably false a priori) are unlikely to hold up in an abductive reasoning process.

The Pivot Theory not only provides a mechanism by which the set of phonological subcategorization relations can be established, it also provides a handy scheme for typologizing infixes. One of the main goals of the typological survey below, besides showing the range of infixation patterns from a cross-linguistic perspective, is to provide a descriptively adequate system for the purpose of infix classification. The pivot approach provides an efficient mechanism to reduce the complexity of the typology, and it allows generalizations to emerge that might be missed under previous approaches. Take, for example, the cases of English expletive infixation and Ulwa construct-state infixation. In the case of English expletive infixation, the expletive appears to the left of a stressed foot.

(8)   English expletive infixation (McCarthy 1982)
       togéther   to-*bloody*-gether
       advánce   ad-*bloody*-vance
       Bhowáni   Bho-*bloody*-wani
       perháps   per-*bloody*-haps
       enóugh   e-*bloody*-nough
       impórtant   im-*fuckin*-portant
       Kalamazóo   Kalama-*fuckin*-zoo
       Tatamagóuchee   Tatama-*fuckin*-gouchee
       Winnipesáukee   Winnipe-*fuckin*-saukee

As alluded to in earlier chapters, the construct-state (CNS) markers in Ulwa
are affixed to the right edge of an iambic stressed foot.

(9)   Ulwa construct state (Green 1999: 64)
       súːlu   súː-**ma**-lu   'dog-CNS2'
       áytak   áy-**mana**-tak   'paper-CNS22'
       aláːkuṃ   aláː-**ka**-kuṃ   'Muscovy duck-CNS3'
       waráẉwa   waráẉ-**kana**-wa   'parrot sp.-CNS33'
       káːsiráːmah   káː-**ki**-siráːmah 'lizard sp.-CNS1'

According to the theory of pivot points, both the English and the Ulwa cases
are classified under the same pivot point, namely, the stressed foot. However,
in Ultan's (1975) classification scheme, for example, the English and Ulwa
patterns would appear under distinct categories. In particular, Ultan (1975),
who based his survey on seventy-five languages, suggests that there are
basically eight patterns of infixation. (The same typology is adopted in
Moravcsik 2000.)

(10) Ultan's (1975) inventory of infixation
       After initial consonant
       After initial vowel
       After initial syllable
       Before second consonant
       After second consonant
       After second syllable
       Before final consonant
       Before final syllable

Under this classification scheme, English expletive infixation falls under the
Before-a-Stressed-Foot category while the Ulwa construct-state marker falls
under the After-a-Stressed-Foot category. An obvious opportunity is missed
to connect two seemingly disparate patterns.

The pivot approach not only offers a more insightful way to typologize infixes, it often allows a more simplified description of infixal patterns as well. For example, in Paiwanic reduplication, the reduplicant may appear as suffixing when the root is vowel-final and infixing when the root is consonant-final. Since after the final vowel is not amongst the set of possible infixal locations, under Ultan's classification scheme, the Paiwanic pattern would have to be classified as simultaneously suffixing and affixing before the final consonant. The pivot approach, however, treats the reduplicant as appearing after the final vowel and requires no special stipulation about the nature of the final consonant.

(11) Paiwan (Chen and Ma 1986; Ferrell 1982)

kupu	'tea cup'	kupu**kupu**	'a kind of small tea cup'
kuva	'a type of bean'	kuva**kuva**	'large bean'
daŋas	'upper side'	daŋa**daŋas**	'bedside'
kadz̢aj	'a small basket'	kadz̢a**kadz̢aj**	'very small basket'
kadz̢uŋ	'bamboo water basket'	kadz̢u**kadz̢uŋ**	'a kind of bee'
ɭuʔul	'coffin'	ɭuʔu**ɭuʔul**	'a little box'
kamuraw	'pomelo'	kamura**muraw**	'a very small pomelo'
guŋtsuj	'tobacco-pipe'	quŋtsu**ŋtsuj**	'Rauwolfia verticilla'

For the remainder of this chapter, I lay out the typology of infixation using the pivot point classification schema. In what follows, I shall first focus on infixes that target the edge-pivots before proceeding to the prominence pivots. Before diving into the typological survey, however, I will briefly review the nature of the typological database from which I draw my observations.

4.2 Sampling procedures

This survey is based on a database of 154 infixation patterns from 111 languages of 26 different phyla and isolates. A summary of the languages surveyed can be found in the Appendix. In a typological study of any scale, the methodology of sample selection and coding is critical for the ultimate validity of any typological claims derived from the data. Given the relative scarcity of infixation in the world's languages, the main guiding principle in compiling the present database is 'the more the merrier'. Languages without infixes were not surveyed, as the main goal of this research is to consider the internal diversity of languages with infixes, rather than the typological distribution of languages with infixes. This methodological choice has led to certain unavoidable impasses where arbitrary decisions were made. Such decisions will be presented here as clearly as possible in the hope that the reader will be sufficiently informed in order to avoid potential confusion.

Since infixes, more often than not, occupy a relatively small corner of most grammatical descriptions, the thoroughness of their treatment often leaves much to be desired. Thus, I established a minimal requirement for an infixation pattern to be included in the database: the level of description of an infixation construction must be sufficient to address the majority of the main coding categories in the database (i.e., language name, genetic affiliation, infix shape, infix location, and examples). Wherever information is available, basic facts regarding stress assignment and the semantic import of the infix are also recorded. The sources come chiefly from reference grammars, teaching grammars, journal articles, and entries in language handbooks. These materials tend to emphasize the formal aspects of the infix, but give relatively few details regarding the meaning and productivity of the construction. While data from secondary sources, such as short illustrations given in the theoretical literature, are included, I have made an effort to confirm the data from original sources when possible. Patterns where the original source was unavailable are included in the database only if enough data are provided in the secondary source to support the description given.

The genetic affiliation information of each language recorded is based on the Web edition of the *Ethnologue*, published by the Summer Institute of Linguistics. The *Ethnologue* is employed here mainly for its comprehensiveness and its easily searchable database. No attempt was made *a priori* to form a genetically balanced database, but this situation is not as problematic as it might seem; the final corpus nevertheless contains languages from twenty-five language phyla from all major geographic areas. (See the Appendix for the genetic affiliation of languages with infixation.)

Furthermore, it is interesting to note that, while a set of infixation patterns might have a single historical source, the patterns' synchronic manifestations, more often than not, diverge quite markedly across daughter languages. The infix -*um*- found in the many languages of the Austronesian family is a case in point. Despite the fact that the function of this infix varies dramatically across the daughter languages, it is well established that this infix must be reconstructed in Proto-Austronesian (Dahl 1976). This infix invariably appears toward the left edge of the stem. However, individual daughter languages differ on the treatment of this infix with respect to stems that contain an initial onset cluster. Consider the following data from three Austronesian languages, Atayal, Chamorro, and Tagalog.

(12) Atayal animate actor focus (Egerod 1965: 263–6)

qul	qmul	'snatch'
kat	kmat	'bite'
kuu	kmuu	'too tired, not in the mood'
hŋuʔ	hmŋuʔ	'soak'
skziap	kmziap	'catch'
sbil	smbil	'leave behind'

Chamorro verbalizer, actor focus (Topping 1973: 185)

gupu 'to fly'	gumupu i paharu	'the bird flew'
tristi 'sad'	trumisti	'becomes sad'

Tagalog focus construction (Orgun and Sprouse 1999)

gradwet	grumadwet	~	gumradwet	'to graduate'
plantsa	plumantsa	~	pumlantsa	'iron'
preno	prumeno	~	pumreno	'to brake'

A quick comparison between three daughter languages of the Austronesian family reveals several interesting observations. The infix surfaces variably across these languages, namely, as -*m*- in Atayal, but as -*um*- in Chamorro and Tagalog. The distributional variation of the infix is more striking, however. In Atayal, -*m*- appears invariably after the first consonant.[1] In Chamorro, -*um*- appears after the initial onset cluster. In Tagalog, on the other hand, the infix can appear either after the initial consonant or after the onset cluster. Many more intriguing variations in the appearance and distribution of historically related infixes exist within typologically and genetically distinct language families. Thus, the inclusion of samples from closely related languages not only does not confound the validity of this study, it enriches the database further.

Finally, the use of the terms 'first' and 'last' deserves some qualification here. Many earlier studies have invoked these terms. It is perhaps implicitly understood but never explicitly stated what the reference domain is. The notions of 'first' and 'last' are defined relative to the root or the stem to which the infix attaches, not to its position in a fully formed word. An infixed stem may acquire additional adpositional affixes. The SBM approach to affixation captures the cyclic nature of affixation handily (Inkelas 1998; Inkelas and Zoll 2005; Orgun 1998, 1999; Orgun and Inkelas 2002; Yu 2000). Also, I use 'first' and 'last' interchangeably with 'leftmost' and 'rightmost' respectively. The notions of 'first' and 'last' refer to units that are closest to the left and the right edges of a stem respectively, although they need not be edge-most. With these disclaimers in mind, let us begin our discussion with the first pivot point, the first consonant.

---

[1] As noted in Chapter 2, there is some disagreement on the underlying presentation of this morpheme in Atayal. Some contend that the morpheme is /əm/ rather than /m/. (See *n*. 11.)

4.3 First consonant

Much research on syllable structure has suggested that the internal complexity of the syllable onset matters little phonologically. However, in the case of infixation, the distinction between the first consonant and the onset cluster is indispensable, as infixes may appear to the right of the first consonant. For instance, in Maricopa, a Hokan language, one method of plural formation is by adding -*uu*- after the first consonant, regardless of whether or not the first consonant is part of a cluster.[2]

(13) Maricopa
    shmank   shuumanshIk   'get up'   (Thomas-Flinders 1981)
    shtuutyk   shuutuutyk   'pick'   (Thomas-Flinders 1981)
    chmii-m   chuumiish-k   'put'   (Gordon 1986: 96)
    kmii-m   kuumiish-k   'bring'   (Gordon 1986: 96)

In Mlabri, a Mon-Khmer language, the nominalizing morpheme -*rn*- appears after the first consonant of the stem (14a). When the stem begins with a consonant cluster, the allomorph -*r*- is used (14b). When the initial contains a rhotic, the allomorph -*n*- is used instead (14c).[3]

(14) Mlabri nominalization (Rischel 1995: 85)
    a. gɯh   'to be ablaze'   grnɯh   'flames'
         kap   'to sing'   krnap   'singing, song'
         peelh   'to sweep the ground/floor'   prneelh   'a broom'
         tɛk   'to hit'   trnɛk   'a hammer'
    b. kwɛl   'to be rolled up'   krwɛl   'spiral'
         gla?   'to speak'   grla?   'speech, words'
         pluut   'to peel'   prluut   'layer'
         klaap   'to hold'   krlaap   'forceps of
                                                split bamboo'
         gwɛɛc   'to poke'   grwɛɛc   'finger'
    c. chrɛɛt   'to comb'   chnrɛɛt   'a comb'

---

[2] The infixation of -*uu*- is only one of many markers of verbal dual/plural stem formation in Maricopa. Others possibilities include prefixation, suffixation, ablaut, or various combinations of all these devices. See Gordon (1986: section 2.14) for more discussion.

[3] Rischel 1995 mentions a fourth allomorph, -*mn*-, which, along with -*n*-, may be used over -*rn*- or -*n*- respectively due to a tendency toward nasal harmony (e.g., *bliiŋ* 'raw, unripe' → *bnliiŋ* 'green, raw' not *brliiŋ*). However, Rischel also notes that this generalization is not robust since -*mn*- and -*n*- may also appear with roots that contain no nasal (e.g., *ɟuur* 'to descend' → *ɟuur ɟmnuur* 'to go downhill' (1995: 85)). Moreover, the function of these nasal 'allomorphs' does not always match the nominalizing function of -*rn*- (according to Rischel, -*mn*- creates expletive adverbials). This would suggest that -*mn*- might be best analyzed as a separate morpheme from -*rn*- and that the -*n*- in *bnliiŋ* is an allomorph of -*mn*-, not of -*rn*-.

To be sure, many cases of infixing after the first consonant may be amenable to alternative analysis. For example, in Classical Arabic, the Measure VIII template of the verbal derivational morphology, which generally signifies the passive or the mediopassive, involves the infixation of -*t*- after the first consonant of the Measure I CVCVC template. However, since Measure I verb stems do not begin with a consonant cluster, the infix may be equally well described as prefixing to the first vowel of the verb stem. Examples in (15) are taken from Aryan (2001); Measure VIII verbs are cited with the prefix *i* which signifies the third-person singular.

(15) Measure I   Measure VIII
      katab 'to write'   'iktatab 'he copied'
      basim 'to smile'   'ibtasim 'to smile'
      kasab 'to acquire'   'iktasab 'to gain'
      kashaf 'to uncover'   'iktashaf 'to discover'
      garr   'to mislead someone'   'igtarr   'to be blinded'
      faraq 'to separate, part, or   'iftaraq 'to split into many parts
             divide a group of   or group, to become
             entities'   divided'

In the cases mentioned thus far, the infix invariably appears to the right of the first consonant. In certain cases, the infix might end up 'breaking up' an onset cluster. Analytically, I assume that affixes that subcategorize for the first consonant of some domain have the following subcategorization requirement:

(16) Post-first consonant affixation
      ALIGN (Affix, L, C_1-X, R)
      'The left edge of the affix is aligned to the right edge of the first consonant of domain X.'

For example, the Mlabri nominalization construction is analyzed as follows:

(17)
$$
\begin{bmatrix}
\textit{deverbal-noun-stem} & \\
\text{SYNSEM} & \text{NOUN} \\
\text{PHON} & \boxed{3}\, \varphi(\boxed{1}, \boxed{2}\,/\text{rn}/) \\
\text{SUBCAT} & \text{ALIGN}\,(\boxed{2}, \text{L}, \text{C}_1\text{-}\boxed{3}, \text{R})
\end{bmatrix}
$$

$$
\begin{bmatrix}
\textit{verb-stem} & \\
\text{SYNSEM} & \text{VERB} \\
\text{PHON} & \boxed{1}
\end{bmatrix}
$$

This construction specifies that the verb may become a noun as a result of affixing some exponent of -*rn*- after the first consonant of the output verb stem (i.e., C_1-$\boxed{3}$). Thus, for example, the deverbal noun *krnap* 'singing, song' in Mlabri is derived from the *verb-stem* sign of *kap* 'to sing'.

(18)

$$
\begin{bmatrix}
\textit{deverbal-noun-stem} & \\
\text{SYNSEM} & \textit{singing} \\
\text{PHON} & \boxed{2}\ \varphi(\textit{krnap}) \\
\text{SUBCAT} & \text{ALIGN}(/\text{rn}/,\text{L},C_1\text{-}\boxed{2},\text{R})
\end{bmatrix}
$$

$$
\begin{bmatrix}
\textit{verb-stem} & \\
\text{SYNSEM} & \textit{to sing} \\
\text{PHON} & \boxed{1}\ \textit{kap}
\end{bmatrix}
$$

Recall that the declarative nature of signs forbids outputs that fail to satisfy conditions that are specified in each sign. Focusing on the subcategorization information in particular, any potential outputs that show the exponent of /rn/ away from the right edge of the first consonant are automatically ruled out from further consideration. The declarative constraint evaluation can be illustrated using what I refer to as a Declarative Tableau (D-Tableau). Take, for example, the D-Tableau in (19). Here, candidate (19b) fails because the exponent of the nominalizing affix precedes the first consonant, rather than following it. Candidate (19a), the attested output, satisfies the subcategorization restriction, but so does candidate (19e), despite the fact that (19e) does not faithfully realize the nominalizing marker. This is because the declarative evaluation component is only concerned with the alignment properties of the candidates, not their phonological composition. Any candidates that satisfy the subcategorization restriction specified by the *deverbal-noun-stem* sign are checked, while candidates that do not are eliminated (indicated by '✘'). As such, while failed candidates indicated in the D-Tableau will not be considered further (e.g., (19b–d)), all candidates that satisfy the subcategorization requirement (e.g., (19a) and (19e)) must be subjected to further evaluation by the constraint ranking associated with the φ-function.

(19)

	ALIGN(rn, L, C_1-STEM, R)
a. krnap	✓
b. rnkap	✗
c. karnp	✗
d. karp	✗
e. krap	✓

The declarative component thus serves as a first round of elimination, as it were. The phonological component is only required to consider candidates that satisfy the prespecified subcategorization restriction.[4] The allomorphy between *rn*, *r*, *n* is in turn determined by the φ-function, which is the phonological grammar of the language.[5] This is what I will turn to next.

Mlabri stress being always on the final syllable, and never on the initial, yields a basic iambic foot structure. The pretonic syllable may contain a full vowel or a syllabic consonant. Following Rischel's terminology, the pretonic syllable that contains a syllabic consonant is referred to as the minor syllable. A minor syllable may contain one of the following voiced sonorants, /m, n, ɲ, ŋ, r, l/, optionally preceded by another consonant. Onset consonant clusters are not allowed in minor syllables; thus the maximum number of consonants in sequence is three. The constraints in (20) are most relevant for the purpose of determining the shape of the deverbal nominalizing affix.

(20) *CCCC   Quadri-consonantal sequences are prohibited.
      MAX$_{ROOT-IO}$-SEG   Do not delete any root segment.
      MAX$_{AFFIX-IO}$-SEG   Do not delete any affix segment.
      *GEMINATE$_{Rhotics}$ Geminate rhotics are prohibited.
      *n   Assign a violation mark for every instance of /n/.
      *r   Assign a violation mark for every instance of /r/.

---

[4] Like the CONTROL function proposed in Orgun and Sprouse 1999, the declarative subcategorization requirement illustrated above prevents certain candidates from ever surfacing in a language. But unlike the CONTROL function, which rejects winning outputs predicted by what is equivalent to the φ-function here, the declarative subcategorization requirement here regulates the candidate set that 'feeds' the φ-function.

[5] It should be emphasized that there is no intrinsic temporal relation between the declarative constraint evaluation and the constraint evaluation involved in the φ-function. The only difference between constraints in the φ-function and those stated in an Attribute-Value Matrix (AVM) is that the constraints in the φ-function are violable, while the constraints in the AVM are not. I only employ the separate tableau presentations here to highlight this (non)violability distinction.

Outputs with quadri-consonantal sequence are eliminated by the dominating *CCCC constraint, which penalizes four consonants in a row. This constraint must dominate $\text{MAX}_{\text{AFFIX-IO}}$-SEG since *CCCC violations are ameliorated by reducing the number of segments in the affix. $\text{MAX}_{\text{ROOT-IO}}$-SEG must dominate $\text{MAX}_{\text{AFFIX-IO}}$-SEG as well since deletion never affects the root (see failure of (21d).[6] The choice of which segment in the affix is to be deleted is determined by constraints on phonotactics and segmental markedness. Since /r/ is generally preserved over /n/ in the affix /rn/, the markedness constraint, *n, which penalizes all instances of the segment /n/, must dominate *r, which penalizes all instances of /r/.

(21)

p-**rn**-luut	$\text{MAX}_{\text{ROOT-IO}}$-SEG	*CCCC	$\text{MAX}_{\text{AFFIX-IO}}$-SEG	*n	*r
a. prnluut		*!		*	*
b. ☞prluut			*		*
c. pnluut			*	*!	
d. prnuut	*!			*	*

The segment /r/ may be deleted over /n/, however, when the preservation of /r/ would create geminate /r/ (22b).[7] This suggests that the *GEMINATE$_{\text{Rhotics}}$ must outrank *n.

(22)

ch-**rn**-rɛɛt	*CCCC	*GEMINATE$_{\text{Rhotics}}$	$\text{MAX}_{\text{AFFIX-IO}}$-SEG	*n	*r
a. chrnrɛɛt	*!			*	*
b. chrrɛɛt		*!	*		*
c. ☞chnrɛɛt			*	*	

---

[6] The relative ranking between $\text{MAX}_{\text{ROOT-IO}}$-SEG and *CCCC is not clear at this point. Rischel (1995) reports that quadri-consonantal sequences are possible in lexicalized reduplicated forms (e.g., *trŋtuuŋ* 'bamboo "drum"'). Thus, if these forms are treated as non-derived, then $\text{MAX}_{\text{ROOT-IO}}$-SEG must dominate *CCCC. Since root segments are always faithfully realized on the surface, I shall assume that $\text{MAX}_{\text{ROOT-IO}}$-SEG must always be satisfied and will not be considered further in subsequent tableaux.

[7] While Mlabri does not generally allow geminates, Rischel (p. 75) notes that, when a short syllabic /r/ precedes a labial stop, the labial stop sounds rather like it is geminated (e.g., [rpaːʔ] ~ [rɯp.paaʔ]).

The -*rn*- allomorph is most faithfully realized when no high-ranking phonotactic constraints are violated. The affix may not be reduced to satisfy the various low-ranking segmental markedness constraints since they are crucially dominated by $\text{MAX}_{\text{AFFIX-IO}}$-SEG (see the failures of (23b and c)).

(23)

k-**rn**-ap	*CCCC	*GEMINATE_{Rhotics}	$\text{MAX}_{\text{AFFIX-IO}}$-SEG	*n	*r
a. ☞ krnap				*	*
b. krap			*!		*
c. knap			*!	*	

Phonologically conditioned allomorphy, like that in Mlabri, is very common among infixation patterns. What is crucial is that the allomorphs all conform to the subcategorization requirement. In the present case, all allomorphs appear after the first consonant of the verb stem. The phonological grammar (i.e., the φ-function in SBM) only determines the shape of the allomorph, never its position.

As mentioned earlier, the notion of the pivot point is designed to eliminate any directional bias in classification. That is, given a said pivot, one expects the possibility of an infix appearing before or after the pivot or being coextensive with it. Certain cases of infixing reduplication fit the profile of an affixing-to-the-left-of-the-first-consonant pattern. For examples, in Pangasinan, a Malayo-Polynesian language spoken in the Philippines, two patterns of infixing reduplication are found. One strategy of plural formation in noun is by prefixing a CV reduplicant to a C-initial stem. When the stem is vowel-initial, the reduplicant appears after the initial vowel (24b).

(24) CV-plural formation in Pangasinan (Benton 1971: 99–100)

	singular	plural	gloss
a.	kanáyon	kakanáyon	'relatives'
	kúya	kukúya	'older brother'
	maéstro	mamaéstro	'teacher'
	nióg	ninióg	'coconut'
	pláto	papláto	'plate'
	láta	laláta	'can'
	báso	babáso	'glass'

lópot	lolópot	'rag'
bálbas	babálbas	'beard'
b. amígo	amimígo	'friend'
amíga	amimíga	'female friend'

Numerals of limitation are also marked by reduplication. In this case, a CVC reduplicant is prefixed to C-initial stems (25a), but is lodged after the initial vowel in vowel-initial stems (25b).

(25)   Numerals of limitation in Pangasinan (Benton 1971: 151)

	Numeral	'only'	gloss
a.	sakéy	**sak**sakéy	'one'
	taló	**tal**talóra	'three'
	waló	**wál**walóra	'eight'
	siám	**sia**siamíra	'nine'
b.	apát	a**pát**patíra	'four'
	aném	a**ném**nemíra	'five'

Within the framework laid out in this work, such cases of infixing only after an onsetless syllable can be treated as the reduplicant aligning to the left of the first consonant of the input stem. For example, plural formation via CV-reduplication can be analyzed as follows:

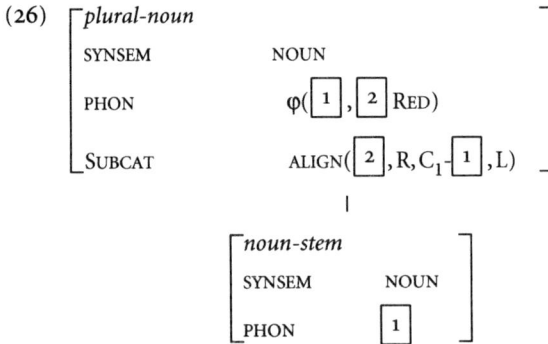

(26)

$$
\begin{bmatrix}
\textit{plural-noun} & \\
\text{SYNSEM} & \text{NOUN} \\
\text{PHON} & \varphi(\boxed{1}, \boxed{2}\,\textsc{Red}) \\
\text{SUBCAT} & \textsc{Align}(\boxed{2}, \text{R}, \text{C}_1\text{-}\boxed{1}, \text{L})
\end{bmatrix}
$$

|

$$
\begin{bmatrix}
\textit{noun-stem} & \\
\text{SYNSEM} & \text{NOUN} \\
\text{PHON} & \boxed{1}
\end{bmatrix}
$$

The subcategorization restriction of the reduplicative plural prohibits prefixing reduplication (see failures of (27d) and (27e) but favors infixation (see (27a) and (27b)) when the input stem is vowel-initial. (The reduplicant is bold-faced and underlined.) To be sure, peripheral prefixation of the reduplicant may also satisfy the subcategorization restriction if the initial vowel is not faithfully realized on the surface (see (27c)). Such a candidate is ruled out by the co-phonology of this construction. This is what we shall turn to next.

(27)

	Align($\textsc{Red}$,R,C_1,L)
☞a. a-**mi**-migo	✓
b. a-**migo**-migo	✓
c. **migo**-migo	✓
d. **a**-amigo	✗
e. **mi**-amigo	✗

The size of the reduplicant is assumed to be the consequence of an emergence-of-the-unmarked ranking pattern. The CV shape of the reduplicant is derived via the ranking, Realize-Morpheme, Max-IO >> NoCoda, *Struc-μ >> Max-BR. Thus the effect of a structure-minimizing constraint emerges when Input-Output faithfulness is not relevant (Kurisu 2001; McCarthy and Prince 1994*a*; Spaelti 1997; Walker 2000*b*).

(28) Realize-Morpheme   Let α be a morphological form, β be a morphosyntactic category, and $F(\alpha)$ be the phonological form from which $F(\alpha + \beta)$ is derived to express a morphosyntactic category β. Then RM is satisfied with respect to β iff $F(\alpha + \beta) \neq F(\alpha)$ phonologically. (Kurisu 2001: 39)

*Struc-μ Assigned a violation to each mora present in the output.

Max-IO   An output segment must have an input correspondent.

Max-BR   A base segment must have a correspondent in the reduplicant.

NoCoda   Coda consonants are prohibited.

Realize-Morpheme (RM) is a type of faithfulness constraint that requires every underlying morpheme to receive some phonological exponence (Kurisu 2001). The high ranking of RM guarantees that the plural reduplicant must have some overt exponent in the output (see the failure of (29d)).[8] The dominance of *Struc-μ, a markedness constraint that penalizes the presence of any moraic structure on the surface, over Max-BR forces the reduplicant to be no larger than a monomoraic syllable (see the failure of (29c)). To be sure, Max-BR violations cannot be minimized by reducing the size of the base (see (29e)) since

---

[8] The syllable boundary is indicated by a period.

it is more crucial to be faithful to the input than to the base (i.e., MAX-IO >> MAX-BR). The reduplicant is always CV in shape due to the dominance of NOCODA over MAX-BR (see (29b)). While the coda consonant in the reduplicant is assumed to be weightless in (29b), whether or not codas are moraic in Pangasinan is inconsequential to the present analysis; a candidate with a moraic coda in the reduplicant would have incurred a fatal violation of *STRUC-μ.

(29)

Input = amigo	RM	MAX-IO	NOCODA	*STRUC-μ	MAX-BR
☞a. a$^\mu$.-**mi$^\mu$**.-mi$^\mu$.go$^\mu$				μμμμ	go
b. a$^\mu$-**mi$^\mu$g**.-mi$^\mu$.go$^\mu$			*!	μμμμ	o
c. a$^\mu$.-**mi$^\mu$.go$^\mu$**.-mi$^\mu$.go$^\mu$				μμμμμ!	
d. a$^\mu$.mi$^\mu$.go$^\mu$	*!			μμμ	
e. **mi$^\mu$**.-mi$^\mu$.go$^\mu$		*!		μμμ	go

Within OT-PR, cases of reduplicant infixing after an onsetless syllable have been analyzed as the result of the infixation of a reduplicative prefix after the initial vowel in order to avoid duplicating ONSET violations. A celebrated example that has been analyzed under this rubric is Timugon Murut reduplication. Like the cases introduced above, Timugon Murut, an Austronesian language spoken in Sabah, Malaysia, marks diminutive and frequentative actions via CV-prefixation when the stem is consonant-initial (30a); when the stem is vowel-initial, the reduplicant appears after the first syllable (30b).

(30)   Timugon Murut (Prentice 1971: 121–2)
      a. tulu?   'index-finger'   tu-tulu?   'S points at O'
         limo   'five'   li-limo   'about five'
         bulud   'hill'   bu-bulud   'ridges in which
                                                             tuberous crops
                                                             are planted'

      b. abalan   'S bathes in T/A' a-ba-balan   'S often bathes in T/A'
         ompodon 'S will flatter T/O' om-**po**-podon 'S always flatters T/O'

Previous analysts working within the framework of OT-PR assume the CV reduplicant to be underlyingly prefixing (McCarthy 2000; McCarthy and Prince 1993*a* and 1993*b*). As illustrated in the tableau below, since straightforward prefixing reduplication would have introduced two ONSET violations in the output when the stem is vowel-initial (31b), the position of the reduplicant is minimally adjusted inward in order to minimize ONSET violations (31a).

(31)

/RED, abalan/	ONSET	ALIGN-RED-L
☞a. a.ba̲.balan	*	*
b. a̲.a.ba.lan	**!	

A closer examination of the source data reveals that the Timugon Murut pattern is more complicated than has been previously assumed. To begin with, it is not the case that infixation only takes place when the first syllable is onsetless. As shown below, infixing reduplication takes place when the verb stem is prefixed.[9]

(32) Reduplication with prothetic consonant (Prentice 1971: 121–2).

mag-ansaŋ   'T/S (two people)   magagansaŋ   'T/S (many people)
            will quarrel with   will quarrel with e.o.'
            e.o.'

maŋ-ila?   'T/S will teach'   maŋiŋila?   'T/S teaches frequently'
                                             or 'T/S is a teacher'

indimo   'five times'   indidimo   'about five times'
< limo 'five'

Prentice also points out that infixing reduplication is not observed in all vowel-initial roots. Certain vowel-initial roots reduplicate with a prothetic consonant (Prentice 1971: 121).

(33) Reduplication with prothetic consonant (Prentice 1971: 121–4).

insilot   'S removes   **gi**ginsilot 'toothpick'
           O from crevice'
abas   'S is adrift'   i-**ga**gabas   'S (swimmer) floats'

---

[9] Some might question whether the reduplicants are infixed in these forms at all. Under the Correspondence Theory of Reduplication, the data can be analyzed as the result of backcopying. For example, in the case of *maŋiŋila?* 'T/S teaches frequently', the final consonant of the prefix *maŋ-* is assumed to have syllabified as part of the reduplicant, which is then backcopied onto the vowel-initial root to ensure Base-Reduplicant faithfulness.

ila?	'S teaches O'	i-**gi**gila?	'S learns'
a**ŋ**kup	no gloss	gaga**ŋ**kup	no gloss
ansip	'S nips/pinches O'	i-**gi**giansip	'S dances between two poles which are moved rhythmically together and apart.'

Finally, there is evidence to suggest that the distribution of Timugon Murut reduplication might be stress-governed. Primary stress in Timugon generally falls on the penultimate syllable.[10] Given the fact that the reduplicant tends to appear in the antepenultimate position in the above examples, the reduplicant might be analyzed as prefixing to the stressed syllable (or the stressed foot). Unfortunately, stress is not generally marked in Prentice's transcriptions, so it is not possible to ascertain the validity of this analysis at this juncture. If this stress-based analysis of Timugon Murut reduplication is proven accurate, however, it will not only obviate the need for an OT-PR analysis of such infixing reduplication patterns, but CV reduplication in Timugon Murut must also be reclassified as targeting a prominence pivot.

Like Timugon Murut, pluractional reduplication in SiSwati (34a) and Kinande (34b), Bantu languages spoken in Swaziland and Zäire respectively, also show a similar type of post-initial-onsetless-syllable distribution. In these languages, pluractionality is generally marked by prefixing a bimoraic foot reduplicant to the verb stem. However, when the verb stem is vowel-initial, the reduplicant appears infixing.

(34) a. SiSwati pluractional formation (Downing 1999: 74)

-tfutséla	-**tfutse**-tfutséla	'move for'
-khulúma	-**khulu**-khulúma	'talk'
-kála	-**kalá**-kala	'weigh'
-enyéla	-e-**nyelá**-nyela	'be hurt'
-engetisa	-e-**ngeti**-ngetisa	'cause to increase'
-endlulána	-e-**ndlula**-nldulána	'pass by each other'
-etsaméla	-e-**tsame**-tsaméla	'bask'

  b. Kinande pluractional formation (Downing 1999: 64)

-huma	-**huma**-huma	'beat'
-ohera	o-**hera**-hera	'pick for'
-esera	e-**sera**-sera	'play for'

Despite the surface resemblance, this infixation pattern is neither a matter of onsetless-syllable-minimization, as argued by OT-PR advocates, nor a matter

---

[10] There are lexical exceptions to this generalization (e.g., *madadá?* 'dislike' (Prentice 1971)).

of aligning with respect to the first consonant of the stem. Downing (1999) reports that, while infixing reduplication is observed when the stem begins with a vowel, it is only so if the stem is underlyingly more than two syllables long. Data from SiSwati are given below.

(35) Infixing reduplication in 3–5 syllable vowel-initial stems in SiSwati
      (Downing 1999: 78)
      a. -enyéla   -e-**nyelá**-nyela   'be hurt'
         -eyáma   -e-**yamá**-yama   'lean'
         -etsaméla   -e-**tsame**-tsaméla   'bask'
         -eyamísa   -e-**yami**-yamísa   'cause to lean'

      b. -ehlukánisa -e-**hluka**-hlukánisa   'distinguish'

When the stem is disyllabic (36a) or is derived from disyllabic stems (36a), the reduplicant appears as prefixing even when the stem is vowel-initial.

(36) Prefixing reduplication in disyllabic vowel-initial stems in SiSwati
      (Downing 1999: 78)
      a. -ókha   -**okhá**-yokha   'light (a fire)'
         -énya   -**enyá**-yenya   'soak'
      b. -okhéla -**okhe**-yokhéla   'light for'
         -enyéla -**enye**-yenyéla   'soak for'

The data in (36) point to the fact that the reduplicant can appear prefixing even when the input stem is vowel-initial. A glide is inserted between the final vowel of the reduplicant and the initial vowel of the base to prevent hiatus. (36) also shows that the reduplicant is not targeting the first consonant of the input stem (e.g., *-enyéla* 'soak for' → *-enye-yenyéla* / *-e-nyela-nyéla*). Instead, as argued in Downing (1998, 1999, 2000), the reduplicant is prefixing to a P-Stem (cf. Crowhurst 2004). Following Inkelas's (1990, 1993) theory of prosodic misalignment, Downing assumes that the left edge of the reduplicant must align with the left edge of the P-Stem. P-Stems are generally co-extensive with the morphological stem. However, the left boundary of the P-Stem in a vowel-initial stem is misaligned with respect to the left edge of the morphological boundary since the P-Stem must begin with a syllable that begins with an onset in SiSwati and Kinande (e.g., *tfutséla* 'move for' in SiSwati → [$_{PS}$*tfutséla* but *etsaméla* 'bask' → *e*[$_{PS}$*tsaméla*). Infixing reduplication in cases like (35) is thus analyzed as a consequence of the extraprosodicity of the stem-initial vowel. The reduplicant is targeting a P-Stem, rather than the first consonant of the stem, as evidenced by the examples in (36). Downing argues that the P-Stem is independently motivated by the assignment of the rightmost high tone in stems. In particular, the location of the high tone is determined by the size of the stem. Two- and three-syllable stems have the rightmost high tone on the penult (see (35)) while longer stems have the rightmost high tone on the antepenult (see (37)).

(37)   High-tone assignment on > three-syllable stems in SiSwati (Downing 1999: 78)
    a. -onákala   'get spoilt'
       -atísana   'introduce each other'
    b. -khulumísana 'talk to each other'
       -hlanyélela   'plant for'

Of particular importance is the fact that vowel-initial stems that take infixing reduplication have high tone on the penult even in four-syllable stems (see (35a)). This evidence suggests that the domain for tonal assignment is also the base of reduplication; the tonal patterns of the infixing verb stems may be straightforwardly accounted for if the initial vowel in such stems does not count toward the stem size calculation.

    Whether this Prefix-to-P-Stem analysis can be extended to Timugon Murut and Pangasinan remains a matter of further research. It is unclear at this point if there is independent evidence that supports the P-Stem domain in these languages. As I alluded to earlier, Timugon Murut might turn out to be a case of prefixing to a stressed pivot. However, the available resources on Timugon Murut do not offer enough conclusive evidence in support of this analysis. In regard to Pangasinan, the mechanism of stress assignment has not been worked out. Benton notes that there exists minimal pairs in the language that are distinguished by the location of stress alone (i.e., stress may be on the penult or the ultima), but he also intimates that stress assignment may interact with the morphology (Benton 1971: 27–8).

    The need to appeal to the P-Stem for analyzing infixation raises the question of how the P-Stem fits into the present typology of infixation. Recall that a P-Stem is generally co-extensive with the morphological stem; the P-Stem is only minimally misaligned with the morphological stem under restrictive circumstances. Given that the P-Stem is always near the periphery of some morphological host, it is licensed by the Pivot Theory since the edges of a P-Stem fall on salient edge positions. It is noteworthy that the present case of aligning with respect to the P-Stem comes from a set of tonal languages and that the base of reduplication coincides with the domain of tone assignment. This suggests that in non-stress-marking languages, the P-Stem might be equivalent to the stress domain. In connection with this, it is also interesting to note that the stems that show infixation in (35) invariably begin with /e/. Downing argues that there is no evidence to suggest that /e/ is morphologically distinct from the stem synchronically speaking. However, rather than treating this as a mere coincidence (the interpretation favored by Downing), it seems likely that the initial /e/ in these infixing vowel-initial stems might have been historically a distinct morpheme. Infixation reduplication might have been the result of entrapment (see Chapter 5 for more discussion on this mechanism) where original prefixing reduplication was reanalyzed as infixing when /e/ lost its meaning and became part of the stem. Further research is needed to ascertain the viability of this analysis, particularly with respect to the morphological status of /e/ in the ancestral language.

No unequivocal cases of a reduplicative infix appearing to the right of the first consonant are found. All potential instances of infixing a reduplicant after the first consonant can equally well be analyzed as subcategorizing for the first vowel of the output. For that reason, such ambiguous examples will be discussed in more detail in the next section.

4.4 First vowel

Another common pivot for infixation is the first vowel. For example, in Chamorro, an Austronesian language, the actor focus marker -*um*- appears before the first vowel of the root, whether the stem begins with an onsetless syllable or a consonant cluster.

(38) Chamorro verbalizer, actor focus (S. Anderson 1992: 208; Topping 1973: 185)

epanglo	'hunt crabs'	umepanglo	'to look for crabs'
gupu	'to fly'	gumupu i paharu	'the bird flew'
tristi	'sad'	trumisti	'becomes sad'
planta	'set the table'	plumanta	'sets (table) (nom. wh-agreement form)'

A similar case is found in Yurok, an Algic language spoken in northwestern California. The intensive infix -*eg*- appears before the first vowel when the stem is cluster-initial. There are no vowel-initial roots in this language.

(39) Yurok intensive (Garrett 2001)

Base		Intensive
laːy-	'to pass'	legaːy-
koʔmoy-	'to hear'	kegoʔmoy-
tewomeł	'to be glad'	tegewomeł
łkyorkʷ-	'to watch'	łkyegorkʷ-
trahk-	'to fetch'	tregahk-

Another example of prefixing to the first vowel of the root is found in Toratan (Ratahan), an Austronesian language spoken in Sulawesi. Here, the past tense agent voice marker -*um*- must appear before the first vowel. Crucially, this pattern cannot be analyzed as inserting to the right of the first consonant, as could those mentioned in the last section, since the allomorph *m*- is prefixed to the first vowel when the stem is vowel-initial.

(40)   Toratan Agent Voice in Past Tense (Himmelmann and Wolff
        1999: 13, 41)

kukuk	'cry out'	kumukuk
suq	'enter'	sumúq
lompuq	'go out'	lumompuq
empo	'sit'	mempo

Following Crowhurst (2004), alignment with respect to the leftmost vowel is analyzed as alignment with respect to the leftmost mora. For example, recall that in Leti nominalization has eight allomorphs: three infixes -*ni*-, -*n*-, -*i*-; three prefixes *ni*-, *i*-, *nia*; a parafix *i*-+-*i*-; and a zero allomorph. The nominalizer appears infixing when the root begins with a consonant. Thus, the allomorph, -*ni*-, appears before the leftmost vowel of the stem when the stem has an initial non-nasal or non-alveolar consonant followed by a non-high vowel (41a). It is realized as -*n*- when the stem contains a high vowel after the initial consonant (41b) and as -*i*- when the initial consonant is a sonorant or an alveolar consonant (41c). Leti examples cited below are all taken from Blevins (1999).

(41)   Nominalizing -*ni*- in Leti

a.	kasi	'to dig'	k-ni-asi	'act of digging'
	polu	'to call'	p-ni-olu	'act of calling, call'
	n-sai	'to climb, rise, III (3SG)'	s-ni-ai	'act of climbing, rising'
	n-teti	'to chop, III (3SG)'	t-ni-eti	'chop, chopping'
b.	kili	'to look'	k-n-ili	'act of looking'
	surta	'to write'	s-n-urta	'act of writing, memory'
	tutu	'to support'	t-n-utu	'act of supporting, support'
	n-virna	'to peel, II (3SG)'	v-n-irna	'act of peeling'
c.	mai	'to come'	m-i-ai	'arrival'
	n-resi	'to win'	r-i-esi	'victory'

davra	'cut'	d-i-avra	'act of cutting, cut'
dèdma	'to smoke'	d-i-èdma	'act of smoking'

When the stem is vowel-initial, however, the nominalizer is prefixed.

(42)

n-osri	'to hunt'	i-osri, ni-osri	'act of hunting'
n-otlu	'to push'	i-otlu, ni-otlu	'act of pushing'
n-atu	'to know'	i-atu, ni-atu	'knowledge'
n-odi	'to carry'	i-odi, ni-odi	'pole, load, act of carrying'
n-èmnu	'to drink'	i-èmnu, ni-èmnu	'act of drinking, drink, beverage'
n-òra	'to be with'	i-òra, ni-òra	'companion'

As noted in Chapter 2, the fact that the nominalizer is infixed is puzzling within a prosodic optimization view of infixation since infixation actually creates initial onset clusters and vowel-vowel sequences[11] that could otherwise be avoided with simple prefixation (e.g., *ni-teti* instead of *t-ni-eti* 'chop, chopping'). Leti infixation cannot be analyzed as the result of edge-avoidance (e.g., Kaufman 2003) similar to that proposed for Dakota infixation (McCarthy and Prince 1993a and 1993b), since the nominalizer may appear prefixing when the root is vowel-initial (42).

The distribution of the nominalizing markers in Leti finds natural expression in the present theory, however. Following Crowhurst's (2004) proposal of mora alignment, I assume that the right edge of the nominalizing marker in Leti must align with the left edge of the first mora of the input verb stem (i.e., μ_{R1}), as stated in (43).

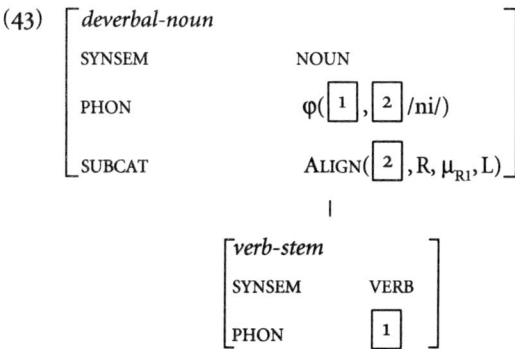

(43)

$$
\begin{bmatrix}
\textit{deverbal-noun} \\
\text{SYNSEM} \qquad\qquad \text{NOUN} \\
\text{PHON} \qquad\qquad \varphi(\boxed{1},\boxed{2}\,/ni/) \\
\text{SUBCAT} \qquad\qquad \textsc{Align}(\boxed{2},\text{R},\mu_{R1},\text{L})
\end{bmatrix}
$$

$$
\mid
$$

$$
\begin{bmatrix}
\textit{verb-stem} \\
\text{SYNSEM} \qquad \text{VERB} \\
\text{PHON} \qquad \boxed{1}
\end{bmatrix}
$$

Thus when the root is consonant-initial, the nominalizing marker appears infixing (following Hayes's (1989) proposal that the onset is linked directly to

---

[11] The high vowel in a vowel-vowel sequence is realized as a glide phonetically.

the syllable, rather than to the mora; root morae are indexed with the subscript 'R'; the mora introduced by the infix is circled).

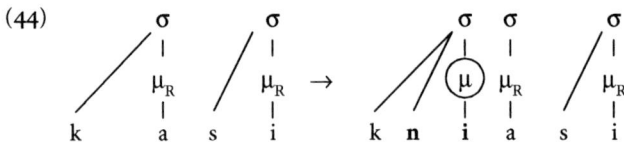

(44)
```
      σ         σ                σ  σ        σ
     /|        /|               //|  |      /|
    / μ_R     / μ_R    →       // (μ) μ_R   / μ_R
   /  |      /  |             //   |   |   /  |
  k    a  s   i            k  n    i   a  s   i
```

The fact that the nominalizer is realized as prefixing when the root is vowel-initial follows straightforwardly from this analysis as well, as illustrated in (45).

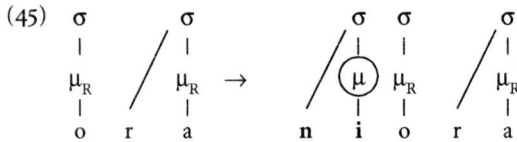

(45)
```
  σ         σ               σ  σ        σ
  |        /|              //|  |      /|
  μ_R     / μ_R    →      // (μ) μ_R   / μ_R
  |      /  |            //   |   |   /  |
  o    r   a          n  i    o   r  a
```

As noted in the preceding section, many cases of internal reduplication after the first consonant can also be classified as appearing before the first vowel. For example, in many aboriginal Australian languages, plurality and adjective intensification are marked by VC(C) reduplicants (46).

(46)   Mangarayi (Kurisu and Sanders 1999; Merlan 1982)
       gurjag   gurjurjagji   'having a lot of lilies'
       gabuji   gababuji   'old person'
       yirag   yirirag   'father'
       waŋgij   waŋgaŋgij   'child'
       jimgan   jimimgan   'knowledgeable one'

Two interpretations are possible here. The reduplicant could be described as appearing after the first consonant (47a) or before the first vowel (47b), as schematized below.

(47)   a. ROOT   ⟶   PIVOT-**RED**-BASE
          gurjag   ⟶   g-**urj**-urjag
       b. ROOT   ⟶   **RED**-PIVOT/BASE
          gurjag   ⟶   g-**urj**-urjag

Crowhurst (2004) argues in favor of the prefix-to-the-first-vowel analysis in (47b). Working within the OT-Phonological Readjustment paradigm, she assumes that Mangarayi internal reduplication is induced by edge avoidance (see also Kurisu and Sanders 1999; McCarthy and Prince 1994*b*). In particular, the infixation of RED is motivated by the dominance of LEFTMOST-ROOT$_{SEG}$ over LEFTMOST-RED$_{SEG}$.

(48) a. LEFTMOST-RED$_{SEG}$: Align$_{SEG}$-Left(RED, PrWd)
'The leftmost segment of RED is aligned with the leftmost segment of some PrWd.'

   b. LEFTMOST-ROOT$_{SEG}$: Align$_{SEG}$-Left(Root, PrWd)
'The leftmost segment of root is aligned with the leftmost segment of some PrWd.'

(49)

RED + jimgan	LEFTMOST-ROOT$_{SEG}$	LEFTMOST-RED$_{SEG}$
☞ a. j-**im.g**-im.gan		j
b. **ji.**-jim.gan	j!i	
c. **jim.**jim.gan	j!im	

The prefixation of the reduplicant to the root and the size of the reduplicant are derived by ranking LEFTMOST-RED$_\mu$, which requires that the leftmost mora of the reduplicant be lined up with the leftmost mora of some prosodic word, over LEFTMOST-ROOT$_\mu$, which requires the leftmost mora of the root be aligned with the leftmost mora of some PrWd.

(50) a. LEFTMOST-RED$_\mu$: Align$_\mu$-Left(RED, PrWd)
'The leftmost mora of RED is aligned with the leftmost mora of some PrWd.'

   b. LEFTMOST-ROOT$_\mu$: Align$_\mu$-Left(Root, PrWd)
'The leftmost mora of root is aligned with the leftmost mora of some PrWd.'

Briefly, as shown in (51), the reduplicant must line up with the leftmost mora; otherwise, it fatally violates the dominating LEFTMOST-RED$_\mu$ constraint (51c). LEFTMOST-RED$_\mu$ crucially dominates LEFTMOST-ROOT$_\mu$ since it is more important to align the reduplicant with the leftmost more than to respect the proper alignment of the root. The reduplicant may copy as much of the base as possible as long as it does not incur more LEFTMOST-RT$_\mu$ violations than it is necessary. In essence, the size of the reduplicant is restricted to no larger than a mora (Crowhurst assumes that coda consonants are weightless).

(51)

Red + jimgan	LEFTMOST-RED$_\mu$	LEFTMOST-RT$_\mu$	MAX-BR
☞ a. j-**i$^\mu$m.g**-i$^\mu$m.ga$^\mu$n		μ	an
b. j-**i$^\mu$m.ga$^\mu$.n**-i$^\mu$m.ga$^\mu$n		$\mu\mu$!	
c. ji$^\mu$m.-**ga$^\mu$**-.ga$^\mu$n	μ!		
d. j-**i$^\mu$m.**-i$^\mu$m.ga$^\mu$n			gan!

The main intuition captured in Crowhurst's analysis of Mangarayi reduplication is the idea that the proper realization of the plural reduplicant, both in terms of its alignment and in the size of the reduplicant, is determined at the level of the mora, in addition to the canonical segmental level. While infixation is forced by edge avoidance, the size of the reduplicant is derived from the tension between the prosodic alignment of the reduplicant and the root at the moraic level. In particular, it is the leftmost mora that is of the utmost importance.

On the view of the present theory, internal reduplication patterns like that found in Mangarayi are also analyzed as a matter of moraic alignment. However, I differ from Crowhurst in assuming that infixation falls out from the morpho-phonological mismatch inherent in the subcategorization restriction specified by the plural construction, rather than as a matter of affix displacement. In particular, I assume that the sign for plural formation in Mangarayi specifies that the left edge of the reduplicant be aligned with the leftmost mora of the PrWd (52).

(52)

$$
\begin{bmatrix}
plural & \\
\text{SYNSEM} & \iota_{\{plural\}}(\boxed{2}) \\
\text{PHON} & \varphi(\boxed{1},\boxed{3}\,\text{RED}) \\
\text{SUBCAT} & \text{ALIGN}_\mu\text{-Left}(\boxed{3},\text{PRWD})
\end{bmatrix}
$$

$$
\begin{bmatrix}
stem & \\
\text{SYNSEM} & \boxed{2}\ \text{NOUN OR VERB} \\
\text{PHON} & \boxed{1}
\end{bmatrix}
$$

Straightforward prefixing reduplication is therefore disallowed because the left edge of the reduplicant does not coincide with left edge of the leftmost mora of the output (53).

(53)

Pr Wd   *j   i   **m**   j   i   m   g   a   n

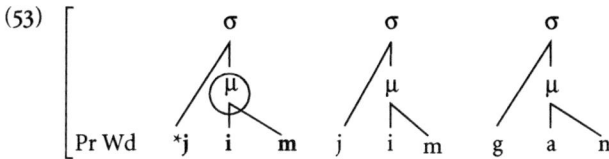

Internal reduplication obtains when the leftmost segment of the output does not match up with the leftmost segment subcategorized by the plural morpheme. That is, when the input verb stem is consonant-initial, the leftmost segment is an onset, which is not mora-bearing. Since the left edge of the reduplicant must match up with the left edge of the leftmost weight-bearing segment, the reduplicant has no choice but to line up with the nucleus of the first syllable (54).

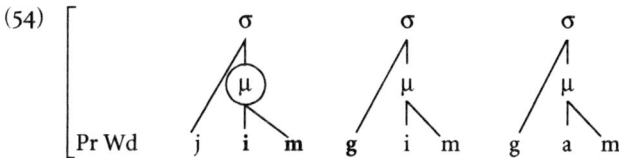

(54)

Pr Wd   j   i   **m**   **g**   i   m   g   a   m

The present analysis is superior to Crowhurst's OT-PR analysis for two reasons. First, it obviates the need to rely on a gradient evaluation of alignment, in keeping with the declarative nature of alignment required by the present theory and also with the recent call to eliminate gradiently evaluated alignment constraints in Optimality Theory (McCarthy 2003*b*). More problematic is the fact that Crowhurst's analysis, indeed the edge-avoidance approach to edge-oriented infixation in general, makes an erroneous prediction regarding the behavior of the reduplicant in vowel-initial roots. While Mangarayi does not contain vowel-initial roots, a similar plural reduplication construction in Kugu Nganhcara, another Australian aboriginal language, demonstrates that the edge-avoidance approach is untenable. As shown in (55b), when the root is vowel-initial, the reduplicant appears prefixing, rather than after the first segment of the root (i.e., the first vowel in this case) as predicted by the logic of edge avoidance (the predicted illegitimate outputs are given to the right of the attested forms in (55b)).

(55) Kugu Nganhcara plural (I. Smith and Johnson 2000: 382)
     a. thena   'stand'   thenena
        pukpe   'child'   pukukpe
        nunpa   'run'   nuntunpa

b. iiru-ma 'here-EMPH'   iiriiru-ma   *iiruru-ma

ungpa 'break'[12]   **ungk**ungpa   *ungpangpa

As illustrated in (56), the reduplicant is prefixing when the root is vowel-initial because the leftmost segment of the reduplicant coincides with the leftmost mora of the PrWd. The alignment requirement of the reduplicant is thus satisfied. As predicted by the Phonological Subcategorization approach, when there is no mismatch in edges, no infixation is predicted.

(56)

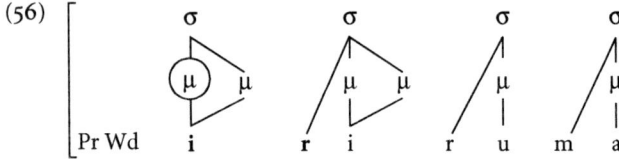

The size of the reduplicant is assumed to be the consequence of an emergence-of-the-unmarked ranking pattern similar to the analysis of Pangasinan plural reduplication in the last section (also similar in spirit to Crowhurst's analysis). In particular, the VC(C) shape of the reduplicant is compelled by the ranking, REALIZE-MORPHEME, MAX$_{IO}$Seg >> *STRUC-μ >> MAX-BR. As illustrated in (57), the size of the reduplicant is kept to no more than one mora due to the dominance of *STRUC-μ over MAX-BR (57b). The structure-minimizing effect of *STRUC-μ is checked by the dominance of REALIZE-MORPHEME (RM) (57d) and MAX-IO (57e). While the reduplicant

(57)

j-Red-imgan	RM	MAX-IO	*STRUC-μ	MAX-BR
☞a. j-i^μ**m.g**-i^{μ}m.ga^{μ}n			3μ	an
b. j-i^μ**m.ga^μ.n**-i^{μ}m.ga^{μ}n			4μ!	
c. j-i^μ**m.**-i^{μ}m.ga^{μ}n			3μ	gan!
d. ji^{μ}m.ga^{μ}n	*!		2μ	
e. j-i^μ**m.**-i^{μ}m		*!**	3μ	

[12] Kugu Nganhcara reduplication may exhibit the reduction of the labial in root-internal heterorganic stop+labial sequence (e.g., *pukpe → pukukpe* 'child'; *wegbe → wegegbe* 'keep'). Also, in heterorganic nasal+labial stop clusters, the labial in the reduplicated cluster is replaced by a stop homorganic with the nasal (e.g., *nunpa → nuntunpa* 'run'; *thanpa → thantanpa* 'cough'; *wunpa → wuntunpa* 'gather, get'). These additional complications are not relevant to the point made here.

cannot be more than a mora long, it nonetheless may copy as much of the base at the segmental level as long as it does not increase the mora count (57c).

Like the Australian aboriginal languages, many Salishan languages have a VC reduplicant; it signifies what is referred to as 'Out-of-Control' in the literature. Examples from Lushootseed, a Central Salish language, are given in (58).

(58)   Lushootseed (Urbanczyk 2001: 56)

a. ʔaɬ   'fast, quickly'   ʔaɬaɬ   'hurry up!'
   dᶻaq'   'fall, topple'   dᶻaq'aq'   'totter, stagger'
   čəχ   'split'   sčəχəχ   'cracked to pieces'

b. haʔkʷ   'for a long time'   haʔaʔkʷ   'a little while ago'
   hawɬ-əd   'improvise'   hawawɬ-əd   'improvise'

c. ʔuluɬ   'travel by water'   ʔululuɬ   'boat riding'
   s-ɬadəyʔ   'woman'   s-ɬadadəyʔ   'woman living alone'
   wəliʔ   'be visible'   wələliʔ-il   'become visible'
   ʔəχid   'what happened'   ʔu-ʔəχiχ-əd   'what's he done?'

Working within the Generalized Template Theory of reduplication (McCarthy and Prince 1994*b*), which eschews morpheme-specific templatic requirements in favor of generalized morphology-prosody interface constraints specifying the unmarked prosodic shape of each morpheme category, Urbanczyk (1996) posits that the Out-of-Control marker belongs to the affixal category, whose canonical shape is generally no larger than a syllable. This reduplicative marker is analyzed as suffixing (i.e., *ʔaɬ-aɬ* 'hurry up!'). As illustrated by the failure of (59b), the VC, rather than CVC, shape of the reduplicant follows from the ranking of NoCoda over BR-Max-Afx, a constraint that demands the full copying of the base. Despite the dominance of NoCoda over BR-Max-Afx, the reduplicant nonetheless ends in a coda consonant due to the high-ranking Anchor-R constraint, which demands that the base and the reduplicant share a correspondent at the right edge (59c).

(59)

ʔaɬ-OC	Anchor-R	NoCoda	BR-Max-Afx
☞a. ʔa.ɬ-aɬ		*	*
b. ʔa.ɬ-ʔaɬ		**!	
c. ʔa.ɬ-a	*!		**

When the verb stem ends in a cluster, the reduplicant appears infixing in order to minimize violations of NoCODA. As such, NoCODA must dominate the suffixing requirement of the OC reduplicant, EDGEMOST-R.

(60)	haʔkʷ-OC	NoCODA	EDGEMOST-R
☞a. ha.ʔa̲ʔkʷ		*	*
b. haʔ.kʷa̲ʔkʷ		**!	

This OT-PR approach to Out-of-Control reduplication runs into two intriguing problems, however. First, while OT-PR predicts minimal displacement, as shown in (58c) where the stem is polysyllabic, the reduplicant actually appears further inward in the stem than predicted (i.e., *s-ɬadada̲yʔ* 'woman living alone' not *s-ɬadəya̲yʔ*). The second problem concerns the shape of the reduplicant itself. Recall that Urbanczyk assumes no specific templatic requirement of the reduplicant per se. The shape of the reduplicant is determined partly by a generalized morphology-prosody interface constraint that specifies the unmarked prosodic shape of the affixal category (i.e., an affix cannot be larger than a syllable) and partly by constraint interaction. As such, it is unclear why the reduplicant does not appear as CV in polysyllabic stems. For example, why is *s-ɬaɬady* not possible for 'woman living alone'? Urbanczyk resolves the first problem by appealing to the effect of BR-MAX-Afx, which maximizes the correspondence between the base and the affixal reduplicant. Since affixes in Lushootseed may not exceed the size of a syllable (see the failure of (61c)), BR-MAX-Afx may be maximized by reducing the size of the base (61b).

(61)	s-ɬadəyʔ-OC	AFX≤σ	BR-MAX-Afx	EDGEMOST-R
☞a. sɬad-a̲d-əyʔ			**	***
b. sɬadəy-ə̲y-ʔ			***!*	*
c. sɬadəy-a̲dəy-ʔ		*!	**	*

The second problem, however, proves to be more recalcitrant. As illustrated in (62), the hypothetical candidate *s-ɬaɬada̲yʔ* is more well-formed with respect to BR-MAX-Afx than the attested output since the base in (62b) is smaller than that in (62a).

(62)

s-ɬadəyʔ-OC	Afx≤σ	BR-Max-Afx	Edgemost-R
☞a. sɬad-**ad**-əyʔ		**!	***
●*b. s-ɬa**ɬ**adəyʔ		*	****

To this end, Urbanczyk proposes that candidates like (62b) are suboptimal because the part of the verb root that corresponds to the base of the reduplicant does not end in a consonant. The best root structure in Lushootseed is consonant-final because an overwhelming number of roots are consonant-final. The constraint, C-Final-Root, requires all output exponents of a root to be consonant-final. A root interrupted by an infix, according to Urbanczyk, has two root components (e.g., s-{ɬad}$_{Root}$-**ad**-{əyʔ}$_{Root}$). The root component to the left of the infix must end in a consonant, just as the root component to the right of the infix. Candidates like (62b) are less well-formed than the attested output, since the root component to the left of the OC marker (i.e., s{ɬa}$_{Root}$**ɬa**{dəyʔ}$_{Root}$) is not consonant-final.

On the view of the present theory, the size and the distribution of the reduplicant fall out naturally from a prefixing analysis of the reduplicant. The OC marker is analyzed as prefixing at the moraic level (63). Like the case of Mangarayi, the OC reduplicant appears after the first consonant of the verb stem (e.g., ʔ**a**ɬaɬ 'hurry up!', h**aa**ʔkʷ 'a little while ago', s-ɬ**a**dadəyʔ 'woman living alone') because the left edge of the reduplicant must share the same edge with the first mora of the output Prosodic Word. Hypothetical outputs where the reduplicant is perfectly aligned with respect to the left edge of the output (e.g., *s-ɬ**a**ɬadəyʔ) or too far to the right of the left edge of the first mora (e.g., *s-ɬad**ad**əyʔ) would therefore be untenable under the present analysis.

(63)

$$\begin{bmatrix} \textit{Out-of-Control} \\ \text{SYNSEM} \quad \iota_{\{\text{OUT-OF-CONTROL}\}}(\boxed{2}) \\ \text{PHON} \quad \varphi(\boxed{1},\boxed{3}\text{RED}) \\ \text{SUBCAT} \quad \text{ALIGN}_\mu\text{-Left}(\boxed{3},\text{PRWD}) \end{bmatrix}$$

$$|$$

$$\begin{bmatrix} \textit{stem} \\ \text{SYNSEM} \quad \boxed{2}\,\text{NOUN OR VERB} \\ \text{PHON} \quad \boxed{1} \end{bmatrix}$$

The fact that the reduplicant appears as VC falls out from the ranking: Realize-Morpheme, Max-IO >> NoCoda, *Struc-μ >> Max-BR. Since Realize-Morpheme and Max-IO are assumed to be undominated under the present analysis, candidates that violate these constraints will not be considered in the following tableaux. As illustrated in (64), the dominance of NoCODA over MAX-BR ensures that the reduplicant may only copy up to one postvocalic consonant; copying any additional postvocalic consonant would incur extra, thus fatal, violations of NoCODA (64b).

(64)	h-OC-aʔkʷ	NOCODA	*STRUC-μ	MAX-BR
☞ a. h-a̲ᵘ.ʔ-aᵘʔkʷ		*	μμ	kʷ
b. h-a̲ᵘʔ.kʷ-aᵘʔkʷ		**!	μμ	

Reduplicative copying of more than one syllable is prohibited due to the dominance of *STRUC-μ over MAX-BR, as illustrated by the losing of (65b).[13]

(65)	s-ɬ-OC-adəʔ	NOCODA	*STRUC-μ	MAX-BR
☞ a. sɬ-a̲ᵘd-aᵘdəᵘʔ		*	μμμ	əyʔ
b. sɬ-a̲ᵘdəᵘy-aᵘdəᵘyʔ		*	μμμμ!	ʔ

There appear to be exactly two 'counterexamples' to the present analysis, although these examples (66) are also counterexamples to Urbanczyk's suffixal analysis. It is noteworthy that both of these 'counterexamples' begin with ʔə-, suggesting that they might be better analyzed as prefixed roots. If such a morphological analysis proves tenable, then these forms would be accounted for straightforwardly by the present analysis.

(66) a. dxʷ-ʔəhad   'talk'
          dxʷ-ʔəhádad   'discuss'
      b. ɬu-ʔəkʷyiqʷ   'great-great-grandparent/grandchild'
          ɬu-ʔəkʷiqʷiqʷəb   'will have great-great-grandchildren'

---

[13] Coda consonants are assumed to be weightless in Lushootseed. Urbanczyk argues that Lushootseed stress assignment is sonority based.

The moraic alignment analysis developed above is superior to Urbanczyk's suffixing reduplication analysis both in terms of analytic simplicity and typological generality. The moraic alignment analysis is less complex since it does not require the stipulation that roots be consonant-final in Lushootseed and that such a requirement has to be applicable even to the subpart of a root. The VC shape of the reduplicant falls out straightforwardly from the alignment property of the affix and its interaction with other constraints. The moraic alignment analysis is also typologically general since the constraint ranking, REALIZE-MORPHEME, MAX-IO >> NOCODA, *STRUC-μ >> MAX-BR, is common to both the analyses of Mangarayi and Lushootseed, two typologically and genetically distinct languages. When two analyses have similar empirical coverage language-internally, the one with greater cross-linguistic portability (i.e., the moraic alignment analysis) should be preferred.

Unequivocal cases of infixing after the first vowel are exceedingly rare. Such cases are hard to locate because it is not always possible to ascertain whether the infix is placed to the right of the first vowel or of the first syllable, as the right edges of these two phonological pivots often coincide due to the lack of word-internal codas in the language. Pluractional infixation in Bole, a Chadic language spoken in Nigeria, is a case in point. In this language, one of the several possible indicators of pluractionality is the infix *-gi-*. Since the stems that take this infix invariably contain an open initial syllable, it is difficult to ascertain whether the infix should be considered appearing after the first mora or the first syllable.

(67) Bole pluractional (Gimba 2000: ch. 10)

ngórúu	ngògìrúu	'tied'
'yórúu	'yògìrúu	'stopped'
ngáɗ	ngàgìɗ úu	'eat (meat)'
kàráa	kàgìráa	'slaughter'
'àwáa	'àgìwáa	'open'

Many such ambiguous examples abound. In Uradhi, an Australian language, and in Quileute, a Chimakuan language, the distribution of the respective pluractional reduplicative marker is consistent with both a post-first vowel and post-first syllable distribution.

(68) Uradhi pluractional reduplication (Crowley 1983: 364)

wili	wilili	'run'
aŋa	aŋaŋa	'dig'
ipiɲi	ipipiɲi	'swim'

wamp	wampampa	'float'
ikya	ikikya	'speak'
uɲɟa	uɲɟaɲɟa	'sleep, lie down'
uŋya	uŋiŋya	'eat'

(69)   Quileute pluractional (Andrade 1933: 188)

qaːleʔ	'he failed'	qaqleʔ	frequentative
tˢiko	'he put it on'	tˢ itˢko	frequentative
kʷeːtˢaʔ	'he is hungry'	kʷekʷtˢaʔ	'several are hungry'
tukoːyoʔ	'snow'	tutkoːyoʔ	'snow here and there'

In Dakota, a Siouan language spoken in the northern area of the United States and its neighboring regions in Canada, there are more than twenty inflectional infixes that appear after the first vowel (Boas and Deloria 1941; Moravcsik 1977; Shaw 1980). What is interesting about Dakota is that the first vowel may be followed by a consonant sequence, yet such sequences are parsed as the onset of the following syllable (Shaw 1980). Consequently, the right edge of the first vowel is effectively the right edge of the first syllable as well.

(70)   Dakota 1st person (Boas and Deloria 1941; Moravcsik 1977)

ća.pa	'stab'	ća.**wa**.pca	'I stab'
ʔi.kto.mi	'Iktomi'	ʔi.**ma**.ktomi	'I am Iktomi'
ma.nų	'steal'	ma.**wa**.nų	'I steal'
na.pca	'swallow'	na.**wa**.pca	'I swallow it'
la.kᶜota	'Lakota'	la.**ma**.kᶜota	'I am a Lakota'
na.wizi	'jealous'	na.**wa**.wizi	'I am jealous'

Infixes that appear in invariably monosyllabic stems are also difficult to classify. For example, in Tzeltal, a Mayan language, the intransitivizing marker -*h*- appears after the root vowel.

(71)   Tzeltal (Nida 1949: 68; Slocum 1948)

puk	'to divide among'	puhk	'to spread the word'
kuč	'to carry'	kuhč	'to endure'
k'ep	'to clear away'	k'ehp	'to be clear'

Similarly, in Tzutujil, another Mayan language, the simple passive, -*j*-[14] (72a), and the mediopassive, -*ʔ*- (72b), must surface after the root vowel.

(72)   Tzutujil simple passive/mediopassive (Dayley 1985: 55, 113–14)

   a. loq' 'buy'   lojq'ik   'to be bought'

     ch'ey 'hit'   xch'ejyi 'it was hit'

---

[14] *j* = [χ].

    b. toj   'pay'   toʔjik   'to be paid'
        k'is   'finish'   k'iʔseem 'to end, finish'
        tij   'eat, consume' tiʔjik   'to be paid'

In Ancient Greek, some present stems are formed partly by infixing a homorganic nasal after the root vowel.

(73)   Greek present stem formation (Garrett forthcoming)

Aorist stem	Present stem	Gloss
e-dak-	daŋk-an-	'bite'
e-lab-	lamb-an-	'take'
e-lat^h-	lant^h-an-	'escape notice'
e-lip-	limp-an-	'leave'
e-pat^h-	pant^h-an-	'suffer'
e-put^h-	punt^h-an-	'inquire'
e-p^{h}ug-	p^{h}uŋg-an-	'flee'
e-t^{h}ig-	t^{h}iŋg-an-	'touch'
e-mat^h-	mant^h-an-	'learn'

These infixes may be described as appearing after the first or the last vowel of the root since roots are monosyllabic in these languages.

    To be sure, unequivocal cases of infixing to the right of the first vowel are indeed observed. For example, the durative marker -r- in Budukh, a Daghestanian language, is one such example. The durative -r-, which has the allomorph -l-, is found after the first vowel on the surface. As such, the durative marker always serves as the coda of the first syllable.

(74)   Budukh durative (Alekseev 1994a: 273)

čo.šu	čor.šu	'to stab (downwards)'
sa.q'a	sar.q'ar	'to die'
ču.qul	čul.q'ul	'to rinse'
sa.ʔa	sar.ʔar	'to become dry'
ʕa.q'al	ʕal.q'al	'to fall'

In the Southern Muskogean languages, which include Alabama, Koasati, Chickasaw, Choctaw, Hitchiti, and Mikasuki (Munro 1987, 1993), the mediopassive marker must surface after the first vowel of the stem, regardless whether or not the first vowel is followed by a coda in the stem.

(75)   a. Choctow passive (Lombardi and McCarthy 1991)

aapitta	'to put into a container'	→	alpitta
takči	'to tie'	→	talakči
hoyya	'to be dripping'	→	holoyya

b. Chickasaw (J. B. Martin and Munro 2005)

apiːsa	'measure'	aɬpisa	'be measured'
oːti	'kindle'	oɬti	'be kindled'
hocifo	'name(v.)'	hoɬcifo	'be named'
takci	'tie'	talakci	'be tied'

In Miskitu, a Misulmalpan language spoken in Nicaragua and Honduras, the placement of the conjugation markers signifies a difference in the alienability of nouns. In the alienable nouns, the person markers appear suffixing (76b). However, when the noun is inalienable, the person markers surface after the first vowel of the stem, regardless of whether the initial syllable is open or closed (76a).[15]

(76)   Miskitu nominal conjugation (Rouvier 2002)[16]

	person	inalienable		alienable
a.		byara 'abdomen'	b.	bip 'cow'
	1st	bya-i-ra		bip-k-i
	2nd	bya-m-ra		bip-ka-m

Suffixation of a person marker in inalienable nouns is possible whenever the infixation of a person marker creates illicit surface syllable structures. For example, the second-person marker -*m*- cannot be infixed when the first syllable ends in a consonant (77a) or a glide (77b); when the initial syllable ends in a palatal glide or contains a high vowel (i.e., /i/ or /u/), the first-person marker -*i*- is suffixed (see (77b–d)). (Miskitu vowels include one diphthong /iɛ/ and short and long /i, u, a/; syllable boundaries are demarcated by periods).

(77)   Miskitu inalienable noun conjugation (Rouvier 2002)

	1st person	2nd person
a. kak.ma 'nose'	ka-i-k.ma	kak.ma-m/ *ka-m-k.ma
b. may.sa 'cintura'	may.s-i /*ma-y-y.sa	may.sa-m/ *ma-m-y.sa
c. bi.la 'mouth'	bi.l-i	bi.la-m
d. pu.sa 'lung'	pu.s-i	pu.sa-m

The fact that the suffixal person conjugation is used only when infixation is disprefered suggests that the person conjugation in inalienable nouns is intrinsically infixal and the peripheral suffixal distribution is secondary.

---

[15] Since stress is always on the first syllable in Miskitu, the person markers in an inalienable noun may also be characterized as infixing after the stressed vowel.

[16] There is no morphological marking on the noun in the third person. The suffix /ka/ is added to the root when the noun is inflected (i.e., the construct state). The final /a/ is deleted when followed by /i/.

Following the moraic alignment analysis presented above, an affix that appears to the right of the first vowel is analyzed as appearing to the right of the first mora. Such an analysis thus makes the prediction that coda consonants in these languages must be moraic (see, e.g., (78a)). Otherwise, weightless codas would be grouped under the same mora as the first vowel (see (78b)).

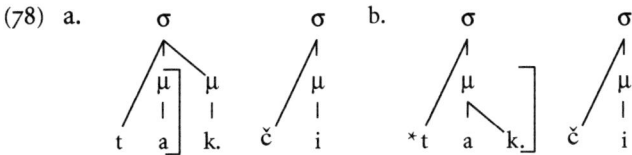

(78) a.   σ   σ   b.   σ   σ

              μ μ   μ   μ   μ

            t a k.   č   i   *t a k.   č   i

While the moraicity of coda consonants in Miskitu is not known at this point, the prediction is borne out in the Muskogean case. Lombardi and McCarthy (1991) observe that CVC and CVV syllables are equivalent under various phonological and morphological conditions. For example, when the first vowel is long, the infixal marker induces closed-syllable shortening (e.g., Choctow *aapitta* 'to put into a container' → *alpitta/*aalpitta*; Chickasaw *o:ti* 'kindle' → *olti/*oolti*). Also, while the vowel of every other CV syllable is lengthened due to a rule of iambic lengthening, no such vowel lengthening occurs in CVC or CVV syllables (e.g., /či+pisa+či+li/ 'thee+see+cause+I' → *čipiisačiili*).

Bunun

A particularly striking example of infixing with respect to the first vowel comes from the Isbukun dialect of Bunun, an Austronesian language spoken in Taiwan. In this language, completed action is indicated by the inserting -*i*- or -*in*- into the verb stem. All Bunun examples below are taken from Lin (2001). What is peculiar about this case is the distribution of the allomorphs; the completive marker may appear after the first vowel of the verb (79a) or before it (79b).

(79)	Verb	Gloss	Completed
a.	kałumah	'to build a house'	ka-i-łumah
	savai	'to win'	sa-i-vai
	makavas	'to conquer'	ma-i-kavas
	saŋkułan	'to be wounded by shooting'	sa-i-ŋkułan
	tałdanav	'to face-wash'	ta-i-łdanav
b.	hud	'to drink'	h-in-ud
	kiłim	'to find'	k-in-iłim
	łusʔan	'to celebrate a religious event'	ł-in-usʔan

simuɬ	'to borrow'	s-in-imuɬ
minhaðam	'to transform into a bird'	m-in-inhaðam
pisʔuɬʔuɬ	'to make rice soup'	p-in-isʔuɬʔuɬ

At first glance, the distributions of -*i*- and -*in*- appear to be complementary: -*i*-surfaces after the first vowel if the first syllable of the root contains an /a/, otherwise, -*in*- is inserted before the first mora of the root. To be sure, the affix -*i*- cannot be analyzed as subcategorizing the first syllable since -*i*- is inserted after the first vowel whether or not the first vowel is in a closed syllable (e.g., *taɬ.da.nav* 'to face-wash' → *ta-i-ɬ.da.nav*). Further examination of the available data suggests that the distribution is much less straightforward, however. To begin with, some verbs whose first syllable contains the nucleus /a/ take the post-initial-consonant -*in*- variant rather than -*i*- (80a). The allomorph -*in*- may also appear after the first nucleus /a/ in verbs that begin with an /ai/ or /au/ vowel sequence (80b). To be sure, not all verbs that begin with an /ai/ or /au/ sequence admit -*in*- in the post-/a/ position (80c).

(80) a. taŋtaŋ   'to shatter'   t-in-aŋtaŋ   *ta-i-ŋtaŋ
          tahis   'to mend cloths'   t-in-ahis'   *ta-i-his
          manah   'to shoot'   m-in-anah   *ma-i-nah

      b. tausʔuvað   'to give birth'   ta-in-usʔuvað
          taimuhus   'to bring dry food' ta-in-imuhus
          haiðuŋðuŋan   'to tangle'   ha-in-iðuŋðuŋan

          *t-in-ausʔuvað
          *t-in-aimuhus
          *h-in-aiðuŋðuŋan

      c. saipuk   'to feed livestock' s-in-aipuk   *sa-in-ipuk
          painuk   'to get dressed'   p-in-ainuk   *pa-in-inuk

The data thus suggests that the completive in Isbukun Bunun has two allomorphs with completely different subcategorization requirements: one appears after the first mora of the root while the other appears before. I shall refer to these as the post-μ_{R_1} allomorph and pre-μ_{R_1} allomorph respectively. Since the class membership of lexical items that take the post-μ_{R_1} versus the pre-μ_{R_1} allomorphs is arbitrary, two inflectional classes in the lexical type hierarchy are posited: *class 1* and *class 2*. Each verb root belongs to one of these two classes. The completive form of each verb class is licensed by a different construction. These two constructions are shown below:

(81)   a. The post-μ_{R1} allomorph

$$
\begin{bmatrix}
\text{\textit{class 1 completive verb}} & \\
\text{SYNSEM} & \iota(\boxed{1}) \\
\text{PHON} & \varphi(\boxed{2},\boxed{3}\text{-}in\text{-}) \\
\text{SUBCAT} & \text{ALIGN}\,(\boxed{3},\text{L},\mu_{R1},\text{R})
\end{bmatrix}
$$

$$
|
$$

$$
\begin{bmatrix}
\text{\textit{class 1 verb}} & \\
\text{SYNSEM} & \boxed{1} \\
\text{PHON} & \boxed{2}
\end{bmatrix}
$$

b. The pre-μ_{R1} allomorph

$$
\begin{bmatrix}
\text{\textit{class 2 completive verb}} & \\
\text{SYNSEM} & \iota(\boxed{1}) \\
\text{PHON} & \varphi(\boxed{2},\boxed{3}\text{-}in\text{-}) \\
\text{SUBCAT} & \text{ALIGN}(\boxed{3},\text{R},\mu_{R1},\text{L})
\end{bmatrix}
$$

$$
|
$$

$$
\begin{bmatrix}
\text{\textit{class 2 verb}} & \\
\text{SYNSEM} & \boxed{1} \\
\text{PHON} & \boxed{2}
\end{bmatrix}
$$

This analysis assumes that the post-μ_{R1} allomorph is underlyingly string-identical to the pre-μ_{R1} variant. The post-μ1 -i- allomorph, a phonologically conditioned allomorph of -in-, results from the deletion of the nasal to avoid the creation of an extra coda consonant on the surface (e.g., *savai* 'to win' → *sa-in-vai* → *sa-i-vai*).

The Isbukun Bunun case illustrates two important points concerning the analysis of infixes. First, phonological similarity between infixal allomorphs is no guarantee that they are phonologically relatable variants of each other. Often, multiple subcategorization frames must be assumed for string-identical allomorphs (see also the analysis of Ulwa construct state affixation discussed in Chapter 3). Second, infixation occurs even when a *post hoc* rationale is not readily available.

4.5 Final syllable

Toward the right edge of a domain, two pivots can be identified: the final syllable and the final vowel. In this section, I shall first focus on the final syllable as an infixal pivot. Consider, for example, the intensive marker in KiChaga, a Bantu language spoken in Tanzania. The intensive is formed by infixing a nasal before the final syllable. The intensifying nasal infix assimilates in place to a following velar. In the following examples, the adjectives are monomorphemic; the verbs end in a final vowel suffix, -*a*; the last form has a reciprocal -*an*- before the final vowel.

(82) KiChaga intensive (Sharon Inkelas p.c.; data from Lioba Moshi p.c. originally)

	Plain	Intensive	Gloss
a.	u.wi.ni	uwi-n-ni	
	lyi.an.gu	lyian-n-gu	'light'
	mu.il.i	mui-n-li	'white'
	-ka.pa	-ka-n-pa	'hit'
	-o.lon.ga	-olon-n-ga	'point'
b.	mu.i.u	mui-n-u	'black'
	-aam.bi.a	-aambi-n-a	'look at'
	-aam.bi.a.na	-aambia-n-na	'look at each other'

Another clear example of affixing to the left of the final syllable is found in two subgroups of the Muskogean languages, Creek-Seminole and Hitchiti-Mikasuki. The plural affix, -*ho*-, appears before the final syllable. Crucially, the singular stem is monomorphemic.

(83) Mikasuki (Martin 1994; Martin and Munro 2005)
hi.ca 'see'   ci-hiːhoːca-laːka   'he will see you all'
im.pa-   imhopa-   'eat (PL)'

Similar to its Muskogean cousins, one strategy for forming verbal pluralization in Koasati is to infix -*s*- before the final syllable. (The forms in (84) are cited in their third-person indicative form, followed by the switch-reference marker -*n*. When the penultimate syllable is light (CV), the vowel is lengthened in the indicative and is usually marked with a high pitch (acute) accent.)

(84) Koasati verbal plurality (Kimball 1991: 327)

Singular	Plural	Gloss
akáːnon	akásnon	'to be hungry'

akopí:lin	akopíslin	'to knock something away'
imanó:kan	imanóskan	'to be winded'
maká:lin	makáslin	'to open the eyes'
stipí:lan	stipíslan	'to be sexually attractive'

The punctual reduplicant in Koasati is a -*Co*- sequence that must appear before the final syllable of the stem. The consonant of the reduplicant is a copy of the first consonant of the stem.[17] The reduplicant contains a long vowel due to an independent effect of penultimate lengthening associated with the indicative.

(85)   Koasati punctual reduplication (Kimball 1991: 325)

aló:tkan	alotló:kan	'to be full'
cofóknan	cofokcó:nan	'to be angled'
copóksin	copokcó:sin	'to be a hill'
lapátkin	lapatló:kin	'to be narrow'
polóhkin	polohpó:kin	'to be circular'
taháspin	tahastó:pin	'to be light in weight'
talásban	talastó:ban	'to be thin'

A somewhat more complicated pattern of infixing before the final syllable is found in Tigre, an Ethiopian Semitic language. Both the intensive -*a:*- and the frequentative -*Ca:*- are infixed before the final syllable of a regular verb stem. (Many other Ethiopian Semitic languages show similar intensive/ frequentative morphology. See Rose (2003*a*, 2003*b*) for more discussion.)

(86)   a. Tigre intensive (Rose 2003*b*: 112, 115)

dənzəz-	'be numb'	dəna:zəz-	'be very numb'
dəngəs'-a:	'be scared'	dəna:gəs'-a:	'be very scared'
mərmər-a:	'examine'	məra:mər-a:	'examine thoroughly'
fəntər-a:	'scatter (seeds)'	fəna:tər-a:	'scatter many seeds'
k'ənt'əb-a:	'pick, be brave'	k'əna:t'əb-a:	'pick many things'

   b. Tigre frequentative (Rose 2003*b*: 112, 115)

dəngəs'-	'become scared'	dənəga:gəs'-	'become slightly scared'
dənzəz-	'be numb'	dənəza:zəz-	'be a little numb'
gərf-a:	'whip'	gera:rəf-a:	'whip a little'
nəsḥ-a:	'advise'	nəsa:səḥ-a:	'advise a little'

[17] Koasati is a pitch-accent language. Since the pitch accent is generally on the penult, the Koasati examples might also be analyzed as affixing to some accented unit. However, since the metrical phonology of this language is not well understood, I shall leave this potential alternative interpretation for future research.

| məzz-aː | 'give responsibility' | məzaːzəz-aː | 'give a little responsibility' |
| saʕan-aː | 'load' | saʕaːʕan-aː | 'load a little' |

Rose (2003*b*) argues that the actual surface form of the frequentative is governed by several additional requirements, as summarized in (87). This approach to the Tigre frequentative finds natural expression in the present theory. In addition to the infix's subcategorization restriction, the frequentative construction also imposes additional templatic requirements (presumably encoded in the associated φ-function) on the output. Crucially, the pre-final syllable distribution of the infix is never violated on the surface.

(87) Enriched infixation hypothesis (Rose 2003*b*: 118–19)
   i. Templatic match
      An output form with four (five) consonants must conform to a quadric- (quinqui)-consonantal template, matching the position and nature of the aspectual vowels.
   ii. Root realization
      All root segments must be represented in the output.
   iii. Frequentative realization
      Reduplication and the affix [aː] must be realized in the frequentative preceding the final syllable of the stem (= preceding the penultimate output root consonant).

It is sometimes difficult to determine whether certain cases should be classified as attaching before the final syllable or after the final vowel. The output is often indistinguishable. Consider the example from Ineseño Chumash, a Hokan language. The infixing reduplication pattern may be described as the placement of a CV reduplicant before the final syllable (e.g., *tašušun* 'to be fragrant') or after the final vowel (e.g., *tašušun* 'to be fragrant'). The function of this reduplication pattern is unclear.

(88) Ineseño Chumash (Applegate 1976: 275)
tašušun	'to be fragrant'
iwawan	'to cut with a sawing motion'
oxyoyon	'to be crazy'
yuxwowon	'to be high, tall'
muc'uc'uʔ	'kind of very small bead' (muc'uʔ 'young, small')
mixixin	'to be hungry' (mixin 'to be hungry')

The classification of patterns such as this remains ambiguous since the available data do not provide conclusive evidence to argue for one interpretation over the other.

4.6 Final vowel

The final vowel as a pivot is most relevant to cases of internal reduplication. For example, in Kamaiurá, a Tupi language spoken in Brazil, the disyllabic plural reduplicant appears after the final vowel. When the stem is consonant-final, the reduplicant appears as infixing.

(89) Kamaiurá plural reduplication (Everrett and Seki 1985)
      omotumuŋ   omotumu**tumuŋ**   'He shook it repeatedly'
      omokon   omoko**mokon**   'He swallowed it frequently'
      ohuka   ohuka**huka**   'He kept on laughing'
      oje?apahʷat   oje?apahʷ**apahʷat** 'He rolls himself up repeatedly'
      jeumirik   jeumiri**mirik**   'I tie up repeatedly'
      oetun   oetu**etun**   'He keeps on smelling'
      apot   apo**apot**   'I jump repeatedly'
      oekɨj   oekɨ**ekɨj**   'He pulls repeatedly'

A similar pattern is found in Korean. Onomatopoetic reduplication involves infixing a CV copy of the right edge of the stem after the final vowel.

(90) Korean Onomatopoetic (Jun 1994)
      culuk   culu**luk**   'dribbling'
      allok   allo**lok**   'mottled'
      tʰak   tʰa**tak**   'with a slap'[18]
      t'aŋ   t'a**taŋ**[19]   'bang'
      wacak   waca**cak**   'munching'

A particular interesting type of internal reduplication with reference to the final vowel is found in many of the Paiwanic languages, part of the Austronesian family, spoken in Taiwan. For example, in Amis, plurality is often marked by reduplicating the final C(V)CV of the stem (91a). When the stem is consonant-final, the reduplicant appears as an infix (91b). Curiously, if the penultimate syllable is closed, only the final CCV sequence is reduplicated (91c).

(91)   Amis (Ho *et al.* 1986)
     a. ʃamaɬu 'card'   ʃamaɬu**maɬu** 'cards'
     b. luma?   'house'   luma**luma?**   'houses'
        kaput   'group'   kapu**kaput**   'groups'

---

[18] Note that the aspirated and fortis onsets are lost in the reduplicant.
[19] ['] indicates the tenseness, rather than ejection.

| wiɬaŋ | 'friend' | wiɬawiɬaŋ | 'friends' |
| niaruʔ | 'village home' | niaruaruʔ | 'village homes'[20] |

c.

ɬaŋka	'sesame'	ɬaŋkaŋka	'pile of sesame'
lamlu	'die'	lamlumlu	'dice'
pawti	'bag'	pawtiwti	'bags'
ʔuŋtʃuj	'rock'	ʔuŋtʃuŋtʃuj	'pile of rocks'
taŋkuj	'winter melon'	taŋkuŋkuj	'winter melons'
tamɬaw	'person'	tamɬamɬaw	'people'

Similar C(V)CV reduplication is found in Thao and other Paiwanic languages.

(92)   Thao (Chang 1998)[21]

a.

| kikaɬi | 'to ask' | ma-kikaɬikaɬi | 'to ask around' |

b.

| quliuʃ | 'long' | mia-quliuliuʃ | 'to straighten, stretch out' |
| patihaul | 'a spell, a curse' | matihauhaul | 'to cast a spell on s.o.' |

c.

agqtu	'to contemplate'	agqtuqtu	'think about'
m-arfaz	'to fly, be flying'	m-arfarfaz	'to keep flying around'
m-armuz	'to dive'	m-armurmuz	'to dive repeatedly'
buqnur	'anger, hatred'	mia-bugnuqnur	'to be irritable'
ma-kutnir	'compact'	mia-kutnitnir	'to harden'

The proper treatment of this type of reduplication has generated much controversy in the Formosan linguistic literature due to the unusual shape of the CCV reduplicant. Chang (1998) assumes that forms like those in (a) reflect what is referred as 'full reduplication' in the Formosan literature while the data in (b) and (c) are considered instances of the so-called 'rightward' reduplication. However, the semantic and functional similarities between rightward reduplication and full reduplication have prompted some to question the necessity for making a distinction between the two patterns (e.g., Lee 2005; Li and Tsuchida 2001).

Here, I submit that the Formosan data above can be understood under a unified analysis within the framework laid out in this work. The analysis mirrors the analysis of reduplicative infixes that align with respect to the leftmost mora introduced earlier. Suffixing to the last vowel is treated as an instance of

---

[20] Vowel clusters are treated as vowel sequences in Amis. The syllabification of *niaru* 'village home' is *ni.a.ru*, for example.

[21] Examples are presented in IPA transcription, rather than in the orthographic convention assumed in the source. Particularly, IPA [ɬ] is represented as 'lh', while [ʃ] as 'sh' in the source.

alignment with respect to the rightmost mora (the analysis proposed here is similar in spirit to Crowhurst's (2004) moraic alignment treatment of Kamaiurá reduplication). A preliminary version of this analysis is stated in (93).

(93)   Plural reduplication (Preliminary version)

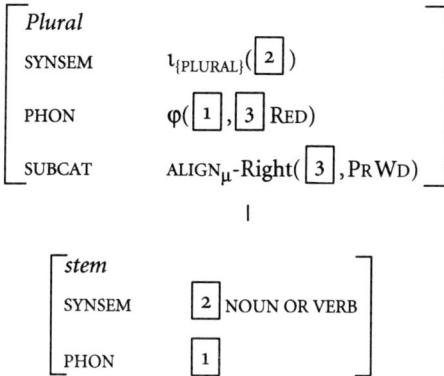

$$
\begin{bmatrix}
\text{\textit{Plural}} \\
\text{SYNSEM} \quad \iota_{\{\text{PLURAL}\}}(\boxed{2}) \\
\text{PHON} \quad \varphi(\boxed{1},\boxed{3}\,\text{RED}) \\
\text{SUBCAT} \quad \text{ALIGN}_\mu\text{-Right}(\boxed{3},\text{PrWD})
\end{bmatrix}
$$

|

$$
\begin{bmatrix}
\text{\textit{stem}} \\
\text{SYNSEM} \quad \boxed{2}\,\text{NOUN OR VERB} \\
\text{PHON} \quad \boxed{1}
\end{bmatrix}
$$

The construction specifies that the rightmost mora of the plural marker for both nouns and verbs must align with the rightmost mora of some prosodic word. As such, any output candidates that show the reduplicant away from the right edge at the moraic level will be ruled out automatically (e.g., (94b and d)). (Examples in the tableaux below are all taken from Amis; the reduplicant is underlined and boldfaced).

(94)

ʃamaɬu-PL	ALIGN$_\mu$-Right(RED, PRWD)
a. ʃa$^\mu$(ma$^\mu$ɬu$^\mu$)(**ma$^\mu$ɬu$^\mu$**)]$_{\text{PrWd}}$	✓
b. ʃa$^\mu$(**ma$^\mu$ɬu$^\mu$**)(ma$^\mu$ɬu$^\mu$)]$_{\text{PrWd}}$	✗
c. (ʃa$^\mu$ma$^\mu$)(ɬu$^\mu$**ʃa$^\mu$**)(**ma$^\mu$ɬu$^\mu$**)]$_{\text{PrWd}}$	✓
d. (**ʃa$^\mu$ma$^\mu$**)(ɬu**ʃ**a$^\mu$)(ma$^\mu$ɬu$^\mu$)]$_{\text{PrWd}}$	✗

The fact that the reduplicant may be either CVCV, CVV, or CCV in shape renders a uniform prosodic characterization and a templatic analysis of this pattern untenable.[22] Instead, the size of the reduplicant itself is derived through constraint interaction; no templatic restriction is imposed onto the

---

[22] The reduplicant may be characterized as bimoraic, but two moras do not form a coherent prosodic constituent.

plural morpheme itself. Like the analysis of Mangarayi and Lushootseed, I assume that REALIZE-MORPHEME and MAX-IO are high-ranking and cannot be violated in the output. This guarantees that the segmental content of the input will always be faithfully realized in the output. Full reduplication is prohibited by virtue of the fact that the size restrictor constraint, *STRUC-Ft, which penalizes any foot in the output, is ranked above MAX-BR. Foot structure in Formosan languages is generally trochaic, parsed from right to left at the level of the syllable. Full reduplication, as illustrated in (95), would have resulted in more feet than partial reduplication.

(95)

ʃamaɬu-PL	*STRUC-Ft	MAX-BR
☞ a. ʃa(maɬu)(**maɬu**)	**	fa
b. (ʃama)(ɬu**ʃa**)(**maɬu**)	***!	

The fact that the reduplicant never copies the final consonant of the root is attributed to the dominance of NOCODA over MAX-BR. A candidate such as *kaputkapu* is ruled out presumably due to a high-ranking ANCHOR$_{BR}$-R, which requires the right edges of the base and the reduplicant to correspond.

(96)

kaput-PL	NOCODA	*STRUC-Ft	MAX-BR
☞ a. (ka$^{\mu}$pu$^{\mu}$)(**ka$^{\mu}$pu$^{\mu}$**t)	*	**	t
b. (ka$^{\mu}$pu$^{\mu}$t)(**ka$^{\mu}$pu$^{\mu}$**t)	**!	**	

While the reduplicant may not be more than a foot long, it crucially cannot be smaller than two moras either. Some as yet unmentioned constraint, X, must favor bimoraic reduplication over monomoraic reduplication.

(97)

kaput-PL	CONSTRAINT-X	NOCODA	*STRUC-Ft	MAX-BR
☞ a. (ka$^{\mu}$pu$^{\mu}$)(**ka$^{\mu}$pu$^{\mu}$**t)		*	**	t
b. ka$^{\mu}$(pu$^{\mu}$**pu$^{\mu}$**t)	*!	*	*	ka

Here, I propose that candidates with a reduplicant smaller than two moras are actually ruled out by another subcategorization requirement of plural reduplication, stated below:

(98)   RED-PrWd$_{\text{HEAD}}$
     The leftmost segment of a reduplicant is dominated by the head of a prosodic word.

RED-PrWd$_{\text{HEAD}}$ states that the leftmost segment of a reduplicant is dominated by the head of a prosodic word.[23] Since a minimal prosodic word cannot be smaller than a foot, as required by the prosodic hierarchy, and since a foot must be trochaic and disyllabic in these languages, the reduplicant must be disyllabic. As shown in (99), monosyllabic reduplication is eliminated by the declarative component. To be sure, (99c) fails not because the declarative component imposes size restrictions on the reduplicant per se. Candidates with a reduplicant smaller than two moras simply have no way of satisfying the two subcategorization requirements of the plural construction simult- aneously; (99d) shows that when the monomoraic reduplicant is part of the head, thus satisfying RED-PrWd$_{\text{HEAD}}$, it will nonetheless violate the other alignment restriction, ALIGN$_\mu$-Right(RED, PrWD).

(99)

kapu-PL-t	RED-PrWd$_{\text{HEAD}}$	ALIGN$_\mu$-Right(RED, PrWD)
a. (ka$^\mu$pu$^\mu$)(**ka$^\mu$pu$^\mu$**t)	✓	✓
b. (ka$^\mu$pu$^\mu$)(**a$^\mu$pu$^\mu$**t)	✓	✓
c. ka$^\mu$(pu$^\mu$**pu$^\mu$**t)	✗	✓
d. ka$^\mu$(**pu$^\mu$**pu$^\mu$t)	✓	✗

Note that, while candidate (99b) satisfies the subcategorization restrictions just as well as the winning candidate, as shown in (100), it nonetheless remains sub- optimal since it incurs more violations of MAX-BR than the winning candidate.

(100)

kapu-PL-t	NOCODA	*STRUC-Ft	MAX-BR
☞ a. (ka$^\mu$pu$^\mu$)(**ka$^\mu$pu$^\mu$**t)	*	**	t
b. (ka$^\mu$pu$^\mu$)(**a$^\mu$pu$^\mu$**t)	*	**	kt!

---

[23] The current analysis is similar in spirit to Crowhurst's analysis for Kamaiurá where the bisyllabic size of the reduplicant is captured by the RED-augment alignment constraint, RED-PrWd-LEFT$_\mu$, which states that the leftmost segment in every RED is the leftmost segment of a PrWd.

The current analysis offers a straightforward understanding of the CCV reduplication pattern as well.

(101)

pawti-PL	NoCoda	*Struc-Ft	Max-BR
☞ a. pa$^\mu$w$^\mu$(ti$^\mu$**w$^\mu$ti$^\mu$**)	**	*	**pa**
b. (pa$^\mu$w$^\mu$ti$^\mu$)(**pa$^\mu$w$^\mu$ti$^\mu$**)	**	**!	

As illustrated in (101), full reduplication (101b) is ruled out since it incurs more *Struc-Ft violations than the attested candidate. Candidates with monomoraic reduplication (e.g., *pa$^\mu$w$^\mu$ti$^\mu$ti$^\mu$*) are undesirable since they will always violate the Red-PrWd$_{HEAD}$ requirement. The optimal candidate (101a) satisfies Red-PrWd$_{HEAD}$, since Red-PrWd$_{HEAD}$ only requires that the leftmost segment be dominated by the head of a prosodic word. Thus, the leftmost segment of the reduplicant need only be part of, rather than coextensive with, a head syllable (the diagram in (102) illustrates this point).

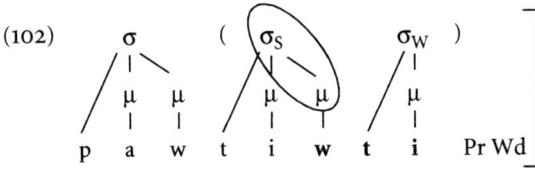

(102)

To summarize, the reduplicative plural construction in the Paiwanic languages is as stated below. This construction has two subcategorization requirements: Red-PrWd$_{HEAD}$ and Align$_\mu$-Right(Red, PrWd).

(103)   Plural reduplication (Final version)

As illustrated above, moraic alignment offers just the tool needed to provide a uniform analysis of the C(V)CV reduplication pattern. The plural reduplicant is atemplatic; the size variation of the reduplicant is a consequence of the interactions between constraints on the subcategorization restriction of the plural marker and constraints on phonotactic and general markedness.

Now, let us turn to infixation before the final vowel. While such infixes are rare, they are nonetheless observed. For example, as mentioned in Chapter 2 (Section 2.1), the applicative *-il-* in ChiBemba (and other Bantu languages) appears before the last vowel of a causativized stem (e.g., *-leef-es-į-* 'to lengthen for/at' from *-leef-į-* 'to lengthen'). Likewise, in Levantine Arabic, a copy of the initial consonant appears before the final vowel to signify intensification.

(104)   Levantine Arabic intensification (Broselow and McCarthy 1983/84; Cowell 1964)

barad	barbad	'shaved unevenly'
šaraħ	šaršaħ	'criticized severely'
ħalat	ħalħat	'sheared unevenly'
daħal	daħdal	'rolled gradually'

In Zuni, a copy of the stem-initial consonant appears before the final syllable, marking medio-passive and repetitive.

(105)   Zuni (Broselow and McCarthy 1983/84; S. Newman 1965: 55)

čolo	'to make the sound of crackling paper'
čolčo+ʔa	'it makes irregular crackling sounds (-ʔa=PRES)'
tomo	'to strike the skin drum'
čuwapi tomto+k'+e+ʔa	'who is making noises on the skin drum (-k'=CAUS, -e = CONT)

As already mentioned earlier, cases of fixed-segment infixation after the final vowel are rare and are often ambiguous. For example, in Huave, a Huavean language spoken in Mexico, the indefinite actor morpheme can be treated as either appearing after the first vowel or after the final vowel of the root since the size of the roots is monosyllabic (see (71) - (73) for other examples of such ambiguous cases).

(106)   Huave indefinite actor (Stairs and Hollenbach 1969: 52)

šom	'to find'	šoram	'to find'
haw	'to know'	a-haraw	'someone knows it'
ndok	'to fish'	a-ndorok	'somebody fishes it'
ndig	'to string'	a-ndiriːeg	'somebody string it up'

Examples of this indefinite actor infixing construction in Huave are scarce since the more common indefinite actor marker is the suffixal allomorph -*aran*.

4.7 Stress and related metrical units

Units of stress often serve as pivot points for infixes. Infixes may target the stressed foot, the stressed syllable, or, in some cases, even the stressed vowel. Logically, there are six possible edges an infix can target: the left edges of a stressed foot, a stressed syllable, or a stressed vowel, and the right edges of those respective units. However, clear examples that can substantiate this six-way typology are hard to locate. This is because it is not often clear what edge an infix subcategorizes for, as the stressed pivots are in a hierarchical relationship with one another and thus the edges of the different stressed pivots often coincide. For example, when the stressed foot is trochaic, the left edge of the stressed foot is also the left edge of the stressed syllable. Likewise, when the stressed foot is iambic, the right edge of the stressed foot is the right edge of the stressed syllable. Infixes that target such edges are therefore amenable to either a stressed-foot or a stressed-syllable pivot analysis. For example, in Samoan, a Polynesian language, the plural is marked by reduplicating the penultimate, thus stressed, syllable. Syllables are always open, and so the reduplicant is CV in shape. When the stem is more than two syllables long, the reduplicant appears to infix before the stressed syllable. (In the following examples, stress is marked to facilitate the presentation, even though it is not marked in the source.)

(107) Samoan plural (Mosel and Hovdhaugen 1992: 221–2)

'toa	'brave'	to'toa
'maː	'ashamed'	ma'maː
a'lofa	'love'	aːlo'lofa
ga'lue	'work'	gaːlu'lue
aː'vaga	'elope'	aːva'vaga
ata'mai	'clever'	atama'mai
maʔa'lili	'cold, feel cold'	maʔali'lili
to'ʔulu	'fall, drop'	toʔu'ʔulu

It is not immediately obvious whether the pivot should be construed in terms of the stressed foot or the stressed syllable. Either characterization would seem to be adequate in accounting for the pattern in Samoan. A similarly ambiguous case is found in Ulwa. As already mentioned in several occasions in the earlier chapters, the infixal variant of the construct-state markers in Ulwa must surface after the leftmost iambic foot of the stem. An SBM analysis of this pattern using the stressed foot as the pivot was developed in Chapter 3. It is equally plausible to analyze the pivot as the stressed syllable, however, since the right edge of an iambic foot coincides with the right edge of the stressed syllable.

(108)   Ulwa construct state (Green 1999: 61, 64)
   a.   súːlu   súː-**ma**-lu   'dog-CNS2'
        áytak   áy-**mana**-tak   'paper-CNS22'
        aláːkuṃ   aláː-**ka**-kuṃ   'Muscovy duck-CNS3'
        waráy̯wa   waráy̯-**kana**-wa   'parrot sp.-CNS33'
        káːsiráːmah   káː-**ki**-siráːmah   'lizard sp.-CNS1'

   b.   awa, awáː   awáː-**ki**   'silkgrass-CNS1'
        súru, surúː   surúː-**kina**   'log-CNS11'
        (?)yápu, yapúː   yapúː-**kana**   'crocodile-CNS3'
        (?)ábu, abúː   abúː-**ma**   'stingray-CNS2'

To be sure, it is possible to tease apart the foot-based analysis from the syllable-based analysis. For example, Ulwa has a distributive reduplication pattern where the CV reduplicant copies the head syllable of an iambic foot (109a). When the root is larger than a syllable, the reduplicant appears infixed (109b) since the left edge of the stressed foot and the left edge of the stressed syllable do not coincide. As such, the reduplicant is analyzed here as targeting a stressed-syllable pivot, rather than a stressed-foot pivot.

(109)   Ulwa adjective distributive reduplication (Green 1999: 51)
   a.   yám-ka   'good-ADJ'   yayámka
        páw-ka   'red-ADJ'   papáwka
        píː-ka   'extinguished-ADJ'   pipíːka

   b.   baraː-ka   'dark-ADJ'   bararáːka
        bisíː-ka   'small-ADJ'   bisisíːka
        ihír-ka   'erect-ADJ'   ihihírka
        waláŋ-ka   'corpulent'   walaláŋka
        barás-ka   'black-ADJ'   bararáska
        burím-ka   'firm-ADJ'   buririmka
        saháw-ka   'nake-ADJ'   sahaháwka

Another prime example that illustrates the disassociation between the stressed foot and the stressed syllable is observed in the case of English expletive infixation. Recall that, in general, the expletive must appear to the left of a trochaic foot. However, based on data like those in (110), the expletive may equally well be analyzed as targeting the stress-syllable pivot.

(110) English expletive infixation (McCarthy 1982)
    a. togéther   to-*bloody*-gether
       advánce   ad-*bloody*-vance
       Bhowáni   Bho-*bloody*-wani
       perháps   per-*bloody*-haps
       enóugh   e-*bloody*-nough
       impórtant   im-*fuckin*-portant
    b. Kalamazóo   Kalama-*fuckin*-zoo
       Tatamagóuchee Tatama-*fuckin*-gouchee
       Winnipesáukee Winnipe-*fuckin*-saukee

As it turns out, words in (110b) may have alternative infixal patterns. Crucially, the expletive may appear before or after the third syllable of an initial dactylic sequence. This distribution suggests that the expletive is not targeting the left edge of the stressed syllable *per se*. Rather, the distribution of the expletive is foot-based. Depending on how the initial dactyl is analyzed, the expletive in English has been analyzed as targeting the left edge of a stressed foot (Davis 2005) or as lodging at the boundary of two feet (McCarthy 1982).

(111) Kalamazóo   Kalama-*fuckin*-zoo   Kala-*fuckin*-mazoo
     Tatamagóuchee Tatama-*fuckin*-gouchee Tata-*fuckin*-magouchee
     Winnipesáukee Winnipe-*fuckin*-saukee Winni-*fuckin*-pesaukee

It should be noted that, since the expletive may appear to the left of a foot boundary, words like *Popocatepetl* or *anticipatory* have two possible expletive-infixed variants. This is because there are two feet with left edges internal to the word (the infixal locations are indicated by the downward arrow, ↓).

(112) (* .)↓ (* .)↓ (*.)
     Popo cate   petl

Before turning to examples of infixes that target the stressed vowel, it is worth mentioning that, like the edge pivots, same-edge alignment is also possible with respect to a prominence pivot. Plural reduplication in Washo is a case in point.

    Washo is a language spoken in an area in California and Nevada around Lake Tahoe. In this language, partial internal reduplication denotes plurality in nouns and pluractionality in the verbal domains.

(113) Singular Plural   Gloss
     dáʔa   daʔáʔa   'mother's brother'
     ʔélel   ʔelélel   'mother's father'

géwe	gewéwe	'coyote'
bík'ɨ	bɨk'ɨ́k'ɨ	'grandmother's sister'
súkuʔ	sukúkuʔ	'dog'
gúšuʔ	gušúšuʔ	'pet'
gúʔu	guʔúʔu	'mother's mother's'
dámal	damámal	'to hear'
bókoŋ	bokókoŋ	'to snore'
bíŋil	biŋíŋil	'to try'
p'ísew	p'isésew	'ear'

At first glance, this plural formation pattern appears to be a straightforward instance of root-final syllable reduplication with final-consonant extrametricality. That is, /p'isésew/ 'ear' can be parsed as /p'isé-se-w/. However, when a root contains an internal consonant sequence, the reduplicant is lodged before the sequence, thus obfuscating the straightforward pre-final syllable analysis.

(114)

Singular	Plural	Gloss
ʔéw.ši?	ʔešíw.ši?	'father's brothers'
nén.t'uš	ne.t'ún.t'u.š-u	'old women: -u=nominalizing'
sák.sag	sa.sák.sag	'father's father's brother'
mók.go	mo.gók.go	'shoe'

The placement of the reduplicant has also been a subject of much debate. Some argue that the reduplicant appears before the stressed vowel (Jacobsen 1964; Winter 1970), while others contend that the reduplicant appears after the first consonant (Broselow and McCarthy 1983/84) or after the first CV (Urbanczyk 1993) of the root. In Yu 2005*a*, I demonstrate that the placement and the size of the plural reduplicant depend crucially on the interaction between constraints on affix anchoring, stress, and weight assignments. The reduplicant must be analyzed as anchoring with respect to the left edge of the stressed syllable. The reduplicant always appears in the penultimate syllable because main stress must be on the penult in polysyllabic words in Washo. The fact that the reduplicant appears before the word-internal consonant sequence in (114) follows from the fact that stressed syllables must be heavy in the language (Yu 2005*a*, 2006). Thus, short of geminating the post-tonic intervocalic consonant (e.g., *ʔewšíši? 'father's brother'), Washo satisfies the stress-to-weight requirement by lodging the reduplicant where the first consonant of the internal consonant sequence can function as the coda of the stressed syllable.

Infixes that illustrate the stressed-vowel pivot are exceedingly rare. Many of the Northern Interior Salish languages mark the diminutive by infixing a reduplicative copy of the pre-tonic consonant after the stressed vowel, regardless of whether the stressed syllable is open or closed. Some examples from Shuswap are given in (115).

(115)   Shuswap diminutive (Anderson 1996: 209; van Eijk 1990: 231)

pésəɬkʷe	'lake'	pépsəɬkʷe	'small lake'
cq'éɬp	'tree'	cqéq'ɬp	'small tree'
sqéx̣he	'dog'	sqéqx̣he	'little dog'
qéʔce	'father'	ɣnqéqʔece	'my father'
səp'-ús	'hit-face'	səpúp'skn	'I am hit in the face'

Chamorro continuative CV reduplication is potentially an instance of infixing after the stressed vowel. The traditional analysis of Chamorro reduplication (e.g., Broselow and McCarthy 1983/84; see also de Lacy's (1996) analysis of Maori reduplication) assumes that the reduplicant appears before the final disyllabic foot (e.g., *hu(gando)* → *huga(gando)*). Unlike Samoan, however, the final foot of the continuative in Chamorro does not coincide with the stressed foot, as the main stress is on the antepenult.[24] Consequently, previous analyses rely on the notion of a final disyllabic prosodic stem, defined specifically for the purpose of reduplication only. The post-stressed-vowel analysis of the continuative reduplicant avoids the need to appeal to the notion of a prosodic stem completely.

(116)   Chamorro continuative reduplication (Topping 1973: 259)

Non-continuative		Continuative		Traditional analysis
'saga	'stay'	'sasaga	'staying'	'sasaga
hu'gando	'play'	hu'gagando	'playing'	hu'gagando
'taitai	'read'	'tataitai	'reading'	'tataitai
'eggaʔ	'watch'	'eʔeggaʔ	'watching'	'eʔeggaʔ

The clearest example of infixing after the stressed vowel comes from a case of fixed-segment infixation sound in Upriver Halkomelem, a Coast Salish language spoken in British Columbia, Canada. Plurality in this language may be marked by either CVC-reduplication (117a) or -*l*- infixation (117b). In a few cases, plurality is indicated by ablaut (117c). Of particular interest here is the fact that the -*l*- infix, which may appear as -*l*- or -*le*-, must appear after the stressed vowel of the root.

---

[24] Note that the unreduplicated form has penultimate stress (e.g., *hu'gando* 'play' vs *hu'gagando* 'playing'). Non-lexical antepenultimate stress appears to be specific to continuative reduplication patterns only since fixed affixes cause stress-shift to the default penultimate position (e.g., *nána* 'mother' vs *naná-hu* 'my mother').

(117) Plural in Upriver Halkomelem (Galloway 1993; Thompson 2005)

a.	lémet	'fold something'	lemlémet	'fold lots of things'
	t'eméls	'chop'	t'emt'emels	'chop something in different places'
b.	lhóqwet	'wet something'	lhóleqwet	'wet many things'
	kw'és	'get burned'	kw'éles	'both burned, many got burned'
c.	thíyeltxwem	'build a house'	tháyeltxwem	'building a house/houses'
	tl'éwels	'bark'	tl'áwels	'do lots of barking'

In Nakanai, an Austronesian language spoken in New Britain, nominalization is formed by inserting -*il*- before the stressed vowel in words containing exactly two syllables (118a). In longer words, nominalization is formed by suffixing -*la* instead (118b).

(118) Nakanai nominalization (Johnston 1980)

a.	iláu	'steering'
	tilága	'fear'
	gilógo	'sympathetic'
b.	sagegéla	'happiness'
	vikuéla	'fight'
	vigilemulimulíla	'story'

On the present theory, the distribution of -*il*- and -*la* can be handled easily as a matter of differences in subcategorization restrictions. The infixal allomorph has the following subcategorization requirements: (i) -*il*- right-subcategorizes for the stressed mora of the stressed foot (i.e., μ'), and (ii) the left edge of -*il*- must coincide with the left edge of the leftmost mora of the Prosodic Word (see McCarthy 2003 for similar alignment requirements).

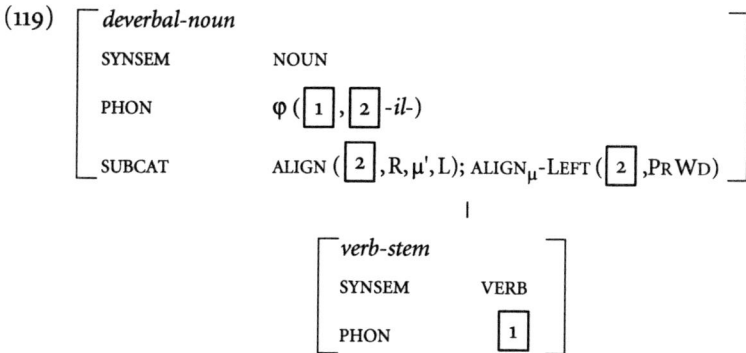

(119)

$$
\begin{bmatrix}
\textit{deverbal-noun} \\
\text{SYNSEM} \quad \text{NOUN} \\
\text{PHON} \quad \varphi(\boxed{1},\boxed{2}\text{-}il\text{-}) \\
\text{SUBCAT} \quad \text{ALIGN}(\boxed{2},\text{R},\mu',\text{L}); \text{ALIGN}_\mu\text{-LEFT}(\boxed{2},\text{PrWD})
\end{bmatrix}
$$

$$
\begin{bmatrix}
\textit{verb-stem} \\
\text{SYNSEM} \quad \text{VERB} \\
\text{PHON} \quad \boxed{1}
\end{bmatrix}
$$

If the subcategorization restrictions of -*il*- cannot be satisfied simultaneously, the suffixal allomorph, -*la*, is used. The fact that the suffixal allomorph is never used with disyllabic roots suggests that -*la* is the 'elsewhere' allomorph that the grammar defaults to when the infixal -*il*- is not possible. Following Bonet, Lloret, and Mascaró (2003), I assume that affix alternants are extrinsically prioritized (see also McCarthy and Wolf 2005; Paster 2006). The subcategorization requirement of -*il*- is thus assumed to take precedence over that of the suffixing -*la*.

4.8 Other potential pivots

Thus far, I have focused on phonological pivots that are well motivated by infix patterns in the world's languages. A summary is given below:

(120)   Attested pivot inventory
  a. *Edge pivots*
     First consonant
     First vowel
     Final syllable
     Final vowel

  b. *Prominence pivots*
     Stressed syllable
     Stressed foot
     Stressed vowel

An asymmetry is immediately apparent given the set of edge pivots. All else being equal, one might expect the first syllable and the final consonant to be among the set of edge pivots given the need for the final syllable and the first consonant as pivot points. In fact, both Ultan and Moravcsik admit infixes before the final consonant and after the first syllable. However, convincing patterns of infixation illustrating the need for those pivot points are not very forthcoming. I review potential evidence for these two pivot points in this section.

4.8.1 *Final consonant*

I begin by first considering cases that might exemplify the final consonant pivot. Note that affixation to the right of a final consonant is not discussed here since it is trivially satisfied by cases of regular suffixation.[25]

---

[25] To be sure, infixation may obtain when an affix subcategorizes for the right edge of the final consonant of stems that are invariably vowel-final (e.g., a root *CVCV* is *CVCAV* when affixed with *A*). I have not been able to locate such a case, however.

4.8.1.1 *Takelma frequentative reduplication*   Takelma, a Penutian language formerly spoken in southwest Oregon, has several strategies for forming frequentatives. The more general method is to mark the frequentative via suffixing C_1C_2-reduplication, where C1 and C2 are copies of the first and second consonants of the verb stem, respectively (121).

(121) C_1aC_2-frequentatives in Takelma[26] (Sapir 1922: 128)

loho-n-	'cause to die'	loho'laha$^\varepsilon$n	'I used to kill them'
wog-	'arrive'	wogowa'k'	'many arrived'
hen-d-	'wait for'	jene'hana$^\varepsilon$n	'I always used to wait for him'
hog-	'run'	hogo'hak'de$^\varepsilon$	'I am always running'
he$^\varepsilon$l-	'sing'	hele'hal$^\varepsilon$	'he used to sing'
odo-	'hunt for'	odo'$^\varepsilon$at'	'she always hunted for them'
og-	'give to'	ogo'$^\varepsilon$ak'i	'he always gave them'
sgīp!-	'cut'	sgī$^{i\varepsilon}$p'sga'p'am	'they had been all cut up'
dō^{u}m-	'kill'	dō^{u}mda`mk'	'he used to kill them' (inferential)
lebe-	'pick up and eat (seeds)'	le'$^\varepsilon$p'lap'	(non-aorist) 'pick and eat many seeds!'

Of particular interest here is the frequentative formation strategy found in a restricted set of verbs in the language. As shown in (122), this type of frequentative appears to be a case of VC reduplicant lodging before the final consonant of the verb stem (e.g., *hem-em-g*). Broselow and McCarthy (1983/ 84), for example, analyze the reduplicant as surfacing in the $[C_0V_-(C)]$ environment in the stem. Yet, in light of the reanalysis of Lushootseed presented above, the VC reduplicant may also be analyzed as lodging after the initial consonant (e.g., *h-em-emg*). This analytic ambiguity is artificial, however. Upon closer examination, a different analysis emerges once the morphology of the language is taken into account.

(122)   Takelma infixal frequentatives (Broselow and McCarthy 1983/84: 71; Sapir 1922: 73, 131–2)

Verb stem		Frequentative
hemg-	'take out'	heme$^\varepsilon$mg-
masg-	'put'	mats!a^{a}sg-
baxm-	'come'	baxa^{a}xm-

[26] Sapir transcribed a glottal stop as a raised 'ε'. Consonants with '!' are pronounced with a glottal release, while aspirated obstruents are indicated with a backward apostrophe.

| ts!a-im- | 'hide' | ts!aya-im- |
| yawī- | 'talk' | yāwa-iy- |

Frequentative formation in (122) is best analyzed as a case of C-reduplication infixing after the root-final vowel. In order to appreciate this analysis, a brief overview of the verbal morphology is in order. The following exposition draws heavily on Lee's (1991) reanalysis of Takelma phonology and morphology based on Sapir's materials.

Takelma verbal morphology is templatic, similar to those found in Semitic languages and various Native American languages (e.g., Yawelmani and the Miwok-Costanoan languages). There are two types of verb stem. Following Lee's terminology, the base for future, inferential, imperative, conditional, and potential affixation is referred to as the 'aorist stem', while the base for all other tense and mode forms is referred to as the 'non-aorist stem'. Depending on the tense-mode, the prosodic shape of the verb may vary. Consider, for example, the non-aorist CVC stems in (123). Certain non-aorist stems have corresponding CVVC aorist stems (123b) while others have CVCV (123b).

(123)   Non-aorist   Aorist   (B. Lee 1991: 90)
   a. CVC   CVVC   (Sapir's Type 1)
      wok   wook[27]   'arrive'
      niw   niiw   'be afraid'
   b. CVC   CVCV   (Sapir's Type 2)
      t'an   t'ana   'hold'
      yal   yala   'lose'
      t^{h}kis-(m)[28]-   t^{h}kisi-(m)-   'get green'
      k'iy-(k^h)-   k'iyi-(k^h)-   'come'
      kin-(k^h)-   kini-(k^h)-   'go'
      xut-(m)-   xutu-(m)-   'whistle'

Furthermore, there are several patterns of non-aorist/aorist correspondence for verbal stems, as summarized in (124). It is unclear at this point why certain verbs follow one mapping pattern and others do not.

(124)   Non-aorist   Aorist
   CVC   CVVC
      CVCV
   CVCV   CVVC

---

[27] Examples cited from Lee 1991 are given in Lee's interpretation of Sapir's original transcription.

[28] The consonants in parentheses are what Sapir refers to as 'petrified suffixes', which are essentially frozen suffixes with varying degrees of semantic transparency.

CVVC   CVCV
         CVVC
         CVC$_i$VC$_i$

What is of importance here is the fact that the frequentative forms in (122) are based on the CVCV(C) aorist stems, rather than the CVC(C) non-aorist counterparts, as assumed in Broselow and McCarthy's analysis.[29] Lee analyzes the frequentative as the result of the mapping of an uneven iambic templatic (i.e., $\sigma_\mu\sigma_{\mu\mu}$) onto a verbal root with the simultaneous spreading of the second consonantal melody to the final consonant of a CVCVVC surface form (Lee, 1991: 137). This templatic analysis suffers from two inadequacies, however. To begin with, it is unclear what the status of the CVCVVC template is with respect to the $\sigma_\mu\sigma_{\mu\mu}$ template. Given that the bimoraicity of the head of the iambic template can be satisfied by the long vowel, it is unclear why the extra final consonant is needed. Moreover, Lee's analysis crucially assumes that the final consonant of all CVCC roots can be reanalyzed as CVC+C. That is, while the infrequentative forms in (122) invariably end in two consonants, Lee assumes that the final consonant in such clusters is analyzed as a petrified suffix. The CVCC roots in (122) are thus assumed to be CVC roots in disguise. This assumption is crucial to Lee's templatic analysis since the final consonant of the CVCVVC template would otherwise have been filled by the third consonant of consonantal melody (i.e., *hem-k* 'take out' → *hemeem-k*, not **hemeek*). This assumption is untenable, however. While some of the forms that participate in this frequentative pattern end with a demonstrable petrified suffix (125a), others may not (125b).[30] Contrary to the prediction of the templatic analysis, the reduplicative consonant appears after the final vowel regardless of whether or not the final cluster ends in a petrified suffix (125b).

(125)	Non-repetitive		Repetitive	(B. Lee 1991: 137–8)
a.	Non-aorist	Aorist	Aorist	
	k'os-k	k'oso-k	k'osoos-k	'pinch'
	hiim-t	himi-t	himiim-t	'talk to'
	p'al-k	p'ala-k	p'alaal-k	'tell a myth'
	kay-w	kaya-w	kayaay-w	'eat'
	hen-t	hene-t	heneen-t	'wait for'
	hem-k	heme-k	hemeem-k	'take out'
	kin-k	kini-k	kiniin-k	'go to'

[29] According to Sapir, the CaC-frequentative formation in (121) takes non-aorist stems as inputs.
[30] Lee analyzes all forms in (125) as ending with a petrified suffix. However, I find no support for such an analysis for the forms in (125b) based on Sapir's description (Sapir 1922: 118–43).

b. paxm	paxam	paxaaxm	'come'
mask	mats'ak	mats'aask	'put'
wism	wits'im	wits'iism	'move'
skelw	skelew	skeleelw	'shout'
kʰewkʰaw	kʰewekʰaw	kʰeweekʰaw	'bark'

In sum, Takelma frequentative formation is the result of affixation of a monoconsonantal reduplicant to the right of the final vowel of a verb root that is then mapped onto an uneven iambic template. If roots with a petrified suffix are treated as polymorphemic, then Takelma infixing frequentative formation is best analyzed as an instance of affixing to the right of the stem-final vowel, rather than before the stem-final consonant.

4.8.1.2 *Hunzib* Another potential example of infixing before the last consonant is found in Hunzib, an East Tsezic language of the Daghestanian sub-branch of Nakh-Daghestanian. According to van den Berg (1995), there are two patterns of infixation before the last consonant of the stem in this language. Interrogation in finite verb forms is marked by a suffix, -*y*, after V, and −*i*, after C or by an infix, -*y*-, which is inserted before the last C of the stem (van den Berg 1995: 113). Verb forms with an interrogative infix may have a negative nuance, indicating that the action mentioned by the verb should not have been done or conversely should have been done but has not (e.g., *čáx* 'to write'; *čáyx-is* 'did X (really) not write? (X should already have written)'; *čáyx-er*? 'did X (really) write? (Why did X, X should not have)').[31] Based on van den Berg's examples, the distribution of -*y*- is amendable to multiple analyses (e.g., the pivot might be the stressed vowel, the final vowel, the initial vowel, or the final consonant).

Hunzib also has a set of infixing plural markers which exhibit a pre-last-consonant distribution, regardless of whether the last consonant appears word-finally or before a final vowel. For example, as illustrated in (126), -*baa*-invariably appears before the last consonant of the root regardless of whether the root ends in a C (i.e., (126a)) or a CV sequence (i.e., (126b)). This pre-last consonant distribution is observed even in derived stems, regardless of whether the derivational morphology is synchronically productive (126c) or not (126d).[32]

(126)   a.   -ūčααx   -ūčαbaax[33]   'slumber'
            āgaš   āgabaaš   'talk'
            tαdααx   tαdαbaax   'get tired'

---

[31] Van den Berg cites only one example of such infixed questions.

[32] Van den Berg differentiates productive and unproductive derivational affixes by '-' and ':' respectively.

[33] Vowel length is contrastive only in the stressed syllable. Thus when a long vowel is deaccented, it shortens. /α/ = [ɑ]; λ = [ɨ]; λ̃ = [ɨ̃]; x = [x̱].

b. haxsə   haxbaasə   'hurry'
   k'arƛe   k'arbaaƛe   'turn'
   kɑkɑƛe   kɑkɑbaaƛe   'laugh without restraint'
   laxƛe   laxbaaƛe   'move, crawl'

c. ẽdu-k(e)   ẽdubaa-k(e)   'go in'
   gišo-k(e)   gišobaa-k(e)   'go out'

d. ãzaa.k'   ãzabaa.k'   'stain'
   k'ot'.le   k'ot'baa.le   'be good'
   -ežaa.k'   -ežabaa.k'   'slide'

While the examples in (126) represent the exhaustive list of verbs that take the
-*baa*- infix, many verbs are pluralized by the infix -*á*-. This infix has several
allomorphs (van den Berg 1995: 81–3): the infix is -*yá*- when the vowel before
the last consonant is *i* or *e* (127a), -*wá*- when the pre-last consonant vowel is *i*,
ə, *o*, or *u* (127b), -*á*- when preceded by *α*, and -*á*- when preceded by *a* (127b).
The plural marker is always stressed on the surface.

(127)   Singular   Plural   Gloss
   a.   -iƛ'e   -iyαƛ'e   'kill'
        -ek   -eyák   'fall'
   b.   -ok'(o)   -owák'(e)   'call'
        ƛĩq'ə   ƛĩwɑq'ə   'end'
        -uč'e   -uwčáč'e   'cut'
        -uhu   -uwɑhe   'die'
   c.   -ɑhu   -ɑɑhu   'take'
        -ãc'ə   (m-)aac'ə[34] 'see'

The pre-final consonant distribution of the infixal plural marker is most
transparent when the root contains a consonant sequence. As illustrated in (128),
-*á*- is consistently inserted in front of the last consonant. The only exception is the
plural of *uhle* 'kill, destroy', which is *uwahle*, rather than *uhale*.

(128)   Singular   Plural   Gloss
        -ɨx.lə   -ɨxale   'warm'
        -ɨq'.lə   ɨq'ale   'grow'
        -ĩc'.k'ə   ĩc'ak'e   'make new'
        -ek.le   -ekale   'let fall'

The pre-final consonant distribution is observed even when the plural is
indicated via vowel replacement. The infix replaces the vowel before the last

[34] Van den Berg analyzes long vowels as a sequence of identical vowels.

consonant of the root. The only exception to this generalization is the plural of *-eżerič* 'be glad', which is *-eżarič* rather than **-eżerač*.

(129) Singular   Plural   Gloss
       -əxə.l   -əxál   'hang'
       -ok'o.l   -ok'ál   'gather'
       -īčox(e)   -īčáx(e) 'stay'
       -acə-k'   -acá-k'   'clean'
       haλ'u.k'   haλ'ák'   'look'

While the plural *-á-* is invariably stressed on the surface, the distribution of the marker itself cannot be derived from stress placement alone. Stress generally falls on the penultimate syllable. However, when the plural marker appears in the final syllable, the final syllable, rather than penultimate syllable, is stressed instead. To the extent that stress is prespecified to be on the infix, thus genuinely unpredictable in the plural forms, Hunzib offers a strong case for the last consonant pivot.

4.8.1.3 *Hausa Class 5 plural formation*   Another promising infixal pattern that argues for the final consonant as a phonological pivot comes from Hausa, a Chadic language spoken in Niger, Nigeria, and neighboring countries. Class 5 plurals in this language are formed by infixing the vocalic plural morpheme *-aa-* before the final consonant of the root followed by the suffixing of the final vowel *-uu* (130) (Newman 2000: 443–4). Thus when the root ends in a consonant cluster, the plural morpheme *-aa-* is straightforwardly infixed before the root-final consonant.

(130)   root   singular   plural   gloss
        CVC_iC_j gurb   gurbìi   guràabuu   'hollow place'
                    kurm   kurmìi   kuràamuu   'copse, jungle'
                    turk   turkèe   turàakuu   'tethering post'
                    giyɓ   giiɓìi   giyàabuu   'tooth gap'
                    miyk   miikìi   miyàakuu   'ulcer'

The problem with claiming that the plural marker is infixed before the final consonant is that such an analysis cannot be straightforwardly extended to roots without final consonant clusters. That is, when the root ends in a single consonant, the final consonant is duplicated.

(131) CVC gaɓ   gaɓàa   gaɓàaɓuu   'joint, limb'
            ƙaf   ƙafàa   ƙafàafuu   'foot'
            tsuw   tsuwèe   tsuwàawuu   'testicle'
            guy   gwiiwàa   gwiyaayuu   'knee'

Thus, whether Hausa Class 5 plural formation should be treated as a case of infixation is a matter of debate. Some scholars have treated Hausa plural formation as a matter of prosodic template satisfaction (Rosenthal 1999), akin to the broken plural in Arabic (McCarthy and Prince 1990). The problem posed by the CVC roots in (131) for the pre-final-consonant analysis is reconcilable within the current theory, however. Class 5 plural formation can be analyzed as follows:

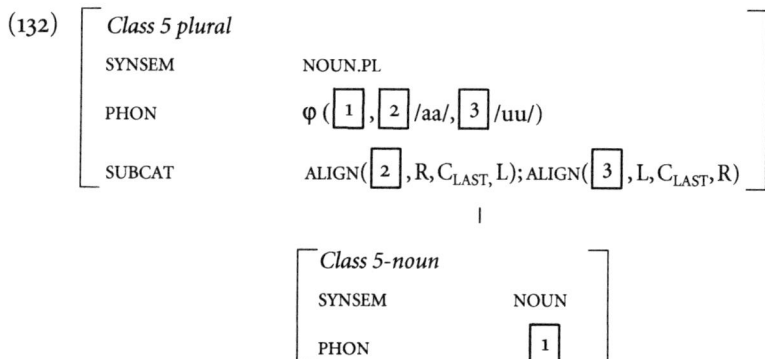

(132)

$$
\begin{bmatrix}
\text{\textit{Class 5 plural}} & \\
\text{SYNSEM} & \text{NOUN.PL} \\
\text{PHON} & \varphi\,(\boxed{1}\,,\boxed{2}\,/\text{aa}/,\boxed{3}\,/\text{uu}/) \\
\text{SUBCAT} & \text{ALIGN}(\boxed{2}\,,\text{R},\text{C}_{\text{LAST}},\text{L});\text{ALIGN}(\boxed{3}\,,\text{L},\text{C}_{\text{LAST}},\text{R})
\end{bmatrix}
$$

|

$$
\begin{bmatrix}
\text{\textit{Class 5-noun}} & \\
\text{SYNSEM} & \text{NOUN} \\
\text{PHON} & \boxed{1}
\end{bmatrix}
$$

The two exponents of the Class 5 plural formation have different alignment requirements. Both exponents take the final consonant as the pivot. One exponent, -*aa*-, appears to the left of the last consonant while the other exponent, -*uu*-, aligns to the right of the last consonant of the root. When a root is cluster-final, -*aa*- fulfills its alignment obligation by breaking apart the root-final consonant sequence. When the root ends in a single consonant, however, the root-final consonant must undergo compensatory reduplication to prevent hiatus (i.e., *gaɓ* 'joint, limb' → *gaɓàaɓuu*, not **gaàaɓuu*). Compensatory reduplication (CR) refers to a type of reduplication pattern which takes place with no obvious semantic import or serves only a secondary role in a morphological construction (Bissell 2002; Goad 2001; Inkelas 2005; Inkelas and Zoll 2005; Kawu 2000; Nelson 2003; Rose 1997; Yu 2004*d*, 2005*b*; Zuraw 2002). It is invoked only to compensate for potential inadequacies of the output. In the case of Hausa Class 5 plural formation, CR is needed to prevent the emergence of onsetless syllables on the surface. Formally, compensatory reduplication in Hausa is modeled as the result of some CR-triggering constraint outranking the relevant FAITH constraints (e.g., INTEGRITY). Default segmental insertion is blocked in favor of CR when DEP$_{\text{IO}}$ outranks INTEGRITY (see the failure of (134c)).

(133)   INTEGRITY-IO   No element of the input has multiple correspondents in the output. (McCarthy and Prince 1995)

(134)

/ga-àa-ɓ-uu/	ONSET	DEP$_{IO}$	INTEGRITY
☞ a. gaɓ$_C$àaɓuu			*
b. gaàaɓuu	*!		
c. gaʔàaɓuu		*!	

Since the traditional B(ase)-R(eduplicant)-ANCHOR analysis does not apply here due to the lack of an abstract morpheme, RED, in the input, a surface correspondence method of evaluating the relationship between the 'redupli-cant' and the 'base' (cf. Bat-El 2002; Yip 1999; Yu 2003, 2004, 2005*b*; Zuraw 2002) is adopted here. The idea behind this approach is that output-identical segments stand in a correspondence relationship (Hansson 2001; Rose and Walker 2004). Following Rose and Walker (2004) and Hansson (2001), I assume that directionality is stated in a correspondence relationship.[35]

(135)   IDENT-S$_R$S$_L$[36]
'Let S$_R$ be a segment in the output and S$_L$ be any corresponding segment of S$_R$ such that S$_L$ precedes S$_R$ in the sequence of segments in the output (L > R).'

The constraint in (135) requires the 'base' of reduplication to follow the reduplicant, not the other way around. An illustration of this analysis is given in (136).

(136)

/ga-àa-ɓ-uu/	IDENT-S$_R$S$_L$
☞ a. gaɓ$_C$àaɓuu	
b. gag$_C$àaɓuu	*!
c. gaɓàaɓ$_C$uu	*!

Candidate (136b) fails under IDENT-S$_R$S$_L$ since the 'reduplicant' follows the 'base'. (The 'copy' is indicated by the subscript *C*). Even though (136c) is string-identical to (136a), it is nonetheless ruled out by IDENT-S$_R$S$_L$ since the

---

[35] The idea that directionality is crucial in a correspondence relationship has been pointed out previously for the input-output relationship (i.e., IDENT-IO vs IDENT-OI; (Morén 2000, 2001; Pater 1999)) and in other applications of surface segmental correspondence, for example, in consonant harmony (Hansson 2001; Rose and Walker 2004).

[36] This constraint is a generalized version of the IDENT-CC(F) constraint proposed in Rose and Walker (2004).

copy follows the base. Given this analysis, Hausa Class 5 plural formation may be considered additional evidence for the last-consonant pivot. Notwithstanding the data from Hunzib and Hausa, the evidence for the last-consonant pivot remains scant, however. Further investigation is obviously needed to substantiate the need for a final consonant pivot. From a diachronic perspective, it is not surprising why such cases are hard to come by. Languages often have restrictions on codas. In particular, coda clusters are often disfavored or banned altogether. Thus the contexts in which a final consonant pivot can be unequivocally established are difficult to obtain.

4.8.2 First syllable

Another phonological pivot hinted at in Ultan and Moravcsik but not appealed to here is the first syllable. Such a pivot should be logically possible, particularly given the need of a final-syllable pivot. As mentioned earlier, evidence for affixing after the first syllable is hard to come by, partly because many potential cases may also exemplify the first-vowel pivot. Moreover, I cannot appeal to cases of affixing before the first syllable as diagnostic evidence since such cases can also be trivially analyzed as straightforward prefixation.

Despite the abovementioned difficulties, there is some suggestive evidence for the first-syllable pivot. For example, in Koasati, a Muskogean language, one method of marking punctual plural is by lodging -*ho*- after the initial syllable of the stem. The data reproduced in (137) are all that were cited in Kimball 1991.

(137)   Koasati punctual plural (Kimball 1991: 326)

ok.cay.yan	'to be alive'	okhocayyan
ok.cák.kon	'to be blue'	okhocákkon
ak.łát.lin	'to be oversize'	akhołátlin
stok.hát.kan	'to be gray'	stokhohátkan

How compelling this pattern is as evidence for the first-syllable pivot is confounded by several peculiarities of this data set. The general method of marking the punctual plural in Koasati is infixing reduplication (see (85) above). The -*ho*- infix is used only when the initial syllable of the stem is closed. The range of coda consonants is vast in Koasati, and no special restriction on the coda inventory of the initial syllable is reported. Thus, the fact that stems that take the -*ho*- infix all begin with a syllable that ends in *k* raises suspicion that the initial syllable might be a separate morpheme or that *k* might be part of the infix itself. The available published account of this pattern offers no further information than what is recounted here. Thus, further research is needed to ascertain the nature of the -*ho*- affix in Koasati.

The most promising set of evidence in support of the initial syllable as a phonological pivot comes from a surprising set of languages. In Mandarin, for example, the syllable -*li*- may be infixed after the first syllable in a mono-morphemic disyllabic root (e.g., *hwudu-de* 'muddled' → *hwu-li*-hwudu-de 'good and muddled'; (Chao 1968)). The Mandarin data are problematic since the -*li*- infixation construction is rather restricted in Mandarin. It is possible that the 'infixed' forms are lexicalized phrases, rather than the products of genuine infixation.

A more robust pattern of infixation is found in Cantonese, however. The word, *kwai* 'ghost', for example, may appear inside certain monomorphemic disyllabic adjectives to signify intensification.

(138)   Cantonese (Matthews and Yip 1994: 43)
   lœntsœn 'clumsy'   lœn-kwɐi-tsœn 'downright clumsy'
   jʊksyn   'ugly'   jʊk-kwɐi-syn   'downright ugly'

Another productive pattern of infixation in Cantonese is observed with certain *wh*-words. For example, *mɐtkwɐi* 乜鬼 or *mɛ* 咩 'what' may appear inside a word to signify uncertainties the speaker might have about a word or a proposition (139). The post-initial syllable distribution of this infix is confirmed by the examples in (139b). Here, the infix is applied to loanwords, which arguably have no internal morphological structure. Crucially, the infix may only occur after the first syllable of the loanword, never after the penultimate syllable. To be sure, the *wh*-infix may not appear internal to a syllable either. That is, *jʊ-mɐt⌐.kwɐi-k.syn* is not a possible output of the word 'ugly' in Cantonese.

(139) a. jʊk⌐.syn   jʊk-mɐt⌐.kwɐi-syn   'ugly'
    ku.hɔn   ku-mɐt⌐.kwɐi-hɔn   'stingy'

   b. mɔ.lɔk⌐.kɔ   mɔ-mɐt⌐.kwɐi-lɔk⌐.kɔ/ 'Morocco'
           *mɔ.lɔk⌐.-mɐt⌐.kwɐi-kɔ

    lɔk⌐-tsʰam-kei lɔk⌐-mɐt⌐.kwɐi-tsʰam.kei/ 'Los Angeles'
           *lɔk⌐.tsʰam-mɐt⌐.kwɐi-kei

   c. ma.ji.toi.fu   ma-mɐt⌐.kwɐi-ji.toi.fu, 'Maldives'
          ma.ji -mɐt⌐.kwɐi-toi.fu/
          *ma.ji.toi.-mɐt⌐.kwɐi-fu

    ki.li.ku.lu   ki.-mɛ-li.ku.lu,   'gibberish'
          ki.li.-mɛ-ku.lu/
          *ki.li.ku-mɛ-lu

The exact distribution of this infix is complicated by the fact that it might also interact with foot structure. Some quadrisyllabic words show variation in the distribution of the infix; the infix may appear after the first syllable or after the first disyllabic string (139c). One interpretation of this variation is that the infix wants to be after the first prosodic constituent of a string. Assuming that quadrisyllabic words are analyzed as consisting of two disyllabic feet, the *wh*-word may appear after the first foot or the first syllable. Thus, while it is difficult to substantiate the need for a first-syllable pivot on the strength of one set of evidence, the Cantonese evidence nonetheless provides a strong case for such a pivot. Future research might turn up more supporting evidence for this pivot.

4.9 Conclusion

This chapter elaborates the theory that phonological subcategorization may target only a restricted set of phonological pivots. Members of the set of phonological pivots share the characteristic of being psycholinguistically salient. Subcategorizations involving this set of phonological pivots are more reliable than subcategorizations involving other conceivable pivot points. Edge pivots dominate the set of salient phonological pivots because they are psycholinguistically salient and are conducive to resulting in more reliable subcategorization restrictions. To exemplify the Pivot Theory, I review numerous cases of infixation instantiating the type of pivots predicted by the theory and how such cases may be analyzed within a declarative theory of the morphology-phonology interface.

A full understanding of the Edge-Bias Effect is not yet complete, however. In addition to a theory of phonological subcategorization and a theory of inductive bias in phonological subcategorization formation, it is equally important to understand the contexts in which the inductive bias is called into play. The next chapter deals with this final dimension of a holistic theory of infix distribution—the mechanisms of infix genesis.

5

The secret history of infixes

In Chapter 3, I argued that a full understanding of the distribution of infixes requires a theory of phonological subcategorization and its interaction with grammar-external constraints or filters. Two types of filters are most relevant in the present context: inductive biases in morphological learning and constraints on language change. In the last chapter, I introduced a type of inductive bias that constrains the types of phonological subcategorization relations a learner might set up. The force of this inductive bias is most apparent, however, when the learner is confronted with a situation where straightforward adpositional morphological subcategorization is not possible.[1] This chapter is dedicated to elucidating the range of known infix-creating ambiguities in language. As such, it is also a diachronic typology of infixation. I will show that edge-oriented infixes ultimately originate from adpositional affixes (i.e., prefixes or suffixes). Their peripheral origins give rise to their synchronic edge-oriented profile. Ultimately, it is the preponderance of such infixes with adpositional origin that gives rise to the observed Edge-Bias Effect.

5.1 Background

The study of morphological change in language began in earnest with the Neogrammarians, who made major advances in the understanding of the role analogy plays in morphological change. In particular, much effort was focused on matters of allomorphy reduction and paradigm uniformity as responses to sound change. However, little attention was paid to the origins of infixation. There are notable exceptions, however. For example, Schmidt (1906) discussed the possible origin of Mon-Khmer infixes as the result of entrapment; Ferdinand de Saussure (Ultan, 1975) intimated an explanation of the origin of the nasal infix in Indo-European in terms of entrapment

---

[1] To be sure, inductive biases presumably apply regardless of the type of morphology involved. But in cases of simple concatenative morphology (e.g., prefixation and suffixation), the type of inductive bias maintained by the Pivot Theory might be less important since subcategorization can be stated solely at the morphological level (e.g., with respect of the root or the stem).

(see Section 5.2.2 for a discussion of this mechanism). Sporadic mentions of the possible origins of infixes also appear in traditional grammatical descriptions. For example, Boas and Deloria (1941) suggested that the inflectional infixes in Dakota resulted from the fusion of the locative prefixes with the root. With the notable exception of Ultan (1975), the lack of attention to the origins of infixation persists.[2] However, there are signs that researchers are beginning to recognize the importance of understanding the origins of infixes; several reports on the origins of infixes in various languages have appeared in recent years (Anderson 1996; Garrett 2001; Haiman 1977, 2003; Harris 2002; Martin 1994; Nichols 2005; Yu 2004*b*).

Ultan, in his pioneering work on the typology and origin of infixation (1975), discussed two main processes that give rise to infixes: phonological/ morphological metathesis and entrapment. These processes will be discussed in detail later in the chapter. Briefly, he cited the Hebrew reflexive -*t*-, Common Indonesian active and passive -*um*- and -*in*-, and Delaware third-person -*wə*-, as instances of metathesis. Entrapment refers to the fusion of an outer affix with the stem, causing the intervening affix to become an infix. He gave Dakota pronominals, Northwest Caucasian pronominals, Indo-European -*n*-, Trukese -*Vkk*- durative, Miskitu construct state formation, and Austro-Asiatic infixations as instances of entrapment. While metathesis and entrapment are certainly two major sources of infixation, the precise nature of these mechanisms remains largely unexplored in Ultan's seminal paper.

This chapter builds on the insight of these earlier works to expand on and, along the way, to revise the understanding of the diachronic landscape of the genesis of infixes. The chapter provides a state-of-the-art overview of the current understanding of the development of infixation. As in any study on diachronic typology, one is invariably restricted by the amount of materials available in the literature. Despite the recent surge of reports, the literature on the diachronic change of infixation remains far from ideal. Thus, in what follows, some of the case studies are the results of original historical investigations.

5.2 Toward a diachronic typology of infixation

Four diachronic pathways can be adduced from the available literature: phonetic metathesis in Section 5.2.1, morphological entrapment in Section 5.2.2,

---

[2] The lack of attention to the historical development of morphological change might partly have to do with the development of the field of linguistics in recent years. As Joseph and Janda (1988) observed, morphology and historical linguistics were in complementary distribution during the Generative era, for example; morphology is in vogue while Generative historical linguistics has just gone out of fashion.

reduplication mutation in Section 5.2.3, and morphological excrescence in Section 5.2.4. Each section contains a general discussion on the respective mechanism of change and examples to illustrate more precisely the mechanism in question. The focus below will be to elucidate the pathways through which ambiguities in morphological parsing arise and which, through the general mechanisms of reanalysis and analogical extension, ultimately lead to the emergence of an infix. Since the focus is the inception of infixation, as such, I shall have little to say regarding to the propagation or regularization of the pattern once it is started.

5.2.1 Metathesis

Metathesis refers to the transposition between two segments, which can be schematized as AB > BA. An example of phonological metathesis can be found in Cayuga, a Northern Iroquoian language, where, according to Foster (1982) (cited in Blevins and Garrett 1998: 509–10), /VʔV/ → [ʔV] and /Vh/ → [hV] in odd-number non-final syllables. The relevant segments are underlined.

(1) Cayuga (Foster 1982; Blevins and Garrett 1998: 510)
    a. /kahwistaʔeks/ → [kʰąwísdʔaes] 'it strikes, chimes (a clock)'
    b. /akekahaʔ/ → [agékhaaʔ] 'my eye'
    c. /koʔnikōhaʔ/ → [gʔoníkhwaʔ] 'her mind'
    d. No change:
      /akahwitáʔek/ → [agahwisdáʔek] 'it struck, chimed'

Many have suggested that infixation can be the result of morphological metathesis (e.g., Ultan 1975), that is, when morphemes A and B were in one linear order historically, but their linear positions are found in the reverse in the daughter language(s).

(2) *A+B > B+A

For example, the glottal stop mediopassive infix that appears after the root vowel in Tzutujil appears to have originated from a type of metathesis similar to that found in Cayuga.

(3) Tzutujil mediopassive (Dayley 1985: 55, 113–14)
    toj 'pay' toʔjik 'to be paid'
    kʼis 'finish' kʼiʔseem 'to end, finish'
    tij 'eat, consume' tiʔjik 'to be paid'

In Yucateco, which is a Mayan language distantly related to Tzutujil, the passive of transitive root has the shape CVʔC. The glottal stop used to be a suffix /b'/ in the sixteenth century (i.e., *CVC-b' > *CVC-ʔ > CVʔC) (Terry Kaufman p.c.). The suffix /b'/ is still found in Mopan, a closely related language.

The third-person marker in Copainalá Zoque, a Mixe-Zoque language spoken in Southern Mexico, is realized as palatalization of the initial consonant of a root if it begins with an alveolar consonant (i.e., *d, ts, s, n*) (4). Otherwise, a palatal glide is infixed after the initial consonant of the root (4) (Wonderly 1951).

(4) a. tsʌhk-   'to do'   tʃahku   'he did it'
         sʌk   'beans'   ʃʌk   'his beans'
         swerte   'fortune'   ʃwerte   'his fortune'
         nanah   'mother'   ɲanah   'his mother'
     b. pata   'mat'   pjata   'his mat'
         burru   'burro'   bjurru   'his burro'
         faha   'belt'   fjaha   'his belt'
         mula   'mule'   mjula   'his mule'
         wakas   'cow'   wjakas   'his cow'
         gaju   'rooster'   gjaju   'his rooster'
         ʔaci   'older brother' ʔjaci   'his older brother'
         hajah   'husband'   hjajah   'her husband'

The third-person marker was historically a prefix *i- (e.g., Sierra Popoluca ʔikaːmaː 'his cornfield' < Proto-Zoque *kämä(k) 'cornfield'), which lenited into a glide (e.g., South Zoque *kajkama* 'cornfield'). However, a general palatal metathesis affected the language and turned all *j + C sequences into Cj in Copainalá Zoque (CZ), North Zoque (NZ), and Northeast Zoque (NeZ). The non-metathesized reflex of *j can still be observed in Sierra Popoluca (SP), South Zoque (SZ), and West Zoque (WZ) (Elson 1992).

(5) CZ, NZ: popja 'he runs'   (SP, SZ: *pojpa* < PZoq *poj + pa)
     CZ, NZ: hapja 'he writes'   (SP, WZ: *hajpa* < PZoq *haj + pa)
     CZ, NZ: hʌpja 'he weeps'   (SP: *hʌjpa* 'he speaks' < PZoq *hʌj + pa)
     CZ, NZ: homi 'tomorrow'   (SP, SZ: *hojmʌ* < PZoq *hoj + mʌ)

Morphological metathesis as such is not a useful concept for the understanding of infix origin, however, since it is merely a restatement of the fact. It offers no greater insight into the mechanisms through which infixation develops. In what follows, I build on a phonetic interpretation of metathesis advanced in Blevins and Garrett (1998, 2005). Grounding the origins of metathesis on articulatory and perceptual factors provides a more restrictive theory of metathesis as a pathway of infix emergence.

5.2.1.1 *The phonetic origins of metathesis* In a series of papers on the origins of metathesis, Blevins and Garrett (1998, 2005), furthering the listener-oriented theory of sound change (cf. Ohala 1993), propose that there are four main types of metathesis: perceptual, compensatory, coarticulatory,[3] and auditory. They summarize these four types of metathesis as follows:

[Perceptual metathesis] involves features of intrinscially longer duration (e.g. pharyngealization); in multisegmental strings, such features are spread out over the entire sequence, allowing them to be reinterpreted in non-historical positions. [Compensatory metathesis] is prosodically conditioned: within a foot, features in a weak syllable undergo temporal shifts into the strong syllable. [Coarticulatory metathesis] arises in clusters of consonants with the same manner of articulation but different places of articulation; the place cues do not necessarily have long duration, and we will suggest that metathesis results from coarticulation facilitated by shared articulatory gestures. [Auditory metathesis] results from the auditory segregation of sibilant noise from the rest of the speech stream.' (Blevins and Garrett 2005: 120–1)

Of the four known triggers of phonological metathesis, perceptual metathesis seems to be the only form of metathesis that gives rise to infixation. A closer look at Blevins and Garrett's survey of metathesis reveals that there is a simple explanation for this connection. To begin with, perceptual metathesis makes up the bulk of the attested metathesis cases. Thus, it is not surprising that there are more instances of infixes that come from perceptual metathesis than other metathesis triggers. Second, compensatory and coarticulatory metatheses are best viewed as more restricted subtypes of perceptual metathesis (6). Both types of metathesis result from perceptual confusion induced by extreme coarticulatory effects. Compensatory metathesis differs from general perceptual metathesis in terms of its reference to prosodic conditioning (i.e., the extreme coarticulatory overlap between a pair of stressed and unstressed vowels). The so-called coarticulatory metathesis, which involves extreme coarticulation, involves the overlapping of consonant sequences. Thus, the fundamental mechanisms behind compensatory and coarticulatory metatheses are no different from that behind perceptual metathesis—perceptual confusion induced by gestural overlaps.

(6) **Mechanism of metathesis** Subtypes
  Perceptual metathesis Compensatory metathesis
    Coarticulatory metathesis
  Auditory metathesis

---

[3] The label 'coarticulatory metathesis' is potentially confusing since, with the exception of auditory metathesis, the other types of metathesis all involve coarticulation in one form or another. An alternative label might be 'obstruent gestural overlap metathesis'.

Crucially, the phonetic understanding of the origins of metathesis makes predictions about possible types of metathesis-induced infixes that are not possible under the morphological view of metathesis. To begin with, the set of potential metathesis-induced infixes is restricted to the set of segments with 'stretch-out' phonetic features that are amenable to perceptual confusion. This class of phonetic objects with elongated acoustic cues includes labials, palatals, pharyngeals, laryngeals, liquids, and rhotics. The phonetic origin of metathesis also predicts that only a single segment can be involved in a 'transposition' at a given time. Infixations that involve the transposition of *groups* of segments do not lend themselves readily to a phonetic misinterpretation account of metathesis (see also Janda 1984). Another major feature of metathesis-induced infixations is that their synchronic exponents often do not match their historical sources. This unfaithful nature of the metathesized segment finds a natural explanation under this phonetic view of metathesis. I elaborate on this point in the next section.

5.2.1.2 *Metathesis without faithfulness*   The mismatches in form between metathesis-induced infixes and their historical sources are commonplace. For example, in Lepcha, a Tibeto-Burman language spoken in Sikkim on the southern fringe of Tibet, the alternation between intransitive and transitive verbs can be marked by the infixing of -*j*- after the initial consonant (Benedict 1943; Ultan 1975; Voegelin and Voegelin 1965).

(7) pok   'cast down'   pjok   'cause to cast down'
     thor   'escape, get free'   thjor   'let go, set free'
     rop   'stick, adhere'   rjop   'affix, attach'
     nak   'to be straight'   njak   'make straight'
     nom   'smell (intr.)'   njom   'smell (tr.)'

Benedict (1943) found that the infix originated from the Tibeto-Burman causative prefix *s-, as illustrated by the following cognate forms in Tibetan:

(8) Lepcha   nom   'smell (intr.)'   Tibetan   mnam-pa
     Lepcha   njom   'smell (tr.)'   Tibetan   snam-pa

The change from *s- to -*j*- might seem anomalous at first glance. However, this outcome is to be expected given the phonetic mechanism that gave rise to metathesis in the first place. No segment was ever transposed. The palatal glide infix in Lepcha was originally conditioned by the coarticulatory effect of the initial *s*. When *s was lost in initial consonant clusters, the listener reinterpreted what was previously coarticulatory palatalization as morphological. As predicted by the phonetic explanation of metathesis, the metathesis-induced change that affected the intransitive/transitive alternation also affected other parts of the Lepcha lexicon. As shown in (9), other words reconstructed to begin with an *s*-initial consonant cluster show reflexes that contain a post-consonantal palatal.

(9) Tibeto-Burman   Lepcha
    *s-na   'nose'   >   njo   'snot'
    *s-nam   'daughter-in-law'   >   njom   'daughter-in-law'
    *s-min   >   mjăn   'to be ripe'

Thus the Lepcha example highlights an important aspect of metathesis-induced infixation. The term 'metathesis' is often defined as the reordering of segments or features within the phonological string (e.g., Blevins and Garrett 2005; Hume 2001). The 'reordering' metaphor gives the impression that the metathesized segment is ontologially one and the same as the 'original' segment. The Lepcha example points to a major problem with such an interpretation of metathesis. The infix in Lepcha did not strictly speaking transpose from one linear position to another. There was never a transitivizing palatal glide morpheme in Tibeto-Burman. The source of palatality came from the coarticulatory effect of the initial alveolar sibilant. This type of 'unfaithful' metathesis is actually rather typical of metathesis in general and especially of metathesis-induced infixes. For example, while the glottal infix in Tzutujil was previously understood as the result of the reordering of the glottal stop (*CVC-bʼ > *CVC-ʔ > CVʔC), the phonetic view of metathesis invites an alternative interpretation. Since the cues for glottalization often stretch out across long distances, at the time when the suffix -bʼ- was still present, we could expect some degree of laryngealization on the root vowel (i.e., *CV̰C-bʼ). The disappearance of the -bʼ- suffix prompted the listener to attribute the laryngealization on the root vowel to the presence of an intrinsic glottal stop (i.e., CVʔC). This scenario obviates the need to posit an intermediate stage where the original -bʼ- suffix reduced to a glottal stop (*CVC-ʔ) first before metathesizing to its contemporary post-root vowel distribution. Under the present theory, the pathway is much more direct: *CV̰C-bʼ > CVʔC. To be sure, an important feature of this theory is its reliance on the mechanism of coarticulation as the ultimate source of metathesis. This theory thus predicts the co-existence of the coarticulatory effect and its source within the same language, all else being equal. Such a prediction is confirmed in the case of the class 3 noun infix in several Benuo-Congo languages. In these languages, the infix -w- came from the reconstructed prefix *u.

(10)   Noni class 3/4 nouns (Blevins and Garrett 1998; Hyman 1981)

Singular (cl. 3)	Plural (cl. 4)	
kwen	ken	'firewood'
gwέŋ	gέŋ	'root'
mbwesɛm	mbesɛm	'green grasshopper'
twéŋ	téŋ	'vine branch'
fwέw	fέw	'thorn'

The reflex of this coarticulatory stage is found in the cognate construction in Aghem, where class 3 nouns are marked by a prefix ó-, as well as an infix -*w*-.

(11)   Aghem class 3 (singular) nouns (Blevins and Garrett 1998; Hyman 1979)

Singular (cl. 3)	Plural	
ó-kwíŋ	é-kíŋ (cl. 4)	'mortar'
ó-kwâʔ	é-káʔà (cl. 4)	'hill, mountain'
ó-twíi	ń-tíi (cl. 12)	'medicine'

Given the propensity for metathesis-induced infixes to be formally unfaithful to their historical antecedents and since telescoping often obscures the original contexts of the change, tracing the source of metathesis-induced infixes is not an easy task. Yet the reward can be impressive if such an endeavor is successful. This point is most effectively demonstrated in the case of diminutive infixation in the Pingding dialect of Mandarin.

5.2.1.3 *Infixation in Pingding Mandarin*   Pingding is a dialect of Mandarin Chinese spoken in the Shanxi province of China. Like most Mandarin dialects, Pingding has a diminutive/hypocoristic affixation process. However, unlike other dialects, in which this process is marked by the suffixing of a retroflexed morpheme (i.e., -*er*), the cognate morpheme in Pingding, realized as a retroflex lateral -*ɭ*-, is infixed between the onset and the rhyme of a syllable.

(12)   Pingding *ɭ*-infixation (Xu 1981)

mən	tuɤŋ	+	ɭ	⟶	mən	tɭuɤŋ	'hole on the door'
lɔ	tʰɤu	+	ɭ	⟶	lɔ	tʰɭu	'old man'
çiɔ	pɤŋ	+	ɭ	⟶	çiɔ	pɭɤŋ	'small notebook'
xɤu	mɤŋ	+	ɭ	⟶	xɤŋ	mɭɤŋ	'back door'
çiɔ	kuɤ	+	ɭ	⟶	çiɔ	kɭuɤ	'small work'
xuaŋ	xua	+	ɭ	⟶	xuaŋ	xɭua	'yellow flower'
	ŋɤ	+	ɭ	⟶		ŋɭɤ	'month'

This infixation pattern is puzzling in several respects. First, the syllable structure of Chinese languages is generally straightforwardly (C)(G)V(C), where 'G' stands for a glide (i.e., *j* or *w*). Thus, it is surprising that infixation should create onset clusters which are otherwise not attested elsewhere in the language. On top of that, a retroflex lateral is not commonly found in descriptions of Mandarin phonetic inventory (e.g., Chao 1968; Duanmu 2000; Li and Thompson 1981). The appearance of a retroflex lateral only in forms with infixation also demands an explanation.

Yu (2004*b*) explains the development of Pingding infixation as follows: Pingding infixation was the result of metathesis of the suffix -*r* from post-vocalic to pre-vocalic position. Rhotic metathesis is commonplace in the world's languages. This is, for example, found in the history of English (e.g., *third* < OE *þridda*, *bird* < OE *brid*). Blevins and Garrett (1998, 2005) attribute the cause of rhotic metathesis to listener misperception fueled by the long phonetic cues of rhotics (e.g., lower F3). That is, the coarticulatory acoustic cues of the rhotic permeate the neighboring vowel, making it difficult for the listener to recover the actual location of the rhotic. In English, what apparently happened was that some speakers misinterpreted the location of the rhotic as pre-vocalic, rather than as post-vocalic, thus resulting in the current metathesized forms. Similarly, the fact that the post-vocalic diminutive suffix -*r* in Mandarin surfaces in pre-vocalic positions in Pingding Mandarin is analyzed as a hypercorrective response (Ohala 1993) to the extensive anticipatory effect of -*r*. That is, the unintentional anticipatory effect of -*r* causes the preceding vowel to be heavily rhoticized. This presents to the listener a problem in localizing the source of the coarticulatory effect since rhoticization could be caused by either a pre-vocalic or post-vocalic retroflex. The ancestral Pingding speakers opted for a pre-vocalic analysis, hence the seed of diminutive infixation in Pingding. One crucial difference between Pingding rhotic metathesis and similar sound changes such as in English, is that rhotic metathesis in Pingding has grammatical consequences. That is, a previously suffixing morphological process is now an infixing phenomenon. One puzzle that remains unresolved is why the diminutive infix is not a straightforward -*r*- in Pingding. Where does the retroflexed lateral -*l*- come from? The answer lies in a similar construction found in the Yanggu dialect of Mandarin.

The diminutive construction in Yanggu, a dialect of Mandarin spoken in Shandong, varies depending on the shape of the lexical host to which it is attached. Dong (1985) reports that, in general, [ɭ] is suffixed to the root.

(13)		Root	Diminutive	Gloss		Root	Diminutive	Gloss
	a.	tʂʐ̩	tʂɤɭ	'stick'	m.	kʰɤŋ	kʰɤɭ	'ditch'
	b.	tʂʰa	tʂʰaɭ	'fork'	n.	pu	puɭ	'cloth'

c.	kɛ	kɛɹ	'cover'	o.	kua	kuaɹ	'melon'
e.	tʂʰə	tʂʰəɹ	'car'	p.	kuɛ	kuɛɹ	'cane'
f.	kɤ	kɤɻ̩	'pigeon'	q.	uɤ	uɤɹ	'pot'
g.	ʂɤi	ʂɤɻ̩	'color'	r.	xuɤi	xuɤɻ̩	'dust'
h.	pao	paoɹ	'bun'	s.	uãn	uɛɹ	'bowl'
i.	xou	xouɹ	'monkey'	t.	uɤ̃n	uɤɻ̩	'wrinkle'
j.	pãn	pɛɹ	'class'	u.	kʰuãŋ	kʰuaɹ	'basket'
k.	kɤ̃n	kɤɻ̩	'root'	v.	kũŋ	kuɤɹ	'bow'
l.	kãŋ	kaɹ	'basin'				

However, when the word begins with a dental/alveolar consonant, [t, t^h, n, ts, ts^h, s], an [l][4] appears pre-vocalically after the initial consonant concomitant with the suffixing of [ɹ].

(14)	Root	Diminutive	Gloss		Root	Diminutive	Gloss
a.	tsa	tslaɹ	'yesterday'	g.	tʰãŋ	tʰlaɹ	'soup'
b.	tsʰɛ	tsʰlɛɹ	'vegetable'	h.	tʰu	tʰluɹ	'rabbit'
c.	tao	tlaoɹ	'knife'	i.	tsuɤ	tsluɤɹ	'seat'
e.	tsou	tslouɹ	'walk'	j.	tuãn	tluɛɹ	'group'
f.	sãn	slɛɹ	'three'	k.	tũŋ	tluɤɹ	'cave'

It should be emphasized that [l] only appears after a dental consonant, not after coronals in general, as [l] is not found in retroflex-obstruent-initial words.

(15)	Root	Diminutive	Gloss		Root	Diminutive	Gloss
	tʂʐ̩	tʂɤɹ	'stick'	vs	tsa	tslaɹ	'yesterday'
	tʂʰa	tʂʰaɹ	'fork'	vs	tao	tlaoɹ	'knife'
	ʂɤi	ʂɤɹ	'color'	vs	sãn	slɛɹ	'three'

In Yu (2004*b*), I argue that the appearance and the distribution of the lateral in Yanggu diminutive formation just in the case where the initial consonant is dental is the result of the drastic transition from an anterior sound to the rhotacized vowel.[5] This abrupt transition apparently yielded a percept of a

---

[4] While Dong transcribes the Yanggu infixing lateral as a plain lateral he does acknowledge the fact that this lateral is slightly further back, and very similar to a retroflex sound (Dong 1985: 276, *n.* 3). Dong also points out that the vowels that follow the inserted [l] are invariably rhotacized (Dong 1985: *n.* 5), suggesting that the sound represented as *l* might be more accurately transcribed as [ɭ].

[5] The distribution of the retroflexed lateral is more complicated than what is reproduced here. See Yu (2004*b*) for more details of the Yanggu pattern and the historical analysis.

transitional approximant, which was reinterpreted as a purposeful gesture and was subsequently phonemicized as a retroflex lateral.

The Yanggu pattern thus represents the missing link between Standard Chinese *r*-suffixation and the present-day Pingding infixing pattern. The development of Pingding infixation is schematized below:

(16) A summary of the development of *l*-infixation in Pingding

Stage	Pattern	Notes	Example
1	r-suffixation		Pekingese
2	r-suffixation plus allophonic [l] insertion	Conditioning factors of [l] insertion present	Yanggu
3	r-suffixation vs *l*-infixation	Conditioning factor lost	Unattested
4	*l*-infixation	Leveling	Pingding

Original suffixation of -*r* (Stage 1) gave rise to the conditioned emergence of a prenucleus lateral like that found in Yanggu (Stage 2). Before the development of a full-blown infixing pattern in Pingding, the original final -*r* must have been lost at some point, leaving an alternation between retroflex lateral infixation in words that begin with anterior sounds, and regular *r*-suffixation in other forms (Stage 3). The available Pingding data does not provide evidence for the independent loss of syllable-final rhotics. However, such a change is observed in neighboring dialects of Mandarin Chinese. Qian *et al.* (1985) report that the words 'child, ear, two', all pronounced as [ɚ] in Standard Chinese, are pronounced as [lə] in some dialects of Mandarin in the Pingdu county of the Shandong Province, while other dialects within the same county vary between [ɚ] and [lə]. Once the rhotic metathesis sound change was complete, the pressure of paradigm leveling must have regularized the infixing pattern (Stage 4). The resultant infixation pattern requires -*l*- be inserted before the nucleus. Thus, when a word is vowel-initial, -*l*- appears as prefixing (e.g., in Pingding *uɤ* 'pot' → *luɤ*).

5.2.1.4 *Summary* The phonetic interpretation of metathesis presupposes the listener's misidentification of the source of certain elongated phonetic cues. This emphasis on long phonetic cues makes two crucial predictions. It restricts the class of metathesizable segments, and by extension the class of metathesis-induced infixes, to labials, palatals, pharyngeals, laryngeals, liquids, and rhotics. It also suggests that metathesis can 'transpose' only one segment at a time. The listener-misperception view of metathesis also explains why the 'transposed' object does not always resemble its original source: metathesis, for the most part, stems from misparsing introduced by coarticulation, and coarticulatory effects often do not exhibit the same phonetic features as their sources.

In this section, I introduced the mechanism of metathesis-induced infixation and explained its properties. The source of reanalysis in the case of metathesis ultimately stems from the infix itself; that is, the ambiguities develop out of the affix in question. In the next section, I review a class of infixes which emerge as victims of their environment. They are helpless orphans, as it were, caught in the fusional forces of grammaticalization.

5.2.2 *Entrapment*

Entrapment refers to the scenario in which a morpheme is stranded between a fossilized composite of an affix and a root. That is, in a composite zyX where z and y are historical adpositional affixes (i.e., prefixes and suffixes), z merges with the root X to form a new root zX, where the independent existence of z or X is no longer recoverable synchronically. The morpheme y is said to be *entrapped* in a form like xyZ, between the historical adfix z and the historical root X. Entrapment is the most often invoked explanation of infix emergence. As noted earlier, Schmidt, Saussure, Boas and Delaria, and Ultan all discuss possible instances of entrapment-based infixation, even if they do not explore the precise mechanism of this process in detail. Many other cases of entrapment have since been proposed, most notably the pronominal infixes in the Nakh-Daghestanian languages (Harris 2002; Nichols 2005). Here, I focus on an example of entrapment found in the languages of the Muskogean family.

5.2.2.1 *Muskogean infixation*   The Muskogean languages of the southeastern United States are divided into four subgroups (classification based on Martin and Munro 2005):

(17) a. Chickasaw and Choctaw (the 'Western' languages)

      b. Alabama and Koasati (and possibly Apalachee)

      c. Hitchiti and Mikasuki

      d. Creek (including Muskogee, Oklahoma Seminole, and the Florida Seminole dialect of Creek)

Several infixation patterns are found in these languages. While their functions range from agreement marking to punctuality, their locations are remarkably restricted. For examples, the plural marker (18a) in Mikasuki and the subject pronominal 'actor' markers (18b) in Koasati appear as the penultimate syllable of the inflected stem.

(18) a. Mikasuki (Martin 1994; Martin and Munro 2005)
          hica 'see' ci-hiːhoːca-laːka 'he will see you all'
          impa-   imhopa-   'eat (PL)'

      b. Koasati   (Haas 1977: 531)
                    huhca 'to dig'

Singular	Plural
1 huhcalí	hulihcá
2 hucihcá	huhacihcá
3 huhcá	huhuhcá

On the other hand, the mediopassive -l- has a post-initial vowel distribution.

(19) Mediopassive -l- infixation (Martin and Munro 2005: 316)
      a. Alabama   oːti 'make a fire'   oːlti 'kindling'
         Chickasaw   oːti 'kindle'   ołti 'be kindled'
      b. Alabama   takco 'rope (v.)'   talikco 'be roped'[6]
         Chickasaw   takci 'tie'   talakci 'be tied'

The pre-final syllable distribution of the Muskogean infixes in (18) is the result of historical fusion of a verb-auxiliary complex. That is, affixes that were historically prefixed to the auxiliary verb are now 'trapped' between the main verb and the historically separate auxiliary. To explain this development more concretely, a brief overview of Proto-Muskogean verbal morphology is in order.

Proto-Muskogean (PM) had an 'active' system of person marking with two series of person markers. Subjects of most transitives and agentive intransitives were marked by Series I markers, while transitive objects and subjects of non-agentive intransitive verbs were marked by Series II. I shall focus on the development of the Series I markers since only the reflexes of this series may appear infixing in the daughter languages. Booker (1979: 33) reconstructs the Proto-Muskogean 'actor' Series I markers as follows:

(20) | | Singular | Dual | Plural |
      |---|---|---|---|
      | 1 | *-li | Excl. *ili- | *ha-ili- |
      | | | Incl. *ili-ho- | |
      | 2 | *či- | | *ha-či- |

There were four voice-related morphological classes of PM verbs: neutral verbs (with no overt marking of voice), middle verbs (with the middle auxiliary *-ka), active verbs (with the active auxiliary *-li), and causative

---

⁶ An epenthetic *i* is inserted before consonant clusters in Alabama and Koasati while a copy of the preceded vowel is inserted in the Western languages.

verbs (generally with causative auxiliary *-či). PM is also reconstructed to
have two verbal paradigms, the DIRECT vs PERIPHRASTIC paradigms. In the
direct paradigm, the person markers were prefixed to the last auxiliary in the
voiced verb class or directly to the lexical verb in the neutral verb class. In
the periphrastic paradigm, an extra auxiliary was added to the main verb and
the person markers were prefixed to this extra auxiliary. The two verbal
paradigms and their person-marking patterns are illustrated in (21). The
schemas are adopted from Martin and Munro (2005), who analyze the
person markers as clitics (CLT). The *-t marker in (21b) indicates same-
subject switch-reference.

(21) a. Proto-Muskogean Direct Paradigm
	Base	Person-marked form
Neutral verb	VERB	CLT-VERB
Voiced verb	VERB AUX	VERB CLT-AUX

 b. Proto-Muskogean Periphrastic Paradigm
	Base	Person-marked form
Neutral verb	VERB	VERB-t CLT-AUX
Voiced verb	VERB AUX	VERB AUX-t CLT-AUX

The infixal distribution of the person markers illustrated in (18b) emerges
partly from the grammaticalization of the once distinct auxiliary verbs. That
is, when the auxiliary fused with the main verb, the person markers previously
prefixed to the auxiliary verb now obtained a penultimate distribution since
the auxiliaries were all monosyllabic. This penultimate distribution of the
person marker was analogically extended to verbs that were neutral and
monomorphemic, like *huhca* 'to dig' in (18b). The Proto-Muskogean plural
*oho- affix developed into a pre-final syllable infix, -*ho*-, in Creek-Seminole
and Hitchiti-Mikasuki (Martin 1994) through essentially the same mechanism. As already illustrated in (18a), the plural -*ho*- appears before the
final syllable. Crucially, the singular stem is monomorphemic.

Besides this grammaticalization-induced pre-final syllable infixation
pattern, as noted earlier, certain affixes in the Muskogean languages show a
post-first vowel distribution (see (19)). For example, the mediopassive
proclitic *il- in PM appears after the applicative *a- and the plural
*oho-. In the Southern Muskogean languages, however, it appears as an
infix. (Data in (22) are drawn from Martin and Munro 2005: 315–16.)

(22) a. PM   *a-p/hica 'look at'   *a-il-p/hica 'be looked at'
          Alabama   a-hica 'watch over'   a-lhica 'be taken care of'
          Chickasaw a-piːsa 'measure'   a-ɬpisa 'be measured'

b. PM   *oho-icca 'shoot'   *oho-il-icca 'be shot'
    Alabama   hocca 'shoot'   holicca 'be shot'
    Choctaw   hõssa 'shoot at'   holisso 'be speckled'

Martin and Munro (2005) attribute the synchronic distribution of this med-iopassive infix to the reanalysis of the prefixes, *a- and *oho-, as part of certain neutral verbs, thus trapping the intervening affix *il-. Subsequent analogical extension to etymological monomorphic forms gives rise to the post-first vowel distribution observed in (19).

5.2.2.2 *Symptoms and predictions of entrapment*   Entrapment as understood in the present work makes several important predictions. To begin with, unlike metathesis (and the other mechanisms to be reviewed below), where the source of ambiguity that triggers reanalysis ultimately stems from the infix itself (i.e., affix-internal pressure), entrapment comes from changes that occur in the environment (i.e., affix-external pressure). The encroachment of the surroundings results in the entrapment of an historical adpositional affix. This means that any adpositional affixes that ordinarily appear in the imperiled location are going to be trapped regardless of their functions or forms. The rise of the pronominal infixes in the Muskogean languages exemplifies this; when the main verb and the auxiliary undergo univerbation, all affixes that were originally prefixed to the auxiliary now appear internal to the univerbated verb+auxiliary complex. This scenario also predicts that languages with entrapment-induced infixes may show what might be referred to as the *Stem-class effect*. That is, an affix might appear in an arbitrary class of stem as infixing, while affixing adpositionally in others. This is a ubiquitous prediction of entrapment not shared by any other pathways to infixation. For example, recall that Proto-Muskogean had an 'actor' person paradigm in (20). While the first-person singular marker suffixed to the main verb or the auxiliary, the other person markers were all prefixing either directly to the main verb or to the auxiliary. As illustrated in (18b), the reflexes of the PM person markers in Koasati may appear infixing within certain verbs. However, person markers may also appear prefixing with respect to other verbs (see (23)). Whether a verb takes prefixal or infixal person markers must be lexically determined. The two classes of verbs cannot be distinguished phonologically.

(23)   *há:lon* 'to hear'   (Kimball 1991: 58)

	Singular	Plural
1	há:lo-l	il-há:l
2	is-há:l	has-há:l
3	ha:l	

Similarly, pronominal affixes in Lakhota (also known as Dakota), a Siouan language, appear infixed in some forms, but not in others, even though phonologically speaking, such stems are nearly identical (24).

(24)   Prefixed stem   Infixed stem   (Albright 2002: 89)
                       nuni 'be lost'   *mani* 'walk'
       1 sg.   wa-nuni   ma-**wa**-ni
       2 sg.   ya-nuni   ma-**ya**-ni

Likewise in Dargi, which belongs to the Lak-Dargi subgroup of the Daghestanian branch of the East Caucasian languages, gender markers (25) may be prefixed (e.g., *B-ak'* 'come', *B-it* 'hit', *B-elč* 'read'), infixed (e.g., *ka<B>iʔ* 'sit down', *ka<B>ac* 'descend', *a<B>ac* 'ascend', *če<B>aʔ* 'see'), or suffixed (e.g., *sa-B* 'be (exist)', *le-B* 'be present (here)').[7]

(25)   Gender affixes in Akusha Dargi (van den Berg 1999)

	Singular	Plural	
		1, 2	3
M	w	d-, -r-, -r	-b
F	r		
N	b	d-, -r-, -r	

Stem-classes are found beyond the domain of person affixes as well. For example, the imperfect in Kentakbong, an Austro-Asiatic language, is marked by the prefixing of *ʔən-* to monosyllabic stems (26a), while infixing *-ən-* to disyllabic stems (26b) (Omar 1975).

(26)   a.   /co/ 'speaks'   ʔənco 'speaks.IMPRF'
             /cãs/ 'excretes'   ʔəncãs 'excretes.IMPRF'
       b.   /citɔh/ 'cooks'   cənitɔh 'cooks.IMPRF'
             /sapoh/ 'sweeps'   sənapoh 'sweeps, is sweeping'

Why does *-ən-* infix to disyllabic words but not to the monosyllabic ones (e.g., *co* 'speaks' → *ʔənco* not **cəno*)? To be sure, the predicted pattern is found in Katu, a language related to Kentakbong, where a VC affix, *-an-*, can be infixed to monosyllabic stems (27), as well as in polysyllabic forms (Costello 1998).

---

[7] Following the notation of van den Berg (1999), the sign < > indicates an infix and a gender class marker is represented by capital *B*.

(27) kui   'to carry on back'   kanui   'something carried on back'
      tôl   'to put post in'   tanôl   'post'
      pó   'to dream'   panó   'a dream'
      kuôl   'to have resources'   kanuôl   'resources, strength'
      têêng 'to work'   tanêêng 'work'
      pók   'to make idol'   panók   'idol'

This stem-class phenomenon is a natural corollary of entrapment. As mentioned above, entrapment results from external pressures operating independently of the entrapped affix in question. As such, the stranded affix falls victim, as it were, to the grammaticalization and fusion of other affixes with the stem. While this scenario predicts the eventual emergence of an infixal distribution of the stranded affix, it also crucially allows for the possibility of the would-be-stranded affix to remain adpositional under the appropriate circumstances. For example, the reason why certain verbs in Koasati conjugate with a prefixal pronominal paradigm rather than an infixal one is because, when inflected in the Direct Paradigm, person markers in PM were prefixed to neutral verbs directly (28a). Verbs in Koasati admit infixal person markers only if the verbs are reflexes of PM voiced verbs inflected in the Direct Paradigm (28b) or verbs, voiced or otherwise, inflected in the Periphrastic Paradigm (28c and d). While the infixal distribution of person markers has apparently been analogically extended to certain original directly inflected neutral verbs, many neutral verbs continue to inflect person information prefixally.

(28)   Direct   Base   Person-marked form   Modern reflex
      a. Neutral verb   VERB   CLT-VERB   >   PREFIX
      b. Voiced verb   VERB AUX   VERB CLT-AUX   >   INFIX
          Periphrastic   Base   Person-marked form   Modern reflex
      c. Neutral verb   VERB   VERB-t CLT-AUX   >   INFIX
      d. Voiced verb   VERB AUX   VERB AUX-t CLT-AUX >   INFIX

The situation in Kentakbong can be understood in a similar way. Schmidt (1906) proposes that infixes in Austro-Asiatic languages today are the result of the fusion of certain historical prefixes with roots. Thus, all else being equal, roots that do not take prefixes historically (e.g., monosyllabic roots today) should not give rise to any infix, as no entrapment could have taken place. On the other hand, the Katu pattern can be understood as the result of a subsequent analogical extension of the infixing pattern to historical monomorphemic forms. Finally, in the case of Dargi, van den Berg notes that the infixal class is likely the result of the development of the local and directional prefixes on the verb into synchronic petrified elements (van den Berg 1999: 167, *n.* 5)

In sum, given our understanding of entrapment, it is not surprising that affixes might develop divergent subcategorization requirements despite their surface homophonous realizations. This balkanizing view of the lexicon and treatment of infixes is supported by the fact that many, if not all, known or suspected cases of entrapment-induced infixation (e.g., Dakota, Lezgian, and the Muskogean languages) only apply to a subset of stems in the language.

A key feature of reanalysis is that ambiguities can often be resolved in multiple ways (cf. CHOICE in Blevins 2004). Morphological parsing ambiguities resulting from entrapment are no different in this regard. An affix that is stranded within a univerbated verb-auxiliary complex can be analogically restored to its adpositional location if the affix's original adpositional distribution is preserved elsewhere in the language. Thus, in the Muskogean case, given the fact that the person markers are realized as strictly prefixing to the formerly directly inflected neutral verbs, the stranded person markers at the stage of univerbation could have been analogically restored to their prefixal patterns with respect to the newly formed verbs. Yet, in Koasati, it is the infixal pattern that is extended, rather than the prefixal paradigm. Why is one analysis preferred over the other? Under such a circumstance, resolution often depends on other factors independent of the affixes in question. In the last chapter, I have advanced one such factor—the Pivot Theory. However, besides considerations from learning, language-internal factors may also tilt the balance toward one analysis over another. A case from Hua illustrates this point.

5.2.2.3 *Hua*   In Hua, a language in the Eastern Highlands of Papua New Guinea, pronominal affixes on transitive verbs and inalienable possessed nouns are generally prefixed, as illustrated in the following paradigm:

(29)			Nominal		Verbal	
Sg.	1		d-za?	'my hand'	d-ge	'he sees me'
	2		g-za?	'your hand'	g-ge	'he sees you'
	3		Ø-za?	'his/her hand'	Ø-ge	'he sees him/her'
Du.	1		ra?-za?	'our hand'	ra?-ge	'he sees us two'
	2/3		pa?-za?	'your/their hand'	pa?-ge	'he sees you/them'
Pl.	1		r-za?	'our hand'	r-ge	'he sees us'
	2/3		p-za?	'your/their hand'	p-ge	'he sees you/him'

However, in a small number of extremely common nominal and verbal roots, all beginning with the stressed sequence *há*, these pronouns are sometimes infixed. There are approximately two dozen such words, but it can be

productively extended even to roots which do not usually occur with
pronouns for semantic reasons (e.g., *háivuva* 'root of tree' → *ha-nd-áivuva*).

(30)   Hua person markers (Haiman 1980: 561)

Person	haipai- 'explain, tell'	hamu?	'namesake'
1 sg.	ha-**nd**-apai-	ha-**nd**-amu?	
2 sg.	ha-**g**-apai-	ha-**g**-amu?	
3 sg.	hapai-	hamu?	
1 du.	ha-**raʔ**-apai-	ha-**raʔ**-amu?	
2/3 du.	faʔapai-	faʔamu?	
1 pl.	ha-**r**-apai-	ha-**r**-amu?	
2/3 pl.	fapai-	famu?	

The person markers must have been historically prefixal, as comparative
evidence from closely related languages suggests. Thus the question one
must address is why infixation only takes place with words that begin with a
há sequence.

Based on the pairs of examples in (31), Haiman (1977) argues that *ha* was
historically a prefix, although its original function is now lost. The prenasalization of *d-* in the 1 sg. form in (30) also suggests that *ha* might have been
originally a proclitic since prenasalization of *b* and *d* generally only occurs
word-initially, not word-internally. Thus, the fact that the 1 sg. form of
'namesake' is *ha-nd-amuʔ* and not **ha-d-amuʔ* shows that *d* must have
been word-initial at some point. The historical prefix *ha-* must have fused
with the root, trapping the pronominals in the process.

(31)

gai	'look after'	ha'gai	'stuff'
u	'go'	'hau	'go up'
to	'leave'	ha'to	'scoop'
go	'see'	ha'go	'well up, gather'
kro	'alight, perch'	ha'kro	'pick leaves'
pai	'harden in fire'	ha'pai	'wring out'
tgi	'split (wood)'	ha'tgi	'finish'

The entrapment analysis predicts, however, that the first-person singular form
of *hamuʔ* 'namesake' should be **ha-nd-muʔ*, not *ha-nd-amuʔ*, as attested.
There is an extra *-a-* in the infixed form that is unaccounted for. Haiman
hypothesizes that pre-Hua speakers, using abductive reasoning (Andersen
1973), must have reinterpreted all words beginning in the stressed *há* as
underlyingly a sequence of *ha+á*, based on the existence of an independent
rule of vowel coalescence that reduces a sequence of identical vowels through
the deletion of the unstressed vowel (e.g., *ha#á* → *há*). This analysis creates an

ambiguity in the third-person singular words. Take, for example, the 3 sg. form of *hámu?* 'namesake'. Following the logic of Watkins' Law, which refers to a situation where a 3 sg. form provides the basis for a visible restructuring of its entire paradigm since it is susceptible to more than one analysis by virtue of a null third-person singular marker (Watkins 1962), Haiman argues that two analyses of *hámu?* 'his namesake' are possible. The third-person singular marker could be analyzed as prefixing (i.e., *Ø+ha+ámu*) or between the prefix *ha* and a hypothetical stem *ámu* (i.e., *ha+Ø+ámu*). Haiman argues that a prohibition of *C+h* sequences in Hua provided the incentive for choosing the infixal over the prefixal analysis. That is, whenever *C+h* sequences might be generated as a result of morpheme concatenation, a periphrasis construction is used instead. For example, when the transitive verb *háko* 'look for' takes a benefactive case, instead of **dhake*, one finds *dgaisi?hake*. A strictly semantic explanation would not be able to account for why *háke* with the null third-person marker is possible (i.e., *háke* 'he looked for him'). In the case of *hámu?* 'namesake', Haiman argues that the analytic ambiguities afforded by the null third-person singular marker must have extended to the other person markers in the paradigm as well. Thus in the case of 'your namesake', two possible analyses became available (i.e., **g+ha+ámu* or **ha+g+ámu*). The prefixing option is duly discouraged as a result of the ban on *C+h* sequences (i.e., **g+ha+ámu*).

The Hua example highlights the fact that the mechanism of entrapment is often part of a larger story behind the creation of new infixes. The main ingredient of an entrapment scenario is the obscuring of morphological boundaries due to morphological fusion between distinct stems and affixes. Harris (2002) refers to such developments as 'univerbation'. But as we have seen in this section, not all entrapment cases involve the fusion of a verb stem with a verbal affix. While entrapment creates the impetus for reanalysis, other aspects of the phonology and morphology of the language might come into play in shaping the destiny of a burgeoning infix.

5.2.2.4 *Summary* This section has introduced and exemplified the mechanism of entrapment. Unlike metathesis, the forces that drive this type of reanalysis originate external to the affix in question. As such, the infixes that have emerged are the victims of happenstance. They are in the wrong place at the wrong time, as it were, and are merely passive participants that are caught in the current of grammaticalization. It is this defenselessness of the affixes that allows entrapment to affect more than one affix at a time. It is also the passivity of the affixes that allows them to preserve their phonological composition, unlike in the case of metathesis. In the next section, I review a class of infixes that is affected by another kind of externally imposed change, but the outcome is far more drastic than in the case of entrapment.

5.2.3 Reduplication mutation

Thus far, I have considered only cases of infixation that developed out of historical adpositional fixed-segment affixes. This section looks at a class of infixes that can all be traced back to some historical adfixal reduplication process. However, the resultant infix often does not bear a close resemblance to its source. To understand this type of change, *reduplication mutation,* let us first look at a simple illustration that does not involve the creation of an infix.

5.2.3.1 *Hausa pluractionals* Pluractional reduplication in Hausa, a Chadic language spoken in Nigeria, historically involved reduplicating the two rightmost syllables of the verb, with the concomitant deletion of the original stem-final vowel (Newman 1971). The reduplicant is bold-faced in the following examples.

(32) *yagala   yagal**gàlaa**   'tear to shreds'
       *kucina   kucin**cìnaa**   'break pieces off'
       *taƙare   taƙar**ƙàree**   'strive hard'

In Hausa today, however, most pluractional verbs are formed by reduplicating the initial CVC of the stem, where C_2 assimilates to the following abutting consonant or undergoes rhotacization.

(33) | Singular | Pluractional | Gloss |
      | --- | --- | --- |
      | tunàa | **tun**tùnaa | 'remind' |
      | gaskàtaa | **gas**gaskàtaa | 'verify' |
      | kaamàa | **kan**kàamaa [**kaŋ**kàamaa] | 'catch' |
      | bugàa | **bub**bùgaa | 'beat' |
      | raatàyaa | **rar**raatàyaa | 'hang' |
      | fita | **fir**fita | 'go out' |

The question here is why the original disyllabic suffixing reduplication pattern was replaced by a prefixing CVC-reduplication pattern. Newman (1971) attributes this shift to the reinterpretation of surface ambiguous output strings. Specifically, stem-final vowel dropping in the environment of suffixation, a process that is still active today, created favorable conditions for various phonological processes that target preconsonantal consonants. These phonological processes had many effects on the stem consonant (e.g., the result of final vowel dropping) immediately preceding the reduplicant. A summary with illustrations of these processes is given in (34). The affected segment is underlined.

(34)   Rhotacization of a coda consonant: **gadgadaa > gar̃gadaa* 'rutted road'
Place assimilation of a coda nasal: **jàar̃ùmtakàa > jàar̃ùntakàa* 'bravery'
Complete assimilation of certain consonants: **zàafzaafaa > zàzzaafaa* 'very hot'
Shortening of long vowels and lowering of mid vowels in closed syllables:
*saaboon gidaan àbookiinsà > saaban gidan àbookinsà 'his friend's new house'

Some examples illustrating these processes in pluractional reduplication are given below:

(35)

Singular	Historical Pluractional	Actual Pluractional	Gloss
fita	→ **fitfita*	> fir̃fita	'go out'
bugáa	→ **bugbuga*	> bubbúgaa	'beat'
jéefaa	→ **jeefjeffa*	> jájjeefáa	'throw'
soomáa	→ **soomsooma*	> sansóomaa	'begin'

Newman argues that the reduplicant of the pluractional forms retains the full form of the underlying verb in the case of the disyllabic stems due to these phonological processes, while the original stem was deformed, in some cases, quite drastically. Thus, presumably due to the effect of paradigm uniformity between the singular and pluractional forms (e.g., *bugàa/bubbùgaa* 'beat'; *soomàa/sansòomaa* 'begin'), the pluractional form is reanalyzed morphologically in such a fashion that the positions of the stem and the reduplicant are reversed, as illustrated by the examples below.

(36)

*bubbúgaa	> bubbúgaa	'beat'
*fir̃fita	> fir̃fita	'go out'
*jájjeefáa	> jájjeefáa	'throw'
*sansóomaa	> sansóomaa	'begin'

Thus Hausa pluractional construction illustrates the general phenomenon of reanalysis induced by ambiguities between the identities of the base and the reduplicant. In the present case, it is the historical base of reduplication that is altered by sound changes, which prompted speakers to identify the historical reduplicant as the base, as it resembles more closely the non-reduplicated stem than the actual historical base.

(37)
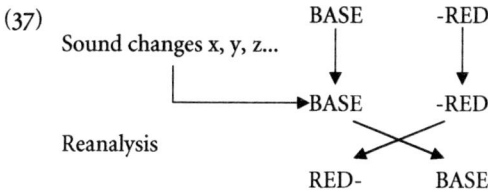

Sound changes x, y, z...

Reanalysis

This type of morphological change comes close to being an instance of morphological metathesis since reduplication-mutation involves morphemes exchanging linear position, say, from suffixing to prefixing (e.g., *Xa* > *aX*, where X is the root, while *a* denotes an affix). As illustrated in the next section, this appearance of morphological metathesis is less clear when the result of reduplication-mutation is internal reduplication, however.

5.2.3.2 *Hopi plural formation*   An infixal analog to the Hausa example is found in Hopi. The plural in nouns is traditionally marked by prefixing CV-prefixing reduplication in Hopi (Jeanne 1982). In the plural, the root vowel is shortened if it is underlyingly long (38a), otherwise, it disappears (38b).[8]

(38) a. | Singular | Plural | Gloss |
|---|---|---|
| saaqa | saasaqa | 'ladder' |
| tooci | tootoci | 'shoe' |
| siivɨ | siisivɨ | 'pot' |
| sooya | soosoya | 'planting stick' |
| nova | noonova | 'food' |
| moosa | moomosa | 'cat' |

b. | koho | kokho | 'wood' |
|---|---|---|
| como | cocmo | 'hill' |
| leŋu | lelŋi | 'tongue' |
| poyo | popyo | 'knife' |

[8] Jeanne (1982) argues that vowel reduction is the result of interconsonantal vowel deletion (V → Ø / VC __ C0V), although this rule applies to a subset of lexical items only (e.g., *pitanakci* 'hat' not *pitnakci*). However, upon closer examination, it seems possible that vowel reduction is stress-conditioned. In particular, this appears to be an instance of post-tonic vowel reduction. In the reduplicated forms, stress is always on the first syllable. This means that, prior to the development of vowel reduction, stress would have been on the root vowel. Thus a form like *láho* 'bucket' would have been reduplicated as *lálaho* (the reduplicant is underlined). Assuming that post-tonic vowel reduction caused the root vowel to disappear, then the modern-day reflex should be *lálho*. This prediction is borne out. This historical analysis crucially assumes that the stress assignment on reduplicated forms differs from that of the unreduplicated forms in Pre-Hopi, however. In Hopi today, stress is on the initial syllable if the initial syllable is heavy (= CVː, CVC), otherwise, stress is on the second syllable. Thus, stress is on the second syllable in words like *laqána* 'squirrel' and *tayáti* 'to laugh', not *láqana* or *táyati* respectively. Further research is needed to ascertain the validity of this post-tonic vowel reduction analysis.

laho	lalho	'bucket'
caqapta	cacqapta	'dish'
kɨyapi	kɨkyapi	'dipper'
melooni	memlooni	'melon'

c.

Singular	Plural	Gloss
patŋa	paavatŋa	'squash'
poosi	poovosi	'eyes'
paasa	paavasa	'fields'
paahɨ	paavahɨ	'water'

According to Kershner (1999), younger speakers of Hopi have developed internal reduplication. The evidence concerns the behavior of the set of p-initial forms in (38c). The main contention with respect to the examples in (38c) concerns the status of ν in Hopi. According to Jeanne (1982), ν is an allophone of /p/ in the speech of the older speakers of Hopi (OG). This is evidenced by the alternation of root-initial /p/ to [v] under prefixation (39). In contrast, younger speakers of Hopi (YG) have innovated a phoneme /v/, as shown by the non-alternation of /p/ and /v/ in intervocalic position (e.g., *ʔipava* 'my elder brother').

(39)

Bare		OG	YG	
poosi	'eye'	ʔi-vosi	ʔi-posi	'my eye'
poyo	'knife'	ʔi-voyo	ʔi-poyo	'my knife'
paasa	'field'	ʔi-vasa	ʔi-pasa	'my field'
pono	'stomach'	ʔi-vono	ʔi-pono	'my stomach'
paava	'elder brother'	ʔi-vava	ʔi-pava	'my elder brother'

The restoration of [p] in intervocalic position by the young Hopi speakers renders the allophonic status of ν opaque, which in turn obscures the original prefix-plus-root relationship in the case of reduplication. The prefixal analysis of the reduplicant is no longer recoverable based on the surface forms. A schematic representation of the shift from prefixing reduplication to internal reduplication in Hopi is shown in (40).

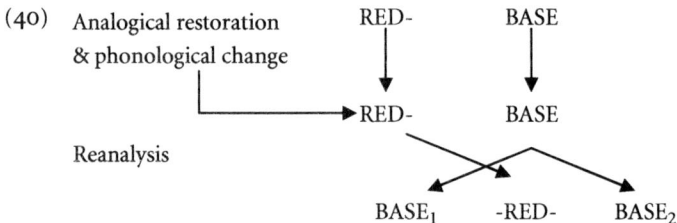

(40)   Analogical restoration
        & phonological change   RED-   BASE

        Reanalysis   RED-   BASE

        BASE$_1$ -RED-   BASE$_2$

Previously, a form like *poovosi* 'eyes' could be analyzed as the result of prefixing reduplication with lenition of the root-initial /p/ and shortening of the root-vowel. After the phonemicization of /v/, it is no longer clear how *v* can be related to the bare form *poosi* 'eye'. In fact, [p] appears to have become an allophone of /v/. That is, /v/ 'hardens' to [p] in coda position (e.g., *heeva* 'to find' becomes *hepnɨ́* 'to find.FUT'). Pressures of paradigm uniformity should therefore favor analyzing the internal -*vo*- string as the exponent of the plural feature (i.e., *poosi*: *poo-vo-si*, not *poo-vosi*) since the infixing analysis offers a more transparent mapping from the singular to the plural. To be sure, the precondition for an internal reduplication analysis of Hopi nominal plural formation is already present in the speech of the older generation of Hopi speakers. That is, as a result of vowel reduction, the root vowel may be completely eliminated in the reduplicated form when the root vowel is underlyingly short (see (38a)). But since vowel reduction is a productive phenomenon in the language, the disappearance of the root vowel is to be expected. Thus whether or not the reduplicative pattern of the older generation Hopi speakers should be considered an instance of internal reduplication is a matter of theoretical debate. Many languages show reduplicative alternation similar to that found in Hopi (see also the discussion on Northern Interior Salish diminutive reduplication below). Depending on their theoretical inclinations, analysts often differ in their interpretations of such patterns. For example, in Pima, a Uto-Aztecan language related to Hopi, plurality is marked by C or CV reduplication similar to that found in Hopi. (Examples are taken from Riggle 2006.)

(41) a.
Singular	Plural	Gloss
mavit	mamvit	'lion'
koson	kokson	'pack rat'
sipuk	sispuk	'cardinal'

   b.
havol	hahavol	'lima bean'
ʔiput	ʔiʔiput	'circle'
gogs	gogogs	'dog'

While Pima plural reduplication may be analyzed as a case of prefixing reduplication (i.e., root vowel deletion applied to (41a) but not in (41b)), Riggle (2006) argues that an infixal interpretation offers a more straightforward and theoretically more restrictive analysis.[10] This type of analytic

---

[9] The shortening of long vowels is due to a productive rule of closed syllable shortening in the language.

[10] Riggle considers infixing -C- reduplication to be the primary strategy of plural formation in Pima. CV- reduplication only takes place when the result of C- reduplication would create illicit codas or consonant sequences.

ambiguity is to be expected from the perspective of language change. The changes that obscure the identity relations between the reduplicant and the base are blind to the global consequences induced by the change. The ramifications are for subsequent learners to sort out. In the present context, whether a reduplicative pattern should be analyzed as prefixing or infixing is underdetermined based on the corpus available to the learner (and to the linguist). It is often the case that only upon further changes to the language will learners converge on a uniform analysis.

I review below a variety of scenarios that can give rise to reduplication mutation. This presentation makes no pretense to be a comprehensive survey of all instances of reduplication mutation. Such an exhaustive survey would be untenable, in my view, since the effects of sound change in a language are invariably confounded by the phonological and morphological system of the language. The illustrations below are meant to demonstrate the intricacies involved in the development of an infix under reduplication mutation. Unlike entrapment, the shape of the resultant infix can be quite different from the historical source. This brief survey begins with a case of reduplication with fixed segmentism in Trukese.

5.2.3.3 *Trukese durative*   In Trukese, an Austronesian language spoken in Micronesia, pluractionality is generally marked by CVC reduplication on consonant-initial verbs, as illustrated below (Goodenough and Sugita 1980):

(42) fætæn 'walk'   → fæf-fætæn   'be in the habit of walking'
      mɔːt   'sit'   → mɔm-mɔːt   'be sitting'
      sɔtu- 'attempt' → sɔs-sɔt   'be sitting'

However, when the verb begins with a vowel or *w* (the only word-initial glide), the infix or prefix -*Vkk*-, where 'V' is a copy of the following vowel, is used instead. The verb 'drink' illustrates an instance of the *w*-insertion sound change (i.e., *inu > *wɨn*).

(43) wɨn   'drink'   → w-ɨkk-ɨn   'be in the habit of drinking'
      wiik   'week'   → w-ikk-iik   'be for a number of weeks'
      isɔni   'keep it'   → ikk-isɔni   'be keeping it'
      ɔsɔmʷoːnu   'pay chiefly → ɔkk-ɔsɔmʷoːnu   'be in the habit of paying
                       respects to'   chiefly respects to'

This infix is the result of the general loss of word-initial *k in durative verbs with original initial *k (i.e., **kVk-k-* > *Vkk-) (Garrett 2001; Goodenough and Sugita 1980; Goodenough 1963).

(44) Pre-Trukic   Trukese
      *kana-   ana-   'classifer: food'
      *kakaká:su   əkkə:s   'treat as a sibling-in-law of the same sex'
      *kasam^{w}ó:nu ɔsɔm^{w}o:nu 'pay chiefly respect to'

The reason for the *kVk-k- > *Vkk- reanalysis can be most effectively
illustrated with a word like ɔsɔm^{w}o:nu 'pay chiefly respect to'. Historically, it
was *kasam^{w}ó:nu and its reduplicated form would presumably be *kak-
kasam^{w}ó:nu. After the dropping of the initial *k, the reduplicated form
became *ak-kasam^{w}ó:nu, which was then reanalyzed as *akk-asam^{w}ó:nu, as
*kasam^{w}ó:nu would have become *asam^{w}ó:nu. This -Vkk- prefix was then
generalized to originally vowel-initial verbs. The -Vkk- infix did not emerge
until a subsequent change of w-insertion, however.

(45) *kóta   wo:t   'coconut-husking stick'
     *ínu   wɨn   'drink'
     *kuku   wɨ:k   'fingernail'
     *kúru   wur   'play'

This prevocalic w-insertion process, which affected certain vowel-initial
words, created synchronic base → durative alternations of the pattern wV-
→ wVkkV-. For example, the reduplicated form of the word wo:t 'coconut-
husking stick' would have been *kok-kota historically. It became *ok-kotta as a
result of initial-k dropping. The w-insertion process took place, giving rise to
*wokkotta. Since -Vkk- can be independently established based on other vowel-
initial forms that remain vowel-initial, *wokkotta was analyzed as *w-okk-otta.

   Ultan (1975) takes this to be a case of entrapment. But as the above
diachronic explanation illustrated, -Vkk- was never a morpheme in
Pre-Trukese, and so the notion of entrapment does not apply here. The
emergence of the -Vkk- infix was the result of a series of isolated developments in the phonology of Trukese that obscured the reduplicative morphology of Trukese durative formation. This aspect of the development of
the -Vkk- infix in Trukese is particularly noteworthy because it resulted in a
reduplication pattern with fixed segmentism. As will be illustrated in the next
section, reduplication mutation may also give rise to fixed-segment infixes
that have lost their reduplicative characters completely.

5.2.3.4 *Yurok intensive* Yurok is an Algic language spoken in northwestern
California. Intensification is marked by the insertion of -eg- after the onset
of the stem, including onset clusters. The orthographic 'g' represents
phonetically a voiced velar fricative [ɣ]. There are no vowel-initial roots in this
language. The intensive is an event-external repetition marker that produces a

variety of meanings (e.g., frequentative with activity verbs or intensity with verbs of experienced state; for more discussion, see Wood and Garrett 2003).

(46)   Yurok intensive (Garrett 2001: 269)

Base		Intensive
laːy-	'to pass'	legaːy-
koʔmoy-	'to hear'	kegoʔmoy-
tewomeł	'to be glad'	tegewomeł
łkyork^w-	'to watch'	łkyegork^w-
trahk-	'to fetch'	tregahk-

Garrett (2001) argues that the -*eg*- infix arose from the reinterpretation of historical monosyllabic *Ce*-reduplication. He argues that Yurok *C(C)e*-intensive reduplication is a reflex of Algic *C(C)eː*- reduplication (47).

(47)   Algic *C(C)eː*->Ritwan **C(C)a*-> Yurok **C(C)e*- (Garrett 2001: 293)

Garrett argues that the -*eg*- infix has its origin in the reduplicated form of *h*-initial stems. Several pieces of evidence illustrate this point. To begin with, only *h in *h*-initial stems, but no other initial consonant (48), was absorbed when combined with pronominal prefixes, creating surface forms such as those schematized in (48c) (examples taken from Garrett 2001: 289).

(48)   a.

helomey-	'to dance'	ʔnelomeyekʷ	'I dance'
hunkeks	'to open'	ʔnunkeksokʷ	'I open'
hoːloh	'basket'	kʼoːloh	'your basket'
haʔaːg	'rock'	ʔwaʔaːg	'her, his, etc. rock'

   b.

tmoːl-	'to shoot'	ʔne-tmoːlokʷ	'I shoot'
skewipʼ-	'to put in order'	kʼe-skewipʼakʷ	'you (sg.) put in order'
tepoː	'tree'	ʔwe-tepoː	'her, his, etc. tree'

   c.   Original *h*-initial stem:
   verb *hVC- → intensive *he-hVC-
   Pronominal perfixes:
   *ʔn-VC (etc.) → intensive *ʔn-e-hVC- (etc.)

A subsequent intervocalic *h > *g* change, as partially demonstrated by the data in (49a), yielded intensive forms that seem to be formed by -*eg*- infixation (49b).

(49)   a.   /ʔo heʔm/ → ʔo geʔm 'there s/he said'   (Robins 1958: 157)
          /ʔo hoːkʼʷc/ → ʔo goːkʼʷc 'there s/he gambled' (Robins 1958: 155)

   b.   Original *h*-initial stems:
   verb *hVC-   →   intensive *heg*VC-
   *ʔnVC- (etc.) →   intensive **ʔneg*VC- (etc.)

Garrett argues that it is based on these apparent infixation patterns that the -*eg*- infix was extended to other consonant-initial stems. Some contemporary *h*-initial forms still preserve the original pattern without any morphological change (50a), while other isolated examples preserve relics of the *Ce*- intensive reduplication pattern (50b) (examples taken from Garrett 2001: 293–5).

(50)   Base verb   Intensive

    a. heʔwoniɬ-   'to wake up' (intr.)   *he-heʔwoniɬ->*hegeʔwoniɬ-
                                                >huːʔwoniɬ-

        hohkum-   'to make'   *he-hohkum>hegohkum-
        hoʔomah   'to make fire together'   *he-hoʔomah>hegoʔomah-
        hoːkʷc-   'to gamble'   *he-hoːkʷc->hegoːkʷc-

    b. ckɪkɪː?   'to pierce'   ckɪckɪkɪː?   'to pierce repeatedly'
        kelomen-   'to turn' (trans)   kekelomen-   'to turn several things'
        *keʔy-   kekeʔy(eɬ-)   'to shine'
        *lek-   'to fall down'   leɬken-   'to throw, to scatter'
        ʔekol-   'to hover'   ʔeʔekol-   'to hover repeatedly'

The origins of the -*Vkk*- durative infix in Trukese and the -*eg*- infix in Yurok illustrate an important point. Infixes resulting from reduplicant mutation have their origins in the obscuring of the reduplicant-base boundary. While the sources of ambiguity may stem from quite different motivations—initial-*k* deletion and subsequence *w*-insertion in Trukese, intervocalic *h > *g* in Yurok—the nature of the end effect is comparable: the precise juncture between the reduplicant and the base is blurred. As the original morphological analysis is no longer readily recoverable from the data, the learner, through abductive reasoning (Andersen 1973; Haiman 1977), develops his/her own theory of morphological composition. In the present case, the infixing analysis prevailed.

    An important factor that increases the opacity between the reduplicant and base is lexical stress. The influence of stress on the development of internal reduplication has already been alluded to in the case of plural reduplication in Hopi. Here, I consider the case of infixal diminutive reduplication in several North Interior Salish languages. This case study also provides an instructive example of how prominence-driven infixes may come about.

5.2.3.5 *Northern Interior Salish diminutives*   The Interior Salish languages, divided into the Northern and Southern branches, consist of the following languages:

(51)   **Northern**   **Southern**
        Lillooet   Coeur d'Alene

Thompson River Salish   Kalispel-Spokane-Flathead
Shuswap   Colville-Okanagan
Columbian

In the Northern Interior Salish languages, diminutives are often marked by infixing a copy of the pretonic consonant after the stressed vowel. In some instances, a copy of the stressed vowel appears in the reduplicant as well.

(52) a. Thompson River Salish (Thompson and Thompson 1996)

Base		Diminutive	
cʔyʔé	'basket'	cʔyʔeyʔ	'favorite (or cute) basket'
s+xénʔx	'rock'	sxéxnʔx	'small rocky hill'
s+mɣéwʔ	'lynx'	smɣéɣuʔ	'lynx cub'
kʔʷáxʷe	'box'	kʔʷákʔʷxʷe	'small box'
twít	'he grows'	twíwʔt	'young man 18–30 years old'
xéʔ	'up high'	xéxeʔ	'a little higher'

b. Shuswap (Kuipers 1974)

sícʔm	'blanket'	síscʔm	'small blanket'
kykéyt	'chickenhawk'	kykékyt	'small chickenhawk'
cwéx	'creek'	cwéwx	'small creek, brook'
twít	'he grows up'	twíwt	'young boy'
cítxʷ	'house'	cíctxʷ	'little house'
tsún=kʷ-m	'island'	tsúsnkʷm	'small island'

c. Lilloet (van Eijk 1997: 60)

ʔáma	'good'	ʔáʔma	'pretty, cute, funny'
p'aʔxʷ	'more'	p'ə́p'ʔaxʷ	'a little bit more'
ʔawʔt	'late, behind'	ʔáʔwʔt	'a little bit later'
səmɣáw	'lynx'	səmɣə́ɣəwʔ	'little lynx'
s-yáqcaʔ	'woman'	s-yə́yʔqcaʔ	'girl'
twit	'good hunter'	twiwʔt	'boy, young man'

The infixal pattern does not only target the root consonant before the stressed vowel, however. Any consonant immediately preceding the stressed vowel, regardless of whether or not it is part of the root, may be copied (see (53)).

(53) a. Thompson River Salish (Thompson and Thompson 1996)

łaʔχ=áns	'(grown person) eats'	łaʔχáχnʔs
qʷəłqʷłi-n=éłmx	'birch-bark basket'	qʷəłqʷłinénłmx

'(baby or animal) eats'
'small birch-bark baskets'

b. Shuswap (Kuipers 1974)

xʷəxʷy=éwt	'absent, delayed'	xʷəxʷyéywt	'a loan, credit'
x+kʔm=íknʔ	'back side'	xkʔmímknʔ	'upper back'
tʔqʷ=éws	'both, together'	tʔqʷéqʷws	'companion, comrade'
pésəɬ=kʷe	'lake'	pépsəɬkʷe	'small lake'

c. Lillooet (van Eijk 1997: 60)

palʔ-áʔqaʔ   'one-year-old buck'
               (*pála* 'one', *aqaʔ* 'barrel, cylindrical object')

wʔəwʔp-l-ílcʼaʔ   'caterpillar' (√*wəp* 'hair', -*l*- connective,
               -*icʼaʔ* 'skin')

χəcp-qíqənʔ-kst 'hundred'
               (*χəcp* element used in numerical units, -*qinʔ-kst*
               'finger [tip]')

Anderson (1996) argues that the diminutive was historically a CV prefix, particularly since languages outside of the immediate Northern sub-branch of the Interior Salish family have only the prefixing C(V) diminutive reduplication construction.

(54)

Colville	kə-kwápaʔ		'dog'
	s-tə-taɬm		'little dog'
Kalispel	sɬ-kʷ-kʷɬʼus		'little face'
	ɬ-pu-ps		'kitten'
Spokane	χ-χɬʼəcin		'dog'
	lʼúlʼəkʷ		'small stick of wood'
Coeur d'Alene	hin-qʔu-qʔušəmʔíčnʔšənʔ		'dog'
	šə-šəlʔúlʔumʔxʷnʔ		'hoe'

Related languages outside of the Interior Salish family also display prefixing CV diminutive reduplication. Examples from Lushootseed, which belongs to the Central Salish family, are given below:

(55) Lushootseed diminutive (Bates, Hess, and Hilbert 1994)

Singular		Plural	
s-qʷəbáyʔ	'dog'	s-qʷíqʷəbayʔ	'puppy'
s-tiqíw	'horse'	s-títiqiw	'pony'
tʃáləs	'hand'	tʃátʃaləs	'little hand'
s-túbʃ	'man'	s-tútubʃ	'boy'
χáhəb	'cry'	χáχahəb	'an infant crying'

Anderson hypothesizes that the infixing reduplicative pattern in the Northern Interior Salish languages is the result of the copying of an historical stressed reduplicative prefix that got reinterpreted as a stress-targeting reduplication pattern. While Anderson's analysis is reasonable, it remains unclear how the reinterpretation might have come about. In what follows, I show that reinterpretation toward the infixal analysis was the result of post-tonic vowel reduction/deletion in the Northern Interior Salish languages. Post-tonic vowel reduction can still be observed in certain completely lexicalized forms (i.e., the ones where diminutive meaning is no longer transparent) in these languages. Some examples from Lillooet are given in (56), showing that the post-tonic vowel is reduced to a schwa (see also the discussion below on Spokane).

(56)   Lillooet (van Eijk 1997: 60)
      púpən 'to find by accident'   (*pun* 'to find')
      cícəl 'new'   (*cil-kst* 'five' with -*kst* 'hand')
      lúləm 'jealous in matters of love' (*lúm-ən* 'to accuse, suspect smb., tr.')
      qíqəlʔ 'weak'   (no simplex, but cf. *qlil* 'angry'[11])

Stress is morphologically governed in the Northern Interior Salish languages, and in Interior Salish languages in general. Prefixes do not normally attract stress. Why then was the prefixing diminutive reduplicant stress-bearing? Based on evidence from a cognate diminutive reduplication pattern in Spokane, a Southern Interior Salish language, I argue that the stress-bearing property of the diminutive prefix is to be expected, at least prior to the development of the infixal pattern.

Spokane diminutive reduplication. Diminutives in Spokane are marked by prefixing reduplication of the first CV of the root and the glottalization of the resonants in the resulting word. The data below show strong and weak CVC roots under the diminutive construction.

(57)   a. Strong roots (Bates and Carlson 1998: 118)
        kʷúkʷʼlʼ   'something small is created, made'
        lʼúlʼkʷ   'it's a little stick of wood'
        nʼínʼčʼ-mʼnʼ   'knife, jackknife'
        s-xʷúxʷyʼ-eʔ   'an ant'

     b. Weak roots
        ššílʼ   'a small thing is chopped'
        cʼcʼúrʼ   'a little thing is sour/salty'
        qqép   'soft, diminutive'
        ppínʼ   'a little bent'

---

[11] This is likely to be a form derived from the Out-of-Control -VC reduplication, although van Eijk does not explicitly clarify this.

Two aspects of these examples must be highlighted. The fact that the diminutive prefix is stressed in the presence of a strong root but not in the weak roots is important; it is in accordance with the rules of stress assignment in Spokane. Stress is generally morphologically determined in Interior Salish languages. We can distinguish between roots that are stressed in the presence of suffixes ('strong' roots) and those that are unstressed in the presence of suffixes ('weak' roots). In Spokane, strong roots are stressed when no strong suffixes are present (58a). Various suffixes are stressed when they occur with weak roots or suffixes (58b), but are unstressed with both strong roots and suffixes (58a). Weak suffixes contain no vowels and are never stressed. Weak roots are stressed when they occur without suffixes or with weak suffixes (58c).

(58)   Examples of Spokane stress assignment (Carlson 1989: 205)

      a. $/\sqrt{k'}ul'$-nt-ex^w/[12]   [k'úl'ntx^w]

             S -W-V   'You made it'

             make, do-TRANS-2S

      b. $/\sqrt{}$šil-nt-ex^w/   [šlntéx^w]

             W-W-V   'You chopped it'

             chop-TRANS-2S

      c. /hec-$\sqrt{}$šil/   [hecšíl]

             -W   'It's chopped'

             PROG-chop

Bates and Carlson (1998) analyze Spokane stress as follows: stress is on the left of a strong root's domain, while weak roots are 'post-stressing', building a foot starting immediately to the root's right. However, when a weak root lacks a vowel to its right, as in the reduplicated forms above, the default final stress obtains. As Bates and Carlson argue, the diminutive reduplicant is within the domain of stress assignment. Another issue related to stress concerns the phenomenon of vowel deletion. As illustrated in the diminutive forms of the strong roots (57a), there is a productive process of unstressed vowel deletion in Spokane, which also applies to reduplicative as well as non-reduplicative forms (e.g., $k^w úl'ntex^w \rightarrow k^w úl'ntx^w$ 'make, 2nd person'; Bates and Carlson 1998: 103).

    Here, I propose that the seed for infixing reduplication can be found in the reduplicated strong roots in Spokane. Specifically, it is the reduction of unstressed vowels that is the smoking gun. Historical CV-prefixing diminutive reduplication (i.e., $'C_iV$-$\sqrt{}C_iVC$)[13] was reinterpreted as infixing -C- reduplication due to the absence of the root vowel (i.e., $*'C_iV$-$\sqrt{}C_i(\vartheta)C >$ $'\sqrt{}C_iV$-C_i-C). In particular, what appears to have happened is that the

---

[12] The root is indicated by the $\sqrt{}$ sign.   [13] The reduplicant is underlined.

reduplication pattern of weak roots has leveled toward the pattern of the strong roots in the Northern Interior languages. The question here is why leveling favored the strong roots' reduplicative pattern, rather than that of the weak roots. The answer lies in the interaction of stress and vowel deletion with double reduplication. (59) illustrates what happens when a root undergoes double reduplication (i.e., CV-prefixing diminutive and VC-suffixing out-of-control reduplication). Recall that stress is on the diminutive prefix when a strong root is reduplicated, while stress is on the weak roots itself when diminutivized.

(59)   Diminutivized out-of-control forms in Spokane (Carlson 1989: 210)
    a. m'é-m'ł'-ł'   'A little thing got mixed by accident'
       DIM-mix-OC

    b. š-šl'-íl'   'Small things got all cut up'
       DIM-chop-OC

As shown in (59a), stress is on the diminutive reduplicant of the strong root /meł'/ 'mix' (i.e., *m'ém'łł'*), while stress is on the out-of-control suffix following the weak root /šil/ 'chop' (59b) (i.e., *ššlíl'*). What is of particular interest here is that no trace of the vowel of the weak root remains in (59b), which gives rise to a potential ambiguity in the morphological analysis of the diminutive and the root. It is this ambiguity that serves as the pivotal context which tilts the balance toward analyzing diminutive reduplication as infixing. To clarify this scenario, a schematic representation of the development of Northern Interior Salish infixing diminutive reduplication, particularly in the out-of-control context, is given in below.

(60)   The proposed origin of North Interior Salish infixing diminutive reduplication

	Strong roots	Weak roots	
Stage 1	$'C_iV$-√C_iVC-VC	C_iV-√C_iVC-$'VC$	Pre-Northern Interior Salish
Stage 2	$'C_iV$-√$C_i(ə)C$-$(ə)C$	$C_i(ə)$-√$C_i(ə)C$-$'VC$	Vowel reduction/deletion
Stage 3	$'C_iVC_iC$-C or	C_iC_iC-$'VC$ or	Ambiguity betweenin fixing vs
	$'C_iVC_iC$-C	C_iC_iC-$'VC$	prefixing reduplication
Stage 4	$'√C_iVC_iC$-C	$'√C_iC_iC$-$'VC$	Leveling toward infixation

Diminutive reduplication in pre-Northern Interior Salish was originally prefixing. The diminutive reduplicant was stressed in the strong roots (Stage 1), causing the root vowel to be reduced or deleted (Stage 2), thus creating an opaque situation in which the historical prefixing nature of the diminutive reduplicant was no longer straightforwardly recoverable. This opaque situation gave rise to the possibility of an infixing analysis of diminutive reduplication (Stage 3) due to the absence of the root vowel. Crucially, the diminutive form of the weak root is consistent with the infixing analysis. Finally, the infixal pattern won out over the prefixal pattern presumably due to the paradigm uniformity effect (e.g., *meƛ'* 'mix' vs *m'ém̓ƛ'* 'DIM-mix').

Northern Interior Salish infixal diminutive reduplication thus emerged out of an ambiguity in the relationship between the reduplicant and the root introduced by the post-tonic deletion of root vowels. This case study illustrates how a prominence-driven pattern emerges out of an original non-stress-related prefixing reduplication. One aspect of this pattern deserves special emphasis. Unlike the other cases reviewed, stress is the main source of ambiguity that led to morphological reanalysis. However, the antecedent construction itself is not prominence-driven. The association between diminutive reduplication and stress assignment observed today is a coincidence of history. To be sure, the transformation from a non-prominence-driven pattern to a prominence-driven one is not a priori a necessary outcome. In the case of the Northern Interior Salish languages, the prominence-driven analysis prevails because not all roots contain a root vowel. The lack of consistency in the segmental pivot might have prompted listeners to opt for the more reliable prominence-driven analysis.

5.2.3.6 *Summary*   This section illustrates how phonological and morphological 'erosions' can obscure the relationship between the base and the reduplicative affix, which ultimately may force a reanalysis of the morphological structure of the base+reduplicant complex. A unique characteristic of infixes that emerges from reduplication mutation is that the resultant infix not only may be unfaithful to its historical antecedent, but also might not be reduplicative at all. This gives the impression that the resultant infix sprang out of nowhere. Fixed-segment infixation that has a reduplicative antecedent is therefore generally difficult to detect. It is important to note that, while reduplication mutation gives rise to fixed-segment infixation, fixed-segment infixation does not seem to ever give rise to internal reduplication. This asymmetry is to be expected. A fixed-segment infix emerges out of reduplication due to the dissociation between the reduplicant and the base, which results from the loss of identity between the reduplicant and base caused by independent sound changes. On the other hand, a robust identity relation between a fixed-segment affix and the stem is far less likely to obtain since the phonological composition of the stem often does not coincide with that of the affix. This asymmetry may have contributed to the overwhelming number of fixed-segment infixes relative to internal reduplication.

The diachronic typological survey thus far reveals that many infixes originate from adpositional affixes. This coverage is of course incomplete. Many modern-day infixes can be traced back to historical infixes while others may have no historical antecedent at all. This is the topic of the next section.

5.2.4 *Morphological excrescence and prosodic stem association*

Many infixes have infixal antecedents. For example, the -*um*- and -*in*- infixes found in many of the Austronesian languages have been reconstructed for Proto-Austronesian (Dahl 1976). Similarly, the -*Vl*- infix in several varieties of Chinese languages are reconstructed for Archaic Chinese as an -**r*- infix.[14] Examples from Yimeng 伊盟, the Chinese name of Ih Ju League, an administrative division of Inner Mongolia, and Huojia 獲嘉 in Henan are given in (61).

(61)   a.   Yimeng -*l*- infixation (Li 1991; cited in Sagart 2000)[15]

pai^3	擺	'to a gitate'	pə(ʔ)lai^3	'to swing, oscillate'
pən^1	奔	'to run'	pə(ʔ)lən^1	'to run on all sides'
xua^4	劃	'to draw'	xuə(ʔ)la^4	'to scribble'
təu^1	兜	'hood, hanging pouch'	tə(ʔ)ləu^1	'cluster(s) of fruit hanging from branches'
khu^3		'box of a wheel'	khuə(ʔ)lu^3	'wheel(s) of a car'

   b.   Huojia -*l*- infixation (He 1989; cited in Sagart 2000)

paʔ	拔	'pull out, choose, select, pick'	pə(ʔ)laʔ	'manipulate an object, as an abacus'
pai	擺	'sway, wave'	pə(ʔ)lai	'move back and forth'
pʰau	刨	'dig'	pʰə(ʔ)lau	'dig repeatedly'
pʰəŋ	篷	'covering, awning, canopy'	pʰə(ʔ)lə ŋ	'covering, awning, canopy (on a chariot; branches and foliage on a tree)'

---

[14] Note that this *-r- infix is not the historical antecedent of the retroflex lateral infix in Pingding and Yanggu discussed in Section 5.2.1.3 (see Yu 2004*b* for details).

[15] Sagart notes that the glottal stop at the end of the first syllable of an infixed form is probably inserted by the original investigators to indicate the shortness of the vowel and is not phonetically realized in normal speech.

Since the infixal distribution of these affixes is inherited, I shall have little to add in regard to the origins of these infixes.

Infixes may also have no historical antecedent, adpositional or otherwise. Haspelmath refers to this type of morphological creation as morphological excrescence (Haspelmath 1995); that is, an affix emerges in a language without an immediately historical antecedent. For example, a set of infixation in Khmer, an Austro-Asiatic language, has been argued to be one such example. The two types of infixation patterns are nominalization (62a) and causativization (62b).

(62) a. Nominalization (Haiman 2003: 111–12)

      a.

t-umn-ɛək	'connection'	< tɛək	'connect'
k-am-hoh	'mistake'	< khoh	'wrong'
c-amn-eh	'knowledge'	< ceh	'know'
p-umn-ool	'recitation'	< pool	'utter'
s-amn-aəc	'(a) smile'	< saəc	'smile'
d-am-nək	'transportation'	< dək	'transport, lead, carry'

      b. Causativization

s-am-ruəl	'facilitate'	< sruəl	'easy'
t-um-lɛək	'drop'	< tlɛək	'fall'
k-am-daw	'heat up'	< kdaw	'hot'
c-am-laaŋ	'help s.o. cross'	< claaŋ	'cross (a river, etc.)'

Haiman (2003) argues that these derivational infixes originate from meaningless -*Vm(n)*- sequences, as evidenced by the following pairs of words that do not have any semantic distinction.

(63)

s-(am)-baəm	'grand, awesome, glorious'
c-(am)-roh	'mixed'
c-(amn)-ah	'mature'
k-(om)-ruu	'teacher'
k-(amn)-aac	'fierce'
t-(um)-roəm	'last, endure, be patient, until'
b-(am)-roŋ	'ready, prepare'

On the basis of the 'more form equals more content' iconic markedness principle, Haiman reasons that the speakers must have folk-etymologized based on the assumption that there is no true synonymy. He also argues that excrescence is plausible since infixation is not attested in all of the Austro-Asiatic languages (e.g., languages of the Viet-Muong subfamily do not have infixation). However, such comparative evidence is inconclusive. Languages lacking infixes today might simply reflect the loss of such operations from changes that affected only those languages. Semantic bleaching and lexicalization are commonplace in language change. That some morphologically marked forms show a lack of semantic distinction from their unmarked counterpart is to be expected, especially with respect to derivational morphology. Furthermore, it seems quite suspect that two sets of grammatical morphemes should emerge from a single ejected string. Also, as alluded to in Section 5.1, Schmidt (1906) had suggested that infixes in the Mon-Khmer languages are the result of entrapment. In light of these complications, whether the infixes in Khmer illustrate a case of morphological excrescence shall remain to be proven. In what follows, I consider instead a case of infixation in English which offers a more robust example of infixation out of morphological excrescence.

5.2.4.1 *The emergence of Homeric infixation*   Recall that Homeric infixation in English, involving the insertion of *-ma-* after a trochaic foot, is a new construction recently introduced into Vernacular American English (a more in-depth synchronic analysis of this pattern appears in Section 6.1 in Chapter 6). A search on the World Wide Web resulted in the tokens shown in (64a). The examples in (64b) were encountered in daily conversations. The meaning of this construction indicates roughly attitudes of sarcasm and distastefulness, although, it can also used as a form of language play.

(64)   a. edu-ma-cate   b. Urs(a)-ma-la
           sophisti-ma-cated   vio-ma-lin
           syndi-ma-cated   edu-ma-cate
           compli-ma-cated   saxo-ma-phone
           lesser-edge-a-ma-cated

People who are familiar with this construction invariably credit the TV animation series, *The Simpsons*®, particularly the speech of the main character Homer Simpson, for popularizing this construction. Below are some quotes from the animation series:

(65)   Homer: Well, honey, what do you like? Tuba-ma-ba? Oba-ma-bo? That one? Saxa-ma-phone?
           Homer: A hundred bucks? For a comic book? Who drew it, Micha-ma-langelo?

This infix is an instructive example for several reasons. First, *-ma-* has no obvious historical morphological antecedent in English. An understanding of its origin will therefore offer a unique window into the mechanism from which new morphological elements may emerge. As I will show further in

Chapter 6, the Homeric infix is also a rare specimen of what I referred to as true infixation. The morpheme -*ma*- may never appear at the periphery; it must appear internal to a morphological host (e.g., *vio-ma-lin*; but never **oboe-ma*, only *obo-ma-boe*). Since true infixes are rare, it should be illuminating to find out how the origins of true infixes differ from other infixes surveyed in this chapter.

As *ma*-infixation appears to be a colloquialism, it is difficult, if not impossible, to identify the earliest attestation of this construction in the history of English. The proposal defended in this section is that -*ma*- emerged out of an accidental convergence among the different filler-word constructions in English. By filler-word construction, I refer to the set of vague, nonsense, filler words English provides when one has a hard time recalling a word, name, or phrase to fill the gap. A list of such words is given below (McArthur 1992):

(66) Fillers for moments of haste or forgetfulness: Put the *thingummy* on the *whatsit.*
      Phrase words based on a question: *whadyamecallit, what's-his-name/face, whatsit, whoosis*
      Variants of thing: Br(itish) E(nglish) *thingie, thingummy,* BrE *thingummybob* Am(erican) E(nglish) *thingamabob,* BrE *thingummyjig* AmE *thingamajig,* AmE *thinkumthankum, chingus, dingbat, dinglefoozie, dingus, ringamajiggen, ringamajizzer, majig, majigger*) extensions of do: *doings, doodah/doodad, doflickety, dofunnies, doowillie, doowhistle*

The theory proposed here is that *ma*-infixation emerges out of the accidental resemblance between two particular sets of these filler words: the variants of thing and the phrase words based on a question.

(67) a. Variant of things:
          thingamabob, thingmabob, thingamajig, ringamajiggen, ringamajizzer
      b. Phrase words based on a question:
          Whatdyamecalli, whatchamacallit

As illustrated above, these two sets of filler words/phrases all contain the medial sequence -*ma*-. The source of this sequence is not always recoverable from the forms themselves. At some point of the history of the English language, some listeners who encountered these sets of words together must have concluded that these words are all related by an infix -*ma*- since they share similar pragmatic meanings of casualness and imprecision. This infix -*ma*- was then extended to other domains to indicate the speaker's casual and non-committal attitude (i.e., subjectification, Traugott 1989, 2004). It is a small step to extend this usage of -*ma*- to indicate sarcasm.

Given this understanding of how -*ma*- came about, what is important to demonstrate at this point is, first, how these two sets of words are related and, second, what the source of the sequence -*ma*- is in each of these sets. These questions will be tackled in order. To begin with, the words in (67) are noun phrases. While the internal syntax of forms in (67b) resembles that of *wh*-questions in English, their external distribution shows that they behave more like noun phrases since they are substituted for the names of either persons or things. The forms in (67) were already used interchangeably as early as the seventeenth/eighteenth centuries, as illustrated in the following quotes taken from the Oxford English Dictionary.

(68)   To speak of Mr. What-d'ye-call-him, or Mrs. Thingum, or How-d'ye-call-her, is excessively awkward and ordinary.

(**1741** CHESTERFIELD *Let. to Son* 6 Aug.)

He would answer... To 'What-you-may-call-um?' or 'What-was-his-name!' But especially 'Thingum-a-jig!'

(**1876** L. CARROLL *Hunting of Snark* I. ix)

The quote from Lewis Carroll's *Hunting of Snark* also illustrates the source of the -*ma*- sequence in both *whatchamacallum* and *thingamajig*. The -*ma*- in *whatchimacallum* comes from the word 'may' in 'what you may call him'. In contrast with *whatchacallum* 'what you call him', *whatchamacallum* would appear as if there is an inserted extra syllable *ma*. The *ma* sequence in *thingumajig*, on the other hand, is a reanalysis of the last consonant of the word *thingum* and the excrescent vowel between *thingum* and the word *jig*. The fact that *thing* and *thingy* exist as words in English might have prompted some speakers to analyze *thingumajig* as *thingy-ma-jig*. This reanalysis is likely to have been strengthened by the possible alternative pronunciation of *thing-amabob* as *thingmabob* (thus possibly analyzed as *thing-ma-bob*).

Besides the semantic closeness and formal resemblance of the -*ma*-sequence, the association between these two types of filler words might have also been facilitated by their similar stress patterns. In both *whatchamacallit* and *thingumabob*, -*ma*- appears between two metrical feet (i.e., (ˈwhatcha)*ma*(*callit*) and (ˈthingu)*ma*(*bob*)). This accidental metrical convergence might have prompted some listeners to perceive the convergence as non-accidental, which in turn may have facilitated the extraction of the -*ma*- morpheme. What is crucial here is the fact that the prominence-driven analysis is prompted by the inability to recover the placement of a morpheme through segmental means. That is, in *whatchamacallit*, roughly transcribed as [wʌ(tˀ)tʃəməcɑlitˀ], -*ma*- was flanked by four to five segments to its left and five segments to its right, while in *thingumajig* [θɪŋəmədʒɪg], -*ma*- is flanked by four segments to its left and three segments to its right. Thus, what appears to the right or the left of -*ma*- is not constant, segmentally speaking. However, it can be coherently characterized in metrical terms. In this case, a syllabic trochee is identified as the left pivot.

5.2.4.2 *Summary* The 'Homeric' infix emerged as the result of morphological excrescence (Haspelmath 1995). That is, the infix -*ma*- cannot be traced back to any known historical affixes in English. This case study thus shows that infixes may have non-adpositional origins, although such an infix does not appear to have a peripheral distribution either. The reason appears to be that no coherent segmental pivot is identifiable in the surrounding environment.

5.3 Conclusion

In this chapter, I have illustrated how the set of infixation patterns may be bounded by the forces of history. In particular, this diachronic typological survey reveals that infixes can often be traced back to historical adpositional affixes. This observation is based on diachronic investigations on genetically and geographically diverse languages. If this observation holds up, then the Edge-Bias Effect can be understood as a corollary of this property of infix development. Just as an apple never falls far from the tree, an infix has an edge-oriented profile because it hails from some original adpositional location. Thus, for example, when an adpositional affix metathesizes as an infix (e.g., Lepcha transitive -*j*- infixation), the resultant infix is likely to remain close to one edge of the stem given the fact that most cases of phonetic metathesis are local. That is, the transposed segment remains a segment away from its original etymological position. Even if metathesis were long distance, the transposing segment would migrate into relatively prominent positions (i.e., initial or stressed), never into less prominent ones (Blevins and Garrett 2005). For example, in certain South Italian dialects of Greek, prevocalic *rs* or *ls* in a non-initial syllable have been transposed into the initial syllable.[16]

(69) Classical Greek South Italian Greek (Rohlfs 1924: 15–16, 1933: 19
cited in Blevins and Garrett 2005)

*bóthrakos	vrúθako	'frog'
gambrós	grambó	'son-in-law'

[16] This metathesis only occurs when the liquid was positioned after an obstruent, when the initial syllable had a prevocalic non-coronal obstruent, and when the liquid was *r* and the initial syllable had a prevocalic *t*.

kópros	krópo	'dung'
pastrikós	prástiko	'clean'
kapístrion	krapísti	'halter'
pédiklon	plétiko	'fetter'

Crucially, the set of prominent positions targeted by long-distance metathesis is within the set of potential infixal pivots (i.e., within the initial or stressed syllable). Thus, given that long-distance metathesis is relatively rare, infixes that develop from long-distance metathesis should be even more difficult to find.

Likewise, much research on morphologization and grammaticalization (e.g., Bybee 1985*b*) has shown that grammatical morphemes tend to be small, mainly due to reduction in stress and prominence. An infix resulting from entrapment is unlikely to appear deep inside the stem since the prefix or suffix that fused with the stem is unlikely to be much larger than a syllable either. As the infixes in the Muskogean languages illustrate, the pivots referred to by the infixes were themselves historical grammatical prefixes (e.g., the first vowel/syllable pivot < historical plural *ho- and applicative *a- prefixes) and suffixes/enclitics (e.g., the final syllable pivot < historical post-verbal auxiliaries *ka, *li, *ci). Similarly, infixes resulting from reduplication muta-tion cannot lie far from the edges (of course, with the caveat that such infixes might become stress-dependent as in the case of the Northern Interior Salish languages) since the reduplicant itself was originally adpositional; 'mutations' that obscure the reduplicant-stem identity take place within the reduplicant or around the reduplicant/base boundary.

Of course, not all infixes are edge-oriented nor must they all originate from adpositional affixes. As shown in this chapter, an adpositional affix may become prominence-driven, as in the case of Northern Interior Salish diminutive reduplication; on the other hand, an infix itself may have no historical precedent at all, as in the case of Homeric infixation. Since the pathways to prominence-driven infixes are far fewer than edge-oriented ones, it is not surprising that prominence-driven infixes are cross-linguistically far fewer than edge-oriented ones.

As noted in Chapter 3, the goals of the diachronic and the synchronic research programs are one and the same since the range of possible language changes is bounded by the same constraints that hold on languages in the synchronic sense. As such, the range of possible infixes delineated by the filter function of diachrony must be within the proper subset of all possible human languages. Plausible infixes or pivots may remain unattested because no diachronic pathways lead to their creation straightforwardly. Thus, pivots such as the 'third vowel' or the 'sixth consonant' are not found because the diachronic scenario in which someone would treat the third vowel or the sixth consonant as a viable pivot is vanishingly hard to obtain. Thus while the GA formalism introduced in Chapter 3 and elaborated in detail in Chapter 4 does not preclude the existence of such subcategorization requirements being formulated, the formal system has no business in ruling out this possibility a priori.[17] The diachronic engine creates only a small range of possible morphological parsing ambiguities that ultimately led to the emergence of infixes. However, we should not lose sight of the fact that the trajectory of change is often non-deterministic and ambiguities can often be resolved in multiple ways. Infixation is often only one of many competing solutions. Recall, for example, that the Muskogean languages have markers (70a) that appear as the penultimate syllable of the verb stem, while others appear after the first vowel (70b).

(70) Infixes in Muskogean languages (Martin and Munro 2005)
      a. Mikasuki   hica 'see'   ci-hiːhoːca-laːka 'he will see you all'
                    impa-   imhopa-   'eat (PL)'
      b. Alabama   oːti 'make a fire' oːlti 'kindling'
         Chickasaw oːti 'kindle'   oɬti 'be kindled'

These Muskogean instances exemplify not only the mechanism of entrapment, but also an important aspect of the genesis of infixes. While the historical *plural* and *pronominal proclitics* gave rise to *pre-final syllable infixes* due to the monosyllabicity of the grammaticalized auxiliary verbs, the historical *mediopassive proclitic* gave rise to a *post-initial vowel infix*. The mapping from a morpheme's historical antecedent to its synchronic distribution is thus not direct. Why, then, do the Proto-Muskogean inflectional proclitics subcategorize to their right, while the mediopassive proclitic subcategorizes to its left in the daughter languages? The answer to this question brings us back to the Pivot Theory advanced in Chapter 4. Speakers may settle on a unique solution with the assistance of inductive biases on phonological subcategorization. Thus, while diachronic forces introduce the type of ambiguous situation critical to the emergence of an infix, it is these inductive biases inherent in the morphological learning process that ultimately determine

---

[17] The apparent non-occurrence of the 'third syllable' pivot might also be due to the fact that such a pivot could be analyzed in the reverse. That is, given a language with, say, a two-disyllabic foot minimal-word-size requirement, a potential 'third syllable' pivot from the left might also be analyzed as a monosyllabic pivot on the right edge. The real question here is why languages tend to single out pivots that are shorter than a syllabic foot. Some researchers have, for example, asserted that the language faculty is incapable of counting higher than two.

what type of infix might result. In particular, the factor that determines what pivot an infix should subcategorize for rests on the relative robustness of the competing potential subcategorization requirements. The fact that the mediopassive infix takes the initial vowel as its pivot rather than the material following it (i.e., the historical root) has to do with the size inconsistency of the historical roots (e.g., PM *kaxa 'to sit (PL)' was disyllabic but *moxoθi 'to boil' was trisyllabic (Booker, 2005: 252–3)). Thus, what appeared to the right of the entrapped infix, the historical root, was not a reliable constituent for subcategorization. On the other hand, the material preceding the infix was either *a- or *ho (< *oho), which was invariably monosyllabic.

Thus, it is from this multifaceted perspective that the Edge-Bias Effect can be fully understood. The Edge-Bias Effect is neither the consequence of the formal grammar nor is it the accidental product of diachrony alone. While language change creates the necessary preconditions, infixes may only come about given the right analytic tools (i.e., a theory of phonological/morphological subcategorization) and principles (i.e., a theory of morphological learning).

6

Beyond infixation

This last chapter is devoted to exploring some of the ramifications of the phonological subcategorization approach to infixation. To begin with, the idea that infixation is the result of edge misalignment raises the question: does true infixation exist? That is, are there infixes that are demonstrably incapable of appearing adpositionally? The evidence suggests the answer is positive. While most infixes are 'fake' in the sense that their subcategorization restrictions do not call for an intrinsically intramorphemic distribution, 'true' infixes do occur. Homeric infixation in English is a case in point and will be explored in some detail in Section 6.1. Section 6.2 looks at how language games and disguises that involve infixation differ from grammatical infixation. I show that infixing games and disguises can be insightfully analyzed in terms of phonological subcategorization, even in the context of iterative infixing ludlings. Like infixes, clitics are said to have intramorphemic distribution in some languages. Section 6.3 reviews two such cases of endoclisis. I argue that the propensity for endoclitics to 'lean' on an edge- and/or a prominence-based unit lends itself naturally to a phonological subcategorization analysis. In Section 6.4, I explore the possibility of featural subcategorization. I argue that, while features may govern allomorph selection, they do not seem to trigger infixation. Throughout this book, I have defended the idea that infixation obtains when two conditions are satisfied: (i) when the morphological host of affixation is larger than the size of the phonological constituent subcategorized by the affix and (ii) when the language tolerates morpheme interruptions. While much attention has gone into illustrating the variety of outcomes that result when condition (i) is met, little has been said about the effect of condition (ii). As this book draws to a close, I discuss in Section 6.5, albeit briefly, other cases of phonological subcategorization that do not result in infixation.

6.1 Fake vs. true infixation

A central idea argued in this work is that infixes are nothing more than phonological affixes. That is, they subcategorize for phonological units rather than morphological ones. Infixation obtains when the edge of phonological alignment does not coincide with a morphological boundary. When the edge of phonological subcategorization coincides with an edge of the morphological host, the affix in question will appear adpositionally. Not all infixes show an alternating distribution between infixation and adpositional affixation, however. Certain subcategorization restrictions, for all intents and purposes, preclude an adpositional realization of a phonological affix. For example, the intensive marker, -*eg*-, in Yurok will always appear after the root-initial consonant(s) since roots are never vowel-initial. Thus -*eg*- invariably appears infixal because the necessary precondition for its adpositional realization is not available (i.e., vowel-initial verbs). The source of the phonological affix's invariable infixal distribution is, therefore, external; certain properties of the language conspire against an adpositional realization of the phonological affix. As such, this type of phonological affix can be referred to as a 'fake' infix. There is no intrinsic requirement preventing the phonological affix from appearing peripherally. On the other hand, some phonological affixes are inherently infixal. That is, under no circumstance can such affixes appear adpositionally. These are 'true' infixes since they can never be realized without causing the morphological host to become discontinuous. A prime example of a true infix is the case of Homeric infixation introduced in the earlier chapters.

Recall that the infix -*ma*- in English subcategorizes for a disyllabic trochaic foot to its left. For example, in words which bear input stress on the first and third syllables only, the infix, -*ma*-, invariably appears after the unstressed second syllable, whether main stress is on the first (1 a and b) or the third syllable (1 c and d).

(1) a. $'\sigma\sigma_{,}\sigma$ $'\sigma\sigma$-ma-$_{,}\sigma$ c. $_{,}\sigma\sigma'\sigma\sigma$ $_{,}\sigma\sigma$-ma-$'\sigma\sigma$
         saxophone saxo-ma-phone   Mississippi   Missi-ma-ssippi
         telephone tele-ma-phone   Alabama   Ala-ma-bama
         wonderful wonder-ma-ful   dialectic   dia-ma-lectic

     b. $'\sigma\sigma_{,}\sigma\sigma$ $'\sigma\sigma$-ma-$_{,}\sigma\sigma$ d. $_{,}\sigma\sigma'\sigma\sigma\sigma$ $_{,}\sigma\sigma$-ma-$'\sigma\sigma\sigma$
         feudalism feuda-ma-lism   hippopotamus   hippo-ma-potamus
         secretary secre-ma-tary   hypothermia   hypo-ma-thermia
         territory terri-ma-tory   Michaelangelo Micha-ma-langelo

In words which are long enough to have stress on the first, third and fifth syllables, infix placement may vary; the infix can follow either the second syllable or the fourth syllable. Words with essentially the same syllable count and stress pattern may, nonetheless, have different infixation patterns (e.g., (2a) vs. (2b)).

(2) a. $(_\iota\sigma\sigma)('\sigma\sigma)\,(_\iota\sigma)$ $(_\iota\sigma\sigma)('\sigma\sigma)$ -ma-$(_\iota\sigma)^1$
         underestimate   underesti-**ma**-mate

     b. $(_\iota\sigma\sigma)\,('\sigma\sigma)\,(_\iota\sigma\sigma)$ $(_\iota\sigma\sigma)$-ma-$('\sigma\sigma)\,(_\iota\sigma\sigma)$
         unsubstantiated   unsub-**ma**-stantiated

     c. $(_\iota\sigma\sigma)\,(_\iota\sigma\sigma)\,('\sigma\sigma)$ $(_\iota\sigma\sigma)\,(_\iota\sigma\sigma)$-ma-$('\sigma\sigma)$
         onomatopoeia   onomato-**ma**-poeia

The data thus far suggests that the infix must appear to the right of a disyllabic trochaic foot. However, as shown in (3), when the input contains a dactylic pretonic string, -*ma*- does not appear as the third syllable as one would expect if feet are strictly binary (e.g., *(mùl.ti)-ma-pli.(cá.tion)*). Instead, -*ma*- surfaces as the fourth syllable. A simple post-disyllabic-trochee analysis is, therefore, insufficient.

(3) σ̆σ̆σ̆σ́σ̆   a. σ́σ̆σ̆-**ma**-σ́σ̆   b. *σ̀σ̆-**ma**-σ̆σ́σ̆
     multiplication   multipli-**ma**-cation   *multi-**ma**-plication
     Mediterranean   Mediter-**ma**-ranean   *Medi-**ma**-terranean

Here, I analyze the 'Homeric' infix as left-subcategorizing for a *maximal foot*. A maximal foot must be directly dominated by a Prosodic Word. It may dominate another foot, however. A *minimal foot*, on the other hand, cannot dominate another foot. From this perspective, the third syllable of an initial dactyl is assumed to be adjoined to the initial foot (e.g., Hayes 1982; Ito and Mester 1992; Jensen 1993, 2000; McCarthy 1982). Words such as *Tatamagouchee* and *multiplication* are analyzed as in (4).

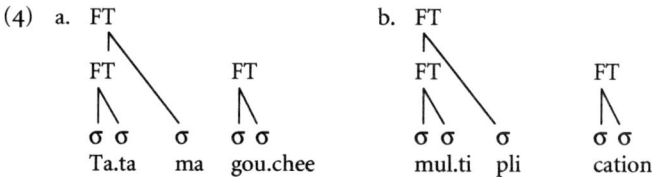

(4) a. FT   b. FT

         FT   FT   FT   FT

         σ σ   σ   σ σ   σ σ   σ   σ σ
         Ta.ta   ma   gou.chee   mul.ti pli   cation

By allowing the infix to left-subcategorize for a maximal foot, the analysis not only captures the infixation pattern in words like *multiplication*, but also excludes unattested patterns such as **multi-ma-plication*.[2]

---

[1] Infixing after the initial foot, i.e., *under-ma-restimate*, is also possible here (i.e., *repa-ma-pellent* vs *repella-ma-lent*), though with concomitant reduplication.

[2] The main issue raised by this understanding of the prosodic organization of words like those in (4) is that it violates the Strict Layer Hypothesis (Nespor and Vogel 1986: 7; Selkirk 1984: 26). However, violations of the Strict Layer Hypothesis seem to be independently motivated regardless of the case discussed here (e.g., Hayes 1982; Jensen 1993, 2000).

The phonological subcategorization analysis predicts that, all else being equal, -*ma*- is expected to surface after the second syllable when the input is disyllabic. Curiously, this prediction is not borne out, as evidenced by the ungrammaticality of following examples.

(5) oboe   *oboe-ma
     opus   *opus-ma
     party   *party-ma
     piggy   *piggy-ma
     purple   *purple-ma
     scramble   *scramble-ma
     stinky   *stinky-ma
     table   *table-ma

In lieu of realizing -*ma*- as a suffix, speakers instead expand the stem in order to accommodate the subcategorization restriction of the infix. Two types of expansion patterns are found. When the stressed syllable is closed, a schwa is inserted to create a disyllabic stressed foot (6). This strategy is referred to as *schwa-epenthesis*. The epenthetic schwa is underlined below.

(6) careful   'kʰɛɹə̲-mə-fəl
     grapefruit 'gɹejpə̲-mə-,fɹut
     graveyard   'gɹejvə̲-mə-'jaɹd
     hairstyle   'hɛɹə̲-mə-,stajl
     lively   'lajvə̲-mə-lɪ
     lonely   'loʊnə̲-mə-lɪ
     Orwell   'ɔɹə̲-mə-wəl

When the first syllable is open, however, a Cə syllable is inserted where the consonant is identical to the onset of the syllable following the infix (7). This is a case of compensatory reduplication.

(7) oboe   oba̲-ma-boe   washing   washa̲-ma-shing
     opus   opa̲-ma-pus   water   wata̲-ma-ter
     party   parta̲-ma-ty   wonder   wonda̲-ma-der
     piggy   piga̲-ma-gy   aura   aura̲-ma-ra
     purple   purpa̲-ma-ple   music   musa̲-ma-sic
     scramble   scramba̲-ma-ble Kieran   Kiera̲-ma-ran
     stinky   stinka̲-ma-ky   joking   joka̲-ma-king
     table   taba̲-ma-ble   listen   lisa̲-ma-sten
     tuba   tuba̲-ma-ba

The distribution of -*ma*- stands in stark contrast with the other infixes reviewed thus far. The fact that -*ma*- can never surface suffixally points to the fact that the proper realization of the Homeric infix is contingent on its appearance as a genuine infix in the output, that is, internal to the transformed word. An adequate analysis of Homeric infixation must account for this fact. To this end, I propose the following SBM analysis.

$$(8) \quad \begin{bmatrix} \text{'}\textit{Homeric'-word} & \\ \text{PHON} & \varphi_2(\boxed{1},\boxed{2}\text{-}ma\text{-}) \\ \text{SUBCAT} & \text{ALIGN}(\boxed{2},\text{L},\text{FT}_{\text{MAX}},\text{R}); \text{ANCHOR}_{\text{IO}}\text{-R} \end{bmatrix}$$

$$|$$

$$\begin{bmatrix} \textit{Free-stem} & \\ \text{PHON} & \varphi_1(\boxed{1}) \end{bmatrix}$$

Several aspects of this construction are noteworthy. First, the construction takes as its input words that are already parsed metrically. That is, the source words to 'Homericization' are free-standing words themselves. Consider, for example, the word *Cánada*. Following the parametric approach to English stress assignment (Hayes 1995), the main stress foot, which is trochaic, is built from right to left. The final syllable is extrametrical (e.g., ('*Cana*)<*da*>)), which explains why main stress is on the antepenult (i.e., word-initial), rather than on the penult. Curiously, primary stress remains initial in the infixed version of this word, *Cána-ma-da*. The preservation of initial stress would be unexpected if stress placement occurs concomitantly with infixation since antepenultimate stress (e.g., Ca(*ná-ma*)-<*da*> similar to *América*) should otherwise be expected. This illustration points to the fact that input foot structure must be preserved in the output. Thus the reason one finds *Cána-ma-da*, not *Caná-ma-da, is because the Homeric infix takes (*Cána*)*da* as the input. The outcome of infixation is (*Cána*)-*ma-da*. This transderivational effect is captured handily in (8). The lexical type *Homeric word* takes the type *free-stem* as input. Crucially, the phonology associated with the type *free-stem* (i.e., φ_1) is stress-assigning. The phonological output of the type *free-stem* is subjected to the co-phonology of the *Homeric word*, abbreviated as φ_2, which is stress-preserving.

Consider now the subcategorization requirements stated in (8). This analysis states that all well-formed Homericized words must satisfy two SᴜʙCᴀᴛ restrictions. As argued earlier, the 'Homeric' marker must take a maximal foot as its left pivot. What remains to be explicated is the non-peripheral restriction. Here, I analyze non-peripherality as a consequence of edge-anchoring. That is, the right edge of the source word must remain as the right edge of the transformed word (9).

(9)   ANCHOR$_{IO}$-R (a.k.a. ANCHOR-R)
'The right edge of the input must coincide with the right edge of the output.'

Infixation in polysyllabic input falls out naturally from this analysis. To illustrate the effect of the declarative subcategorization requirements, consider the declarative tableau in (10). Outputs such as (10b) are banned since the right edge of the input does not coincide with the right edge of the output.[3]

(10)

('tʰɛlə)(ˌfoʊn), mə	ALIGN(ma, L, FT$_{MAX}$, R)	ANCHOR-R
a.☞('tʰɛlə)-mə-(ˌfoʊn)	✓	✓
b. ('tʰɛlə)(ˌfoʊn)-mə	✓	✗

Similarly, when the input is disyllabic, candidates such as (11b) where -*ma*- appears suffixally are ruled out since the final segment of the input fails to appear finally in the output.

(11)   Evaluation of /lively, ma/

	ALIGN(ma,L,FT$_{MAX}$,R)	ANCHOR-R
a.☞('laj.və.)-mə-lɪ	✓	✓
b. ('lajv.lɪ.)-mə	✓	✗

While expansion can be accomplished via schwa insertion when the stressed syllable in the input is closed, when the stressed syllable is open, expansion is realized via the duplication of the post-tonic syllable (i.e., compensatory reduplication).

---

[3] Unlike traditional OT tableaux, tableaux illustrating declarative evaluations have constraints that are not crucially ranked with respect to each other (indicated by the zig-zag line) since all declarative constraints must be satisfied by the output.

(12) Evaluation of /tuba, ma/

'tʰubə, mə	ALIGN(ma,L,FT_{MAX},R)	ANCHOR-R
a. ☞ ('tʰub_iə_j)-mə-b_iə_j	✓	✓
b. ('tʰubə)-mə	✓	✗

Two aspects of this analysis of non-peripherality should be emphasized. First, the edge-anchoring analysis of non-peripherality should not be confused with the type of OT-PR edge-avoidance analysis argued against in Chapter 2. The subcategorization requirements of the Homeric marker are respected in all Homeric words. No 'movement' of any affix is required. Instead, the source form is expanded so that the resulting transformed word may satisfy the two subcategorization restrictions simultaneously. Second, non-peripherality is an idiosyncratic and intrinsic property of the Homeric infix. It cannot be derived from general properties of English phonology and morphology *per se*. For example, non-peripherality is not a general property of infixation in English; expletive formation in English allows both infixing and 'prefixing' variants.

(13) fantastic   fan-bloody-tastic   bloody fantastic
     Minnesota   Minne-bloody-sota   bloody Minnesota
     Alabama   Ala-bloody-bama   bloody Alabama

Neither can non-peripherality be attributed to general rhythmic considerations of English. The rhythmic pattern of the degenerate output *opus-ma ['oupʰəsmə] (−⌣⌣), for example, is identical to that of *cinema* ['sɪnəmə] or *venomous* ['vɛnəməs].

The final aspect of the Homeric infixation construction concerns the issue of source word expansion, in particular, the treatment of compensatory reduplication illustrated in (7). Compensatory reduplication (CR), as illustrated in Chapter 4, must consist of three major components: (i) some CR-triggering factor; (ii) specification of the direction of duplication; and (iii) some way to prevent expansion by default segmental epenthesis. Schematically, compensatory reduplication can be modeled with the following constraint hierarchy schema (Yu 2005*b*):

(14)   CR-triggering constraint, SCORRI$_{L/R}$, DEP$_{IO}$>> INTEGRITY

In the present context, the CR-triggering factor is templatic (i.e., the phonological subcategorization restrictions). When a CR-triggering constraint is inviolable (or, in some cases, is ranked above the relevant FAITH constraints (e.g., DEP$_{IO}$, INTEGRITY)), phonological compensation or some other form of expansion is called for. Default segmental insertion is blocked in favor of CR when DEP$_{IO}$ outranks INTEGRITY (see (15); the inserted string is boldfaced; surface corresponding segments are coindexed).[4]

(15)

tʰub$_i$ə$_j$, mə	DEP$_{IO}$	INTEGRITY
☞a. (tʰu.b$_i$ə$_j$)-mə-b$_i$ə$_j$		**
b. (tʰu.ʔə)-mə-b$_i$ə$_j$	*!*	

The directionality of duplication can be handled using directional surface correspondence constraints. The effect of a constraint like (16) is that the copied material must come from the syllable following, not preceding, the infix (17).

(16)   IDENT-S$_R$S$_L$
    'Let S$_R$ be a segment in the output and S$_L$ be any corresponding segment of S$_R$ such that S$_L$ precedes S$_R$ in the sequence of segments in the output (L > R).'

(17)

tʰ$_x$u$_z$b$_i$ə$_j$, mə	IDENT-S$_R$S$_L$
☞a. (tʰ$_x$u$_z$.**b$_i$ə$_j$**)-mə-b$_i$ə$_j$	
b. (tʰ$_x$u$_z$.**t$_x$ə$_z$**)-mə-b$_i$ə$_j$	*!*

Finally, the fact that words like *lively* Homerize as ['lajvə̱-mə-lɪ], never *['lajvɪ-mə-lɪ] suggests that partial reduplication is not possible without the copying of the onset consonant as well. This preference is captured by the *Surface Correspondence Percolation* in (18).

---

[4] The reduplicant does not copy the content of the infix presumably because the INTEGRITY$_{Affix}$ constraint is ranked above DEP$_{IO}$, which in turn is ranked above INTEGRITY$_{Stem}$; it is better to allow segments in the stem, rather than segments in the affix, to undergo segmental fission.

(18) Surface Correspondence Percolation
'If syllable σ_i contains a segment S_i that is in surface correspondence with segment S_j in syllable σ_j, all segments in syllable σ_i must be in correspondence with segments in syllable σ_j.'

Phonological reduplication without the copying of an onset consonant is not possible in cases like *lively* because the syllable hosting any surface corresponding segments must also be in correspondence. That is, if syllable σ_i contains a segment S_i that is in surface correspondence with segment S_j in syllable σ_j, all segments in syllable σ_i must be in correspondence with segments in syllable σ_j. Such a restriction on surface correspondence is encoded using the theory of Prosodic Anchoring (McCarthy 2000; see also Yip 1999 for a similar proposal). Two syllable-anchoring constraints are posited.

(19) L-Anchor$_\sigma$
'The initial position of two syllables in a surface correspondence relationship must correspond.'
R-Anchor$_\sigma$
'The final position of two syllables in a surface correspondence relationship must correspond.'

Below is an example of an infixed disyllabic input.[5] The analysis predicts the reduplicant to be a CV syllable when the pivot is expanded by reduplication since the source of the copied syllable is also CV in shape. While the copying of the nucleus from the syllable following the infix would be sufficient to satisfy the disyllabic requirement of the pivot, as illustrated by (20b), such a candidate fatally violates L-Anchor$_\sigma$, which demands the matching of the initial segments of the corresponding syllables.

(20)

		L-Anchor$_\sigma$	R-Anchor$_\sigma$
☞a.	$(t^hu.[b_i\partial j]_x)$-mə-$[b_i\partial j]_k$		
b.	$(t^hu.[\partial j]_x)$-mə-$[b_i\partial j]_k$	*!	

The compliance of these two constraints is asymmetric, at least in the case of Homeric infixation (i.e., L-Anchor$_\sigma$ must dominate R-Anchor$_\sigma$) since no reduplication is possible when the initial syllable is closed. For example, (21a)

---

[5] The square brackets indicate syllable boundaries.

is ruled out by virtue of the fact that the onsets of the corresponding syllables do not match. The syllables before and after the infix in (21a) are in correspondence due to the fact that the reduplicative vowel is in a correspondence relationship with the final vowel. (21b) prevails even though it contains an epenthetic schwa. The syllables before and after the infix are not in correspondence in this candidate since none of the segments of the respective syllables invoke surface correspondence.[6]

(21)		L-ANCHOR$_\sigma$	R-ANCHOR$_\sigma$
a. (['laj][vi$_j$]$_k$)-m ə - [l$_j$i$_j$]$_k$		*!	
b.☞ (['laj][və])-mə -[l$_i$l$_j$]$_k$			*

There are various complications to the patterns of Homeric infixation that will remain unexplored here (see Yu, 2003, 2004*b*; 2005*b* for further explications). The main goal of this section is to argue for the distinction between fake and true infixes and how their differences may be captured. True infixes are essentially phonological affixes that have an additional non-peripheral requirement. It should be noted that strict non-peripheral distribution does not appear to be a strong characteristic of grammatical affixes. This state of affairs is no doubt a reflection of the adpositional origin of infixes. That is, since infixes generally originate from previous prefixes and suffixes, it is not surprising that they might betray their etymological adpositional distribution under the appropriate circumstances. On the other hand, as seen in the last chapter, the Homeric infix, a true infix, originates word-internally. The lack of evidence for its peripheral distribution might have prompted speakers to be less inclined to realize it peripherally. In the next section, I consider the types of infixation found in language games and disguises. Unlike grammatical infixes, infixal language games and disguises often impose strict non-peripherality requirements.

6.2 Infixation in language games and disguises

Language games and disguises (also known as ludlings) may come in various different forms. Bagemihl (1988) identifies three types of ludlings in the world's languages: templatic, reversing, and infixing. I shall focus on the

---

[6] L-ANCHOR$_\sigma$ and R-ANCHOR$_\sigma$ must dominate D$_{EP_{IO}}$ since default schwa insertion is allowed when CR is not possible.

infixing ludlings here, which generally involve the insertion of a fully or partially specified sequence of segments into the string of some source forms. The epenthetic material resembles an infixing morpheme but is semantically void. For example, in Estonian, a Finno-Ugric language, one word game involves the insertion of a syllable /pi/ after the first vowel of the word.

(22)   Estonian word game (Lehiste 1985)
     a. sa̯da   sa'b̯ida   'Q1, hundred'

     b. laulus   la'b̯iulus   'Q2, in the song, inessive sg.'
       seadus   se'b̯ia̯dus   'Q3, law, nom. s.g.'
       kauu̯a   ka'b̯iuu̯a   'Q2, for a long time, adv.'
       haige   ha'b̯i:ge   'Q3, sick, nom. sg.'
       maii̯as   ma'b̯i:i̯as   'Q2, fond of sweets, nom. sg.'

As the examples in (22b) illustrate, the infix is left-subcategorizing for the first vowel (which I analyzed here as the first mora), rather the first syllable. Thus when the first syllable contains a diphthong, the infix appears between the two elements of the diphthong. The first-mora-pivot analysis is further supported by the behavior of the infix when the first syllable of the source word contains a long vowel. As is well known, Estonian has three degrees of quantity: Q1 (short), Q2 (long), Q3 (overlong). When the first syllable of the stem begins with a long vowel or an overlong vowel, the long vowel in the first syllable is realized as short in the infixed word and the vowel of the infix surfaces as long (23).

(23)   sa̯da   sa'b̯ida   'Q1, hundred'
      sa:da   sa'b̯i:da   'Q2, send, 2 sg. imper.'
      sa:da   sa'b̯i:da   'Q3, get, -*da* infinitive'

This distribution of vowel length is to be expected if the distribution of the infix is stated at the moraic level. That is, if the left edge of the infix must align with the right edge of the first mora, then the original second mora in the source word is displaced to the second syllable, which coincides with the syllable of the infix itself (24).

(24)

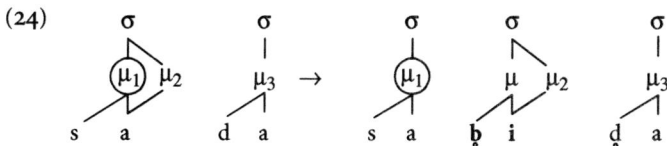

Infixing ludlings also often impose additional prosodic requirements on the output. For example, *Prokem* is a slang adopted by teenagers and students, mostly in Jakarta, the capital city of Indonesia.

(25)   Indonesian *Prokem* slang
  bapak bokap
  malu   mokal
  pembantu pambokat
  rumah rokum
  begitu begokit

As illustrated by the examples above, in this language disguise, the final rhyme of a source word is truncated and the infix *-ok-* is inserted before the final vowel of the truncatum (Slone 2003).

6.2.1 *Iterative infixal ludling*

One feature that distinguishes infixing ludling from grammatical infixation is that infixes in word games may sometimes apply iteratively. That is, the inserted string is found in multiple locations within the source word. Iterative infixing of the same morph is not found in grammatical infixation. Take, for example, a set of ludlings found in Tigrinya. In this language, there are two play languages, both involve the insertion of *-gV-* after each vowel, where V is a copy of the preceding vowel. The two play languages have different output requirements, however.

(26)   Tigrinya (Bagemihl 1988)

Natural Lg	Play Lg 1	Play Lg 2	
s'äḥifu	s'ägäḥigifugu	s'ägäḥigifugu	'he wrote'
bïč'a	bïgïč'aga	bïgïč'aga	'yellow'
ʔintay	ʔigïntagay	ʔigïnïgïtagayïgï	'what'
k'arma	k'agarmaga	k'agarïgïmaga	'gnat'

In Play Language 1, word-internal consonant clusters are left intact. Unlike Play Language 1, all closed syllables in the source words are eliminated via the insertion of *ï* in Play Language 2 and the infix may appear after the inserted *ï*.[7]

 A similar game is found in Tagalog where the sequence *-gVVdV-* is inserted after the nucleus of each syllable. The unspecified vowels of the infix copy the vocalism of the preceding syllable (Conklin 1956, 1959).

(27)   Tagalog *baliktad* speech-disguise game (Conklin 1956)
  hindí? higíidindigíidi?   'not, not'
  taŋháali? tagáadaŋhagáadaligíidi? 'noon'

---

[7] For an in-depth discussion of Tigrinya play languages and their phonological implications, see Bagemihl (1988).

Several approaches to iterative infixation are available within a constraint-based framework. Iterative infixation can be analyzed as a reversal in the quantification relation between aligning elements. Recall that the arguments in a Generalized Alignment constraint are bound by different quantifiers. The first argument is within the scope of a universal quantifier, while the second argument is bound by an existential quantifier. When the infixal materials occupy the universal-quantified argument, the resulting alignment constraint can be satisfied whenever there is at least one appearance of the infixal string in the proper location in the output. While such a constraint does not ban multiple realization of the infix *a priori*, iterative infixation is not expected to occur without additional motivations (see below). However, when a phonological pivot occupies the universally quantified argument and the infixal morph occupies the existential-quantified argument, iterative infixation is predicted. For example, the play languages in Tigrinya can be analyzed as follows:

(28)

$$\begin{bmatrix} play\text{-}lg\text{-}word \\ \text{PHON} \qquad \phi(\boxed{1}, \boxed{2}\text{-}gV\text{-}) \\ \text{SUBCAT} \qquad \text{ALIGN}(\mu_H, R, \boxed{2}, L) \end{bmatrix}$$

$$|$$

$$\begin{bmatrix} Stem \\ \text{PHON} \quad \boxed{1} \end{bmatrix}$$

Ignoring for the moment the analysis of the vocalic element in the infix, the constraint in (28) says that every head mora of a source syllable must be followed by the sequence -*gV*-. As illustrated in Play Language 1, the infix must be analyzed as appearing after the nucleus (29) which is the head of the syllable. The infix does not appear after a moraic coda since codas cannot be the head of a syllable (e.g., *k'ar.ma* → **k'agargamaga*). In Play Language 2, moraic codas in the input may be followed by an infix, but only if a vowel is inserted. Thus, moraic codas are eliminated as a result of vowel epenthesis. As illustrated in (29), the alignment restriction in (28) is satisfied since each input head mora is followed by an infix.

(29)

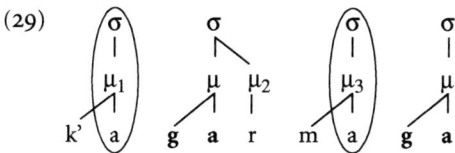

The difference between Play Language 1 and Play Language 2 is that, in Play Language 2, the source word may be expanded in order to avoid surface codas, while Play Language 1 has no such restriction. Crucially, the number of infixes that show up in the output is limited only by the number of head moras there are in the source word.

While iterativity in infixing ludling can be analyzed in terms of a reversal of quantificational relation between aligning elements, such an analysis runs into troubles when iterativity is accompanied by non-peripherality. The *hábà?ábà* game in Hausa offers an instructive illustration of this problem. In this game, -*bV*- is inserted after the head mora of a syllable (i.e., the nucleus), regardless of whether or not that vowel is followed by a coda consonant (30a). Like the other infixing ludlings introduced thus far, the vowel of the infix is a copy of the preceding vowel. What distinguishes the *hábà?ábà* game from the other iterative infixing ludlings mentioned above is that the infix can never appear after the final vowel of the source word, that is, the infix can never appear at the periphery. Thus when the source word is monosyllabic, for example, the infix appears internal to the reduplicated version of the source word (30b).

(30) Hausa word game (Alidou 1997: 34–5)

a.	gidaa	gibìda	'house'
	màskíi	mábàskí	'oily'
	màimúnà	máibàimúbùná	'Maimuna (name)'
	hátsíi	hábàtsí	'millet'
	tàabármáa	tábàbábàrmá	'mat'
b.	Dáa	DábàDá	'son, child'
	râi	ráibàirái	'life'
	cán	cábàncán	'there'

This non-peripheral restriction is problematic since a subcategorization requirement like (28) states that ALL head moras are followed by an infix. As subcategorization requirements are stated declaratively within the present framework and are thus inviolable, the inability of the ludling infix to appear after the final vowel is contrary to the spirit of a declarative analysis of affix placement. To this end, Piñeros's (1998) subcategorizationless approach to iterative infixation provides an intriguing alternative.

Based on a set of Jerigonza word games in various dialects of Spanish, Piñeros (1998) argues that iterative infixing ludling should not be analyzed as infixation at all. The inserted syllables are treated as a matter of phonological epenthesis while iterativity is motivated by output prosodic requirements. Before diving into the specifics of Piñeros's analysis, let us first consider the Spanish Jerigonza data. Examples of the Jerigonza word game are given in (31).

In the Peruvian Spanish version of this game, *cha-* is 'prefixed' to every syllable of the source word. In the Colombian version, *-pV-* appears after every syllable of the word. In the Costa Rican version, however, *-pV-* appears to the right of every head of the syllable, separating the coda from its source syllable affiliation. Crucially, the outputs of Jerigonza always have an alternating stress pattern where every syllable of the source word carries either primary or secondary stress; the contrastive stress pattern of the source word is neutralized.

(31) a.   *Source*   *Gloss*   *Colombian*

can.ción   'song'   càm.pa.cióm.po

ma.és.tro   'teacher'   mà.pa.ès.pe.tró.po

pájaro   'bird'   pà.pa.jà.pa.ró.po

b.   *Source*   *Gloss*   *Costa Rican*

can.ción   'song'   càm.pan.ció.pon

ma.és.tro   'teacher'   mà.pa.è.pes.tró.po

pájaro   'bird'   pà.pa.jà.pa.ró.po

c.   *Source*   *Gloss*   *Peruvian*

can.ción   'song'   cha.càn.cha.ción

ma.és.tro   'teacher'   cha.mà.cha.ès.cha.tró

pájaro   'bird'   cha.pà.cha.jà.cha.ró

Piñeros (1998) analyzes the distribution of the inserted string as the result of prosodic faithfulness constraint interaction. Armed with the assumption that inputs to word games are well-formed words (i.e., syllabified), Piñeros proposes that the edges of each input syllable must align with some output foot (32). On the other hand, feet must be binary at the syllabic level in Jerigonza. Thus, in order to satisfy syllable edge alignment and the binary syllabic feet requirement simultaneously, the source words are expanded by way of the inserted string. For example, in (33), when the foot binarity requirement dominates ANCHOR(σ)R, candidates with monosyllabic feet will lose invariably (see (33b and c)).

(32) ANCHOR(σ)L
'The leftmost element of a syllable in the source form corresponds to the leftmost element of a foot in the output.'
ANCHOR(σ)R
'The rightmost element of a syllable in the source form corresponds to the rightmost element of a foot in the output.'
FOOTBINARITY
'All feet are binary at the syllabic level.'
DEP-σ
'Do not insert a syllable.'

(33)

can.ción, PV	ANCH(σ)L	FTBIN	DEP-σ	ANCH(σ)R
☞ a. (càn.<u>PV</u>)(ción.<u>PV</u>)			**	**
b. (càn)(ción)		*!*		
c. (càn.<u>PV</u>)(ción)		*!	*	

Piñeros's analysis offers a straightforward explanation for the difference in the behavior of codas in the Colombian and Costa Rican versions of Jerigonza. Under his analysis, the distribution of the inserted CV string is not governed by any subcategorization requirements; in fact, the inserted CV is not treated as a morphological entity at all. Rather, it is the result of default consonant epenthesis and compensatory rhyme reduplication. I shall come back to this point in due course. Let us first look at how the constraints in (32) account for the different infixal locations found in the different Spanish dialects. In Colombian Jerigonza, since ANCHOR(σ)L outranks DEP-σ, the inserted syllable (shown as -PV- in the tableau) must appear to the right of a source syllable. As foot binarity is always obeyed in all Jerigonza-transformed words, the FTBIN constraint (and the candidates that violate this constraint) will be left out in the subsequent tableaux to simply the presentation.

(34)

(sol)	ANCH(σ)L	DEP-σ	ANCH(σ)R
☞ a. (sol.<u>PV</u>)		*	*
b. (<u>PV</u>.sol)	*!	*	

In the case of Peruvian Jerigonza, ANCHOR(σ)R dominates DEP-σ and -PV- is inserted to the left of the source syllable.

(35)

[(sol)]	ANCH(σ)R	DEP-σ	ANCH(σ)L
a. [(sol.<u>PV</u>)]	*!	*	
☞ b. [(<u>PV</u>.sol)]		*	*

Crucially, when both ANCHOR(σ)L and ANCHOR(σ)R outrank DEP-σ, -*PV*- is sandwiched, as it were, between parts of the input syllable, as found in Costa Rican Jerigonza, because the peripheral segments of the input syllable must also coincide with the peripheries of the output foot.

(36)

[(sol)]	ANCH(σ)L	ANCH(σ)R	DEP-σ
a. [(sol.<u>PV</u>)]		*!	*
b. [(<u>PV</u>.sol)]	*!		*
☞c. [(so.<u>PVl</u>)]			*

The segmental content of the inserted string, under Piñeros's analysis, is a matter of the emergence of the unmarked (J. McCarthy and Prince 1994*a*). The vocalic content of the inserted syllable is the result of compensatory reduplication (cf. Yip 1999). That is, rather than epenthesizing a default vowel to satisfy the disyllabic foot requirement, Jerigonza prefers the duplication of the nucleus of the source syllable. As shown in (37), default vowel insertion is prohibited because DEP-V is ranked above INTEGRITY. It is therefore better to introduce a copied vowel than to insert a new segment.

(37)

[(sol)]	DEP-V	INTEGRITY
☞a. [(so.<u>Po</u>l)]		*
b. [(so.<u>Pa</u>l)	*!	

Since ONSET, a constraint requiring all syllables to begin with a consonant, dominates DEP-C, an onset consonant must also be introduced to accompany the copied vowel. INTEGRITY must dominate DEP-C since the inserted onset is a fixed segment, rather than a duplicate of the onset of the preceding syllable. The actual phonological content of the inserted onset is governed by the relative ranking between the constraint ONSET and a set of segmental markedness constraints. Crucially, when ONSET ranks above the markedness constraint against labial stops but below the markedness constraints for all other types of segments at syllable margins (abbreviated as *M/C=¬*p* in (38)), *p* emerges as the 'default' epenthetic consonant.

(38)

[(sol)]	*M/C=¬p	Onset	*M/p
☞a. [(so.p̠ol)]	s		*
b. [(so.f̠ol)	sf!		
c. [(so.s̠ol)]	ss!		
d. [(so.ol)	s	*!	

In sum, Piñeros has advanced two proposals. First, he argues that iterative 'infixing' ludling is motivated by prosodic restriction on output structures. Second, the inserted materials should be accounted for by way of phonological epenthesis and compensatory reduplication. As such, the inserted materials are treated as entirely phonologically derived and thus have no lexical entry or subcategorization restrictions. If this compensatory reduplication approach is proven correct, iterative 'infixing' ludling is not a case of infixation at all since the inserted string has no inherent content. They are merely introduced to satisfy output prosodic requirements of the game (e.g., foot binarity and source syllable anchoring). Since no subcategorization restriction is posited in association with the inserted string, the non-peripheral distribution of the inserted string can be handled easily by assuming that the input-output edge-anchoring constraints are highly ranked, similar to the approach taken in the analysis of Homeric infixation above. This emergent approach to iterative infixing ludling makes a strong, but fatal, prediction, however. That is, the inserted string is predicted to be either phonologically unmarked or is some duplicate of elements already in the source word. That is, iterative infixing ludling cannot involve the insertion of a polysyllabic string and the inserted string can never contain different non-reduplicated materials or syllable structures. As demonstrated by the examples in (39), this prediction is easily falsified, however (cf. McCarthy 1991). For example, the insertion of a -*ppV*- string in Cuna is unexpected under the emergent view of iterative infixing ludling since it seems highly unlikely that a geminate -*pp*- should be the unmarked consonant in the language. Worse yet are examples like Cyprus Greek (39d) and Latvian (39e) where the inserted strings in both cases contain consonants of wildly different place and manner of articulations. In particular, in the Cyprus Greek case, the inserted string contains both open and closed syllables.

(39)   a.   Cuna *ottukkuar sunmakke*   -*ppV*-
            merki 'American'   ⇒   mepperki**ppi**
            perkwaple 'all'   ⇒   pepperkwappapleppe

	pia 'where'	⇒	pi**ppi**appa
	ua 'fish'	⇒	u**ppu**appa
b.	Hausa		-gVdV-
	káasúwáa 'market'	⇒	ká**gá**dá**sú**gú**dú**wáa
	búuláaláa 'whip'	⇒	bú**gú**dú**lá**gá**dá**láa
	tàakàlmíi 'shoe'	⇒	tà**gà**dà**ká**gá**dá**lmíi
	màimúnàa 'person name'	⇒	mà**gà**dà**i**mú**gú**dú**nàa
c.	Hausa		-ʔVsVdv-
	ráabìyáa 'personal name'	⇒	ràa**ʔà**sà**dà**abíi**ʔí**sí**díi**yàa[8]
	kàasúwáa 'market'	⇒	kàa**ʔà**sà**dà**sú**ʔú**sú**dú**wáa
d.	Greek (Cyprus)		-kVkVrdVrVkVkV-
	alékos 'Alec'	⇒	a**ka**kár**da**ra**ka**ká**le**ke**kér**de**re**ke**ké-**ko**sko**kór**do**ro**ko**kós
e.	Latvian		-hVlef VC-
	erschlug		er**her**lefe**schlug**hug**le**fug
	Abel		a**ha**lefa**bel**hel**le**fel

In this section, I reviewed two approaches of iterative infixing ludling. The reverse-quantification approach predicts iterative affixation of ludling materials but it fails to accommodate the possibility of non-peripherality. The emergent approach to infixing ludling proposed by Piñeros, on the other hand, denies such ludlings as 'infixing' at all; iterative 'infixing' ludling is treated as an instance of phonological epenthesis. While such an approach appears to work well for iterative infixing of CV syllables, it offers no recourse when the inserted material is internally heterogeneous (e.g., containing consonants of different places of articulation and syllables of different structures). In the next section, I advance a generalized theory of iterative infixation. It combines the strengths of the subcategorization approach and Piñeros's prosodic interpretation of iterative infixation.

6.2.2 *A general theory of iterative infixing ludling*

The theory of iterative ludling infixation advanced here has two main features. First, the treatment of iterative infixing ludlings is formally no different from non-iterative infixing ludlings. All infixing ludlings have subcategorization requirements similar to those of other phonological affixes. Second, the infixal construction itself imposes strict output prosodic

---

[8] Alidou (1997: 46) notes that the behavior of vowel length in this game is not predictable. Certain game forms show lengthening of the original non-final short vowels, while others do not. Some examples also show shortening of original non-final long vowels in the derived words.

restrictions on the transformed word. Thus, for example, I propose that the Hausa *hábà?ábà* game involves the insertion of -*b*-, which is left-subcategorizing for a head mora of a foot (i.e., ALIGN(-*b*-,L,μ_H,R)). (I shall return to the issue of the copied vowel in due course.) Unlike other infixation patterns, the *hábà?ábà* game imposes prosodic well-formedness restrictions on the transformed words. Specifically, outputs of the *hábà?ábà* game must be parsed into disyllabic trochaic tonal feet. Since the head of a tonal foot in Hausa must carry a high tone (cf. Leben 2001), syllables inherited from the source words are invariably associated with a high tone on the surface, while the inserted -*bV*-, which occupied the weak position of a tonal foot, always carries a low tone. Leaving aside the issue of tonal assignment, the proper footing of a transformed word is formalized in terms of the constraints in (40) (see also (32)). Note that all long monophthongs are shortened in this game, including the last, presumably due to the effect of an undominated *LONG VOWEL constraint.

(40) ANCHOR(σ)L
      'The leftmost element of a syllable in the source form corresponds to the leftmost element of a foot in the output.'
      ANCHOR(σ)R
      'The rightmost element of a syllable in the source form corresponds to the rightmost element of a foot in the output.'
      FOOTBINARITY
      'All feet are binary at the syllabic level.'
      PARSE-σ
      'Every syllable must be footed.'

(41) Source word: *màs.kíi* 'oily'

	FTBIN	ANCH(σ)L	ANCH(σ)R	PARSE
☞a. (mábàs)kí		*		*!
b. má(bàskí)		**!		*
c. (másbà)kí		*	*!	*
d. (mábàs)(kí)	*!			
☜e. (mábàs)(kíbì)				

Assuming that -*bV*- must be present in the transformed word (presumably the result of an undominated REALIZE-MORPH constraint (cf. Kurisu 2001)), as illustrated in tableau (41), a well-formed foot in the output candidate must be headed by materials from the source word, otherwise, the candidate (i.e., (41b)) will fatally violate ANCH(σ)L. Inserting -*bV*- after the coda consonant of the source word syllable will fatally violate ANCH(σ)R (i.e., (41c)).[9] As shown by the failing candidate in (41d), not every syllable of the source word is parsed. In particular, the final syllable cannot be parsed into its own foot since it will fatally violate FOOTBINARITY. The analysis in (41) is curiously incomplete, however, since it fails to predict the correct output candidate. That is, candidate (41e) is more well-formed than the attested output (41a) because (41e) left no syllable unparsed on the surface. Note that (41e) satisfies ANCH(σ)R since the rightmost segment of this candidate (i.e., the nucleus of the inserted -*bV*-) stands in correspondence with the rightmost segment of the source word. This correspondence relation is licensed by the fact that the nucleus of the inserted -*bV*- is epenthesized via the mechanism of compensatory reduplication. As shown in the diagram in (42), the final vowel *i* stands in surface correspondence with the preceding vowel, which in turns stands in correspondeance with the final vowel of the source word. By transitivity, the final *i* in the output stands in correspondence with the final vowel of the source word as well. As such, ANCH(σ)R is satisfied in (41e) since the rightmost element of the final foot stands in correspondence with the rightmost element of the final syllable of the source word.

(42) Source:

Ultimately, the reason why candidate (41e) is undesirable has to do with the fact that the *hàbàʔábà* game imposes a non-peripherality requirement on all transformed outputs. Such a non-peripheral restriction is not an intrinsic property of iterative infixing ludling, even in Hausa. The *ʔásàdásà* game in Hausa inserts -*sV*- after each source syllable, for example. Unlike the *hàbàʔábà* game, however, -*sV*- can appear word-finally. Non-finality is, therefore, not an intrinsic property of iterative infixing ludlings *per se*, but rather a feature that must be stipulated for a particular game. In the *ʔásàdásà* game, for example, a candidate like (41e) would be the desired winner.

(43) Hausa *ʔásàdásà* word game (Alidou 1997: 42–3)

| nóonòo | 'milk' | nósònósò |
| sàndáa | 'stick' | sánsàdásà |

---

[9] If the coda consonant is moraic, then such a candidate will be ruled out independently due to its failure to conform to the subcategorization requirement (i.e., -*bV*- left-subcategorizes for the head mora of a foot, which corresponds to the nucleus of a source syllable).

kwáryáa	'calabash'	kwársàyásà
bíŋgèl	'personal name'	bínsìgélsè

Returning to the analysis in (41), what differentiates (41a) from (41e) is the fact that (41e) violates the non-peripheral requirement but (41a) does not. Earlier, in the context of Homeric infixation, I suggested that the non-peripheral restriction is captured by the ANCHOR$_{IO}$-R constraint. This constraint requires the right edge of the source word to coincide with the right edge of the transformed output. Candidates such as (41e) show that such a parochial ANCHOR constraint is insufficient in the present context since the final segment of the source word is indeed in correspondence with the final segment of the output, albeit via the mechanism of compensatory reduplication. A more refined notion of anchoring is needed. Here, I adopt the notion of STRONG-ANCHOR (Ussishkin 1999).The idea behind STRONG-ANCHOR is that relations between STRONG-ANCHOR-ed segments must be unique. That is, no segments regulated by STRONG-ANCHOR can have exponents elsewhere in the output. While STRONG-ANCHOR mimics the effect of INTEGRITY, it is more restrictive than INTEGRITY since STRONG-ANCHOR localizes its ban to just segmental fission. Given a constraint like (44), the previously problematic candidate is duly eliminated (see (45b)). It should be noted that since non-peripherality is an intrinsic property of the *hábà?ábà* game, the STRONG-ANCHOR requirement is stated as part of the declarative component of the construction. The declarative tableau evaluation in (45) reflects this point.

(44)   STRONG-ANCHOR$_{IO}$-R
      $\forall x, y, [(x = \text{Edge}(S_1, R)) \, \& \, (x\mathcal{r}y)] \rightarrow [y = \text{Edge}(S_2, R)]$
      'No internal correspondence of input-right-edge element.'

(45)   Source word: *màs.kíi* 'oily'

	ALIGN($-bV-$, L, μ_H, R)	STRONG-ANCHOR$_{IO}$-R
☞ a. (mábàs)kí	✓	✓
b. (mábàs)(kíbì)	✓	✗

(46) summarizes my analysis of the *hábà?ábà* game thus far. This construction states that -*b*- must appear to the right of some head mora of a syllable and that the right edge of the transformed output must uniquely correspond to the right edge of the source word. Crucially, nowhere in the analysis is iterative insertion of the -*b*- infix required. Rather, iterative infixation falls out as a by-product of the output prosodic requirements, as Piñeros argued

(i.e., output foot binarity and input-output syllable edge alignment). Note also that the inserted material is assumed to be a mere consonant, -*b*-. The vocalism that accompanies the inserted -*b*- is derived from the output prosodic requirements (e.g., FTBIN is satisfied via compensatory vocalic reduplication). I will focus on this aspect of the analysis for the remainder of this section.

(46)

$$\begin{bmatrix} \textit{Disguised word} \\ \text{PHON} \qquad \varphi(\boxed{1}, \boxed{2}\text{-}b\text{-}) \\ \text{SUBCAT} \qquad \text{ALIGN}(\boxed{2}, \text{L}, \mu_H, \text{R}); \text{STRONG-ANCHOR}_{IO}\text{-R} \\ \qquad\qquad\qquad | \\ \qquad\qquad \begin{bmatrix} \textit{Free-stem} \\ \text{PHON} \qquad \boxed{1} \end{bmatrix} \end{bmatrix}$$

Since the co-phonology of the *hábàʔábà* game calls for input-output prosodic correspondence, to minimize such prosodic anchoring violations, a certain strategy is employed to guarantee output foot well-formedness. To understand this, it is best to illustrate the idea with a concrete example. Consider the evaluation in (47).

(47) Source word: *màimúnà* 'Maimuna (name)'

	FTBIN	ANCH(σ)L	ANCH(σ)R	PARSE
☞a. (máibài)(múbù)ná				*
b. (máibài)(múná)		*	*!	
c. mái(múbù)ná				**!
d. (máibài)(mú)(ná)	*!*			

The source word contains three input syllables (i.e., *mài.mú.nà*). In order to maximize the number of footed syllables, every non-final syllable may serve as the head of a foot. Candidates with more than one unparsed syllable (e.g., (47c)) are automatically ruled out by the excessive violations of PARSE-σ relative to the winning candidate. Yet, since FOOTBINARITY is undominated, an input syllable cannot form its own foot, as illustrated by the failure of (47d). Instead, disyllabic feet are made possible via the duplication of the nucleus of the source syllable. (The infix -*b*- is duplicated to supply an onset for the inserted nucleus. See below for more discussion.)

(48)   Source: m   ai_i   m   u_j   n   a

Transformed: m   ai_i   b_k   ai_i   m   u_j   b_k   u_j   n   a

To be sure, this expansion is not motivated by the subcategorization requirement of -*b*- *per se*. As shown in (47b), the subcategorization of -*b*- is fulfilled
as long as there is one instantiation of -*b*- in the output. Nothing in
the construction in (46) requires -*b*- to be present after every head mora.
However, when it does appear in the output, every instance of -*b*- is subject
to the same subcategorization requirement. A candidate like *(máibài)(bù-
mú)ná* would not only violate Anchor(σ)L since the second foot is not
headed by a syllable corresponding to a source syllable, but would also violate
the distributional restriction of -*b*- imposed by the game since the second
instance of -*b*- does not follow a head mora (recall that the head mora is to be
understood as the head mora of the head syllable of a foot).

One question that remains to be addressed is why disyllabic-foot-well-
formedness is satisfied via compensatory reduplication. Recall that compensatory reduplication is motivated by the constraint-ranking schema, Dep_IO >>
Integrity. As illustrated in (49), expansion via non-reduplicative epenthesis
(see (49b)) is ruled out due to the high ranking of Dep_IO. What remains unclear
is why candidates like (49c) are impossible. As noted above, the construction in
(46) imposes no requirement of iterative insertion of -*b*-. Thus as long as -*b*- is
properly realized somewhere in the output, it is unclear why foot expansion
elsewhere in the transformed word cannot be realized through the full copying
of the immediately preceding syllable (i.e., (49c)). This is especially curious since
the rhyme of the inserted syllable is a direct copy of the rhyme of the preceding
syllable anyway; it seems to be a natural step to copy the onset consonant as well.

(49)

	Dep-Seg	Integrity
☞ a. (máibài)(múbù)ná		****
b. (máibài)(mú?a)ná	*!*	**
☜ c. (máibài)(m_júm_jù)ná		****

Onset copying is prevented due to the high ranking of the constraint in (50).
This constraint states that if the leftmost element of an input syllable corresponds with the leftmost element of a foot in the output, the corresponding

output element must be unique. Thus as shown in (51), a candidate with onset copying from the immediately preceding syllable (51b) is undesirable since the onset of the preceding syllable always stands in a prosodic anchoring relation with a source syllable. On the other hand, duplicating -*b*- does not violate S-ANCHOR since -*b*- has no syllable affiliation in the input at all.

(50)   S-ANCHOR (σ)L
       $\forall$x, y, [(x = Edge(σ_I, L)) & (x$\Re$y)] $\rightarrow$ [y = Edge(Σ_O, L)]
       'If the leftmost element of an input syllable corresponds with the
       leftmost element of a foot in the output, the corresponding output
       element must be unique.'

(51)

	DEP-SEG	S-ANCHOR(σ)L	INTEGRITY
☞ a. (máib$_j$ài)(múb$_j$ù)ná			★★★★
b. (máibài)(m$_j$úm$_j$ù)ná		*!	★★★★

The main goal of this discussion is to highlight the fact that iterative infixing ludling can be accounted for using the same mechanism already proposed in this work. The theory advanced in this section provides the necessarily framework for understanding iterative infixing ludlings in general. Crucially, the present treatment of iterative infixing ludling is, at its core, no different from treatments of other phonological affixes argued throughout this work. The infix in question is subcategorizing for a moraic pivot. The multiple appearances of the infix in the output are the by-product of other prosodic requirements independently imposed by the game. Iterative infixation is the result of compensatory reduplication.

Iterativity, I suspect, is impossible as a stand-alone feature of any linguistic phenomenon unmotivated by prosodic or rhythmic factors. Rhythmicity may also be a strategy to reduce the cognitive burden of processing disguised words in infixing ludling. This proposal is motivated by the obser-vation that iterative ludling infixation appears to correlate with a reduction of phonological complexity. That is, outputs of iterative infixing ludling often carry less contrastive information than their source word counterparts. For example, the Hausa *hábà?ábà* game not only requires the insertion of -*bV*- after the nucleus of each non-final syllable in the source word, long monophthongal vowels in the source word are also shortened as a result of infixing ludling. The vowel length contrast in Hausa is, therefore, suspended in the transformed word. More important is the fact that the tonal pattern of the source word is ignored in favor of an alternating high-low tone pattern such that the high tones always fall on syllables of the source word. Contrastive tonal information in the source words is therefore suspended as well in favor of a predictable alternating tone pattern. The dispreference for direct onset copying illustrated in (51) might also be a reflection of this facilitative disposition of iterative infixing ludling. That is, if the inserted syllable is a full copy of its preceding syllable, recovery of the source word might be hindered by the need to factor out duplicated materials at every turn. The insertion of a fixed consonant, on the other hand, provides a level of contrast between the inherited source word materials and the extraneous inserted materials. In particular, the inserted consonant functions as the onset. It not only demarcates the boundary of the inserted syllable, but it might also serve as an invitation to the listener to ignore the content of that syllable. Note that such complexity reduction is, however, characteristic of iterative infixing ludlings only, not of infixing ludlings in general. Complexity reduction might therefore be a strategy to reduce the processing costs of severely disguised words. Obviously, this claim about the complexity reduction aspect of iterative infixing ludling must be tested against a larger corpus of iterative infixing ludling games. More research on ludlings in general is in fact needed. For example, just exactly how are diphthongs and long vowels treated in iterative infixing ludling? In Hausa, for example, there appears to be much variation in the treatment of diphthongs and long vowels. Some games treat diphthongs on the par as monophthongs but as long vowels in other games. The issue of tonal assignment must also be examined in more detail. Again, in Hausa, some games retain the tonal pattern of the source word, but others prefer to impose their own tonal patterns.

In the next section, I turn to a phenomenon that closely resembles infixation—endoclisis. I briefly consider how the theory of phonological subcategorization may be extended to accommodate endocriticized words.

6.3 Endoclisis

Clitics can be broadly defined as a class of linguistic units that are phonologically dependent on some other prosodically independent units. Following the diagnostic conditions laid out in Zwicky and Pullum (1983), clitics must satisfy the majority, if not all, of the following criteria:

(52)   A. Clitics can exhibit a low degree of selection with respect to their hosts, while affixes exhibit a high degree of selection with respect to their stems.

B. Arbitrary gaps in the set of combinations are more characteristic of affixed words than of clitic groups.

C. Morphological idiosyncrasies are more characteristic of affixed words than of clitic groups.

D. Semantic idiosyncrasies are more characteristic of affixed words than of clitic groups.

E. Syntactic rules can affect affixed words, but cannot affect clitic groups.

F. Clitics can attach to material already containing clitics, but affixes cannot.

An intriguing aspect of clitics is that they often appear in places that seem to create apparent discontinuities. Consider the following examples from Serbo-Croatian (data taken from Anderson 2000: 308):

(53) a. Moja =će mladja sestra doći u utorak
my FUT younger sister come on Tuesday
'My younger sister will come on Tuesday'

b. Moja mladja sestra =će doći u utorak
My younger sister FUT come on Tuesday
'My younger sister will come on Tuesday'

c. Lav =je Tolstoi veliki ruski pisac
Leo is Tolstoy great Russian writer
'Leo Tolstoy is a great Russian writer'

d. Lav Tolstoi =je veliki ruski pisac
Leo Tolstoy is great Russian writer
'Leo Tolstoy is a great Russian writer'

The clitics, shown in boldface, are instances of the so-called second-position clitics, which generally appear after an initial syntactic constituent. The point of interest here is that, at least for some speakers, these clitics may appear after the initial word irrespective of constituent unity. For example, the clitic =*je* in (53c) intrudes within the proper name Leo Tolstoy. The ability for certain clitics to create discontinuity extends beyond the syntactic domain. Some clitics may even disrupt the integrity of a lexical word. This section focuses on these so-called endoclitics.

The treatment of clitics varies from being purely syntactically driven to purely phonologically driven. Anderson (2005), who presents the most comprehensive study of the linguistic properties of clitics to date, argues for the view that the nature of clitics is essentially morphological. That is, clitics are phrasal affixes. An important argument for the morphological nature of clitics is its parallelism with regular affixation. Specifically, he observes that, not only are there prefixing and suffixing counterparts of affixation in clitics, but that infixation of a clitic is also possible. That is, like infixes which create discontinuity in their morphological hosts, several languages have been reported to have clitics that show intramorphemic distribution. I review two such cases in this section.

6.3.1 *Udi*

In the most extensive and convincing study of endoclisis to date, Harris (2002) reports that, in Udi, a Lezgic language of the Nakh-Daghestanian family, there is a set of person-marking clitics (PM) that show agreement with the subject of a clause. The choice of the allomorphs of a given PM form is entirely phonologically governed.

(54)

	General	Inversion	Possession	Question
1 sg.	-zu, -z	-za	-bez, -bes	
2 sg.	-nu, -n, -ru,-lu	-va	-vi	
3 sg.	-ne, -le, -re	-t'u	-t'a	-a
1 pl.	-yan	-ya	-beš	
2 pl.	-nan, -ran, -lan	-va, -vạn	-ẹf	
3 pl.	-q'un	-q'o	-q'o	

Under certain specific tense/aspect categories and focus construction, these markers are encliticized to the verb. In other context, however, the distribution of these clitics is more complicated. In most TAM categories (present, imperfect, aorist I, aorist II, perfect, particle conditional, future I, conditional I) PMs appear in a complex verb stem, occurring between the so-called incorporate category and the light verb. (In (55), the incorporate category immediately precedes the (bold) PM clitic, while the light verb is italicized.)

(55) a. zavod-a   aš=**ne**=*b*-sa   (Harris 2002: 122)
         factory-DAT   work-3SG-do-PRES
         'She works in a factory.'

      b. nana-na   bụɣa=**ne**=*b*-e   p'ạ   ačik'alšey
         mother-ERG   find-3SG-do-AORII   two   toy
         'Mother found two toys.'

      c. äyel   kala=**ne**=*bak*-e   (Harris 2000: 596)
         child.ABS   big-3SG-become-AORII
         'The child grew (up).'

When the verb is monomorphemic, however, the PM appears immediately before the final consonant of the verb (56). In the examples below, the root is given first, followed by the endocliticized example (Harris 2000: 598–9).

(56) a. aq'- 'take receive'

    kaɣuz-ax   a=z=q'-e
    letter-DAT   receive1-1SG-receive2-AORII
    'I received the letter'

    b. bašq- 'steal'

    q'ačaɣ-ɣ-on   bez   täginax baš=q'un=q'-e
    thief-PL-ERG   my   money   steal$_1$-3PL-steal$_2$-AORII
    'Thieves stole my money'

    c. bak- 'be, become; be possible'

    ba=ne=k-sa   sa   pašč'aɣ-k'ena adamar
    be1-3SG-be$_2$-PRES one king-like   person.ABSL
    '[Once upon a time, there] is a person like a king.'

To be sure, the distribution of the endoclitic PM cannot be phonologically conditioned. For example, whether a PM is infixed to a monomorphemic verb root is determined by the transitivity of the stem (Crysmann 2000; Harris 1997, 2002). When the verb is transitive, PMs are inserted before the final consonant of the (underlined) verb root. On the other hand, when a verb is intransitive, PMs are encliticized.

(57) Distribution of PMs in transitive and intransitive verbs (Harris 2002: 127)
    Intramorphemic/transitive   Intermorphemic/intransitive

a-t'u-ḵ'-sa	'sees'	aǩ'-ne-sa	'shows, is visible (intr.)'
bi-ne-ṯ'-sa	'sows'	bit'-t'e-sa	'is sown'
bo-ne-x̱-sa	'boils, cooks (tr.)'	box-ne-sa	'boils (intr.)'
la-ne-x̱-sa	'lays, puts'	lax-ne	'lies, is'
u-ne-ḵ-sa	'eats'	uk-ne-sa	'is edible'
u̱-ne-ɣ̱ -sa	drinks'	u̱ɣ -ne-sa	'is drinkable'

The distribution of PM is considerably more complicated, however. Harris observes that the placement of PM may be affected by '(a) specific TAM categories (future II, subjunctive I and II, imperative), (b) syntactic notions, including [focused constituents] and predicate nominals, (c) incorporated status of a morpheme, (d) specific lexical stems…, (e) the phonological structure of verb stems (i.e., the position before the last consonant of the stem)' (Harris 2002: 143). The exact conditions under which these various factors come into play with the placement of PM are summarized in (58).

(58) Rules for Udi PM placement (reproduced from Harris
                  2002: 130)
      Rule 1. PMs are final in the Vx if the verb is in the future II, subjective I, the subjunctive II, or the imperative.[10]
      Rule 2. PMs occur enclitic to a focused constituent.
               a. PMs occur enclitic to a negative particle.
               b. PMs occur enclitic to a questioned constituent.
               c. PMs occur enclitic to other focused constituents.
      Rule 3. In clauses with zero copulas, PMs are enclitic to predicate nominals.
      Rule 4. PMs are enclitic in a complex verbstem, occurring between the IncE and the light verb or verb root.
               a. In a productive causative, PMs occur between the infinite (in -*es*) and the light verb. In the archaic causative, PMs occur between the-ev affix and the light verb or the verb root.
               b. PMs occur between the IncE (noun, adjective, adverb, simplex verb stem, borrowed verb, unidentified element, or locative preverb) and the light verb or verb root.
      Rule 5. For verb stems of class M, in the intransitive, PMs are endoclitic, occurring between the verb stem and the present-tense marker.
      Rule 6. With verb forms of category A and category B, PMs are enclitic to the entire verb form.
               a. Category A consists of verb forms with a stem (or an allomorph of a stem) consisting entirely of a single consonant or a CV sequence.
               b. Category B consists of irregular forms of other verbs: *aba-za* 'I know', *ex-ne* 'she says', *p'ur-e-ne* 'he died', *č'e-re-ne* 'she went out', *a-re-ne* 'she came', and *ci-re-ne* 'she went down'
      Rule 7. PMs are endocliticized immediately before the final consonant in monomorphemic verb roots.

In order to capture the fact that the PM placement rules are prioritized (i.e., Rule 1 takes precedence over Rule 2, Rule 3 takes precedence over Rule 4, etc.), Harris formalizes these placement restrictions within the framework of Optimality Theory. The analysis is summarized below:

---

[10] 'Vx' refers to the complex consisting of the verb and the negative. 'IncE' refers to Incorporated elements;

(59) Align-PM-*al/-a*>>Align-PM-FocC>>Align-PM-IncE>>Align-PM-
VERBSTEM

I shall not reproduce Harris's detailed analysis here. Interested readers should
consult that work directly. Suffice to say that Rule 1 is captured by the Align-
PM-*al/-a* constraint, while Rule 2 is captured by Align-PM-FocC. Rule 4 and
Rule 5 are subsumed by Align-PM-IncE, while Rule 7 is captured by Align-PM-
VERBSTEM. What is of particular interest here is that these alignment constraints are suppletive constraints in the sense that they stipulate the position
of a PM relative to some part of the verbal complex. The constraint hierarchy
in (59) captures the order of importance between these alignment requirements. That is, the optimal candidate is selected based on its compatibility
with the highest relevant ranking constraint. For example, the clitic *ne* appears
after *aš*, an incorporated element, in *aš=ne=b-sa* 'work-3SG-do-PRES'
because neither Align-PM-*al/-a* nor Align-PM-FocC is relevant in this context
since the specific constituents targeted by these constraints (i.e., -*al/a* and a
focus constituent) are not present. However, in the corresponding negative
version of that verb, the clitic does not come after *aš* in *te=ne-aš-b-sa* 'NEG-
3SG-work-do-PRES' because the negative marker *te* is focused (i.e., a FocC).
Since Align-PM-FocC takes priority over Align-PM-IncE, the clitic must come
after the focused constituent even though *aš* is an incorporated element
(IncE). Note that Align-PM-FocC does not conspire with Align-PM-IncE to
derive the position of the endoclitic. The position is already stated in the
constraints themselves. The constraint ranking only specifies which subcategorization restriction should apply in a given situation. As such, at its core,
Harris's analysis is very much within the spirit of the subcategorization
analysis advocated in this work. As already mentioned earlier, prioritization
between allomorphs with differing subcategorization restrictions is independently motivated outside the context of infixation, that is, whenever a structural
condition is targeted by more than one affix alternant or subcategorization
restriction, the grammar must provide some mechanism to allow one
alternant to take precedence over another. (See Bonet, Lloret, and Mascaró
2003, Crysmann 2000, McCarthy and Wolf 2005, and Paster 2006 for more
discussion on how to capture allomorph prioritization effects.)

The only OT-PR component of Harris's analysis concerns the Align-
PM-VERBSTEM constraint. This constraint states that the right edge of a PM
must also be the right edge of the verb stem (indicated by '|' in (60)). This
requirement creates a conflict between the proper realization of the root and
the proper placement of the clitics. According to Harris, when a PM clitic
occupies a position right of the verb root, it is outside the domain of the verb

stem (60d). Assuming that segmental fusion is not possible, the closest the right edge of a PM can be to the right edge of the verb stem is by infixing the clitic before the final consonant of the verb stem (60c). There is no motivation for infixing the PM further inward since such a move would only increase the violation of Align-PM-VERBSTEM (see (60a and b)).

(60)

ad	Align-PM-VERBSTEM
a. ne+beɣl-e	beɣ!
b. b-ne+eɣl-e	eɣ!
☞c. be-ne+ɣl-e	ɣ!
d. beɣl-ne+e	ne!

This OT-PR analysis is not a necessity within Harris's analysis, however. As Harris herself points out, the Align-PM-VERBSTEM analysis can easily be reformulated as in terms of the PM targeting the final-consonant-pivot (i.e., Align(PM, R, C]$_{Vst}$, L) (Harris 2002: 153)). With this substitution, Harris's analysis is perfectly in line with the framework laid out in this work since all output endocliticized words are licensed by at least one of the subcategorization constraints. The positioning of the clitic does not rely on conflicts between subcategorization restrictions as in the case of OT-PR (but see Anderson 2005).

6.3.2 *Pashto*

Another classic example of endoclisis is found in Pashto, an Indo-Iranian language spoken mainly in Afghanistan, and the neighboring regions. The clitics of interest are given below:

(61) Pashto Group I clitics (Tegey 1977: 81)
       Pronominal ergative, accusative, genitive clitics

me	1st singular
de	2nd singular
ye	3rd singular and plural
am	1st and 2nd plural
mo	1st and 2nd plural

       Model clitics

ba	will, might, must, should, may
de	should, had, better, let

Adverbial clitics
xo   indeed, really, of course
no   then

These clitics are second-position clitics, thus generally appear after the first major constituent of the sentence, regardless of its length or grammatical function (contrast (62a) and (62b)). As a result of this strict second-position distribution, the verb might appear initial (62c) even though Pashto is essentially a SOV language. It should be noted that the constituent which a clitic 'leans' on must crucially carry lexical stress. For example, in (62d), the clitic does not come after the initial prepositional phrase (i.e., *ra ta* 'for me') since none of the items inside the prepositional phrase bears stress.

(62) a. xušal   aw   patang =ba ye dər ta rawṛi
                                                (Tegey 1977: 84)
        Khoshal and   Patang will it you to bring
        'Khosal and Patang will bring it to you.'

    b. nə   =ba =de   pezani
       not maybe   you knows
       'Maybe he doesn't know you.'

    c. satə   =me
       keep   I
       'I was keeping it'

    d. ra   ta   prexodə́ =de (Tegey 1977: 116)
       me   for left   you
       'You were leaving it for me.'

That Pashto illustrates second-position cliticization is not disputed. The case for endoclisis is, however, a matter of debate. Evidence of endocliticization comes from two sets of verbs in Pashto. First, there is a set of verbs that begin with /a/ where stress may appear on the penultimate/ultimate syllable or on the initial syllable in the imperfective form. The clitic generally appears post-verbally (63a). However, when stress falls on the first syllable, the clitic appears after the first syllable (63b). According to Tegey, there is no independent evidence to substantiate the claim that the initial /a/ is a separate morpheme from the rest of the stem.

(63) a. axistə́lə=me   b. á=me=xistələ   (Tegey 1977: 89)
        'I was buying them'   'I was buying them'
        aǧustə́=me   á=me=ǧustə
        'I was wearing it'   'I was wearing it'

Likewise, there exists a restricted set of monomorphemic words which form their perfective stem by shifting main stress to the initial syllable. When stress is initial, the clitics appear after the first syllable (64b), otherwise, they appear post-verbally (64a).

(64) a. pacedə́le=ba   b. pá=ba=cedəle   (Tegey 1977: 93)
          'You would be getting up.'   'You would get up.'
          baylodə́=me   báy=me=lodə
          'I was losing it'   'I lost it'
          bowə́=de   bó=de=tə
          'You were taking it'   'You took it'

Whether the examples in (63) and (64) show genuine endoclisis has been a matter of much discussion. The general pattern appears to be that, when endoclisis occurs, the clitics invariably appear after the initial stressed syllable. However, initial stress alone is not enough to predict endoclisis. There are, for example, imperfective verbs that show variable stress assignment that is characteristic of the /a/-initial words, but such verbs do not afford the type of endoclisis option that is observed in the /a/-initial stems above.

(65) satə́m=ye   sátəm=ye   (Tegey 1977: 88)
      'I keep it'   'I keep it.'
      pərebdə́=me   pə́rebdə=me
      'I was beating him' 'I was beating him'

Kaisse (1981) treats /a/-initial verbs analytically as morphologically complex, even though many of the /a/-initial verbs are historically monomorphemic (see also Anderson 2005). She contends that the meaninglessness of /a/ is not sufficient to rule out a bipartite treatment of these verbs since it is the distribution of the morpheme and its ability to undergo rules of allomorphy that are the most reliable criteria for morpheme-hood (cf. Aronoff 1976). The analysis of /a/- as a prefix is, according to Kaisse, supported by the fact that /a/- undergoes vowel coalescence but other vowels do not (i.e., when a ə-final particle precedes an /a/-initial word, the two vowels coalesce to an [a]). If this morphological analysis is proven correct, then the examples in (63) actually illustrate a post-initial morpheme distribution of the clitics; thus Pashto does not have a genuine case of endoclisis, at least with respect to the examples in (63). The reanalysis of monomorphemic forms as bimorphemic, however, seems highly implausible for the forms in (64). As Tegey points out, the syllable after which the clitics are placed is not an identifiable morpheme; neither are there rules of allomorphy that affect the first syllable of these verbs.

The bipartite treatment of the verbs in (63) and (64) misses two important generalizations regarding the distribution of the endoclitics, however. The appearance of endoclisis is tightly correlated with initial stress; no endoclisis occurs when stress is on the penultimate syllable, for example (e.g., *pacedə́le=ba* 'You would be getting up' never **pacedə́=ba=le*). Initial stress is crucially a characteristic property of the perfective stems, thus endoclisis essentially takes place in perfective stems only (save the initially stressed /a/-initial stems in (63)). To illustrate this point, let us briefly review the basic pattern of perfective morphology in Pashto.

Pashto verbs may be in the perfective or imperfective. In the imperfective form, all verbs show main stress on either the ultimate or penultimate syllable (though see below for certain lexical exceptions). However, in the perfective form, stress is always stem-initial. Tegey further divides Pashto verbs into three classes. Class-I verbs form their perfective with the prefix *wə-*. The Class-II verbs are characterized by the fact that the stem always contains a derivational prefix. Since the Class-II perfective stem is marked by a stress shift to the initial position only, stress alway falls on the derivational prefix in the perfective. Finally, Class-III verbs, which comprise the majority of verbs, consist of an auxiliary plus an adjective, an adverb, or a noun. The non-auxiliary component is referred to by Tegey as the 'initial lexical component'. Unlike the other classes where stress is on the initial syllable in the perfective form, Class-III perfective stems invariably have stress on the initial lexical component, although stress might be on the first syllable or the second syllable of the output depending on the nature of the initial lexical component.

Of particular interest here is the distribution of the clitics when the verb is in sentence-initial position. In the imperfective context (save the /a/-initial imperfective verbs discussed above), the clitics invariably appear after the verb, regardless of verb class (66). That is, the clitics are encliticized to the imperfective verb. In the perfective, however, the clitics appear after the stressed perfective prefix in Class I (66a), after the stressed derivational prefix in Class II (66b), or after the stressed initial lexical component in Class III (66c).

(66) Imperfective   Perfective
   a. mačawə́le=ye   wə́=de=pezandə   (Tegey 1977: 86–7)
      'He was kissing you'   'You recognized him'

   b. ṭel-wahə́=me   ṭél=me=wahə   (Tegey 1977: 92)
      'I was pushing it'   'I pushed it'
      pore-westə́=me   póre=me=westə
      'I was carrying it across' 'I carried it across'

c. tawdedá=ba   póx=me=kə   (Tegey 1977: 98–9)
   'It would be getting warm'   'I cook it'
   x̱katakawúm=ye   pórta=me=kə
   'I am bringing it down'   'I brought it up'

Verbs that admit endoclitization in (64) are structurally similar to Class-I verbs (i.e., monomorphemic), but they do not form their perfectives with the prefix *wə-* (thus in this respect, more like the Class-II verbs). Crucially, clitics may only appear after the initial syllable when the verb is in the perfective, never in the imperfective.

A complete analysis of second-position cliticization in Pashto will not be attempted here since such a project would necessarily include discussion of various aspects of Pashto syntax and would therefore bring the present discussion too afar afield. Instead, I shall limit myself to accounting for the intramorphemic behavior of these clitics. To begin with, it must be assumed that there exist different alloclitics in Pashto. These alloclitics have in common the fact that the clitic is phonologically subcategorizing for a leftmost stressed constituent; the clitic must appear to the right of that constituent. The accented constituent may be of different sizes (e.g., DP, PP, PrWd, etc.). Endoclisis obtains when the right edge of the subcategorized phonological constituent does not coincide with the right edge of a morphological boundary. Such a scenario arises when the leftmost accented constituent is a perfective verb. Here, I assume that the co-phonology associated with perfective stem formation projects a minimal PrWd[11] above the stressed constituent (67a), whereas the co-phonology of other stem types do not have such a feature (67b).

(67) a.   Perfective   b.   Imperfective
           $PrWd_{MAX}$

           PrWd   PrWd   PrWd
            | | |
           wə́-   pezandə   pə́rebdə
           'PF-   recognize'   'beat.IMPF'

This analysis captures the systematic connection between endoclisis and the initial stress of perfective stems naturally. Clitics will always have a post-initial syllable or a post-initial morpheme distribution in the perfective since the leftmost accented PrWd coincides with the initial syllable, as in the Class-I verbs and the irregular verbs in (64), or the initial morpheme in

---

[11] I assume here that the minimal PrWd in Pashto is a CV syllable.

Class-II and Class-III verbs. Note, however, that endoclisis, like infixation, is epiphenomenal in the sense that the clitics themselves do not demand an intramorphemic distribution. Endoclisis arises only when the phonological constituent subcategorized by the clitics is smaller than the morphological constituent of the host.

The analysis laid out thus far is silent with regard to endoclisis in the /a/-initial stems, however. As noted earlier, /a/-initial verbs belong to the Class-I category since their perfective counterparts contain the *wə-* prefix. In the imperfective, these stems show variable stress placement. While the analysis I sketched above assumes that only the co-phonology associated with perfective stem formation creates the type of prosodic structures that are conducive to endoclisis, the fact that endoclisis obtains in imperfective /a/-initial verbs when stress falls on the initial syllable, suggests that initially stressed imperfective /a/-initial verbs must share the type of prosodic characteristics found in the perfective stems. My solution here is to assume the co-phonology that produces initial stress in the imperfective /a/-initial stem also projects a minimal PrWd above the stressed syllable, just like the perfective stem co-phonology. Such an analysis, however, leaves unanswered the question why only initially stressed /a/-initial stems allow endocliticization but not other initially stressed stems. That is, why imperfective verbs like *pə́rebdə=me* 'I was beating him' do not have an endocliticized counterpart (i.e., *pə́=me=rebdə*) but the imperfective of /a/-initial verbs do (e.g., *áxistələ=me ~ á=me=xistələ* 'I was buying them')? The answer, I argue, lies in the morpho-phonology of the /a/-initial verbs. Recall that the initial vowel of /a/-initial verbs undergoes coalescence when preceded by a /ə/-final prefix. Thus, in the perfective context, the /ə/ of the perfective prefix coalesces with the initial /a/ of the root, yielding /ɑ/ (68a). No such coalescence occurs with other vowel-initial roots (68b).

(68) a. tə   ye   wɑxla (<√axl)   (Tegey 1977: 149)
          you   it   PF-buy
          'You buy it'
     b. tə   ye   wə-ešawa
          you   it   PF-boil
          'You boil it'

Crucially, when endocliticization takes place in the perfective /a/-initial verbs, the clitic appears after the coalesced vowel, rendering opaque the fact that the root is vowel-initial.

(69) wɑ=ye=xla   (Tegey 1977: 163)
      'Buy it'

In light of the lack of coalescence of the initial vowel in other cliticized vowel-initial stems and the regular behavior of consonant-initial stems under cliticization, learners of Pashto might have erroneously concluded that forms like (69) contain the (bound) root /xla/ (70). When they finally encounter evidence of the presence of the initial /a/, they might conclude that the structure of such roots is like that of the Class-II verbs, thus containing some sort of a lexical prefix. In a nutshell, the ability of /a/-initial stems to project a minimal PrWd above the stressed syllable is coerced by the pseudo-prefixal status of /a/ and the optional initial stress assignment.

(70) skunḍa   : ešawa   : ?   ?= xla
      wə=ye=skunḍa   wə=ye=ešawa[12]   wɑ=ye=xla

In sum, I have argued that endoclisis is the result of certain initially stressed verbs projecting a PrWd above the stressed syllable. Since the second-position clitics are targeting the first stressed constituent of the sentence, the clitics appear endocliticized in (63) and (64) because the right edge of the first stressed PrWd falls within the domain of the morphological host. This analysis thus shares Kaisse's assumption that the /a/-initial stems in (63) are morphologically complex. But no such stipulation is needed for the stems in (64). Endoclisis obtains because of the prosodic structure of the word, not because of the morphological structure per se.

In this section, I have surveyed a number of reported cases of endoclitics. To the extent that endoclitics and infixation share common distributional properties, endoclitics targets phonological constituents that are also at the edge of some domain or some prosodically prominent position. The intra-morphemic distribution of endoclitics, like infixes, is the result of misalignment between the phonological and morphological domains. As such, endoclitics are formally no different from infixes (e.g., Anderson 1992, 2000, 2005; Lengendre 2000). The only substantive divergence is in the phonological constituent subcategorized. In the case of infixes, the phonological domains tend to be within the scope of a word, while in the case of endoclitics, higher phonological domains such as the Phonological Phrase might be relevant.

6.4 Feature and subcategorization

A curious aspect of phonological subcategorization in general is the fact that affixes may sometimes subcategorize at the featural level as well. For example, in English, the inchoative suffix -*en* (e.g., *darken, stiffen, redden*) is restricted

---

[12] This form is constructed based on the information given in Tegey 1977.

to stems ending in obstruents (e.g., **coolen*, **thinnen*, **puren*). Similarly, in Tahitian, the causative/factitive has two allomorphs, *ha'a-* and *fa'a-*. The *ha'a-* allomorph can only be prefixed to roots that begin with a labial while the *fa'a-* is applied elsewhere (Lazard and Peltzer 2000; Paster 2006).[13]

(71) a. fiu   'se lasser'   ha'a-fiu   'ennuyer, s'ennuyer'
           mana'o   'penser'   ha'a-mana'o 'se rappeler'
           veve   'pauvre'   ha'a-veve   'appauvrir'

     b. 'amu   'manger'   fa'a-'amu   'faire manger, nourrir'
           rave   'faire'   fa'a-rave   'faire faire'
           tai'o   'lire'   fa'a-tai'o   'faire lire'

While many such cases of featural conditioning on affixation have been documented in Paster (2006), it remains unclear to what extent infixes are sensitive to information at the featural level. To be sure, cases of feature-sensitive allomorphy involving infixation are not difficult to find (e.g., Crowhurst 1998; Pater 2001; Yu 2004*a*). For example, in Muna, an Austronesian language spoken on Muna Island, located off the southeast coast of the crab-shaped island of Sulawesi, Indonesia, the realis and irrealis distinction on certain verb stems is partly distinguished by the infixation of *-um-* after the initial consonant (72a) or by the prefixation of *m-* to vowel-initial forms (72b). (Muna data cited below are drawn from van den Berg 1989.)

(72)		Realis	Irrealis	Gloss
	a.	dadi	d[um]adi	'live'
		dhudhu[14]	dh[um]udhu	'push'
		gaa	g[um]aa	'marry'
		hela	h[um]ela	'sail'
	b.	ala	m-ala	'take'
		ere	m-ere	'stand up'
		uta	m-uta	'pick fruit'
		omba	m-omba	'appear'

When roots begin with *p* or *f*, these consonants are replaced by *m* (73a), but when the root begins with *b*, *bh*, nasal or prenasalized consonants, there is no formal change in the root (73b).[15] Finally, while the majority of roots with

---

[13] Paster argues that the allomorphy observed in Tahitian is suppletive rather than the result of some general dissimilation process. See Paster 2006: 39–40 for details.

[14] /dh/ = [ɖ]; /bh/ = ɓ.

[15] There are discrepancies in the data; some nasal initial roots appear to participate in *um*-infixation. For example, *miina na-n[um]aando-a* 'it is not there', where the verb 'to be' *naando* is infixed with *-um-* (p. 159).

initial *w* behave like the non-changing roots (73c), others require nasal substitution instead (73d).

(73)

	Realis	Irrealis	Gloss
a.	pong	mongko	'kill'
	pili	mili	'choose'
	foni	moni	'climb, go up'
	futaa	mutaa	'laugh'
b.	baru	baru	'happy'
	bhala	bhala	'big'
	manda	manda	'repent'
	nale	nale	'soft, weak'
	mbolaku	mbolaku	'steal'
	ndiwawa	ndiwawa	'yawn'
c.	wanu	wanu	'get up'
	wei	wei	'clear (a field)'
d.	waa	maa	'give'
	wora	mora	'see'

Feature-sensitive infixal allomorphy of the sort found in Muna provides an instructive example of how the featural composition of the stem may determine, if only partly, the shape of the allomorph (Pater 2001) or the selection of suppletive allomorphs (Yu 2004*a*). But beyond allomorphy, there are also claims that certain cases of infixation might be governed by factors at the featural level. In what follows, I evaluate the evidence from two languages: Kashaya Pomo and Tiene.

6.4.1 *Kashaya Pomo*

Buckley (1997) reports that the exponents of the Plural Act feature in Kashaya Pomo, a Pomoan language of northern California, may be infixed to improve the featural content of the coda and to prevent the deletion of distinctive features. For example, the -*ta*- allomorph is suffixed to verbs that end in one of the consonants /l, n, ñ, č / (see (74a)) but is infixed when the final consonant is /m, q, qʷ, c/ (see (74b)).

(74)

a.	dahqoṭol-	dahqoṭol-ta-	'fail (to do)'
	diṭ'an-	diṭ'an-ta-	'bruise by dropping'
	duhluṅ -	duluṅ -ta- [dulu?ta-]	'pick (berries)'
	dayeč -	dayeč -ta- [daye?ta-]	'press hand against'

b. bilaqʰam-   bilaqʰa-ta-m-   'feed'
   sima:q-   sima-ta-q-   'go to sleep'
   qašo:qʷ-   qašo-ta-qʷ-   'get well'
   duqa:c-   duqa-ta-c-   'get lost'

At first glance, -*ta*- appears to be targeting roots that end in a non-coronal segment for infixation. Working within the framework of OT-PR, Buckley argues that the infixation of -*ta*- takes place when the stem-final consonant is non-coronal but not when the stem is coronal-final because the phonological grammar of Kashaya Pomo tolerates coronal codas better than it tolerates non-coronal codas. As shown in (75a), when the root ends in a coronal, no infixation is needed since the constraint militating against coronal codas is ranked lower than the suffixing requirement of -*ta*-. On the other hand, infixation is preferable when the root ends in a labial. This is because the infixation of -*ta*- eliminates any labial coda on the surface (see (75d)).

(75)

			*DOR]$_\sigma$	*LAB]$_\sigma$	ALIGNR	*COR]$_\sigma$
a.	☞	di.t'an.ta				*
b.		di.t'a.tan			*!	
c.		bi.la.qʰam.ta		*!		
d.	☞	bi.la.qʰa.tam			*	

Buckley's analysis is only viable, however, if the final labial in candidate (75d) fails to incur a *LAB]$_\sigma$ violation (e.g., *bi.la.qʰa.tam#*). To this end, Buckley contends that the forms cited in (74) are incomplete and that the final consonant is an onset since a following vowel-initial suffix can be assumed (e.g., *bi.la.qʰa.ta.m-V*). When the infixed stem is followed by a consonant-initial suffix (e.g., *bi.la.qʰa.tam.-CV*), Buckley argues, paradigm uniformity requires that the Plural Act affix occupy the same position.

This featural-markedness-driven OT-PR analysis is problematic on two counts, however. First, if paradigm uniformity has an effect on affix placement at all, it is not clear why the uniformity effect does not restore -*ta*- to its underlying adpositional position. All else being equal, the logic of OT-PR always favors inertia. More to the point is the fact that -*ta*- is but one of thirteen possible exponents of the Plural Act feature. As shown in (76), the distribution of these allomorphs is not at all transparent

(Buckley 1994). In many cases, the distributions, at least in terms of the phonological restrictions, are very much overlapping.

(76)   -t-   infixed before the root-final consonant, if any; *Decrement*[16]
       -h-   infixed before root-final /ɬ/ *Decrement*
       -ta-   infixed before root-final /n, q, qʷ, c/; *Decrement*
       -Ø   with some roots ending in /t, ṭ/; *Decrement*
       -ta   after /l, n, nʰ, ṅ, č /; *Decrement*
       -ʔta   after /y/; *Decrement*
       -at   after /l, n/; co-occurs with the Durative
       -m   after a long vowel; *Decrement*
       -m   after a vowel or a consonant
       -aq   after /l/; *sometimes with Decrement*
       -ataq   after /l/; *sometimes with Decrement*
       -w   after a vowel; co-occurs with the Durative
       -w   after a long vowel; co-occurs with the Durative; *Decrement*

The many exponents of the Plural Act feature highlight the fact that this morpho-syntactic operation is unlikely to be a productive process in the language; different subcategorization restrictions must be stated for different allomorphs. On the question of whether the subcategorization restrictions of these allomorphs need to target specific phonological features, the answer seems to be negative. As shown in (76), many of the allomorphs apply to similar environments, suggesting the choice of the Plural Act allomorph is idiosyncratic to the verb and must be stipulated. It is also worth pointing out that many allomorphs of this Plural Act feature contain /q, m/ as their final segments, the very segments that trigger infixation in Buckley's analysis. In fact, one of the allomorphs, -*ataq*, shows essentially the sequence one would expect if -*ta*- is infixed in a *q*-final root. This resemblance between the set of alleged infix-triggering segments and the allomorphs of the Plural Act feature appears to be too regular to be a mere coincidence. Further research may prove this case to be an instance of entrapment. If so, the suppletive subcategorization requirements of the Plural Act allomorphs are the natural results of the entrapment pathway, as noted in Chapter 5.

6.4.2 *Tiene*

Tiene is a Niger-Congo language spoken in the Democratic Republic of Congo. Hyman and Inkelas (1997) report that certain extension suffixes in

---

[16] The Decrement is a morphologically triggered rule that deletes a laryngeal increment (Buckley 1994: 288). Laryngeal increments, on the other hand, are glottal segments (/ʔ/ or /h/) or sometimes vowel length that has the effect of 'strengthening or adding weight to the vowel which it follows' (Buckley 1994: 269).

this language are infixed to the verb roots in order to satisfy certain templatic restrictions. In particular, when the suffix consonant is coronal, such as the applicative and the causative markers, and the root ends in a velar, the coronal affix is infixed into the velar-final root (77a). However, when the root is coronal-final and the suffix consonant is velar, straightforward suffixation is observed (77b).

(77) a. [[CVK]VT] → -CVTVK- [infixation]¹⁷
         lók-a   'vomit'   lósek-ɛ   'cause to vomit'   <PB*-es-[causative]
         yók-a   'hear'   yólek-ɛ   'listen to'   <PB*-ed- [applicative]
     b. [[CVT]VK] → -CVTVK- ['normal' suffixation]
         bol-a   'break'   bolek-ɛ   'be broken'   <PB*-ek- [stative]
         kot-a   'tie'   kotek-ɛ   'be united'   <PB*-uk-[reversive]

Likewise, when the root-final consonant is grave (labial/velar), the stative and reversive would infix their coronal allomorphs (78), instead of selecting the suffixal velar allomorphs shown in (77b).

(78) [[CVK]VK] → -CVTVK- [-VT allomorph used instead of -VK]
     kab-a   'divide'   kalab-a   'be divided'   ?<PB*-ad-[stative]
     sook-ɛ   'put in'   solek-ɛ   'take-out'   <PB*-od- [reversive]

At first glance, this case seems to be an instance of infixing before a grave consonant. However, as shown in (79), when both the root-final consonant and the suffix consonant are coronal, 'imbrication' takes place. That is, C2 and C3 undergo fusion which results in a single surface coronal consonant.

(79) [[CVT]VT] → -CVVT- ['imbrication' (=fusion)]
     mat-a   'go away'   maas-a   'make go away'   ?<PB*-es [causative]
     koɲ-a   'nibble'   kooɲ-ɛ   'nibble for'   <PB*-ed-[applicative]

(80) summarizes the range of behaviors described thus far. Four affixes, the stative, reversive, applicative, and causative, are infixed under certain conditions. The applicative undergoes imbrication in other circumstances. (The /L/ represents the alternation between [l] and [n] according to nasal harmony while the /K/ indicates alternates between [k] and [ŋ].) The question here is under what circumstances infixation and imbrication take place. The answer has to do with the phonology of the DStem and the Base. (In Hyman and Inkelas's terminology, the DStem refers to the derivational stem which

---

¹⁷ Hyman and Inkelas (1997) treat the extension suffixes as purely consonantal since the stem-internal vowels are determined by vowel harmony while the final vowel is determined by a combination of morphological and phonological considerations. Only the vowel in V₁ position is contrastive.

includes the root and the extension suffixes but not the final vowel. The 'Base' refers to both derived and underived stems without the final vowel.)

(80)   Morpheme(s)   UR   Behavior
        a. Stative, Reversive   L~K   infixation (CVC →CV*L*VC)
                                         suffixation (CVC →CVCV*K*)
        b. Applicative, causative L, s infixation (CVC →CV*L*VC)
                                         imbrication (CVC→CVVC)

Hyman and Inkelas argue that the DStem in Tiene must be minimally and maximally bimoraic (i.e., CVVC or CVCVC). The Base, on the other hand, has strict segmental templatic requirements: C_2 must be coronal while C_3 must be grave. Since the DStem is a subtype of Base, DStems must conform to these restrictions as well. As they apply to the Base, these restrictions are also obeyed in non-derived stems. The reconstructed forms below show that the place of articulation restrictions has been enforced diachronically ('GCB' = Guthrie Common Bantu).

(81)   kótok-   'gnaw'   C-t-k-   GCB   *-kókot-
       vútek-   'come back'   C-t-k-   GCB   *-bútok-
       tóleb-   'pierce'   C-l-b-   GCB   *-tóobod-
       dínem-   'get lost'   C-n-m   GCB   *-dímed-

The evidence thus far suggests that the placement of the extension affixes is severely constrained by the phonotactics of the DStem and the Base. The unresolved question here is exactly how these restrictions interact with affix placement. Several approaches are available. From the perspective of phonological subcategorization, suppletive subcategorization frames can be set up for each of the allomorphs. For example, while the K-allomorph of the stative/reversive is suffixing, the L-allomorph is left-subcategorizing for the root vowel. Such an account misses the connections between the observed templatic restrictions and the placement of the extension affix, however. The main issue here is how does an approach that prohibits direct interaction between phonological factors with affix placement capture the link between the observed templatic restrictions and the placement of the extension affixes? This question, however, is misguided. The real question, I maintain, is whether the extensions have subcategorization restrictions at all. The proper placement of the extension affixes is entirely predictable based on the restrictions placed on the realization of the DStem and the Base. There is no need to stipulate any subcategorization requirement for the extension affixes. Formally, I propose that extension affixes in Tiene are underspecified for subcategorization restriction. The placement of the affix exponents is governed solely by the co-phonology of the DStem and the Base. Take, for example, the causative construction below:

(82) $\begin{bmatrix} \textit{causative-stem} \\ \text{SYNSEM} \qquad \iota_{\{\text{CAUSATIVE}\}}(\boxed{2}) \\ \text{PHON} \qquad \varphi_{\{\text{DSTEM/BASE}\}}(\boxed{1}, s) \\ \text{SUBCAT} \qquad -- \end{bmatrix}$

$\begin{bmatrix} \textit{verb-root} \\ \text{SYNSEM} \quad \boxed{2} \\ \text{PHON} \quad \boxed{1} \end{bmatrix}$

Recall that, in SBM, the phonological exponents of affixes are represented as fixed arguments to the phonological function (i.e., the φ-function), specified in affixational constructions. As such, the phonological content of the affix interacts directly with the phonological constraints in the φ-function. In general, the co-phonology is only responsible for selecting the proper allomorphs. However, the causative stem construction in (82) specifies no subcategorization restriction. A stem of the type *causative-stem* must be a combination of a verb root with /s/. Since /s/ has no subcategorization restriction, the proper realization of /s/ with respect the verb root $\boxed{1}$ is left entirely to the co-phonology, which enforces the templatic restrictions of the DStem and the Base. Here, I adopt Hyman and Inkelas's analysis of the templatic restrictions, which are captured by the constraints in (83).

(83) NADIR   'An intervocalic C must be coronal.'
      OCP[Cor].TROUGH 'No two adjacent coronals in the TROUGH.'

NADIR states that intervocalic consonants must be coronal. OCP[Cor] specifies that no two adjacent coronals are allowed. These constraints are crucially relativized to the prosodic TROUGH domain. The TROUGH 'is a substring of the form under review in which (i) contrasts are suppressed and/or (ii) special input-output relations obtain' (Hyman and Inkelas 1997: 101). In Tiene, the TROUGH (τ) is a substring of the base which excludes C₁ and the final vowel (84).

(84) Tiene DStem TROUGH: $<C>\tau<V>$ (where $\tau = $ VCVC, VVC)

As shown in (85), the constraints in (83) conspire to rule out forms that do not conform to the templatic restrictions. NADIR rules out *l(abab) and *l(abas) since the intervocalic consonants within the TROUGH are not coronal. OCP [Cor].Tr eliminates *l(asas) since there are two coronals within the TROUGH domain. (The TROUGH is demarcated in the candidates by parentheses.)

(85)

	NADIR	OCP[Cor].TR
☞a. l(asab)		
b. l(abab)	*!	
c. l(abas)	*!	
d. l(asas)		*!

With regard to the question of infixation, I diverge from Hyman and Inkelas's analysis. Working within the OT-PR approach to infixation, Hyman and Inkelas argue that infixation is the result of certain phonological constraints subverting the underlying suffixing nature of the extension affixes. For example, when the causative /-s/ attaches to a grave-final root such as *lók* 'vomit', the candidate with an infixed causative (86a) is selected because the suffixation of /s/ (86b) would have fatally violated NADIR.

(86)

/lók, s/	NADIR	ALIGN-R
☞a. l(ósek)		*
b. l(ókes)	*!	

Similarly, when a stative or a reversive attaches to a grave-final root, the infixing *L* allomorph is selected (87bii) since candidates with a *K* allomorph invariably violate NADIR fatally regardless of whether *K* is realized suffixally or infixally (87a).

(87)

a.		/kab, -K/	NADIR	ALIGN-R
	i.	k(abak)	*!	
	ii.	k(akab)	*!	*
☞b.		/kab, -L/	NADIR	ALIGN-R
	i.	k(abal)	*!	
	☞☞ii.	k(alab)		*

From the perspective of the present theory (i.e., (82)), there is no 'movement' of any affix *per se* since there is no intrinsic subcategorization restriction specified in the construction. To be sure, neither is there morpho-phonological mismatch in the sense of the theory of phonological subcat-egorization examined in this work. The proper realization of /s/ is determined by the co-phonology alone. When NADIR dominates CONTIGUITY$_{IO}$, a con-straint that prohibits morpheme interruption, 'infixation' of a coronal consonant obtains when the root ends in a grave consonant.

(88)

/lók, s/		NADIR	CONTIGUITY$_{IO}$
☞a.	l(ósek)		*
b.	l(ókes)	*!	

Gratuitous morpheme interruption is not allowed due to the effect of CONTIGUITY$_{IO}$. As illustrated in (89), the *L*-allomorph is never selected when the root ends in a coronal consonant since such output candidates will always fatally violate OCP[Cor].TR, whether or not the allomorph is infixed. The *K*-allomorph will always appear suffixing since there is no motivation for *K* to interrupt the root.

(89)

		/yat, -K/	NADIR	OCP[Cor].TR	CONTIGUITY$_{IO}$
☞a.					
	☞☞i.	y(atak)			
	ii.	y(akat)			*!
b.		/yat, -L/	NADIR	OCP[Cor].TR	CONTIGUITY$_{IO}$
	i.	y(atal)		*!	
	ii.	y(alat)		*!	*

Imbrication obtains when both the root-final consonant and the suffix consonant are coronal. As shown in (90), straightforward suffixation or infixation of the causative /s/ will fatally violate OCP[Cor].TR. The preferred solution in Tiene is the deletion of one of the offending segments. Which consonant is deleted depends on the nature of the root-final consonant and the consonant of the affix. While the root-final consonant is deleted when the affix is the causative -*s* (90), the affixal consonant is deleted in the applicative (e.g., /bot, -L/ → *boot* /*bool). In general, it is preferable to delete a sonorant, rather than an obstruent. Stridents are always preserved.[18]

(90)

/mat, s/	OCP[Cor]. TR	MAX(SEG)
a. m(at-as)	*!	
b. m(a-as-t)	*!	
☞c. m(a-a-s)		*t̞

In sum, infixation in Tiene is a matter of output well-formedness satisfaction. Note that the co-phonology does not determine 'affixing ordering' *per se*. The exponents of the extension affixes are treated fixed arguments to the phonological function with no intrinsic meaning associated; meaning is associated with the construction itself, not with what is specified in the phonological function.[19] It is interesting to note that the present case of subcategorization-less morphological derivation is only possible due to several very specific factors. First, DStems in Tiene may only have one extension at a time. Second, the range of possible locations of extension exponent realization is extremely limited (i.e., either C2 or C3 of a DStem) due to the prosodic size restriction imposed on all DStems (i.e., bimoraic minimality and maximality) and the strict conditions placed on the nature of C2 and C3. This state of affairs suggests that, when phonological factors play a role in affix placement, they do so in a very restrictive fashion. In her survey of over 400 grammars, Paster found only five putative cases of phonologically driven affix ordering, where the ordering of multiple affixes is said to be determined by phonological factors regardless of semantic scope and/or subcategorization restrictions. She demonstrates that all five cases are amenable to alternative, non-phonologically governed, analyses. Note also that the framework advocated in this work offers a natural account for patterns like Tiene. When subcategorization is underspecified, the position of an affixal exponent is determined by the phonological function alone. Subcategorization under-specification is likely motivated by the fact that the phonological template offers a more reliable predictor to affix location than the suppletive subcategorizations otherwise needed to account for the variable placement of the

---

[18] Hyman and Inkelas (1997) account for the variable deletion in imbrication in terms of the following ranking: MAX(Strident) >> MAX(Obstruent) >> MAX(Sonorant).

[19] In SBM, zero derivation is essentially a construction that contributes no additional fixed argument to the phonological function.

allomorphs. The rarity of subcategorization underspecification, on the other hand, can be explained by the fact that the type of strict output well-formedness conditions required to sustain a subcategorizationless analysis is likely to be difficult to obtain diachronically.

6.5 Conclusion

Throughout this work, I have argued for a theory of infixation that casts infixes as essentially epiphenomenal. That is, infixes emerge, for example, when an affix subcategorizes for an edge of a phonological constituent (i.e., a P-edge) that does not match one of the edges of the morphological host. The phenomenon of 'infixation', as it were, is illusory since the intramorphemic distribution of an affix is not intrinsic to the subcategorization information itself. Infixes, at the fundamental level, are no different from their adpositional cousins (e.g., prefixes and suffixes). Since pivots are defined over phonological constituents and constituency at the phonological level is generally derived rather than assumed *a priori*, it is not surprising that misalignment between the phonological edge and morphological boundary takes place. An important prediction of this theory of infixation is that, all else being equal, a phonological-subcategorizing affix is predicted to realize adpositionally whenever the P-edge subcategorized by an affix coincides with one of the edges of the morphological host. Also, this theory predicts that infixes are predominantly edge-oriented because the set of subcategorizable phonological pivots are edge-based (with the obvious caveat of the prominence pivots).

Infixation is not a necessary outcome of phonological subcategorization, however. Infixation is possible only if the language tolerates the creation of derived discontinuous morphs (in OT-terms, infixation is only possible when contiguity of the input string can be violated). When morpheme interruption is prohibited, languages may respond to the failure to satisfy a phonological subcategorization requirement in different ways. Carstairs-McCarthy (1998) identifies three strategies: (a) unsystematic filling of the gaps; (b) systematic morphological filling of the gaps; and (c) systematic syntactic filling of the gaps via periphrasis. For example, abstract noun formation in English is an instance of (a). The deverbal nominalizing suffix *-al* in English is restricted to bases with main stress on the final syllable. Thus, words like *arríval, committal, reférral* and *refúsal* are possible, but **abólishal, *bénefital, *devélopal, *exáminal* are not (Carstairs-McCarthy 1998). On the view of the present theory, the nominalizing suffix *-al* is left-subcategorizing for the stressed syllable. Thus when the stressed syllable falls on the last syllable of the root, *-al* appears suffixing. However, unlike the infixes reviewed in this work, *-al* cannot appear intramorphemically when the stressed syllable is internal to the root (e.g., **exam-al-ine* is impossible). Instead, English verbs whose phonology prevents the attachment of the noun-forming -*al* may form their corresponding abstract noun in alternative ways (e.g., *abolition, development, examination*), even though the choice of these alternative strategies is not systematic. An example of morphological filling of gaps is found in Saami, a Lappic language spoken in Norway. In this language, the exponents of person marking on verbs are determined by the syllable count of the stem. Stems with an even syllable count take the person markers under the 'even' paradigm, while stems with an odd syllable count take the 'odd' paradigm (Dolbey 1997).

(91)   pers/num allomorphy

	'even'	'odd'	jéar.ra- 'to ask'	véah.ke.hea- 'to help'
1 du.	Ø	-tne	je:r.re-Ø	veah.ke.he:-**t.ne**
2 du.	-beahtti	-hppi	jear.ra.-**beaht.ti**	veah.ke.hea-**hp.pi**
2 pl.	-behtet	-hpet	jear.ra.-**beh.tet**	veah.ke.he:-**h.pet**
3 pl. pret	-Ø	-dje	je:r.re-Ø	veah.ke.he:-**d.je**

Finally, languages may fill a gap by syntactic means. For example, adjectives that do not form their comparative and superlative with the -*er* and -*est* suffixes respectively employ a periphrasis with *more* and *most* instead (e.g., *more curious, most sensitive* etc.).

As this book comes to a close, I hope that, while this work provides answers to questions concerning the nature of infixation, it also raises others. The holistic approach to linguistic explanation pursued in this work, which emphasizes the need to consider both grammar-internal and grammar-external forces in shaping the typological profile of a phenomenon, has witnessed some advances in the phonological domains in recent years (e.g., Blevins, 2004; Mielke, 2004). Much work remains if a fuller understanding of many phonological phenomena, especially the source of Prosodic Morphology (but see Niepokuj 1997), is to be obtained. As many mysteries are still waiting to be unveiled, this book shall be a call to arms.

Appendix

Language	Macro-Phylum	Main source(s)
1. Acehnese	Austronesian	Durie 1985
2. Akkadian	Afro-Asiatic	Marcus 1978; Whaley 1997
3. Alabama	Muskogean	Hardy and Montler 1988; Montler and Hardy 1990, 1991
4. Amharic	Afro-Asiatic	Rose 1997, 2003a, 2003b
5. Amis	Austronesian	Ho 1986
6. Arabic (Classical)	Afro-Asiatic	Aryan 2001
7. Arabic (Levantine)	Afro-Asiatic	Broselow and McCarthy 1983/84; Cowell 1964
8. Archi	Nakh-Daghestanian	Kibrik 1998
9. Atayal	Austronesian	Egerod 1965, 1999
10. Birom	Niger-Congo	Bouquiaux 1970
11. Bole	Afro-Asiatic	Gimba 2000
12. Budukh	Nakh-Daghestanian	Alekseev 1994a
13. Bunuba	Australian	Rumsey 2000
14. Bunun (Isbukun)	Austronesian	Lin 2001
15. Cantonese	Sino-Tibetan	Matthews and Yip 1994
16. Chamorro	Austronesian	Topping 1973
17. ChiBemba	Niger-Congo	Hyman 1994
18. Chickasaw	Muskogean	Martin and Munro 2005
19. Choctaw	Muskogean	Lombardi and McCarthy 1991
20. Chontal	Mayan	Waterhouse 1962
21. Chrau	Austro-Asiatic	Thomas 1971
22. Colville	Salishan	Mattina 1973
23. Creek	Muskogean	Martin 1994
24. Dakota	Siouan	Albright 2002; Boas and Deloria 1941; Moravcsik 1977
25. Dargi (Akusha)	Nakh-Daghestanian	van den Berg 1999
26. Djingili	Australian	Chadwick 1975; Fabricius 1998
27. English	Indo-European	McCarthy 1982; Viau 2002; Yu 2004b
28. Greek	Indo-European	Garrett forthcoming a
29. Harari	Afro-Asiatic	Rose 1997, 2003a, 2003b
30. Hausa	Afro-Asiatic	Newman 1990, 2000
31. Hopi	Uto-Aztecan	Jeanne 1982; Kershner 1999
32. Hua	Trans-New Guinea	Haiman 1977, 1980
33. Huave	Huavean	Stairs and Hollenbach 1969
34. Hunzib	Nakh-Daghestanian	van den Berg 1995
35. Ilokano	Austronesian	Vanoverbergh 1955

36. Ineseño Chumash	Hokan	Applegate 1976
37. IsiXhosa	Niger-Congo	Downing 1998
38. Kadazan	Austronesian	Antonissen 1958
39. Kamaiurá	Tupi	Everett and Seki 1985
40. Kamhmʔ	Austro-Asiatic	Anderson 1992; Merrifield, Naish, Resch, and Story 1965
41. Kashaya Pomo	Hokan	Buckley 1994, 1997
42. Katu	Austro-Asiatic	Costello 1998; Costello and Sulavan 1996
43. Kentakbong	Austro-Asiatic	Omar 1975
44. KiChaga	Niger-Congo	Inkelas p. c.
45. Kiliwa	Hokan	Mixco 1985
46. Kinande	Niger-Congo	Downing 1999
47. Kiriwina/Kilivila	Austronesian	Lawton 1993; Senft 1986
48. Koasati	Muskogean	Kimball 1991
49. Korean	Isolate	Jun 1994
50. Kugu Nganhcara	Australian	Smith and Johnson 2000
51. Lepcha (Rong)	Sino-Tibetan	Benedict 1943
52. Leti	Austronesian	Blevins 1999
53. Lilloet	Salishan	van Eijk 1997
54. Lushootseed	Salishan	Urbanczyk 1996
55. Malagasy	Austronesian	Keenan and Polinsky 1998
56. Mandarin (Peking)	Sino-Tibetan	Chao 1948
57. Mandarin (Pingding)	Sino-Tibetan	Xu 1981; Yu 2004*a*
58. Mandarin (Yanggu)	Sino-Tibetan	Dong 1985; Yu 2004*a*
59. Mangarayi	Australian	Merlan 1982
60. Maricopa	Hokan	Thomas-Flinders 1981
61. Mikasuki	Muskogean	Martin 1994
62. Miskito	Misumalpan	Rouvier 2002
63. Mlabri	Austro-Asiatic	Rischel 1995
64. Mojave	Hokan	Munro 1976
65. Muna	Austronesian	van den Berg 1989
66. Nabak	Trans-New Guinea	Fabian, Fabian, and Peck 1971; Kiparsky 1986
67. Nakanai	Austronesian	Johnston 1980
68. Ngizim	Afro-Asiatic	Newman 1990
69. Nicobarese	Austro-Asiatic	Radhakrishnan 1981
70. Noni	Niger-Congo	Blevins and Garrett 1998; Hyman 1981
71. Old Chinese	Sino-Tibetan	Sagart 2000
72. Paiwan	Austronesian	Chen and Ma 1986
73. Palauan	Austronesian	Josephs 1975
74. Pangasinan	Austronesian	Benton 1971
75. Pazeh	Austronesian	Blust 1999
76. Quileute	Chimakuan	Andrade 1933; Broselow and McCarthy, 1983/84
77. Rutul	Nakh-Daghestanian	Alekseev 1994*b*

78. Samoan	Austronesian	Broselow and McCarthy 1983/84
79. Sanskrit	Indo-European	Whitney 1889
80. Shuswap	Salishan	Kuipers 1974; van Eijk 1990
81. SiSwati	Niger-Congo	Downing 1999
82. Sonora Yaqui	Uto-Aztecan	Dedrick and Casad 1999
83. Sundanese	Austronesian	Cohn 1992; Robins 1959
84. Surin Khmer	Austro-Asiatic	Thomas 1990
85. Tagalog	Austronesian	French 1988
86. Takelma	Penutian	Lee 1991; Sapir 1922
87. Temiar	Austro-Asiatic	Benjamins 1976; Gafos 1998
88. Tetun (Ferhan)	Austronesian	van Klinken 1999
89. Thao	Austronesian	Chang 1998
90. Thompson River Salish	Salishan: Interior	Thompson and Thompson 1992, 1996
91. Tiene	Niger-Congo	Ellington 1977; Hyman and Inkelas 1997
92. Tigre	Afro-Asiatic	Rose 2003*b*
93. Tigrinya	Afro-Asiatic	Buckley 1990; Rose 2003*b*
94. Timugon Murut	Austronesian	Prentice 1971
95. Tiriyo	Carib	Meira 1999
96. Toba Batak	Austronesian	Crowhurst 1998, 2001
97. Toratan (Ratahan)	Austronesian	Himmelmann and Wolff 1999
98. Trukese	Austronesian	Garrett 2001; Goodenough and Sugita 1980; Goodenough 1963
99. Tzeltal	Mayan	Nida 1949; Slocum 1948
100. Tzutujil	Mayan	Dayley 1985
101. Ulwa	Misumalpan	Green 1999; Hale and Lacayo Blanco 1989
102. Uradhi	Australian	Crowley 1983; Fabricius 1998
103. Wardaman	Australian	Merlan 1994
104. Washo	Isolate/Hokan	Jacobsen 1964; Yu 2005*a*
105. West Tarangan	Austronesian	Nivens 1992
106. Yagaria	Trans-New Guinea	Renck 1975
107. Yir Yoront	Australian	Alpher 1991; Fabricius 1998
108. Yuma	Hokan	Halpern 1946, 1947*a*, 1947*b*
109. Yurok	Algic	Garrett 2001; Robins 1958
110. Zoque	Mixe-Zoque	Wonderly 1951
111. Zuni	Isolate	Newman 1965

References

Akinlabi, A. (1996). 'Featural affixation', *Journal of Linguistics*, 32 (2): 239–89.

Albright, A. C. (2002). 'The identification of bases in morphological paradigms'. Unpublished Ph.D. (Los Angeles: University of California, Los Angeles).

—— and Hayes, B. (2003). 'Rules vs. analogy in English past tenses: A computational/ experimental study', *Cognition*, 90: 119–61.

Alekseev, M. E. (1994*a*). 'Budukh', in R. Smeets (ed.), *The Indigenous Languages of the Caucasus, Volume 4: North East Caucasian Language Part 2 Presenting the Three Nakh Languages and Six Minor Lezgian Languages* (Delmar, New York: Caravan Books), 259–96.

—— (1994*b*). 'Rutul', in R. Smeets (ed.), *The Indigenous Languages of the Caucasus, Volume 4: North East Caucasian Language Part 2 Presenting the Three Nakh Languages and Six Minor Lezgian Languages* (Delmar, New York: Caravan Books), 213–58.

Alidou, O. D. (1997). 'A phonological study of language games in six languages of Niger'. Unpublished Ph.D. (Bloomington: Indiana University).

Alpher, B. (1991). *Yir-Yoront Lexicon: Sketch and Dictionary of an Australian Language* (Berlin, New York: Mouton de Gruyter).

Andersen, H. (1973). 'Abductive and deductive change', *Language*, 49: 765–93.

Anderson, G. D. S. (1996). 'Interior Salish reduplication in a diachronic perspective', in *Proceedings of the 22nd Annual Meeting of the Berkeley Linguistics Society* (Berkeley: Berkeley Linguistics Society), 11–24.

Anderson, S. (1972). 'On nasalization in Sundanese', *Linguistic Inquiry*, 3: 253–68.

—— (1988). 'Morphological change', in F. Newmeyer (ed.), *Linguistics: The Cambridge Survey*, Vol. 1 (Cambridge: Cambridge University Press), 324–62.

—— (1992). *A-morphous Morphology* (Cambridge: Cambridge University Press).

—— (2000). 'Towards and Optimal account of second-position phenomena', in J. Dekkers, F. van der Leeuw, and J. van de Weijer (eds.), *Optimality Theory: Phonology, Syntax, and Acquisition* (New York: Oxford University Press), 302–33.

—— (2005). *Aspects of the Theory of Clitics* (Oxford: Oxford University Press).

Andrade, M. (1933). *Quileute* (New York: Columbia University Press).

Antonissen, A. (1958). *Kadazan-English and English-Kadazan Dictionary* (Canberra: Government Printing Office).

Anttila, A. (1997). 'Variation in Finnish phonology and morphology'. Unpublished Ph.D. (Palo Alto: Stanford University).

—— (2002). 'Morphologically conditioned phonological alternations', *Natural Language and Linguistics Theory*, 20: 1–42.

—— (2006). 'Variation and opacity', *Natural Language and Linguistic Theory* 24 (4): 893–944.

Applegate, R. (1976). 'Reduplication in Chumash', in M. Langdon and S. Silver (eds.), *Hokan studies* (The Hague: Mouton), 271–83.

Aronoff, M. (1976). *Word Formation in Generative Grammar* (Cambridge, MA: MIT Press).

Aryan, R. (2001). 'Arabic Roots'. Unpublished MA thesis (Dominguez Hills: California State University Dominguez Hills).

Avery, P. and Lamontagne, G. (1995). 'Infixation <and metathesis> in Tagalog'. Paper presented at the Canadian Linguistics Association, Montreal, 3 June.

Bagemihl, B. (1988). 'Alternate phonologies and morphologies'. Unpublished Ph.D. (Vancouver: University of British Columbia).

—— (1995). 'Language games and related areas', in J. A. Goldsmith (ed.), *The Handbook of Phonological Theory* (Cambridge: Blackwell Publishers), 697–712.

Bao, Z.-M. (1990). 'Fanqie languages and reduplication', *Linguistic Inquiry*, 21: 317–50.

Barnes, J. A. (2002). 'Positional neutralization: A phonologization approach to typological patterns'. Unpublished Ph.D. (Berkeley: University of California, Berkeley).

—— (2006). *Strength and Weakness at the Interface* (Berlin and New York: Mouton de Gruyter).

Bat-El, O. (2002). *Hebrew Reduplication: The Interpretation of Forms with Identical Consonants*. Unpublished manuscript.

Bates, D. and Carlson, B. (1998). 'Spokene (Npoqíniscn) syllable structure and reduplication', in E. Czaykowska-Higgins and M. D. Kinkade (eds.), *Salish Languages and Linguistics* (Berlin: Mouton de Gruyter), 99–124.

—— Hess, T. and Hilbert, V. (1994). *Lushootseed Dictionary* (Seattle: University of Washington Press).

Beckman, J. N. (1997). 'Positional faithfulness, positional neutralization and Shona vowel harmony', *Phonology*, 14: 1–46.

—— (1999). *Positional Faithfulness: An Optimality Theoretic Treatment of Phonological Asymmetries* (New York and London: Garland Publishing).

Benedict, P. K. (1943). 'Secondary infixation in Lepcha', *Studies in Linguistics,* 1 (19): 2.

Benjamins, G. (1976). 'An outline of Temiar grammar', in P. Jenner and L. Thompson (eds.), *Austroasiatic Studies* (Honolulu: University of Hawaii Press), 129–88.

Benton, R. A. (1971). *Pangasinan Reference Grammar* (Honolulu: University of Hawaii Press).

Berg, H. van den (1995). *A Grammar of Hunzib (with texts and lexicon)* (Munich, Newcastle: Lincom Europa).

—— (1999). 'Gender and person agreement in Akusha Dargi', *Folia Linguistica*, 33 (2): 153–68.

Berg, R. van den, (1989). *A Grammar of the Muna Language* (Dordrecht-Holland: Foris Publication).

Bergsland, K. (1976). *Lappische Grammatik mit Lesestücken* (Wiesbaden: Otto Harrassowitz).

Bissell, T. (2002). 'Avoidance of the Marked in Miya Pluractional Allomorphy', *MIT Working Papers in Linguistics*, 42: 1–22.

Blevins, J. (1999). 'Untangling Leti infixation', *Oceanic Linguistics*, 38 (2): 383–403.

—— (2004). *Evolutionary Phonology: The Emergence of Sound Patterns* (Cambridge: Cambridge University Press).

—— and Garrett, A. (1998). 'The origins of consonant-vowel metathesis', *Language*, 74 (3): 508–56.

—— —— (2005). 'The evolution of metathesis', in B. Hayes, R. Kirchner, and D. Steriade (eds.), *The Phonetic Basis of Phonology* (Cambridge: Cambridge University Press), 117–56.

Blust, R. (1999). 'Notes on Pazeh phonology and morphology', *Oceanic Linguistics*, 38 (2): 321–65.

Boas, F. and Deloria, E. (1941). *Dakota Grammar* (Washington: United States Government Printing Office).

Boersma, P. (1998). *Functional Phonology: Formalizing the Interactions between Articulatiory and Perceptual Devices* (The Hague: Holland Academic Graphics).

Bonet, E., Lloret, M.-R., and Mascaró, J. (2003). *Phonology-morphology Conflicts in Gender Allomorphy: A Unified Approach.* Paper presented at the GLOW, Lund, Sweden, 9–11 April.

Booij, G. (1985). 'Coordination reduction in complex words: A case for prosodic phonology', in H. van de Hulst and N. Smith (eds.), *Advances in Non-linear Phonology* (Dordrecht: Foris), 143–60.

—— and Rubach, J. (1984). 'Morphological and prosodic domains in lexical phonology', *Phonology Yearbook*, 1: 1–27.

—— —— (1987). 'Postcyclic versus postlexical rules in lexical phonology', *Linguistic Inquiry*, 18: 1–44.

Booker, K. M. (1979). 'Comparative Muskogean: Aspects of Proto-Muskogean verb morphology'. Unpublished Ph.D. (Lawrence: University of Kansas).

—— (2005). 'Muskogean historical phonology', in H. K. Hardy and J. Scancarelli (eds.), *Native Languages of the Southeastern United States* (Lincoln: University of Nebraska Press), 246–98.

Bouquiaux, L. (1970). *La Langue birom (Nigéia septentrional): Phonologie, morphologie, syntaxe* (Paris: Soc. d'édition 'Les belles lettres').

Broselow, E. (1995). 'Skeletal positions and moras', in J. A. Goldsmith (ed.), *The Handbook of Phonological Theory* (Oxford: Blackwell Publishers), 175–205.

—— and McCarthy, J. (1983/84). 'A theory of internal reduplication', *Linguistic Review*, 3: 25–88.

Buckley, E. (1990). 'Edge-in association and OCP "violations" in Tigrinya', *Proceedings of the West Coast Conference on Formal Linguistics*, 9: 75–90.

—— (1994). *Theoretical Aspects of Kashaya Phonology and Morphology* (Stanford: CSLI).

—— (1997). 'Explaining Kashaya infixation', in M. Juge and J. Moxley (eds.), *Proceeding of the 23rd Annual Meeting of the Berkeley Linguistics Society* (Berkeley: Berkeley Linguistics Society), 14–25.

Bybee, J. (2001). *Phonology and Language Use* (Cambridge: Cambridge University Press).

—— (forthcoming). 'Los mecanismos del cambio como universales lingüísticos', in R. Mairal and J. Gil (eds.), *En torno a los universales lingüísticos* (Cambridge: Cambridge University Press).

—— (1985*a*). 'Morphology as Lexical Organization', in M. Hammond and M. Noonan (eds.), *Theoretical Morphology: Approaches in Modern Linguistics* (San Diego: Academic Press), 119–41.

—— (1985*b*). *Morphology: A Study of the Relation between Meaning and Form* (Amsterdam: John Benjamins).

—— (1995). 'Regular morphology and the lexicon', *Language and Cognitive Processes*, 10 (5): 425–55.

Campbell, L. (1986). 'Testing phonology in the field', in J. J. Ohala and J. J. Jaeger (eds.), *Experimental Phonology* (Orlando: Academic Press), 163–74.

Carlson, B. (1989). 'Reduplication and stress in Spokane', *International Journal of American Linguistics*, 46: 21–6.

Carpenter, B. (1992). *The Logic of Typed Feature Structure* (Cambridge: Cambridge University Press).

Carstairs-McCarthy, A. (1998). 'Phonological constraints on morphological rules', in A. Spencer and A. Zwicky (eds.), *The Handbook of Morphology* (Oxford: Blackwell Publishers), 144–8.

Chadwick, N. (1975). *A Descriptive Study of the Djingili Language* (Canberra: Australian Institute of Aboriginal Studies).

Chang, M. L. (1998). 'Thao reduplication', *Oceanic Linguistics*, 37 (2): 277–97.

Chao, Y. R. (1948). *Mandarin Primer* (Cambridge, MA: Harvard University Press).

—— (1968). *A Grammar of Spoken Chinese* (Berkeley, CA: University of California Press).

Chen, K. and Ma, R. (1986). *Gaoshanzu yu yan jian zhi [A Short Description of Formosan Languages: Paiwan]* (Peking: Min tsu chu pan she).

Chiu, B. H.-C. (1987). 'The morphology of the Alabama set I affixes', in P. Munroe (ed.), *Muskogean Linguistics* (Los Angeles: Department of Linguistics), 21–35.

Chomsky, N. (1986). *Knowledge of Language* (New York: Prager).

Clements, G. N. (1985). 'The problem of transfer in nonlinear morphology', *Cornell University Working Papers in Linguistics*, 7: 38–73.

Cohn, A. (1989). Stress in Indonesian and bracketing paradoxes. *Natural Language and Linguistics Theory*, 7, 167–216.

—— (1992). 'The consequences of dissimilation in Sundanese', *Phonology*, 9 (2): 199–220.

Conklin, H. (1956). 'Tagalog speech disguise', *Language*, 32: 136–9.

—— (1959). 'Linguistic play in its cultural context', *Language*, 35: 631–6.

Costello, N. A. (1998). 'Affixes in Katu of the Lao P. D. R', *Mon-Khmer Studies*, 28: 31–42.

—— and Sulavan, K. (1996). 'Preliminary statement of Katu orthography in Lao script', *Mon-Khmer Studies*, 26: 233–44.

Cowell, M. (1964). *A Reference Grammar of Syrian Arabic* (Georgetown: Georgetown University Press).

Crowhurst, M. (1998). 'Um infixation and prefixation in Toba Batak', *Language*, 74: 590–604.

—— (2001). 'Coda conditions and um infixation in Toba Batak', *Lingua*, 111: 561–90.

—— (2004). 'Mora alignment', *Natural Language and Linguistics Theory*, 22: 127–77.

Crowley, T. (1983). 'Uradhi', in R. M. A. Dixon and B. J. Blake (eds.), *Handbook of Australian Languages*, Vol. 3 (Canberra: ANU Press), 306–428.

Crysmann, B. (2000). *On the Placement and Morphology of Udi Subject Agreement.* Unpublished manuscript.

Dahl, O. C. (1976). *Proto-Austronesian*, 2nd edn. (London: Curzon Press).

Davis, S. (1988). 'On the nature of international reduplication', in M. Hammond and M. Noonan (eds.), *Theoretical Morphology: Approaches in Modern Linguistics* (San Diego: Academic Press), 305–24.

—— (2005). ' "Capitalistic" vs. "militaristic": The Paradigm Uniformity Effect reconsidered', In L. Downing, T. A. Hall, and R. Raffelsieffen (eds.), *Paradigms in Phonological Theory* (Oxford: Oxford University Press), 107–21.

Dayley, J. P. (1985). *Tzutujil Grammar* (Berkeley: University of California Press).

Dedrick, J. M. and Casad, E. H. (1999). *Sonora Yaqui Language Structures* (Tucson: University of Arizona Press).

Dixon, R. M. A. (1972). *The Dyirbal Language of North Queensland* (Cambridge: Cambridge University Press).

Dolbey, A. (1997). 'Output optimization and cyclic allomorph selection', *Proceedings of the West Coast Conference on Formal Linguistics*, 15: 97–112.

—— and Hansson, G. (1999). 'The source of naturalness in synchronic phonology', in S. Billings, J. Boyle and A. Griffith (eds.), *CLS 35: The Main Session. Papers from the 35th Meeting of the Chicago Linguistic Society, Vol. 1* (Chicago: Chicago Linguistics Society), 59–69

Dong, S. (1985). 'Yanggu fangyan de erhua [Er-ization in the Yanggu dialect]'. *Zhonggua Yuwen [Chinese Linguistics and Literature]*, 4: 273–6.

Downing, L. J. (1998). 'Prosodic misalignment and reduplication', in G. Booij and J. van Marle (eds.), *Yearbook of Morphology 1997* (Amsterdam: Kluwer Academic Publishers), 83–120.

—— (1999). 'Verbal reduplication in three Bantu languages', in R. Kager, H. van der Hulst, and W. Zonneveld (eds.), *The Prosodic-Morphology Interface* (Cambridge: Cambridge University Press), 62–89.

—— (2000). 'Morphological and prosodic constraints on Kinande verbal reduplication', *Phonology*, 17 (1): 1–38.

Duanmu, S. (2000). *The Phonology of Standard Chinese* (Oxford: Oxford University Press).

Durie, M. (1985). *A Grammar of Acehnese on the Basis of a Dialect of North Aceh* (Cinnaminson: Foris Publications).

Egerod, S. (1965). 'Verb inflexion in Atayal', *Lingua*, 15: 251–82.

—— (1999). *Atayal-English Dictionary*, 2nd edn. (Copenhagen: The Royal Danish Academy of Sciences and Letters).

Eijk, J. P. van (1997). *The Lillooet Language* (Vancouver: UBC Press).

—— van (1990). 'VC Reduplication in Salish', *Anthropological Linguistics*, 32 (3–4): 228–62.

Ellington, J. (1977). *Aspects of the Tiene Language.* Unpublished Ph.D., (Madison: University of Wisconsin).

Elman, J., Bates, E., Johnson, M., Karmiloff-Smith, A., Parisi, D., and Plunkett, K. (1996). *Rethinking Innateness* (Cambridge, MA: MIT Press).

Elson, B. F. (1992). 'Reconstructing Mixe-Zoque', in Shin Ja J. Hwang and William R. Merrifield (eds.), *Language in Context: Essays for Robert E. Longacre*, Summer Institute of Linguistics and the University of Texas at Arlington Publications in Linguistics, 107 (Dallas: Summer Institute of Linguistics and the University of Texas at Arlington), 577–92.

Engelenhoven, A. T. P. G. van (2004). *Leti: A Language of Southwest Maluku*, Vol. 211 (Leiden: KITLV Press).

Everrett, D. and Seki, L. (1985). 'Reduplication and CV skeletal in Kamaiurá', *Linguistic Inquiry*, 16: 326–30.

Fabian, E., Fabian, G., and Peck, C. W. (1971). 'The morphophemics of Nabak', *Kivung*, 4: 147–60.

Fabricius, A. H. (1998). *A Comparative Survey of Reduplication in Australian* (Munich: Lincom Europa).

Ferrell, R. (1982). *Paiwan Dictionary*, Vol. 73 (Canberra, Australia: Research School of Pacific Studies, The Australian National University).

Fife, J. and King, G. (1998). 'Celtic (Indo-European)', in A. Spencer and A. Zwicky (eds.), *The Handbook of Morphology* (Oxford: Blackwell), 477–99.

Fillmore, C. and Kay, P. (1994). *Construction Grammar.* Unpublished manuscript, Berkeley.

Flemming, E. S. (1995). 'Auditory representations in phonology'. Unpublished Ph.D. (Los Angeles: University of California, Los Angeles).

Foster, M. K. (1982). 'Alternating weak and strong syllables in Cayuga words', *International Journal of American Linguistics*, 48: 59–72.

French, K. M. (1988). *Insights into Tagalog: Reduplication, Infixation, and Stress from Nonlinear Phonology* (Arlington, Texas: Summer Institute for Linguistics and University of Texas at Arlington).

Fromkin, V. A. (1980). 'Introduction', in V. A. Fromkin (ed.), *Errors in Linguistic Performance* (New York: Academic Press), 1–12.

Gafos, D. (1998). 'Eliminating long-distance consonantal spreading', *Natural Language and Linguistics Theory*, 16: 223–78.

—— (1999). *The Articulatory Basis of Locality in Phonology* (New York: Garland).

Galloway, B. (1993). *A Grammar of Upriver Halkomelem* (Berkeley and Los Angeles: University of California Press).

Garrett, A. (2001). 'Reduplication and infixation in Yurok: Morphology, semantics, and diachrony', *International Journal of American Linguistics*, 67 (3): 264–312.

—— (Forthcoming). 'Paradigm uniformity and markedness', in J. Good (ed.), *Explaining Linguistic Universals: Historical Convergence and Universal Grammar* (Oxford: Oxford University Press).

Gimba, A. M. (2000). 'Bole verb morphology'. Unpublished Ph.D. (Los Angeles: University of California, Los Angeles).

Goad, H. (2001). 'Assimilation phenomena and initial constraint ranking in early grammars', *Proceedings of the Boston University: Concerence on Language Development*, 25: 307–18.

Goldberg, A. (1999). 'The emergence of the semantics of argument structure constructions', in B. MacWhinney (ed.), *The Emergence of Language* (Mahwah, NJ: Lawrence Erlbaum).

—— (2006). *Constructions at Work: The Nature of Generalization in Language* (Oxford: Oxford University Press).

Goodenough, W. H. (1963). 'The long or double consonants of Trukese', in *Proceedings of the Ninth Pacific Science Congress of the Pacific Science Association, vol. 1, Introductory and International Cooperation in Science* (Bangkok: Department of Science), 77–80.

—— and Sugita, H. (1980). *Trukese-English Dictionary* (Philadelphia: American Philosophical Society).

Gordon, L. (1986). *Maricopa Morphology and Syntax* (Berkeley: University of California Press).

Gordon, M. (1999). 'Syllable weight: phonetics, phonology, and typology'. Unpublished Ph.D. (Los Angeles: University of California, Los Angeles).

—— (2001). 'A typology of contour tone restriction' *Studies in Language*, 25 (3): 423–62.

—— (2002). 'A factorial typology of quantity insensitive stress', *Natural Language and Linguistics Theory*, 20: 491–552.

Green, T. M. (1999). 'A Lexicographic Study of Ulwa'. Unpublished Ph.D. (Cambridge, MA: MIT).

Greenberg, J. H. (1966). 'Some universals of grammar with particular reference to the order of meaningful elements', in J. H. Greenberg (ed.), *Universals of Language* (Cambridge, MA: MIT Press).

—— (1969). 'Some methods of dynamic comparison in linguistics', in J. Puhvel (ed.), *Substance and Structure of Language* (Berkeley: University of California Press), 147–203.

Haas, M. R. (1977). 'From auxiliary verb to inflectional suffix', in C. N. Li (ed.), *Mechanisms of Syntactic Change* (Austin: University of Texas Press), 525–37.

Haiman, J. (1977). 'Reinterpretation', *Language*, 53: 312–28.

Haiman, J. (1980). *Hua: A Papuan Language of the Eastern Highlands of New Guinea* (Amsterdam: John Benjamins).

—— (2003). 'Explaining infixation', in J. Moore and M. Polinsky (eds.), *The Nature of Explanation in Linguistic Theory* (Palo Alto: CSLI Publications), 105–20.

Hale, K. and Lacayo Blanco, A. (1989). *Diccionario Elemental del Ulwa (Sumu Meridional)* (Cambridge, MA: Center for Cognitive Science, MIT).

Hale, M. and Reiss, C. (2000). ' "Substance abuse" and "dysfunctionalism": Current trends in phonology', *Linguistic Inquiry*, 31 (1): 157–69.

—— (2001). 'Infixation versus onset metathesis in Tagalog, Chamorro, and Toba Batak', in M. Kenstowicz (ed.), *Ken Hale: A Life in Language* (Cambridge, MA: MIT Press), 153–68.

—— & Marantz, A. (1993). 'Distributed Morphology and the pieces of inflection', in K. Hale and S. J. Keyser (eds.), *The View from Building 20* (Cambridge, MA: MIT Press), 111–76.

Halpern, A. M. (1946). 'Yuma', in C. Osgood (ed.), *Linguistic Structures of Native America* (New York: Viking Fund Publications in Anthropology), 249–88.

—— (1947a). 'Yuma IV: Verb themes', *International Journal of American Linguistics*, 13 (1): 18–30.

—— (1947b). 'Yuma V: Conjugation of the verb theme', *International Journal of American Linguistics*, 13 (2): 92–107.

Hansson, G. (2001). 'Theoretical and typological issues in consonantal harmony'. Unpublished Ph.D. (Berkeley: University of California, Berkeley).

Hardy, H. K. and Montler, T. R. (1988). 'Alabama radical morphology: H-infix and disfixation', in W. Shipley (ed.), *In Honour of Mary Haas. From the Haas Festival Conference on Native American Linguistics* (Berlin: Mouton de Gruyter), 377–409.

Hargus, S. (1993). 'Modeling the phonology-morphology inteface', in S. Hargus and E. Kaisse (eds.), *Studies in Lexical Phonology* (London: Academic Press), 45–74.

Harris, A. C. (1997). *What's in a Word? The Problem of Endoclisis in Udi*. Unpublished manuscript.

—— (2000). 'Where in the word is the Udi clitic?' *Language*, 76 (3): 593–616.

—— (2002). *Endoclitics and the Origins of Udi Morphosyntax* (Oxford: Oxford University Press).

—— and Campbell, L. (1995). *Historical Syntax in Cross-linguistic Perspective* (Cambridge: Cambridge University Press).

Harrison, K. D. and Kaun, A. R. (1999). 'Pattern responsive lexicon optimization', *Proceedings of the North East Linguistics Society*, 30: 327–40.

—— —— (2001). 'Patterns of pervasive patterns, and feature specification', in T. A. Hall (ed.), *Distinctive Feature Theory* (Berlin: Mouton de Gruyter), 211–36.

Haspelmath, M. (1995). 'The growth of affixes in morphological reanalysis', in G. Booij and J. van Marle (eds.), *Yearbook of Morphology 1994* (Dordrecht: Kluwer), 1–29.

Hawkins, J. A. and Cutler, A. (1988). 'Psycholinguistic factors in morphology asymmetry', in J. A. Hawkins (ed.), *Explaining Language Universals* (Oxford: Basil Blackwell), 280–317.

Hayes, B. (1982). 'Extrametricality and English stress', *Linguistic Inquiry*, 13: 227–76.

—— (1989). 'Compensatory lengthening in moraic phonology', *Linguistic Inquiry*, 20: 253–306.

—— (1995). *Metrical Stress Theory: Principles and Case Studies* (Chicago: University of Chicago Press).

—— (1999). 'Phonetically driven phonology: The role of Optimality Theory and inductive grounding', in M. Darnell, E. Moravcsik, F. Newmeyer, M. Noonan, and K. Wheatley (eds.), *Formalism and Functionalism in Linguistics*, Vol. 1: General Papers, (Amsterdam: John Benjamins), 243–85.

He, W. (1989). *Huojia Fangyan Yanjiu* (Beijing: Beijing Shangwu Yinshuguan).

Himmelmann, N. P. and Wolff, J. U. (1999). *Toratán (Ratahan)* (Munich, Newcastle: Lincom Europa).

Ho, J.-f. *et al.* (1986). *Kao-shan tsu yu yen chien chih. A-mei-ssu yu [A short description of Formosan languages: Amis]* (Peking: Min tsu chu pan she).

Hombert, J.-M. (1986). 'Word games: Some implications for analysis of tone and other phonological constructs', in J. J. Ohala and J. J. Jaeger (eds.), *Experimental Phonology* (Orlando: Academic Press), 175–86.

Hopper, P. and Traugott, E. (1993). *Grammaticalization* (Cambridge: Cambridge University Press).

Huang, H.-c. J. (2005). *Contrast in Syllable Types: The Cases of Isbukun Bunun and Squliq Atayal.* Unpublished manuscript.

Hume, E. (2001). 'Metathesis: formal and functional considerations', in E. Hume, N. Smith, and J. van de Weijer (eds.), *Surface Syllable Structure and Segment Sequencing* (Leiden: HIL), 1–25.

—— (2004). 'The Indeterminacy/Attestation model of metathesis', *Language*, 80 (2): 203–37.

—— and Johnson, K. (2001). 'A model of the interplay between speech perception and phonology', in E. Hume and K. Johnson (eds.), *The Role of Speech Perception in Phonology* (New York: Academic Press), 3–26.

Hyman, L. (1977). 'On the nature of linguistic stress', in L. Hyman (ed.), *Studies in Stress and Accent. Southern California Occasional Papers in Linguistics*, 4 (Los Angeles: Department of Linguistics, University of Southern California).

—— (1979). *Aghem Grammatical Structure* (Los Angeles: Department of Linguistics, University of Southern California).

—— (1981). *Noni Grammatical Structure* (Los Angeles: Department of Linguistics, University of Southern California).

—— (1994). 'Cyclic phonology and morphology in ChiBemba', in C. Kisseberth and J. Cole (eds.), *Perspectives in Phonology* (Stanford: CSLI), 81–112.

—— and Inkelas, S. (1997). 'Emergent templates: The unusual case of Tiene', in V. Miglio and B. Morén (eds.), *University of Maryland Working Papers in Linguistics: Selected Phonology Papers from H-OT-97* (College Park: University of Maryland Department of Linguistics), 92–116.

Inkelas, S. (1990). *Prosodic Constituency in the Lexicon* (New York: Garland Publishing).

Inkelas, S. (1993). 'Deriving cyclicity', in S. Hargus and E. Kaisse (eds.), *Studies in Lexical Phonology* (London: Academic Press), 75–110.

—— (1998). 'The theoretical status of morphologically conditioned phonology: A case study of dominance effects', *Yearbook of Morphology*, 1997: 121–55.

—— (2005). 'Morphological Doubling Theory I: Evidence for morphological doubling in reduplication', in B. Hurch (ed.), *Studies in Reduplication* (Berlin: Mouton de Gruyter), 65–88.

—— Orgun, C. O., and Zoll, C. (1997). 'The implications of lexical exceptions for the nature of grammar', in I. Roca (ed.), *Derivations and Constraints in Phonology* (Oxford: Clarendon Press), 393–418.

—— and Zoll, C. (2005). *Reduplication: Doubling in Morphology* (Cambridge: Cambridge University Press).

Ito, J. and Mester, A. (1992). *Weak Layering and Word Binarity* (Santa Cruz: University of California, Santa Cruz).

—— —— (1999). 'Realignment', in R. Kager, H. van der Hulst, and W. Zonneveld (eds.), *The Prosody-Morphology Interface* (Cambridge: Cambridge University Press), 188–217.

Jacobsen, W. H. J. (1964). 'A grammar of the Washo language'. Unpublished Ph.D., (Berkeley: University of California, Berkeley).

Janda, R. (1984). 'Why morphological metathesis rules are rare: On the possibility of historical explanation in linguistics', in C. Brugman and M. Macaulay (eds.), *Proceedings of the 10th Annual Meeting of the Berkeley Linguistics Society* (Berkeley: Berkeley Linguistics Society), 87–103.

Jeanne, L. M. (1982). 'Some phonological rules of Hopi', *International Journal of American Linguistics*, 48 (3): 245–70.

Jensen, J. T. (1993). *English Phonology* (Amsterdam: Benjamins).

—— (2000). 'Against ambisyllabicity', *Phonology*, 17 (3): 187–235.

Johnston, R. L. (1980). *Nakanai of New Britain: The Grammar of an Oceanic Language* (Canberra: Australian National University).

Joseph, B. D. and Janda, R. (1988). 'The how and why of diachronic morphologization and demorphologization', in M. Hammond and M. Noonan (eds.), *Theoretical Morphology: Approaches in Modern Linguistics* (San Diego: Academic Press), 193–210.

Josephs, L. S. (1975). *Palauan Reference Grammar* (Honolulu: University Press of Hawaii).

Jun, J. (1994). 'Metrical weight consistency in Korean partial reduplication', *Phonology*, 11: 69–88.

Kager, R. (2000). *Optimality Theory* (Cambridge: Cambridge University Press).

Kaisse, E. (1981). 'Separating phonology from syntax: A reanalysis of Pashto cliticization', *Journal of Linguistics*, 17: 197–208.

Kaufman, D. (2003). 'Paradigm effects and the affix-shape/position generalization', *Proceedings of the West Coast Conference on Formal Linguistics*, 22: 273–86.

Kavitskaya, D. (2001). 'Compensatory lengthening: Phonetics, phonology, diachrony'. Unpublished Ph.D. (Berkeley: University of California, Berkeley).

Kawu, A. (2000). 'Structural markedness and non-reduplicative copying', in *Proceedings of NELS 20* (GLSA: University of Massachusetts, Amherst), 377–88.

Keenan, E. L. and Polinsky, M. (1998). 'Malagasy morphology', in A. Spencer and A. Zwicky (eds.), *The Handbook of Morphology* (Oxford: Blackwell), 563–624.

Kehoe, M. and Stoel-Gammon, C. (1997). 'The acquisition of prosodic structure: An investigation of current accounts of children's prosodic development', *Language*, 73 (1): 113–44.

Kenstowicz, M. and Kisseberth, C. (1977). *Topics in Phonological Theory* (New York: Academic Press).

Kershner, T. L. (1999). 'Generational faithfulness in Hopi reduplicative infixation', in K. Baertsch and D. A. Dinnsen (eds.), *IUWPL 1: Optimal Green Ideas in Phonology* (Bloomington, IN: IULC Publications), 11–29.

Kibrik, A. (1989). 'Archi', in R. Smeets (ed.), *The Indigenous Languages of the Caucasus, Volume 4: North East Caucasian Language Part 2 presenting the three Nakh languages and six minor Lezgian languages* (Delmar, New York: Caravan Books), 297–366.

—— (1998). 'Archi (Caucasian—Daghestanian)', in A. Spencer and A. Zwicky (eds.), *The Handbook of Morphology* (Oxford: Blackwell Publishers), 455–76.

—— and Kodzasov, S. (1988). *Sopostavitel'noe izuchenie dagnestanskix jazykov. Glagol* (Moskva: Izdatel'stvo Moskovskogo universiteta).

Kimball, G. (1991). *Koasati Grammar* (Lincoln: University of Nebraska Press).

Kiparsky, P. (1983). 'Word formation in the lexicon', in F. Ingemann (ed.), *Proceedings of the 1982 Mid-America Linguistics Conference* (Lawrence: University of Kansas), 3–29.

—— (1986). *The Phonology of Reduplication*. Unpublished manuscript, Stanford.

—— (2000). 'Opacity and cyclicity', *The Linguistic Review*, 17: 351–67.

Kirchner, R. (1998). 'An effort-based approach to consonant lenition'. Unpublished Ph.D. (Los Angeles: University of California, Los Angeles).

—— (2000). 'Geminate inalterability and lenition', *Language*, 76: 509–45.

Klinken, C. L. van (1999). *A Grammar of the Fehan Dialect of Tetu: An Austronesian Language of West Timor* (Canberra: The Australian National University).

Koenig, J.-P. and Jurafsky, D. (1994). 'Type underspecification and on-line type construction in the lexicon', in *Proceedings of WCCFL 13* (Stanford: CSLI), 270–85.

Kuipers, A. H. (1974). *The Shuswap Language: Grammar, Texts, Dictionary* (The Hague: Mouton).

Kurisu, K. (2001). 'The phonology of morpheme realization'. Unpublished Ph.D. (Santa Cruz: University of California, Santa Cruz).

—— and Sanders, N. (1999). 'Infixal nominal reduplication in Mangarayi. Phonology at Santa Cruz', *Phonology at Santa Cruz*, 6: 47–56.

Kurylowicz, J. (1958). *L'accentuation des langues indo-europeenes* (Wroclaw-Krakow).

Lacy, P. de (1996). *Circumscription Revisited: An Analysis of Maori Reduplication*. Unpublished manuscript, Auckland, New Zealand.

Lawton, R. (1993). *Topics in the Description of Kiriwina* (Canberra: Australian National University).

Lazard, G. and Peltzer, L. (2000). *Structure de la langue tahitienne* (Paris: Peeters).

Leben, W. (2001). 'Tonal feet', in *Proceedings of the Typology of African Prosodic Systems Workshop* (Bielefeld) <http://www.spectrum.uni- bielefeld.de/TAPS/Leben.pdf>.

Lee, A. P. (2005). 'Rightward reduplication in Formosan languages revisited', *UCLA Working Papers in Linguistics*, 12 (September): 227–39.

Lee, B. (1991). 'Prosodic structures in Takelma phonology and morphology'. Unpublished Ph.D. (Austin: The University of Texas at Austin).

Lehiste, I. (1985). 'An Estonian word game and the phonematic status of long vowels', *Linguistic Inquiry*, 16 (3): 490–2.

Lengendre, G. (2000). 'Morphological and prosodic alignment of Bulgarian clitics', in J. Dekkers, F. van der Leeuw, and J. van de Weijer (eds.), *Optimality Theory: Phonology, Syntax, and Acquisition* (New York: Oxford University Press), 423–62.

Li, C. N. and Thompson, S. A. (1981). *Mandarin Chinese: A Functional Reference Grammar* (Berkeley: University of California Press).

Li, P. J.-k. (1980). 'The phonological rules of Atayal dialects', *Bulletin of the Institute of History and Philology*, 51 (2): 349–405.

—— and Tsuchida, S. (2001). *Pazih Dictionary* (Taipei: Academic Sinica).

Li, Z. (1991). 'Yi Meng Fangyan de Fenyinci', *Fangyan*, 1982 (1): 37–46.

Lieber, R. (1980). 'On the organization of the lexicon'. Unpublished Ph.D. (Cambridge, MA: MIT).

Lin, T. (2001). *Isbukun: Bunong yu gou ci fa yan jiu [Bunun word formation]* (Taibei City: Du ce wen hua shi ye you xian gong si).

Lin, Y.-H. (2002). *Faithfulness, Alignment, and Markedness in Pingding Er Infixation.* Unpublished manuscript, Michigan State University.

Lombardi, L. and McCarthy, J. (1991). 'Prosodic circumscription in Choctaw morphology', *Phonology*, 8: 37–71.

Lubowicz, A. (2005). *Infixation as Morpheme Absorption.* Unpublished manuscript, Los Angeles.

MacWhinney, B. (1999). 'The emergence of language from embodiment', in B. MacWhinney (ed.), *The Emergence of Language* (Mahwah, NJ: Lawrence Erlbaum).

Marantz, A. (1982). 'Re reduplication', *Linguistic Inquiry*, 13: 435–83.

Marcus, D. (1978). *A Manual of Akkadian* (New York: University Press of America).

Martin, J. (1994). 'Implications of plural reduplication, infixation and subtraction for Muskogean subgrouping', *Anthropological Linguistics*, 36: 27–55.

Martin, J. B. and Munro, P. (2005). 'Proto-Muskogean morphology', in H. K. Hardy and J. Scancarelli (eds.), *Native Languages of the Southeastern United States* (Lincoln: University of Nebraska Press), 299–320.

Matthews, P. (1974). *Morphology: An Introduction to the Theory of Word-Structure* (Cambridge: Cambridge University Press).

Matthews, S. and Yip, V. (1994). *Cantonese Grammar: A Comprehensive Grammar* (London, New York: Routledge).

Mattina, A. (1973). *Colville Grammatical Structure* (Honolulu: University of Hawaii).

McArthur, T. (1992). *The Oxford Companian to the English Language* (Oxford: Oxford University Press).

McCarthy, J. (1979). *Formal Problems in Semitic Phonology and Morphology.* Unpublished Ph.D. (Cambridge, MIT).

—— (1981). 'A prosodic theory of nonconcatenative morphology', *Linguistic Inquiry*, 12: 373–418.

—— (1982). 'Prosodic structure and expletive infixation', *Language*, 58: 574–90.

—— (1991). 'L'infixation réduplicative dans les langages secrets', *Langages*, 101: 11–29.

—— (2000). 'Faithfulness and prosodic circumscription', in J. Dekkers, F. van der Leeuw, and J. van de Weijer (eds.), *Optimality Theory: Phonology, Syntax, and Acquisition* (New York: Oxford University Press).

—— (2003*a*). 'Optimal paradigms', in L. Downing, T. A. Hall, and R. Raffelsiefen (eds.), *Paradigms in Phonological Theory* (Oxford: Oxford University Press), 170–210.

—— (2003*b*). 'OT constraints are categorical', *Phonology*, 20 (1): 75–138.

—— and Prince, A. (1986). *Prosodic Morphology.* Unpublished manuscript, University of Massachusetts and Brandeis University.

—— —— (1990). 'Foot and word in Prosodic Morphology: The Arabic broken plural', *Natural Language and Linguistics Theory*, 8: 209–83.

—— —— (1993*a*). 'Generalized alignment', in G. Booij and J. van Marle (eds.), *Yearbook of Morphology 1993* (Dordrecht: Kluwer Academics), 79–153.

—— —— (1993*b*). *Prosodic Morphology I: Constraint interaction and satisfaction.* Unpublished manuscript, University of Massachusetts, Amherst, and Rutgers University.

—— —— (1994*a*). 'The emergence of the unmarked', in M. Gonzalez (ed.), *Proceedings of the 24th Annual Meeting of the Northeast Linguistics Society*, (Amherst, MA. GLSA), 333–79.

—— —— (1994*b*). *An overview of Prosodic Morphology: Parts I and II.* Unpublished manuscript, Utrecht University.

—— —— (1995). 'Faithfulness and reduplicative identity', in J. N. Beckman, L. W. Dickey, and S. C. Urbanczyk (eds.), *Papers in Optimality Theory* (Amherst: GLSA), 249–384.

—— and Wolf, M. (2005). *Less than Zero: Correspondence and the Null Output.* Unpublished manuscript.

McCawley, J. (1978). 'Where you can shove infixes', in A. Bell and J. Hooper (eds.), *Syllables and Segments* (Amsterdam and New York: North Holland), 213–21.

Meira, S. (1999). 'A Grammar of Tiriyó'. Unpublished Ph.D. (Houston: Rice University).

Merlan, F. (1982). *Mangarayi* (Amsterdam: North-Holland).

—— (1994). *A Grammar of Wardaman: A Language of the Northern Territory of Australia*, Vol. 11 (Berlin: Mouton de Gruyter).

Merrifield, W. R., Naish, C. M., Resch, C. R., and Story, G. (1965). *Laboratory Manual for Morphology and Syntax* (Santa Ana, CA: Summer Institute of Linguistics).

Mielke, J. (2004). 'The emergence of distinctive features'. Unpublished Ph.D. (Columbus: Ohio State University).

Mikheev, A. (1997). 'Automatic rule induction for unknown-word guessing', *Computational Linguistics*, 23 (3): 405–23.

Mixco, M. (1985). *Kiliwa Dictionary* (Salt Lake City: University of Utah).

Montler, T. R. and Hardy, H. K. (1990). 'The phonology of Alabama agent agreement', *Word*, 41 (3): 257–76.

—— —— (1991). 'The phonology negation in Alabama', *International Journal of American Linguistics*, 57 (1): 1–23.

Moravcsik, E. (1977). *On Rules of Infixing* (Bloomington: Indiana University Linguistics Club).

—— (2000). 'Infixation', in G. Booij, C. Lehmann, and J. Mugdan (eds.), *Morphology: An International Handbook on Inflection and Word-Formation, Volume 1* (New York, Berlin: Walter de Gruyter), 545–52.

Morén, B. (2000). 'The puzzle of Kashmiri stress: implications for weight theory', *Phonology*, 17 (3): 365–96.

—— (2001). *Distinctiveness, Coercion and Sonority: A Unified Theory of Weight* (New York and London: Routledge).

Mosel, U. and Hovdhaugen, E. (1992). *Samoan Reference Grammar* (Oslo: Scandinavian University Press).

Munro, P. (1976). *Mojave Syntax* (New York: Garland).

—— (1987). 'Introduction: Muskogean Studies at UCLA', *UCLA Occasional Papers in Linguistics*, 6: 1–6.

—— (1993). 'The Muskogean II prefixes and their implications for classification', *International Journal of American Linguistics*, 59: 374–404.

Nelson, N. (2003). 'Asymmetric anchoring'. Unpublished Ph.D. (New Brunswick: Rutgers University, New Brunswick).

Nespor, M. and Vogel, I. (1986). *Prosodic Phonology* (Dordrecht: Foris).

Newman, P. (1971). 'The historical change from suffixal to prefixal reduplication in Hausa pluractional verbs', *Journal of African Languages and Linguistics*, 11: 37–44.

—— (1990). *Nominal and Verbal Plurality in Chadic* (Dordrecht, Holland: Foris Publications).

—— (2000). *The Hausa Language: An Encyclopedic Reference Grammar* (New Haven and London: Yale University Press).

Newman, S. (1965). *Zuni Grammar* (Albuquerque: The University of New Mexico Press).

Nichols, J. (2005). 'A bipartite stem outlier in Eurasia: Nakh-Daghestanian', in P. M. Novak, C. Yoquelet, and D. Mortensen (eds.), *Proceedings of the 29th Annual Meeting of the Berkeley Linguistics Society* (Berkeley: Berkeley Linguistics Society), 321–34.

Nida, E. A. (1949). *Morphology: The Descriptive Analysis of Words* (Ann Arbor: The University of Michigan Press).

Niepokuj, M. K. (1997). *The Development of Verbal Reduplication in Indo-European* (Washington: Institute for the Study of Man).

Nivens, R. (1992). 'A lexical phonology of West Tarangan', in D. Burquest and W. Laidig (eds.), *Phonological Studies in Four Languages of Maluku* (Arlington, Texas: Summer Institute of Linguistics & University of Texas at Arlington).

Ohala, J. J. (1983). 'The origin of sound patterns in vocal tract constraints', in P. F. MacNeilage (ed.), *The Production of Speech* (New York: Springer), 189–216.

—— (1993). 'The phonetics of sound change', in C. Jones (ed.), *Historical Linguistics: Problems and Perspectives* (London: Longman), 237–78.

Omar, A. H. (1975). *Essays on Malaysian Linguistics* (Kuala Lumpur: Dewan Bahsa dan Pustaka).

Orgun, C. O. (1996). 'Sign-based morphology and phonology with special attention to Optimality Theory'. Unpublished Ph.D. (Berkeley: University of California, Berkeley).

—— (1998). 'Cyclic and noncyclic phonological effects in a declarative grammar', *Yearbook of Morphology, 1997*: 179–218.

—— (1999). 'Sign-Based Morphology: A declarative theory of phonology-morphology interleaving', in B. Hermans and M. van Oostendorp (eds.), *Derivational Residue in Phonological Optimality Theory* (Amsterdam: John Benjamins), 247–67.

—— and Inkelas, S. (2002). 'Reconsidering Bracket Erasure'. *Yearbook of Morphology, 2001*: 115–46.

—— and Sprouse, R. L. (1999). 'From MParse to Control: Deriving ungrammaticality', *Phonology*, 16: 191–224.

Paster, M. (2006). 'Phonological conditions on affixation'. Unpublished Ph.D. (Berkeley: University of California, Berkeley).

Pater, J. (1999). 'Austronesian nasal substitution and other NC effects', in H. van der Hulst, R. Kager, and W. Zonneveld (eds.), *The Prosody Morphology Interface* (Cambridge: Cambridge University Press), 310–43.

—— (2001). 'Austronesian nasal substitution revisited: What's wrong with *NC (and what's not)', in L. Lombardi (ed.), *Segmental Phonology in Optimality Theory: Constraints and Representations* (Cambridge: Cambridge University Press), 159–82.

Payne, T. (1997). *Describing Morphosyntax: A Guide for Field Linguists* (Cambridge: Cambridge University Press).

Peters, A. M. (1983). *The Units of Language Acquisition* (Cambridge: Cambridge University Press).

Piggott, G. (2000). 'Against featural alignment', *Journal of Linguistics*, 36: 85–129.

Piñeros, C.-E. (1998). 'Prosodic morphology in Spanish: Constraint interaction in word-formation'. Unpublished Ph.D. (Columbus: Ohio State University).

Pollard, C. and Sag, I. A. (1994). *Head-driven Phrase Structure Grammar* (Chicago: University of Chicago Press).

Prentice, D. J. (1971). *The Murut Languages of Sabah* (Canberra, Australia: Linguistic Circle of Canberra).

Prince, A. and Smolensky, P. (1993). *Optimality Theory: Constraint Interaction in generative Grammar* (New Brunswick: Rutgers University and Boulder: University of Colorado).

Qian, Z., Cao, Z., and Luo, F. (1985). 'Phonetic differences and similarities among the dialects of Pingdu county, Shandong province', *Fangyan*, 3: 214–21.

Radhakrishnan, R. (1981). *The Nancowry Word, Phonology, Affixal Morphology and Roots of a Nicobarese Language* (Edmonton, Alberta: Linguistic Research Inc).

Rau, D.-h. V. (1992). 'A grammar of Atayal'. Unpublished Ph.D. (Ithaca: Cornell University).

Renck, G. L. (1975). *A Grammar of Yagaria* (Canberra: Research School of Pacific Studies, Australian National University).

Riggle, J. (2006). 'Infixing reduplication in Pima and its theoretical consequences', *Natural Languages and Linguistics Theory* 24 (3): 857–91.

Rischel, J. (1995). *Minor Mlabri: A Hunter-Gatherer Language of Northern Indochina* (Njalsgade: Museum Tusculanum Press).

Robins, R. H. (1958). *The Yurok Language: Grammar, Texts, Lexicon*, Vol. 15 (Berkeley: University of California Press).

—— (1959). 'Nominal and verbal derivation in Sundanese', *Lingua*, 8: 337–69.

Rohlfs, G. (1924). *Griechen und Romanen in Unteritalien: Ein Beitrag zur Geschichte der unteritalienischen Gräzität* (Geneva: Leo S. Olschki).

—— (1933). *Scavi linguistici nella Magna Grecia* (trans. B. Tomasini) (Rome: Collezione Meridionale Editrice).

Rose, S. (1997). 'Theoretical issues in comparative Ethio-Semitic phonology and morphology'. Unpublished Ph.D. (Montreal: McGill University).

—— (2003*a*). 'The formation of Ethiopian Semitic internal reduplication', in J. Shimron (ed.), *Language Processing and Acquisition in Languages of Semitic, Root-based, Morphology* (Amsterdam and Philadelphia: John Benjamins), 79–97.

—— (2003*b*). 'Triple Take: Tigre and the case of internal reduplication', *San Diego Linguistic Papers*, 1: 109–28.

—— and Walker, R. (2004). 'A typology of consonant agreement as correspondence', *Language*, 80: 475–531.

Rosenthal, S. (1999). 'The prosodic base of the Hausa plural', in R. Kager, H. van der Hulst, and W. Zonneveld (eds.), *The Prosody Morphology Interface* (Cambridge: Cambridge University Press), 344–66.

Rouvier, R. (2002). 'Infixation and reduplication in Misumalpan: A reconstruction'. Unpublished BA Honors Thesis (Berkeley: University of California, Berkeley).

Rumsey, A. (2000). 'Bunuba', in R. M. A. D. Dixon and B. J. Blake (eds.), *The Handbook of Australian Languages, Vol. 5: Grammatical Sketches of Bunuba, Ndjebbana and Kugu Nganhcara* (Oxford, New York: Oxford University Press), 35–154.

Sadtano, E. (1971). 'Language games in Javanese', in J. E. A. Sherzer (ed.), *A Collection of Linguistic Games* (Austin: University of Texas). pp

Sagart, L. (2000). 'Vestiges of Archaic Chinese derivational affixes in Modern Chinese dialects', in H. Chappell (ed.), *Sinitic Grammar: Synchronic and Diachronic Perspectives* (Oxford: Oxford University Press), 123–42.

Sapir, E. (1921). *Language: An Introduction to the Study of Speech* (New York: Harcourt, Brace and Co.).

—— (1922). 'The Takelma language of southwestern Oregon', in F. Boas (ed.), *Handbook of American Indian Languages, Part 2 (Bureau of American Ethnology, Bulletin 40)* (Washington, DC: Smithsonian Institution), 1–296.

Saussure, F. de (1916 [1986]). *Cours de linguistique générale* (trans. R. Harris) (Peru, IL: Open Court Publishing Company).

Schachter, P. and Otanes, F. T. (1972). *Tagalog Reference Grammar* (Berkeley: University of California Press).

Schmidt, P. W. (1906). *Die Mon-Khmer Völker: Ein Bindeglied zwischen Völkern Zentralasiens und Austronesiens* (Braunschweig: Friedrich Vieweg & Son).

Selkirk, E. O. (1982). *The Syntax of Words* (Cambridge, MA: MIT Press).

—— (1984). *Phonology and Syntax: The Relation between Sound and Structure* (Cambridge, MA: MIT Press).

Senft, G. (1986). *Kilivila* (Berlin and New York: Mouton de Gruyter).

Shattuck-Hufnagel, S. (1986). 'The representation of phonological information during speech production planning: Evidence from vowel errors in spontaneous speech', *Phonology Yearbook,* 3: 117–49.

—— (1992). 'The role of word structure in segmental serial ordering', *Cognition,* 42: 213–59.

Shaw, P. (1980). *Dakota Phonology and Morphology* (New York: Garland).

Silverman, D. (1995). 'Phase and recoverability'. Unpublished Ph.D. (Los Angeles: University of California, Los Angeles).

Slocum, M. C. (1948). 'Tzeltal (Mayan) noun and verb morphology', *International Journal of American Linguistics,* 14 (2): 83.

Slone, T. H. (2003). *Prokem: An Analysis of a Jakartan Slang* (Oakland, CA: Masalai Press).

Smith, I. and Johnson, S. (2000). 'Kugu Nganhcara', in R. M. A. Dixon and B. J. Blake (eds.), *The Handbook of Australian Languages, vol. 5: Grammatical sketches of Bunuba, Ndjebbana, and Kugu Nganhcara* (Oxford, New York: Oxford University Press), 357–489.

Smith, J. L. (2002). 'Phonological augmentation in prominent positions'. Unpublished Ph.D. (Amherst: University of Massachusetts).

—— (2004). 'Making constraints positional: Toward a compositional model of CON'. *Lingua,* 114: 1433–64.

Spaelti, P. (1995). 'A constraint-based theory of reduplication patterns', *West Coast Conference in Formal Linguistics,* 14: 477–92.

—— (1997). *Dimensions of Variation in Multi-pattern Reduplication* (Santa Cruz: University of California, Santa Cruz).

Sproat, R. (1985). 'On deriving the lexicon'. Unpublished Ph.D. (Cambridge, MA: MIT).

—— (1986). 'Malayalam compounding: A non-stratum ordered account', *Proceedings of the West Coast Conference on Formal Linguistics,* 5, 268–88.

Stairs, E. F. and Hollenbach, B. E. (1969). 'Huave verb morphology', *International Journal of American Linguistics*, 35: 38–53.

Stemberger, J. P. and Bernhardt, B. H. (1998). 'Contiguity, metathesis, and infixation', in K. Shahin, S. Blake, and E.-S. Kim (eds.), *The Proceedings of the Seventh West Coast Conference on Formal Linguistics* (Stanford: CSLI), 610–24.

Steriade, D. (1994). *Positional Neutralization and the Expression of Contrast.* Unpublished manuscript, UCLA.

—— (1995). *Licensing retroflexion.* Unpublished manuscript, UCLA.

—— (1997). *Phonetics in Phonology: the Case of Laryngeal Neutralization.* Unpublished manuscript, UCLA.

—— (2000). 'Paradigm uniformity and the phonetics-phonology boundary', in M. B. Broe and J. Pierrehumbert (eds.), *Papers in Laboratory Phonology V: Acquisition and the Lexicon* (Cambridge: Cambridge University Press), 313–34.

—— (2001). 'Directional asymmmetries in place assimilation', in E. Hume and K. Johnson (eds.), *The Role of Speech Perception in Phonology* (San Diego: Academic Press), 219–50.

Surintramont, A. (1973). 'Some aspects of underlying syllable structure in Thai: Evidence from Kampuan-A Thai word game', *Studies in the Linguistic Sciences*, 3: 121–42.

Tegey, H. (1977). 'The grammar of clitics: Evidence from Pashto and other languages'. Unpublished Ph.D. (Urbana-Champaign: University of Illinois).

Thomas, D. (1971). *Chrau grammar* (Honolulu: University of Hawaii Press).

—— (1990). 'The instrument/locative and goal affix N- in Surin Khmer', *Mon-Khmer Studies* 16–17: 85–98.

Thomas-Flinders, T. (1981). 'Aspects of Maricopa verbal morphology', in T. Thomas-Flinders (ed.), *Inflectional Morphology: Introduction to the Extended Word-and-Paradigm Theory*, Vol. 4 (Los Angeles: Department of Linguistics, UCLA).

Thompson, J. J. (2005). *Upriver Halkomelem Pluractionality as Event Number.* Unpublished manuscript.

Thompson, L. C. and Thompson, M. T. (1992). *The Thompson Language* (Missoula, Montana: Linguistics Laboratory, University of Montana).

—— —— (1996). *Thompson River Salish Dictionary.* Missoula, Montana: Linguistics Laboratory, University of Montana.

Tomasello, M. (2003). *Constructing a Language: A Usage-based Theory of Language Acquisition* (Cambridge, MA: Harvard University Press).

Topping, D. M. (1973). *Chamorro Reference Grammar* (Honolulu: University Press of Hawaii).

Traugott, E. (1989). 'On the rise of epistemic meanings in English: An example of subjectification in semantic change', *Language*, 57: 33–65.

—— (2004). 'Historical pragmatics', in L. Horn and G. Ward (eds.), *Handbook of Pragmatics* (Oxford: Blackwell), 538–61.

Trubetzkoy, N. S. (1939). *Grundzüge der Phonologie* (Prague: Travaux du Cercle linguistique de Prague).

Ultan, R. (1975). 'Infixes and their origins', in H. Seiler (ed.), *Linguistic Workshop III* (Munchen: Fink (Structura 9)), 157–205.

Urbanczyk, S. C. (1993). 'Infixing and moraic circumscription', in T. Sherer (ed.), *Phonological Representations (University of Massachusetts Occasional Papers 16)*, 319–57.

—— (1996). 'Patterns of reduplication in Lushootseed'. Unpublished Ph.D. (Amherst: University of Massachusetts, Amherst).

—— (2001). *Patterns of Reduplication in Lushootseed* (New York: Garland).

Ussishkin, A. (1999). 'The inadequacy of the consonantal root: Modern Hebrew denominal verbs and output-output correspondence'. *Phonology*, 16 (3): 401–42.

—— (2000). 'The emergence of fixed prosody'. Unpublished Ph.D. (Santa Cruz: University of California, Santa Cruz).

Vago, R. M. (1985). 'The treatment of long vowels in word games', *Phonology Yearbook*, 2: 329–42.

Vanoverbergh, M. (1955). *Iloko Grammar* (Manila: Advocate Book Supply).

Viau, J. (2002). *Accounting for -iz Infixation in Rap and Hip-hop Music*. Unpublished manuscript, Evanston.

Voegelin, C. F. and Voegelin, F. M. (1965). 'Languages of the world: Sino-Tibetan fascicle five', *Anthropological Linguistics*, 7 (6): 2–56.

Walker, R. (2000a). *Nasalization, Neutral Segments and Opacity Effects* (New York: Garland).

—— (2000b). 'Nasal reduplication in Mbe affixation', *Phonology*, 17 (1): 65–115.

Waterhouse, V. (1962). *The Grammatical Structure of Oaxaca Chontal*, Vol. 28 (Research Center in Anthropology, Folklore, and Linguistics).

Watkins, C. (1962). *Indo-European Origins of the Celtic Verb, I: The Stigmatic Aorist* (Dublin: Institute of Advanced Studies).

Weinreich, U., Labov, W., and Herzog, M. (1968). 'Empirical foundations for a theory of language change', in W. P. Lehmann and Y. Malkeil (eds.), *Directions for Historical Linguistics: A Symposium* (Austin, Texas: University of Texas Press), 95–188.

Whaley, L. L. (1997). *Introduction to Typology: The Unity and Diversity of Language* (Thousand Oaks, London and New Delhi: SAGE Publications).

Whitney, W. D. (1889). *Sanskrit Grammar* (Cambridge, MA and London: Harvard University Press).

Winter, W. (1970). 'Reduplication in Washo: A Restatement), *International Journal of American Linguistics*, 35 (3): 190–8.

Wonderly, W. L. (1951). 'Zoque I–IV', *International Journal of American Linguistics*, 17 (1–9): 105–23, 137–62, 235–51.

Wood, E. J. and Garrett, A. (2003). 'The semantics of Yurok intensive infixation', in *Proceedings of WAIL 4*, UC Santa Barbara Papers in Linguistics. (Santa Barbara: UC Santa Barbara), 112–25.

Xu, T. (1981). 'Shanxi Pingding fangyan de erhua he Jinzhong suowei de qian l ci [Er-affixation in Shanxi Pingding dialect and l-infixation]', *Zhonggua Yuwen [Chinese Linguistics and Literature]*, 20: 408–15.

Yip, M. (1982). 'Reduplication and C-V skeletal in Chinese secret languages', *Linguistic Inquiry*, 13: 637–61.

—— (1999). 'Reduplication as alliteration and rhyme', *GLOT International*, 4: 1–7.

—— (2002). 'Necessary but not sufficient: perceptual loanword influences in loanword phonology', in H. Kubozono (ed.), *The Journal of the Phonetics Society of Japan. Special Issue on Aspects of Loanword Phonology*, 6: 4–21.

—— (2003). 'Casting doubt on the Onset/Rime distinction', *Lingua*, 113 (8): 779–816.

—— (2006). 'The symbiosis between perception and grammar in loanword phonology', *Lingua*, 116: 950–75.

Yu, A. C. L. (2000). 'Stress assignment in Tohono O'odham'. *Phonology*, 17 (1): 117–35.

—— (2003). 'The morphology and phonology of infixation'. Unpublished Ph.D. (Berkeley: University of California, Berkeley).

—— (2004*a*). 'Explaining final obstruent voicing in Lezgian: Phonetics and history', *Language*, 80 (1): 73–97.

—— (2004*b*). 'Infixing with a vengeance: Pingding Mandarin infixation', *Journal of East Asian Linguistics*, 13 (1): 39–58.

—— (2004*c*). *The Morphology of Muna Nasal Substitution*. Unpublished manuscript, Chicago.

—— (2004*d*). 'Reduplication in English Homeric infixation', in K. Moulton and M. Wolf (eds.), *Proceedings of the 34th North East Linguistics Society*, Vol. 34 (Amherst: GLSA), 619–33.

—— (2005*a*). 'Quantity, stress, and reduplication in Washo', *Phonology*, 22 (3): 437–75.

—— (2005*b*). 'Toward a typology of compensatory reduplication', in J. Alderete, C.-h. Han, and A. Kochetov (eds.), *Proceedings of the 24th West Coast Conference on Formal Linguistics* (Somerville, MA: Cascadilla Proceedings Project), 397–405.

—— 2006). 'Prosodically-governed segmental fission in Washo', in R. Cover and Y. Kim (eds.), *The proceedings of the 31st Annual Meeting of the Berkeley Linguistics Society* (Berkeley: Berkeley Linguistics Society), 513–24.

Zhang, J. (2001). 'The effects of duration and sonority on contour tone distribution-typological survey and formal analysis'. Unpublished Ph.D. (Los Angeles: University of California, Los Angeles).

Zuraw, K. (1996). 'Floating phonotactics: infixation and reduplication in Tagalog loanwords'. Unpublished MA (Los Angeles: University of California, Los Angeles).

—— (2002). 'Aggressive reduplication', *Phonology*, 19 (3): 395–440.

—— (2005). *The Role of Phonetic Knowledge in Phonological Patterning: Corpus and Survey Evidence from Tagalog*. Unpublished manuscript, Los Angeles.

Zwicky, A. M. and Pullum, G. K. (1983). 'Cliticization vs. inflection: English *n't*', *Language*, 59: 502–13.

Language Index

Aghem 144
Alabama 40, 44, 103, 148–51, 179
Amis 111–12, 113
Apalachee 148
Arabic 131
  Classical 77
  Egyptian 9
  Levantine 117
Archi 42, 44–5
Atayal 2, 34–5, 74–5

Bole 101
Budukh 29, 32–3
Bunun, Isbukun dialect 105–7

Cantonese 134–5, *see also* Chinese
Cayuga 139
Chamorro 74–5, 89, 122
ChiBemba 12–13, 117
Chickasaw 103–5, 148–50, 179
Chinese 144, 172
  Archaic 172
  Standard 147
Chocktaw 103, 148, 151
Chontal, Oaxaca 41–2, 44
Chumash, Ineseño 110
Coeur d'Alene 165, 167, *see also* Interior Salish
Colville 166–7, *see also* Interior Salish
Columbian 166, *see also* Interior Salish
Creek 108, 148, 150
  Florida Seminole 148
  Muskogee 148
  Oklahoma Seminole 148
Cuna 198

Dakota
  agreement infixation 19–21, 29, 37–8, 91, 102, 138, 152
  entrapment 138, 154
Dargi 152, 153
Delaware 138
Dyirbal 22–3

English 13, 48, 53, 174
  expletive infixation 1, 2, 9–10, 21–2, 33, 71–2, 119–20
  Homeric infixation 1, 2, 174–7, 181–90
  internal modification 9–10
  -iz- infixation 1, 2
  morphological subcategorization 14–15, 21–2
  phonological subcategorization 14–15, 21–2, 218, 229–30
  phonologically conditioned allomorphy 56
  rhotic metathesis 145
Estonian 191

Flathead 166, *see also* Interior Salish
French 13

German 13, 22
Greek 2
  Ancient 103
  Classical 177–8
  Cyprus 198–9
  South Italian 177–8

Halkomelem, Upriver 122–3
Hanunoo 36

Hausa
  Class 5 plural formation 130–3
  iterative infixation 31–2, 194, 199–201,
    205
  pluractional reduplication 157–9
Hebrew 138
Hitchiti 103, 108, 148, 150
Hopi 159–61, 165
Hua 29, 154–6
Huave 117–18
Hunzit 128–30, 133
Huojia 172

Ilokano 42–4
Indonesian
  Common 138
  Prokem slang 191–2
Interior Salish
  Northern 121, 161, 165–71, 178
  Southern 165–6, 168

Javanese 36

Kalispel 166–7, *see also* Interior Salish
Kamaiurá 111, 113, 115 n.
Katu 152–3
Kentakbong 152, 153
Khmer 173
KiChaga 108
Kinande 86–7
Koasati 148
  first-syllable pivot 133–4
  mediopassive 41 n., 103
  person markers 148–9, 151, 153–4
  punctual reduplication 110, 133–4
  verbal plurality 109–10
Korean 111
Kugu Nganhcara 95–6

Lakhota 152, *see also* Dakota
Lappish 22
Latin 5
Latvian 198–9

Lepcha 142–3, 177
Leti 28–30, 90–1
Lezgian 154
Lillooet 165–8, *see also* Interior Salish
Lushootseed 97–9, 100 n., 101, 114, 125, 167

Mandarin 36, 134, 147
  Pingding dialect 28–30, 144–7, 172 n.
  Yanggu dialect 145–7, 172 n.
  see also Chinese
Mangarayi 92–5, 99, 101, 114
Maricopa 76
Mikasuki 103, 108, 148–50, 179
Miskitu 104–5, 138
Mlabri 76–9, 80 n., 81
Mopan 140
Muna 219–20
Murut, Timugon dialect 10–11, 22, 24–5,
    84–8, 88

Nakanai 123
Noni 144

Okanagan 166, *see also* Interior Salish
Old Irish 11

Paiwan 73
Pangasinan 81–2, 84, 88, 96
Pashto 212–18
Pima 161
Pomo, Kashaya 220–2
Popoluca, Sierra 140
Pre-Trukese 163
Proto-Austronesian 31 n., 74, 172
Proto-Muskogean 149–51, 179
Proto-Zoque 140

Quileute 101–2

Ratahan, *see* Toratan

Saami 230
Sabah Murut, *see* Murut

Samoan 23–4, 118, 122
Seminole 108, 148, 150, *see also* Creek
Serbo-Croatian 207
Shuswap 122, 166–7, *see also* Interior
   Salish
SiSwati 86–8
Spanish 194–6
   Colombian 195–6
   Costa Rican 195–7
   Jerigonza 194–7
   Peruvian 195–6
Spokane 166–70, *see also* Interior Salish
Sundanese 29 n.

Tagalog
   -*in*- infixation 17–19, 60
   language disguise/game 32, 36, 192
   -*um*- infixation 16 n., 27, 38–40,
      59–60, 74–5
   variable infixation 59–60
Tahitian 219
Takelma 125–8
Thai 36
Thao 112
Thompson River Salish 166, *see also*
   Interior Salish
Tibetan 142
Tiene 220, 222–9

Tigre 109–10
Tigrinya 36, 192–3
Toba Batak 32
Toratan 90
Trukese 138, 162–3, 165
Tzeltal 102
Tzutujil 102, 139, 143

Udi 208–12
Ulwa 54
   adjective distributive
      reduplication 119
   construct state 22, 33–4, 50–1, 55–7,
      71–2, 107, 118–19
   phonological subcategorization 22,
      33–4, 50–1
   suppletive allomorphy 56, 107
Uradhi 51, 101

Washo 120–1

Yawelmani 126
Yimeng 172
Yucateco 139
Yurok 31 n., 89, 182

Zoque 140
Zuni 117

Subject Index

agreement 2, 19–20, 29, 37–8, 89, 148, 208
Akinlabi, A. 40 n.
Albright, A. C. 69–70, 152
Alekseev, M. E. 33, 103
Alidou, O. D. 36, 194, 199 n., 201
allomorphy 22, 37 n., 103, 117–18, 137, 181,
    211, 214
  phonological 23, 28, 32, 56, 76–81, 90,
    103, 129, 208, 219–20, 223, 225–7
  suppletive 56–7, 105–7, 123–4, 219 n.,
    220–2, 224, 228–9
analogy 51 n., 52, 137, 159
  analogical extension 63–4, 139, 147,
    150–1, 153–4, 170
  analogical restoration 154, 160
Andersen, H. 71, 155, 165
Anderson, G. D. S. 122, 138, 167–8
Anderson, S. 6, 21, 26, 30 n., 49, 89, 207,
    212, 214, 218
Andrade, M. 102
Anttila, A. 53
Applegate, R. 110
Aronoff, M. 33, 214
Aryan, R. 77
Avery, P. 60

Bagemihl, B. 36, 190, 192
Bao, Z.-m. 36
Barnes, J. A. 6, 62, 68
Bat-El, O. 132
Bates, D. 167, 168, 169
Beckman, J. N. 68
Benedict, P. K. 142
Benton, R. A. 81–2, 88
Berg, H. van den 128–9, 152–4
Berg, R. van den 219
Bergsland, K. 22

Bernhardt, B. H. 17, 21
Bissell, T. 131
Blevins, J. 6, 28, 63, 90, 139–41, 143–5,
    154, 177, 230
Boas, F. 20, 37 n., 102, 138, 148
Boersma, P. 5
Bonet, E. 124, 211
Booij, G. 15, 26
Booker, K. M. 149, 180
Broselow, E. 4, 35, 51 n., 117, 121, 122,
    125, 127
Buckley, E. 4, 17, 21, 26, 28, 220–2
Bybee, J. 47, 61, 69, 178

Campbell, L. 36
Carlson, B. 168, 169, 170
Carpenter, B. 54
Carstairs-McCarthy, A. 229
Chang, M. L. 112
Chao, Y. R. 134, 145
Chen, K. 73
Chiu, B. H.-C. 4
Chomsky, N. 5
Clements, G. N. 4, 51 n.
clitics 150, 155, 178, 179, 181
  endoclitics 8, 181, 206–18
  second-position 207, 212–13, 216,
    218
Cohn, A. 4, 15, 21, 26
Conklin, H. 32, 36, 192
constraint 40, 53, 79n.
  construction of 18, 61
  declarative/non-violable 56, 59, 78,
    79 n., 186 n., 188
  grammar-external/substantive 8, 48,
    137
  grammar-internal 7, 47, 58, 59, 62

co-phonology 53, 82, 185, 203, 216–17, 225, 227–8
correspondence 87 n., 126, 190, 201n.
    surface 132, 188–9, 190, 201
Costello, N. A. 152
Cowell, M. 117
Crowhurst, M. 4, 87, 90–6, 113, 115 n., 219
Crowley, T. 51, 101–2
Crysmann, B. 209, 211

Dahl, O. C. 31 n., 74, 172
Davis, S. 4, 120
Dayley, J. P. 102–3, 139
Deloria, E. 20, 37 n., 102, 138
diminutive 2, 28, 84, 121–2, 144–6, 161, 165–71, 178
discontinuous morphology 9–10, 13, 45 n., 182, 207–8, 229
Dixon, R. M. A. 23
Dolbey, A. 6, 230
Dong, S. 145, 146 n.
Downing, L. J. 86–9
Duanmu, S. 145
durative 2, 42, 44–5, 103, 138, 162–3, 165, 222

Edge-Bias Effect 3, 8, 34, 47, 57–8, 63–5, 135, 137, 177, 180
Egerod, S. 2, 35, 75
Eijk, J. van 122, 166, 167, 168
Elman, J. 61
Elson, B. F. 140
Engelenhoven, A. T. P. G. van 29
entrapment 8, 12, 64, 89, 137–9, 148–57, 162–3, 174, 178–80, 222
Everett, D. 111
expletive 1, 2, 10, 11, 21–2, 33, 48, 71–2, 76 n., 119–20, 187

Ferrell, R. 73
Fife, J. 11
Fillmore, C. 7, 53

Flemming, E. S. 5
foot structure 71, 86, 135, 179 n., 185, 204
    iambic 33, 50, 56, 72, 79, 118–19
    maximal foot 183, 185
    minimal foot 183
    trochaic 2, 21–2, 115, 118, 119, 174, 182, 183, 185
Foster, M. K. 139
frequentative 2, 84, 102, 109–10, 125–8, 164, *see also* iterative
Fromkin, V. A. 35

Gafos, D. 10
Galloway, B. 123
Garrett, A. 2, 89, 103, 138, 139–41, 143–5, 162, 165, 177
Generalized Alignment (GA) 7, 15, 22, 33, 36, 46, 48–53, 58, 62–3, 193
Generalized Template Theory 97
Gimba, A. M. 101
Goad, H. 131
Goldberg, A. 61
Goodenough, W. H. 162
Gordon, L. 76
Gordon, M. 5, 68
Green, T. M. 33, 50, 72, 119
Greenberg, J. H. 1, 2, 47

Haas, M. R. 149
Haiman, J. 30, 138, 155–6, 165, 173
Hale, M. 6, 56
Halle, M. 4, 5, 17–19, 32
Hansson, G. 132
Hargus, S. 22
Harris, A. C. 6, 138, 148, 156, 208–12
Harrison, K. D. 36
Haspelmath, M. 173, 177
Hawkins, J. A. 3
Hayes, B. 5, 58, 61, 91, 183, 185
He, W. 172
head
    of a foot 23, 34, 49–51, 119, 204
    of a prosodic word 49, 115–16

of a syllable 193–5
Herzog, M. 47, 64
Himmelmann, N. P. 90
Ho, J.-f. *et al.* 111
Hombert, J.-M. 36
Homeric infixation 2, 174–7, 178, 181–90,
  198, 202
Hopper, P. 63
Hovdhaugen, E. 24, 118
Huang, H.-c. J. 35 n.
Hume, E. 6, 61, 62, 143
Hyman, L. 4, 12, 17, 71, 144
hyperinfixation 38–41, 48

infixes
  edge-oriented 3, 4, 23, 57, 63, 95, 137,
    177–8, 229
  prominence-driven 3, 23, 46, 165, 171,
    176, 178
Inkelas, S. 4, 7, 14, 15, 17, 22, 26, 49, 53, 75,
  87, 108, 131, 222–6, 228 n.
intensive/intensivitization 31 n., 89,
  108–9, 163–5, 182
interface 19
  morphology-prosody 26, 97, 98
  morphology-phonology 7, 41, 48,
    53–4, 57–8, 135
iterative 12, 31, 32, 181, 192–206
  infixing ludlings 8, 181, 190, 192–200
Ito, J. 36, 183

Jacobsen, W. H. J. 121
Janda, R. 142
Jeanne, L. M. 159–60
Jensen, J. T. 183
Johnston, R. L. 123
Joseph, B. D. 138 n.
Jun, J. 111

Kager, R. 16 n.
Kaisse, E. 214, 218
Kaufman, D. 4, 17, 35 n., 42–3, 45, 91
Kavitskaya, D. 6, 62

Kawu, A. 131
Kay, P. 7, 53
Kehoe, M. 68
Kenstowicz, M. 44
Kershner, T. L. 160
Kibrik, A. 42, 45
Kimball, G. 108, 109, 133, 151
Kiparsky, P. 4, 14, 22, 49, 51 n., 53
Kirchner, R. 5
Koenig, J.-P. 53
Kuipers, A. H. 166, 167
Kurisu, K. 4, 83, 92–3, 200
Kurylowicz, J. 71

Labov, W. 47, 64
Lacy, P. de 122
language disguises, *see* language games
language games 8, 31–2, 35–6, 181,
  190–206
Lazard, G. 219
Leben, W. 200
Lee, A. P. 112
Lee, B. 126–7
Lehiste, I. 36, 191
Lengendre, G. 218
leveling, *see* analogy
lexically specified subclass
  noun class 56
  stem class 151–3
lexicon 15, 59–60, 143, 154
Li, P. J.-K. 35 n., 112
Li, Z. 172
Lieber, R. 14
Lin, T. 105
Lin, Y.-H. 29
Lloret, M.-R. 124, 211
Lombardi, L. 103, 105
Lubowicz, A. 4, 21

MacWhinney, B. 61
Marantz, A. 4, 51 n.
Martin, J. 108, 138, 149, 150
Martin, J. B. 41, 104, 108, 148–51, 179

Mascaró, J. 124, 211
Matthews, P. 5
Matthews, S. 134
McArthur, T. 175
McCarthy, J. 1, 4, 10, 11, 15–17, 19, 20–1,
    23–7, 33–4, 36, 37 n., 38–41, 43,
    45–6, 49, 51, 56, 62, 72, 83, 85, 91, 93,
    95, 97, 103, 105, 117, 120–2, 123, 124,
    125, 127, 131, 183, 189, 197, 198, 211
McCawley, J. 11, 22 n.
Merlan, F. 92
Mester, A. 36, 183
metathesis 60, 139–48, 151, 156–7, 159,
    177–8
  long-distance 178
  morphological 138–40, 159
  Onset Metathesis 17–19, 32–3
  phonetic 8, 138, 177
  phonological 138–9
  rhotic 145–7
  segmental 17, 19
  types of 141–2
Mielke, J. 6, 62, 230
Mikheev, A. 70
mora(ic) alignment 91, 94, 101, 105, 113,
    117
Moravcsik, E. 3, 4, 5, 10 n., 17, 18, 20,
    37 n., 72, 102, 124, 133
Morén, B. 132 n.
morphological acquisition, *see*
    morphological learning
morphological change 6, 8, 48, 61, 137,
    138 n., 159, 165
morphological excrescence 8, 139, 172–7
morphological learning 7–8, 48, 61, 63–5,
    67, 179–80
Mosel, U. 24, 118
Munro, P. 41, 103, 104, 108, 148–51, 179

Nelson, N. 131
Neogrammarian(s) 137
Nespor, M. 183 n.
Newman, P. 32, 130, 157–8

Newman, S. 117
Nichols, J. 138, 148
Nida, E. A. 9, 102
Niepokuj, M. K. 230
nominalization 2, 22, 28–9, 32, 76–9,
    90–2, 104, 121, 123, 173, 229

Ohala, J. J. 63, 141, 145
Omar, A. H. 152
Optimal Paradigm 44–5
Optimality Theory 4, 15, 19, 23, 25–6,
    45–6, 58, 60 n., 62, 95, 210
Orgun, C. O. 7, 12, 39, 53, 54 n., 59–60,
    75, 79 n.
Otanes, F. T. 17–18
overgeneration 37–45, 55, 58–62, 63

paradigm 42–5, 92, 150–1, 153–4, 156, 230
  leveling 147
  paradigm uniformity 42–3, 137, 158,
    161, 171, 221
  see also analogy
Paster, M. 23, 55–6, 124, 211, 219, 228
Pater, J. 5, 132 n., 219, 220
Payne, T. 9
Peters, A. M. 68
phonological subcategorization, *see*
    subcategorization
Phonological Readjustment 4, 7, 14,
    16–17, 19, 21, 23, 25–46, 57–8, 62, 92
Piggott, G. 41 n.
Piñeros, C.-E. 36, 194–9, 202
pivot 7, 50–2, 54, 60, 64, 170–1, 177–80,
    185, 189, 191, 193, 205, 212, 229
  Pivot Theory 8, 65, 67–135, 137 n., 154
pluractionality 51, 86, 101–2, 120, 157–9,
    162
Pollard, C. 7, 53
prefix(ation) 153, 170
Prentice, D. J. 11, 24, 84, 85–6
Prince, A. 4, 15–17, 19, 20–1, 23, 25–6,
    33–4, 36–8, 45–6, 49, 51, 56, 83, 85,
    91, 93, 97, 131, 197

prosodic circumscription 23–5, 34
Prosodic Hierarchy 16, 34–5, 46, 49–50, 115
Prosodic Morphology 19, 23, 26, 34, 230
prosodic template 10, 26, 34, 77, 131, 188, 190, 223–5, 228

Qian, Z. 147

Rau, D.-h. V. 35 n.
reanalysis 61, 63, 125–6, 139, 148, 151, 154, 156, 158–60, 163, 171, 176, 214
reduplication 25, 51, 73, 82, 84, 86, 94, 96–8, 108–10, 111–17, 119, 120–2, 125–6, 132, 183 n., 189
 compensatory 131, 184, 186–7, 196–8, 210–15
 diminutive 161, 165, 167–71, 178
 double 170
 infixing 81, 85–9, 110, 133, 169
 internal 51, 92, 94–5, 111, 120, 159–61, 165, 171
 mutation of 8, 138–9, 157–72
 prefixing 82, 85, 87, 89, 94, 157, 159–61, 168, 170–1
 suffixing 101, 125, 157
Riggle, J. 161
Rischel, J. 76, 79, 80 n.
Robins, R. H. 164
Rohlfs, G. 177
Rose, S. 4, 109–10, 131, 132
Rosenthal, S. 131
Rubach, J. 15, 26

Sadtano, E. 36
Sag, I. A. 7, 53
Sagart, L. 172
sampling, typological 73–5
Sanders, N. 4, 92–3
Sapir, E. 13, 125–6, 127 n.
Saussure, F. de 54, 137, 148
Schachter, P. 17–18
Schmidt, P. W. 137, 148, 153, 174

Selkirk, E. O. 14, 183 n.
Shattuck-Hufnagel, S. 35, 68
Sign-Based Morphology (SBM) 53–8, 62–3, 65, 75, 81, 119, 185, 225, 228 n.
Silverman, D. 5
Smolensky, P. 4, 21, 36
Slocum, M. C. 102
Slone, T. H. 192
Smith, I. 95
Smith, J. L. 5, 58–9, 61, 68
Spaelti, P. 4, 83
Sproat, R. 14, 15, 26
Sprouse, R. L. 39, 59–60, 75, 79 n.
Stairs, E. F. 117
Stemberger, J. P. 17, 21
Steriade, D. 5, 30
stress 2, 3, 11, 21–4, 33, 48–50, 52, 54–5, 60, 67–8, 70–2, 74, 79, 86, 88, 100 n., 104 n., 118–24, 128–30, 141, 154–5, 159 n., 165–6, 168–71, 176–8, 182, 184–6, 195, 213–30
subcategorization 8, 22–3, 47, 65, 69, 77, 78–9, 81–2, 89, 94–5, 106–7, 110, 114–18, 123–4, 135, 154, 179–80, 183, 191, 196, 198–200, 201 n., 204–5, 211–12, 217, 219–29
 featural 181
 morphological 15, 48, 50, 56, 137, 180
phonological 4–5, 7–8, 14–17, 21–3, 25–50, 52–62, 67, 70–1, 96, 135, 137, 179–82, 184–8, 194, 206, 216, 218, 224, 227, 229
 prosodic 22, 49
susbstantive filter 59, 61
Surintramont, A. 36
syllable 2, 16, 19–25, 27, 29–32, 34, 35 n., 36–41, 43, 50–2, 55, 58, 60, 67–72, 76, 79, 82, 84–9, 92, 95, 97–8, 100–6, 108–11, 114, 116–24, 128 n., 130–1, 133–5, 139, 141, 144, 147–50, 157–8, 159 n., 161 n., 172 n., 176–9, 182–6, 188–206, 213–18, 229–30

Tegey, H. 212–17, 218 n.
template, *see* prosodic
     template
Thomas-Flinders, T. 76
Thompson, J. J. 123
Thompson, L. C. 166
Tomasello, M. 61
Topping, D. M. 75, 89, 122
Traugott, E. 175
Trubetzkoy, N. S. 68
Tsuchida, S. 112
typology 1, 3–5, 22, 30, 47–8,
     52, 138
   diachronic 8, 47, 63, 65, 137–77
   synchronic 48, 63, 65, 67–135

Ultan, R. 1, 2, 12, 72, 73, 124, 133, 137–8,
     139, 142, 148, 157, 163
undergeneration 31–7
Urbanczyk, S. C. 4, 97–101, 121
Ussishkin, A. 10, 202

Vago, R. M. 36
Vanoverbergh, M. 42

variation 5, 47, 59–60, 65, 68–9, 75, 117,
     135, 206, 214, 217, 228
Viau, J. 1
Voegelin, C. F. 142

Walker, R. 5, 83
Waterhouse, V. 41
Watkins, C. 156
Weinreich, U. 47, 64
Winter, W. 121
Wolf, M. 124, 211
Wonderly, W. L. 140
Wood, E. J. 164

Xu, T. 29, 144

Yip, M. 36, 60, 132, 189, 197
Yu, A. C. L. 1, 6, 29, 53, 75, 121, 131, 132,
     138, 145, 146, 172 n., 187, 190, 219, 220

Zhang, J. 68
Zoll, C. 53, 75, 131
Zuraw, K. 59, 60, 131, 132
Zwicky, A. M. 206

IN PREPARATION

The Logic of Pronominal Resumption
by Ash Asudeh

Phi Syntax: A Theory of Agreement
by Susana Béjar

French Dislocation: Syntax, Interpretation, Acquisition
by Cécile De Cat

The Syntax of Sentential Stress
by Arsalan Kahnemuyipour

Stratal Optimality Theory
by Ricardo Bermúdez Otero

The Ecology of English Noun-Noun Compounding
by Ray Jackendoff

Adverbs and Adjectives in Semantics and Discourse
edited by Louise McNally and Chris Kennedy